NUMBER FIFTEEN

The Presidency and Leadership

James P. Pfiffner, General Editor

SERIES BOARD
Peri Arnold
H. W. Brands, Jr.
George C. Edwards III
Fred I. Greenstein
Erwin C. Hargrove
Charles O. Jones
Martha Joynt Kumar
Roger Porter
Stephen J. Wayne

THE PRESIDENCY AND WOMEN

THE PRESIDENCY AND WOMEN

Promise, Performance, & Illusion

Janet M. Martin

TEXAS A&M UNIVERSITY PRESS   COLLEGE STATION

The paper used in this book
meets the minimum requirements
of the American National Standard for Permanence
of Paper for Printed Library Materials, z39.48-1984.
Binding materials have been chosen for durability.

Library of Congress Cataloging-in-Publication Data

Martin, Janet M., 1955–
    The presidency and women : promise, performance, and
illusion / Janet M. Martin.—1st ed.
        p. cm.—(The presidency and leadership ; no. 15)
    Includes bibliographical references and index.
    ISBN 1-58544-245-3 (cloth : alk. paper)
    1. Women in the civil service—United States.   2. United
States—Officials and employees—Selection and appointment.
3. Women in politics—United States.   I. Title.   II. Series.
JK721.M34   2003
352.3'082'0973—dc21   2002014492

To John Winship

CONTENTS

TABLES

BOXES

PREFACE

Research can begin with a carefully focused question in mind, but often that question leads to other questions, and before long a project expands into unexpected territory. This project began in 1989 as a study of women and the presidency with a focus on the impact of women appointed to positions in the executive branch. With so few women appointed to positions until the Carter administration, my intended focus was the last two decades—starting with the Carter administration and proceeding through the Reagan and Bush administrations. However, in looking at those administrations I began to look beyond appointments at the wider web of women's organizations, agenda items, and White House structures, all addressing the question of the inclusion of women in the executive branch. An appropriate starting point would need to extend back in time, before the ERA became a singular focus in the 1970s and early 1980s. I noted a broader agenda for women, one with the same recurring issues (e.g., issues of equal pay, child care, health care, pensions, discrimination, and sexual harassment), recurring year after year.

My research broadened to include these new elements. I began to see my research providing a story, and an historical narrative was the best way to tell that story. An historical narrative has allowed me to lay out, in a systematic and quite comprehensive fashion, the players (presidents, staff, appointees, interest groups, Congress, the courts, and the public), the structures (White House organization, legislative devices, and presidential style), and the issues (Title IX, civil rights, pensions, child care, women in the military, education, jobs, and training) in a manner that opens up a new way of looking at the presidency and also women and politics. The narrative is one that has not been told by those scholars who have focused on one administration such as Franklin D. Roosevelt, or one issue such as the ERA, or more generally on historical evolution of the women's movement. The research here suggests a broader role of the federal government in affecting the course of the women's movement, and at a much earlier point in history than is generally noted, and the important role of the women's movement in broadening the presidential agenda.

The historical narrative of five administrations—Kennedy, Johnson, Nixon, Ford, and Carter—as well as an introductory chapter covering a broader sweep of history lends itself to the inclusion of evolving political movements and public attitudes, and of policy incubation over time. This narrative sweep also facilitates discussion of how a broader political and social context affects presidential decision making. By weaving a story from administration to administration, I am also able to focus on the institution of the presidency.

ACKNOWLEDGMENTS

A project of this scope, worked on over a number of years, generates a list of many people to acknowledge and thank. While I bear full responsibility for any errors, and all interpretations and conclusions in this book, the book has nevertheless greatly benefited from the comments of a number of anonymous reviewers, as well as those listed below.

I am deeply appreciative of the support given to this project by Texas A&M University Press. I also appreciate the comments of anonymous reviewers who provided insight, especially in areas with which I have less familiarity, and detailed comments and corrections which only benefited the manuscript. Nancy Kassop carefully read the manuscript and I am grateful for her overall comments on the manuscript but also for suggesting where clarification was needed. Her expertise in the courts proved especially helpful in both adding and correcting the names of important court cases concerning women.

I received a number of grants which provided me the time and resources needed to do archival research at various sites around the country, including: an American Political Science Association Research Grant, a Gerald R. Ford Foundation Research Grant, a Moody Grant from the Lyndon Baines Johnson Foundation, a John F. Kennedy Library Foundation Grant, and Faculty Development Grants from Bowdoin College, and a William R. Kenan, Jr., Fellowship for Faculty Development from Bowdoin College.

The archivists at the Kennedy, Johnson, Ford, and Carter presidential libraries and the archivists at the National Archives Nixon Materials Project (both in Alexandria, Virginia, and in College Park, Maryland) and the Margaret Chase Smith Library have all provided valuable insight into their collections and friendly assistance in both finding and working with materials.

This project has let me see the evolution of presidential libraries, with a simplification of photocopying processes and search mechanisms over the years. I greatly appreciated the care with which Erika Hafner transferred archive citations from photocopy request forms to individual documents, at a time when self-photocopying was not yet allowed in the libraries, and the work of Jennifer Knaut in organizing materials from archive sources, as well as Erika's and Jennifer's work in searching for material. A number of student research assistants have provided assistance, and their perseverance in tracking down material contributed greatly to the book, including Jennie Kneedler, Bebe Ryan, Stephanie Fine, Jim Bradley, Anubha Sacheti, Chris Stearns, and Brian Guiney. Jennifer Cromwell gave assistance on the index. Emily Ewell's research on Title IX was also helpful in tracing its implementation over time.

Corby Baumann and Jenna Goldman patiently read each platform and carefully recorded each party's position for the appendix. I also wish to thank Melissa Koch, whose research was funded through a Surdna Undergraduate Fellowship, for introducing me to a variety of documents from the early years of the Women's Bureau. Jessica Landis was a most valuable research assistant in preparing for and responding to copy-edit questions, as well as in compiling the index.

Bowdoin's government documents librarian, Ginny Hopcroft, was always enthusiastic in her help in both tracking down material—even obscure appointments of women as lighthouse keepers in the early 1800s—and in introducing me to new collections or websites. In addition, Jeanie Bowles, superintendent in the U.S. Senate Document Room, and her student intern, Danielle Fling, were helpful in providing information and access to congressional documents and bibliographic materials on women.

Katrina Robb provided invaluable assistance in using the archive collection of the Marguerite Rawalt Resource Center at the Business and Professional Women/USA headquarters in Washington, D.C. This archive collection, which I was not familiar with until two-thirds of the way into this project, proved invaluable, offering up materials that are not readily available in other archive collections.

I also want to thank my mother, Mary Martin, and two sisters, Judy Ann and Jean T., and my friends for all of their support. They will no longer need to hesitate in asking, "How is the book?" The warm friendship of MaryAnne Borrelli, who has certainly been a friend indeed, has been most appreciated.

Finally, this book is dedicated to John Winship, whose love, insight, editing, succinctification, and cartoons of a certain researcher engulfed by a never-ending project have provided constant support and encouragement, from the book's conception through to its long-awaited conclusion. Thanks.

THE PRESIDENCY AND WOMEN

Introduction

*"Remember the Ladies, and be more generous and
favourable to them than your ancestors."*
—Abigail Adams to John Adams, March 31, 1776

THE WORDS OF Abigail Adams, a future First Lady, are often quoted by feminist scholars, yet are rarely noted by students of the presidency. Abigail Adams, in writing to her husband, a member of the Continental Congress meeting in Philadelphia, took note of the approaching day when the colonies would declare their independence from England, and commented on the structure of a new government that might emerge following that declaration and war with Great Britain.

> I long to hear that you have declared an independency—and by the way in the new Codes of Laws which I suppose it will be necessary for you to make I desire you would Remember the Ladies, and be more generous and favourable to them than your ancestors. Do not put such unlimited power into the hands of the Husbands. Remember all Men would be tyrants if they could. If perticular care and attention is not paid to the Laidies we are determined to foment a Rebelion, and will not hold ourselves bound by any Laws in which we have no voice, or Representation.[1]

While Abigail Adams appeared by these words to suggest herself an early feminist, she also was resigned to the legal and political status of women at the dawning of a new nation, continuing in the letter: "Why then, not put it out of the power of the vicious and the Lawless to use us with cruelty and indignity with impunity. Men of Sense in all Ages abhor those customs which treat us only as the vassals of your Sex. Regard us then as Beings placed by providence under your protection and in immitation of the Supreme Being make more use of that power only for our happiness."[2]

Abigail Adams would often serve as a political advisor to her husband, who became the first vice president and second president of the United States, yet in this case her words of advice did not influence the legal status of women in this new government, who would not gain the right to vote nationally until 1920, or other legal and political rights until well into the twentieth century. The lack of formal representation as well as descriptive representation in the U.S. Congress, the federal courts, and the executive branch continuing on into the twentieth century resulted in the near absence of substantive policy issues especially of concern to women moving on to the national policy agenda until late in the twentieth century.[3]

Women and politics scholars have often traced the evolution of political power and legal rights for women through a focus on social movements, and in particular, the women's movement, or through case studies focusing on the successful addition of the Nineteenth Amendment to the Constitution granting suffrage to women, or the unsuccessful drive for an equal rights amendment (ERA) beginning during the 1920s, and intensifying in the 1970s. However, by using a case study approach, the historical evolution of White House involvement with women's organizations and "women's issues" is missed. Specifically, the parallel emergence of the modern women's movement with the growth and expansion of the Executive Office of the President, and in particular the White House Office, has created a symbiotic relationship that meets some needs of both the president and women's organizations.

In the chapters that follow, the focus is on the presidency and women. Individual administrations, in particular those of Kennedy, Johnson, Nixon, Ford, and Carter, have been used to organize material and enable identification and examination of variables affecting relationships between the presidency and women over time. This book attempts to provide insight into aspects of each presidency that are often missing in the many biographies, memoirs, and autobiographies that pour out of these administrations. A quick glance at most biographies and studies of the presidency reveals little attention given to discussion of any women, except perhaps the First Lady. Similarly, issues of concern to women such as health care, family leave, dependency care, gender discrimination, equal pay, social security, and pensions[4] are rarely the focus of policy case studies on presidential decision making or presidential-congressional relations. Much has been written about each of these administrations, as well as the women's movement of the 1960s and 1970s, and numerous studies have analyzed both domestic and foreign policy during these same years. For that reason, the well-known history of this period will not be covered, except in providing a contextual background for the analysis at hand.

Scholars can and should continue to broaden analyses to examine the routinization of decision-making processes within the White House to more fully understand the presidency. By focusing on one constituent group and issues of concern to that group we can gain insight into the nature of White House decision-making processes and perhaps insight into presidential involvement itself in the process. This allows for a more accurate representation and understanding of the day-to-day ongoing activity between the White House and outside groups, outside political pressures for a certain policy agenda, as well as internal White House dynamics. Thus the study is not an analysis of any one president's behavior or actions but rather a study of the institution of the presidency vis-à-vis one group in society—i.e., women.

The structure of the book weaves the actions of presidents, their White House staff, and others in government with the actions of women and women's organizations. The result is a longitudinal political narrative of the presidency and women with a focus on the years 1961 to 1981.

While several books on the presidency have included brief mention of the activities of women or women's groups, or the president's position on issues such as the ERA, none has systematically addressed the role of women's groups and organizations as an external force affecting decision making in the White House over time or the White House's institutionalizing of a response to women, with continuity of issues from one administration to the next. The president's national constituency and role as world leader provide a context in which to assess response to one constituency—women.

To understand how and when major change takes place in the relationship between the presidency and women, that is, the time period spanning the administrations of John F. Kennedy through Jimmy Carter (1961–81), Chapter 1 provides a brief historical overview of some of the ways in which women were active participants prior to 1961. Women worked as federal employees in the departments and agencies, and as lobbyists to the president, either for themselves or as representatives of organizations in support of specific reforms or governmental action (e.g., suffrage, child labor laws, protective work legislation, appointment of women to positions in the government, or as federal court judges).

A broad sweep of history is covered in Chapter 1 to lay out the origins of some of the paths whereby women's organizations and issues of concern to women begin to intersect with the presidency. In this analysis I have tried to identify the continuities in the relationship between the White House and women which evolve over time, as well as the dissimilarities observed from one administration to the next, especially in the context of social change. The focus is only on those activities and actions undertaken by women and women's organizations more central to an understanding of the presidency.

In the chapters that follow, the key starting point in the analysis is the Kennedy administration. The focus on the years 1961–81 may be unusual since many presidency scholars begin analysis of the institution of the presidency with the development of increasingly complex and expanded advisory structures, especially the establishment of an Executive Office of the President in the 1930s during the Franklin D. Roosevelt administration.

Also, the time frame does not coincide with the time period and events often used in examining the modern feminist movement, such as the publication of Betty Friedan's *The Feminine Mystique* in 1963 or the formation of the National Organization for Women (NOW) in 1966, and the key events associated with the passage of the ERA in both houses of Congress, or the amendment's failure to win ratification during the 1970s and 1980s.[5]

However, from 1961 to 1981 there is a synchronous movement of the presidency and women to more broadly include women within the work of administrations, in political appointments made, and in policy considered. The Kennedy administration is a particularly important marker in that two dominant issues dividing the women's movement since 1920—the ERA and protective labor legislation—begin to affect decision making within the White House. The Kennedy administration's establishment of a President's Commission on the Status of Women (PCSW) structures the boundaries for debate over the two issues. The commission is a focal point in that its members represent groups and organizations long active in representing the interests of women and in bringing about descriptive as well as substantive representation of women in all three branches of government. In addition, the recommendations of the PCSW and policy issues addressed by the commission in essence set forth an enduring policy agenda for the next forty years. The commission created by Kennedy is the first formal structure established by a president to address issues of concern to women.

This movement forward came to a halt in the 1980s in spite of President Reagan's appointment of the first woman to serve on the Supreme Court, Sandra Day O'Connor, in 1981. The percentages of women appointed to judicial posts in the federal district courts and appeals courts and the percentage of women appointed in the executive branch declined.[6] In addition, ratification of the ERA by the states failed, and there was little action taken in moving forward on the new agenda items of the 1970s addressing issues of concern to women. Efforts instead were made to limit or reduce enforcement of civil rights laws, ban abortions, and reduce spending for programs such as AFDC and WIC.[7]

The 1980s and 1990s are important decades to consider, and are briefly assessed in Chapter 7, but a full analysis is beyond the scope of this book. This natural historical break (1960s and 1970s vs. 1980s and 1990s) and the differences between these decades become more evident when looking at the last two decades of the twentieth century. In the 1990s again there is movement forward with increasing percentages of appointments going to women both in the Bush and Clinton administrations and in the federal courts and in the use of executive orders as well as the passage and implementation of legislation of concern to women (e.g., family leave, funding for women's health research, and implementation of Title IX requirements).[8]

All research projects must be finite in nature in spite of the infinite questions that are raised in the course of one's exploration of a topic. Given the need to bring closure to a project which began while George H. Bush occupied the White House, the analysis of the executive branch focuses on issues of domestic policy, White House advisors, and full-time appointments requiring Senate confirmation to departments and agencies within the executive branch. Civil servants within the executive branch are primarily discussed in terms of relevant interactions with the White House. Given the growing body of work providing in-depth analyses of the State Department and Defense Department, especially in looking at the foreign service, ambassadors, delegations to international conferences and organizations, and women in the military with a focus on personnel and policy issues of concern to women, these topics will receive only brief mention.[9]

Similarly, judicial scholars have extensively studied the president's appointments to the federal courts and have also studied the influence of the solicitor general in structuring and influencing the Supreme Court's agenda on issues of gender and reproductive freedom, and so these areas will also be left for other scholars to continue to explore.[10] Given an interest in the normative questions of representation and inclusion, the focus of analysis is also on the interactions of the White House externally with groups and representatives of organizations, and not with the other two institutions of government—i.e., members of Congress or the courts.

THE CONCEPT OF REPRESENTATION
IN PRESIDENCY STUDIES

Scholarship on the presidency has tended to centralize around several themes, for example, the individual in the office, addressing such issues as personality, strengths, weaknesses, or management style or structures, especially given the growth of the Executive Office of the President and the White House Office. Other studies focus on the organization of the White House staffing system—the president as the "hub" in a "spokes-of-the-wheel" system versus an hierarchical arrangement with a strong chief of staff acting as a gatekeeper to the president. Analysis has also tended to focus on the major historical events of an administration, often providing exciting case studies by which to analyze presidential decision making. And there has been a good deal of scholarship on the presidency vis-à-vis Congress and the courts, as well as the external environment; presidential-congressional relations with a focus on "wins" and "losses" of the president's announced policy agenda, with analysis broadening to include the meaning and role of party; the president's use of a "going public" legislative strategy; and the nature and impact of modern election campaigns, as well as the president's relationship with the media and public approval of the president. Approaches to the study of the presidency have included legal, institutional, psychological, behavioral, and political/power orientations. Scholarship has suggested the importance of representation in analyzing the presidency, but the concept of representation has, perhaps, most explicitly been addressed by those scholars studying the president's appointments, and in particular the president's cabinet. The president's description of cabinet members and the press's focus on constituent representation contributes to a scholarly focus on representation.[11]

Yet representation goes beyond appointments. For instance, the electoral college strategy and wins of a presidential candidate are viewed in terms of constituent groups—thus addressing the issue of representation. Candidates strategize to maximize their support among, for example, labor, a primary constituent group in the battleground states of the Midwest, or from women when a gender gap is identified in voting patterns. As these examples illustrate, the concept of representation in presidency studies has tended to focus on one activity at a certain point in time in isolation—e.g., the 2000 election; or a newly elected president's building of a cabinet; yet representation is ongoing.

The president's relationship to any one demographic group in an ongoing and systematic manner, focusing on activity within the White House and/ or by the presidency, is an area relatively unexplored. Steven Shull's work on civil rights, while not looking at a group, focuses on a single policy area, civil rights, and the president's leadership and influence in making or changing policy which in particular affects certain groups in society, in this case, African Americans.[12] However, with increasing centralization of policy decision making in the White House, the representation of interests becomes an important phenomenon to explore, especially as structures have emerged as part of an institutionalized presidency to enhance representation and assist in agenda setting.

The institution of the presidency fully develops throughout the twentieth century both creating and responding to increasing demands on the president and the executive branch. However, it was not until the 1970s that an Office of Public Liaison was established in the White House.[13]

Charles E. Walcott and Karen M. Hult detail the history of presidential outreach, noting the lack of any White House structure or staff solely responsible for outreach activities to constituent groups until the Nixon administration, with an Office of Public Liaison not formally established until the Ford administration. Although there was little structure, outreach activities did occur in earlier administrations, but more as a response to group interests and demands. For example, a "Minorities Office," during the Truman administration was the name applied to the two staff assistants who "handled most of the contacts with black organizations and executive branch agencies on civil rights matters" during a period of time when discrimination in jobs, housing, education, and voting came to the forefront.[14]

As Walcott and Hult note, with policy decision making becoming centralized in the White House[15] and a move from institutionalized pluralism to individualized pluralism as noted by Samuel Kernell with presidents reaching out to various constituencies, the ad hoc role of group liaison taken on by White House staff in earlier administrations became formalized.[16] Increased federal programs which resulted in an increase in the number of constituent groups outside of Washington, modern technology which allowed greater communication between the White House and those around the country, and the decline of political parties resulted in the necessity for presidents to reach out to various constituencies. The ad hoc role of group liaison taken on by White House staff in earlier administrations became formalized.[17] The presidency has a representative component, and it is in discussions of representation that the inclusion of women can be assessed.

METHODOLOGY

The data for this study comes primarily from documentary material mined from the collections at the presidential libraries and the National Archives (e.g., memos, correspondence, transcripts of meetings, drafts of speeches, reports, and oral histories), the *Public Papers of the Presidents of the United States* series, congressional documents (e.g., hearings, reports, legislation, *Congressional Record* debate), as well as archival material, especially from the historical records kept by the Business and Professional Women (BPW, formerly the National Federation of Business and Professional Women), and memoirs, autobiographies, contemporary news accounts, as well as a variety of secondary sources.[18]

The First Lady is only included in analysis when appropriate from an institutional perspective, especially when issues of representation are addressed—for instance, a symbolic role in a First Lady's reaching out to women's organizations or political appointees in White House meetings or receptions and in enhancing an ongoing relationship between these organizations and the White House; or when the First Lady is playing a private role or public role in advising the president in regards to the appointment of women or supporting issues of concern to women.[19] The focus in this study is more on the routinization of behavior and interactions rather than the idiosyncrasies of each First Lady's actions.[20] The study focuses on those women with formal positions as advisors, heads, or spokespersons of organizations, political appointees, or civil servants when interacting with the White House.

The study also attempts to include the president's own voice regarding representation and inclusion of women and an agenda reflective of the concerns of women especially through examination of the *Public Papers of the Presidents of the United States.*

An institutional approach provides the analytical framework guiding this study. Any analytical framework will influence the nature of data collected for analysis. In this case the focus of both data collection and subsequent analysis is on institutional features of the presidency: White House structures, role and responsibilities, extra-constitutional powers used by presidents, decision-making processes, participants, and interactions and relationships with external forces. An institutional approach also fosters longitudinal analysis which is particularly of value in this study given the evolving women's movement especially in the 1960s and 1970s. Looking at the president's role within this institution singles out the importance of the unilateral powers of the president which provide the office of the presidency some autonomy in action, e.g., the use of executive orders and the "bully pulpit." As Stephen Wayne has noted, although the approach has limitations, "the value of the concept [institutionalization] is that it facilitates the collection of empirical data on a variety of activities. Moreover, its process orientation permits these data to be examined from a longitudinal perspective, which, in turn, allows qualitative analyses that can yield generalizable statements and prescriptive judgments."[21] The search for relationships and interdependencies results in an inductive approach to data collection, especially since women have been virtually ignored in presidency studies.

Ian S. Lustick has addressed the issue of selection bias that can result from the "[u]nself-conscious use of historical monographs" in constructing one's "primary evidentiary base."[22] While Lustick's focus is on the use of historical monographs in constructing an historical or background narrative in the course of developing and testing theories, the points raised are relevant for presidency scholars using a qualitative methodological approach drawing on thousands of pages of documents including oral histories, reports, and transcripts. The conceptual framework or questions underlying a biographical study of and history of a presidency or even the materials saved for and included in a president's memoirs all present a particular perspective. For instance, in looking at President Lyndon B. Johnson's autobiography the only mention of Liz Carpenter, press secretary and staff director for the First Lady, comes in Johnson's retelling of a story told him by his wife, Lady Bird. Johnson writes, "Lady Bird had told me a story when I finally arrived at our home in northwest Washington on the night of November 22 [following the assassination of President Kennedy earlier that day in Dallas, Texas]. She and Liz Carpenter had driven home immediately after our arrival at the White House, while I stayed on to work. On their way to our house, Liz had commented, 'It's a terrible thing to say, but the salvation of Texas is that the Governor [John Connally] was hit.' And Lady Bird replied: 'Don't think I haven't thought of that. I only wish it could have been me.'[23] Carpenter's drafting of Johnson's first words to the nation that tragic night as the newly sworn in president of the United States are not acknowledged. Carpenter is seen as a Texan and friend of the Johnsons in this story. Any other role she played—participating in White House staff meetings, serving as a spokesperson for women's interests, and also offering recommendations on appointments, political activities, and some policy— is not acknowledged as this is her only appearance in an autobiography more than six hundred pages long.

Concepts

In research at the presidential libraries I had to understand the concepts of the time to undertake a search. When I began my research at the presidential libraries many years ago I was guided by the archivists to the "HU" files to gather data on White House activity in the area of "women's issues." In the categorization scheme for the White House Central Files, HU is the designation for "Human Rights." However, in American politics the term "human rights" is rarely applied to a discussion of "women's rights," although President Jimmy Carter and First Lady Hillary Rodham Clinton, among others, have explicitly emphasized that link. I remember at the time thinking this was an odd categorization scheme, but many years later came to realize the appropriateness of that category if one steps back from a pluralist approach where one's research questions and data focus on groups gaining access to and participating in the political system. There also is a normative dimension, through which issues of reproductive freedom, access to and equality in the workforce and in education, equal rights, freedom from sexual harassment, the ending of domestic violence, and dependency care are discussed in the context of basic human rights. These are the issues which should be considered by political leaders, and they are issues the United Nations has been addressing from the beginning.

This difference in perspective became most evident in June, 1998, when President Clinton became the first president to visit China since the Tiananmen Square demonstrations for democracy and the violent government response to the demonstrators. The visit prompted hundreds of articles written by American reporters regarding human rights in China both in anticipation of Clinton's trip and also while covering Clinton in China. In the previous week, and while Clinton was in China, the U.S. Supreme Court handed down rulings on several cases "creating a new national policy" on sexual harassment for the first time.[24] The court's rulings received coverage, but no mention was ever made of this being an issue of human rights. Ironically, at a question-and-answer session with students at Beijing University, the president was asked if there were any "problems in the area of democracy, freedom and human rights" in the United States. President Clinton responded, but only with a focus on discrimination on the basis of race. In asking the question there was a clear attempt to link the issue of human rights with women's rights, yet neither the president nor the press made that link, in spite of the Supreme Court's ruling earlier in the week. During the George W. Bush administration the rights of Afghan women— a human rights issue—in an ironic twist became a means through which

President Bush could reach out to American women for their support in closing the "gender gap" in presidential elections.

As Charles Jones explains in *The Presidency in a Separated System*, government does continue and policy making always goes forward in the face of obstacles, as so vividly demonstrated by the impeachment of President Bill Clinton in December, 1998. Even with a trial set to begin in the Senate as soon as the 106th Congress began in January, 1999, the president was consulting with Congress over the budget, health care reform, and other domestic and foreign policy issues. It is also important to understand that policy can change without congressional action. Executive orders become a way for the president to unilaterally institute change—an avenue presidents have taken especially in ending discriminatory behavior and hiring practices throughout the federal government. But real change in policy can be slow. As Vice President Al Gore accepted his party's nomination in August, 2000, he stated that the budget and personnel needed for enforcement of civil rights laws were both on his agenda. He noted that his twenty-four years of experience in government—as a U.S. representative and senator, and as vice president, had given him the insight to respond to past policy failures. There was a clear and pragmatic recognition of the continuity of policy and the difficulty in bringing about change. Likewise, the focus by scholars on a single administration, and the highlighting of activities within an administration, often leaves us with blinders regarding the inherited agenda already on a president's plate. There exists a cumulative responsibility for a new president—the agenda is in place; how much action a president may take, however, is variable.

As one works with the written legacy of an administration—the reams of paper passed through the Oval Office, around the Oval Office, and through endless corridors in the buildings of the federal government—the role that the institution of the presidency plays becomes evident. While presidents may not be directly involved in each decision that is made, the president is still accountable for actions of his presidency and the management of the executive branch.

As Sidney Milkis has observed, however, under Franklin D. Roosevelt there was "an emergent separation between presidential government and party government."[25] This will become most evident by the 1960s when, as Samuel Kernell has identified, a system of "individualized pluralism" emerges.[26] The women's movement's push into mainstream politics will both contribute to and reflect this transformation. "Roosevelt's party leadership and the New Deal mark the culmination of efforts, which began in the Progressive Era, to loosen the grip of partisan politics on the councils of power, with a view to strengthening national administrative capacities and extending the programmatic commitments of the federal government."[27] The role of the president in shaping the composition of the federal workforce would take on a truly significant dimension following the growth in government resulting from the New Deal legislation of the 1930s and Lyndon Johnson's Great Society programs of the 1960s.

In the chapters that follow, it becomes clear that a president, using the tools of the Office of the President, can include women more broadly in the administration, through management of the career civil service, selection of appointees or department heads, and the composition and structure of a White House office. The president can also influence the lives of women both directly and indirectly through legislative action and executive directives. In turn, the "women's movement" has influenced the president's agenda and actions taken in each administration.

While no woman has served as president or vice president, and only a few have been appointed to the president's cabinet, women have influenced decisions made in the Oval Office. Women have provided both the legitimacy for the president to take unilateral action and the constituency seeking such actions. Especially since 1920, when women greatly expanded the potential electorate, presidents and their advisors have had to respond to this growing constituency long before attention was paid to "soccer moms" in the 1996 election.

Presidential leadership in regards to the inclusion of women can thus be looked at in several areas: presidential direction and leadership via the administration of departments and agencies, the use of executive orders, support for legislation, implementation of policy, and the president's management style—including the selection and use of political appointees and White House staff as advisors and the organization and structure of the White House Office. While the president has no constitutional or formal role in the passage of a constitutional amendment in Congress, or in the ratification process by the states, the president can use the "bully pulpit" to persuade.

These actions contribute to governing. However, the president is part of a larger governmental system, inheriting an agenda, with interest groups, political parties, ongoing executive branch departments, agencies, and programs, Congress, the courts, and the states all part of that system. Throughout the book the emphasis is on the policies of each administration and those who shape that policy.

While this book provides a political narrative, it is not an exhaustive study of all actions, but rather a beginning. It examines the issues of representation and participation: how women have been a part of the presidency, as advisors, appointees, constituents, and finally as voters and beneficiaries of policy, and how the institution of the presidency itself has changed in response to the evolutionary inclusion of women.

Women and the Executive Branch

An Introduction
and Historical Overview

IN AN EARLY MATTER to come to his attention as president, in 1790, George Washington had to decide the fate of a political appointee, Mary Katherine Goddard. Goddard was the postmaster of Baltimore at the time the new government was emerging and had been in that post since 1775. As a printer and newspaper publisher she had been in favor of the revolutionary action following the Stamp Act in 1765, and she owned the printing press that was the first to print a copy of the Declaration of Independence, with all fifty-six signers.[1]

With her position in jeopardy, she petitioned the new president. With the support of several hundred business leaders in Baltimore, she requested that she be allowed to retain the position she had held in the colonial government and under the Articles of Confederation. Members of Congress lobbied on her behalf, even recommending that she be named postmaster general. It was to no avail. Samuel Osgood became the first postmaster general under the Constitution and Washington let each department head have "free rein in dealing with . . . [his] subordinates."[2] Washington wrote to Goddard:

> I have uniformly avoided interfering with any appointments which do not require my official agency, and the Resolutions and Ordinances establishing the Post Office under the former Congress, and which have

been recognized by the present Government, giving power to the Post-master General to appoint his own Deputies, and making him account-able for their conduct, is an insuperable objection to my taking part in this matter.

I have directed your Memorial to be laid before the Postmaster General, who will take such measures thereon as his Judgment may direct.[3]

Osgood did not return Goddard to her post; she had lost her position "on the ground that someone was needed who could visit and superintend the Southern department of the postal system, a responsibility involving more traveling than a woman could manage."[4] Goddard's story points up, on an obvious level, the cultural biases that women have faced. But it also illuminates a constraint that presidents have faced in exercising their appointment power: Washington set an important precedent in letting his department heads select their subordinates.[5] In addition, with the president and Congress of the same party sharing power throughout the mid 1800s, and Congress predominant in the setting of policy, patronage (the "spoils of office") was often shared by the president with individual members of Congress who influenced the appointment process.[6]

Nonetheless, although they lacked the legal and political standing of men, women did win appointments to lower posts. The two departments which had the most work were the Departments of the Post Office and the Treasury.[7] A number of women were listed as working as postmasters and as clerks and assistants in post offices when *A Register of Officers and Agents, Civil, Military, and Naval, in the Service of the United States* was published by the Department of State in 1816. Later listings indicated that women were employed as teachers in the Indian Service and as lighthouse keepers.[8] However, no president included a woman in his cabinet until Franklin D. Roosevelt appointed Frances Perkins as secretary of labor in 1933.

As Abigail Adams so clearly noted, the members of the Continental Congress influenced the role and rights women would have as the new government was created. While it would take more than 140 years from the time of Abigail's admonishment of her husband until all women in the United States won the right to vote, women did begin to participate in this new government from its earliest days, and presidents from George Washington on would influence both their involvement and the policies that concerned them either through the action or inaction of their administrations.

MANAGING THE GOVERNMENT

Students of the presidency have recently focused attention on what a president can do unilaterally—that is, independent of Congress, in an extra-constitutional way. Moe and Howell have provided a theoretical framework in order to analyze

> the president's formal capacity for taking unilateral action, and thus for making law on his own. Often, presidents do this through executive orders. Sometimes they do it through proclamations or executive agreements or national security directives. But whatever vehicles they may choose, the end result is that presidents can and do make new law—and thus shift the existing status quo—without the explicit consent of Congress.[9]

A quick review of government actions in the last century leaves no question that presidents can manage the executive bureaucracy, set the national policy agenda, and more broadly lead a nation independent of Congress, though these actions are subject to future limitations by the courts or Congress. Often cited examples include Franklin D. Roosevelt's executive agreement with England to exchange destroyers for bases, Truman's executive order desegregating the armed forces, and Jimmy Carter's unilateral abrogation of a treaty with Taiwan. For this reason, the inclusion of women as participants in and constituents of government can be greatly influenced by the actions taken by a president and his or her administration. How presidents have shaped governmental participation by women, and how the women's movement has shaped the direction of administrations, is the subject of this book.

Many scholars identify the modern, or "institutional presidency," as emerging during the Franklin D. Roosevelt administration, which brought growth in the role and responsibilities of the federal government in the daily lives of citizens. This administrative state arises shortly after women have won the right to vote. The expansion of government provided opportunities for women, both in terms of employment and benefits received.

Women's participation in government has thus grown over time, as has the president's ability to manage the government. What follows is a brief introduction and overview of how the president's role in gaining control over government personnel and policy has evolved from the "spoils system" to a civil service inclusive of women. For women, access to government developed mainly through interest group activity, since women did not gain status, power, and representation in political parties until the political parties themselves were at their nadir. In addition, presidents and their administrations have responded to the demands and concerns of this new electorate through executive orders, advisory committees and commissions, and White House reorganization, as well as via the "bully pulpit." Presidents have, to varying degrees, therefore, shaped and responded to the women's movement throughout the twentieth century, especially through use of the informal powers of the office.

The Patronage System

From 1816 on, the *Register of Officers and Agents, Civil, Military, and Naval, in the Service of the United States* identifies a number of women on the federal government payroll, but mostly serving in positions in the states and territories. Clara Barton was a pioneer in opening up executive branch positions for women in Washington, D.C. Because her life history is fairly well documented, examining her career in government in some detail illuminates the general experience of women working in the federal government in the nineteenth century.

Barton began work in the summer of 1854 as a clerk in the Patent Office.[10] She was but one of a handful of women working in government. The precise number of women working in the government before the establishment of the civil service is not known since women would often take over a position held by a father or husband upon their death, but would leave his name on the roll.[11] Until the creation of the civil service, a patron was needed. Barton was successful in gaining the support of her representative from Massachusetts. In the case of Barton, while she had the support of Charles Mason, the commissioner of patents, not everyone looked favorably on the employment of women, and so her name was not included in the official roll of federal employees sent to Congress each year.[12] When Mason left his post as commissioner, his successor acted on the wishes of his boss Secretary Robert McClelland and fired Barton and the three other women working in the Patent Office. One historian has noted that McClelland, "an old-line politician . . . considered that the women were taking jobs from deserving men who, even if not more competent, were at least voters. The sight of teapots and hoopskirts in the office irritated him."[13] Barton would regain her position only to lose it when the Democrats gained control of the White House.

During the Pierce administration, when Barton began her work in government, both men and women copyists had been paid at the rate of ten cents for every one hundred words copied. A decade later, women were allowed to "earn only eight cents per hundred words copied,"[14] and in fact, Congress soon statutorily set the pay for women at half that paid to men.[15]

During the Civil War, Barton began working full time ferrying food and medical supplies to Union troops, yet her name was not removed from the federal registers.[16] Her supervisor was a Union sympathizer, and, as was the case for others working for the Union forces, she continued to receive her salary during the war. Her replacement received half the pay, but was not listed on the registers while Barton's name remained on the list.[17] After the war ended, Barton created an Office of Correspondence with Friends of the Missing Men of the United States Army. Three years later the office was closed, having answered 63,182 letters and identified 22,000 men. Though she lost her job at the Patent Office after the war ended, she did receive an appropriation of $15,000 from Congress following her testimony before the Joint Committee on Reconstruction, as reimbursement for money she had spent in providing supplies to Union troops during the war, and to allow her to continue the system of correspondence she had developed to identify the missing men.[18]

Barton acknowledged the role the Civil War had played in facilitating the advancement and recognition of the work of women. "The war . . . had proven the sincerity of women who wanted to contribute to society, had shown them as a political force in every soldiers' aid society and abolitionist rally. And the war had marked woman's worth. 'Only an opportunity was wanting . . . for woman to prove to man that she *could* be in earnest—that she had character, and firmness of purpose—that she *was* good for something in an emergency. . . . The war afforded her this opportunity.'"[19]

Gen. Francis E. Spinner, the treasurer of the United States during the Lincoln administration, increased the numbers of women in government during the war to relieve the increase in vacancies resulting from men joining the war effort.[20] However, given that female clerks were receiving half the pay of male clerks in the department, budget considerations were also a strong motivating factor in Spinner's hiring of women.[21]

The experience Barton had in seeing her own position advance and decline would set the pattern for the next hundred years. In the twentieth century, both during and after the two world wars, women's role in society and in the workforce would see tremendous change.

During this period of time, the president's role was limited. Congressional ascendancy during the 1800s was partially an outgrowth of the presidential nominating system which gave Congress the power to both nominate and select candidates.[22] The size of government in this period was small, although growing. Executive departments and agencies were in direct contact with committees in Congress, seeking support without the White House coordination that would begin to evolve with passage of the Budget and Accounting Act of 1921.[23]

Congress did consider the issue of equal pay for equal work for federal employees, and in 1870 passed a provision referred to as section 165 of the Revised Statutes, which "was watered down to *permit* appointing officers to employ 'female clerks' at the same pay as men."[24] However, although this provision was intended "to benefit women in the matter of pay," for nearly the next ninety-two years, from 1870 until 1962, the act "was construed . . . to give appointing officers the unrestricted right to consider only men (or only women) in appointment."[25] As a result, many jobs in the government remained closed to women. Especially closed to women were high-level posts. This remained the case until Julia Lathrop was appointed to head the Children's Bureau in 1912. The fact that high-level positions were only open to men resulted in Lathrop finding that her new office was "meticulously furnished with every item in the list of standard equipment for high Federal officials—including a spittoon!"[26]

The Impact of a Civil Service System

Following the assassination of President James A. Garfield in 1881 by Charles J. Guiteau, who was described in the *New York Times* in its coverage of the event as a "half-crazed, pettifogging lawyer, who [had] been an unsuccessful applicant for office under the Government,"[27] Congress created a civil service system. The need for a professional workforce, without the "spoils system," became more apparent with the growth of government. The Civil Service Act of 1883 created a merit system in which women were allowed to compete for positions. However, those hiring federal workers remained able to restrict a position to only men or only women applicants. Few women were employed. By 1904, women were only 7.5 percent of the civil service workforce. As was the case elsewhere in society, government positions were opened up to women during World War I. By 1919, women made up one-fifth of the federal workforce. Prior to the war, only 40 percent of civil service exams had been open to women.[28] This changed in 1919, when all competitive civil service exams were opened to women.[29]

Shortly after passage of the Budget and Accounting Act of 1921, Congress moved to solidify the president's responsibility in managing the government with the Classification Act of 1923. This act, coming just three years after ratification of the Nineteenth Amendment giving women the right to vote, reaffirmed the principle of equal pay for equal work in the federal workforce. In fact, salaries were nearly equal for men and women in a study done of appointments made in the 1919–20 fiscal year.[30] Also, up until this point in time, the Congress, through its appropriations process, had set for each agency the number of civil servants at each level and set salaries for each position. However, with the growth in government "for the Congress to pretend to evaluate each job each year, in a growing national government, had become absurd; and to even approach equity in the results— 'equal pay for equal work'—was impossible."[31] The president and executive branch would now be responsible for establishing positions within pay grades and for the composition of the federal workforce.[32]

The status of women in the federal sector during the 1930s was affected by several actions taken by presidents and their administrations, as well as by Congressional legislation. For example, Congress, in responding to the nation's needs at the time of the Great Depression, passed section 213 of the 1932 National Economy Act, which prohibited husbands and wives from working in the federal civil service at the same time, therefore forcing some women to leave government service. (The National Recovery Act, passed a year later, reduced the number of hours of work per week to open up jobs to the unemployed.)[33] Within five years 1,600 married women in the federal government lost their jobs.[34] Yet, in that same year, in December, 1932, after his election defeat, President Hoover signed an executive order which "stipulated that appointing officers may no longer specify either sex as preferred, and that appointments must go to the persons highest on the register unless the work actually is unsuited to their sex."[35] However, in spite of Hoover's executive order change would be slow in coming. His administration would not have the time to implement this directive.

Beginning in 1933 all women in the federal government had to take their husband's married names. With section 213 in place, some women were thus forced to lead double lives following a secret marriage, with two households, different addresses, and even different sets of friends.[36] Section 213 was repealed in 1937 following an intensive lobbying campaign by the National Woman's Party and the Women's Bureau coalition.[37] Even after section 213 was repealed, women serving as political appointees and not under the protection of the civil service system faced loss of jobs as the economy remained an issue.

In addition, under a new administration, Franklin D. Roosevelt's attorney general re-interpreted the 1870 law as "recogniz[ing] the legal right of appointing officers to decide whether to employ a man or woman in a particular Federal job."[38] While civil service exams were open to both men and women, the appointing officer could request a list of eligible men or women only. Table 1.1 reflects the impact of this interpretation on the federal government's hiring practices over the next thirty years with data from the final months of the Eisenhower administration and the beginning of the Kennedy administration.

TABLE 1.1
Requests Received in the Washington, D.C., Office
from September 1960 to February 1961

Grade Level of Positions	Percentage of Requests to Select Men Only
1–4	16%
5–8	56%
9–12	69%
13–15	94%

Source: John Macy, "Employment Policies and Practices of the Federal Government," Feb. 12, 1962. "General Meetings 2/12/62–2/13/62" folder, PCSW, Box 2, John F. Kennedy Library.

During World War II, women were able to increase their ranks in the federal civil service, constituting 40 percent of all federal employees by 1944. Yet after the war, positions were again closed to women, and by 1947, women were only 26 percent of the workforce.[39]

During the latter part of the nineteenth century and early in the twentieth century, while the spoils system was being replaced by a merit system (yet one not fully open to women), women were also beginning to make inroads into the political party structure which had been so important for Clara Barton and others in securing a position in the federal government.

WOMEN AS POLITICAL PARTICIPANTS

Throughout the 1800s, women had become more involved in politics in several distinct, yet overlapping ways, with the Civil War especially providing opportunities for women to enter federal service.[40] Following the Civil War, in spite of the lack of suffrage, women's participation in political party activity began to emerge. However, meaningful participation by women in political activities would come about more quickly through the women's organizations that emerged during the first half of the twentieth century than through the party organizations. Once suffrage for women was achieved nationwide in 1920, the influence and role of women became even more pronounced.

Women and the National Political Parties, 1876–1961

Neither party had moved to include women until the late 1800s.[41] Paula Baker has described the party organizations that emerged with the development of a strong two-party system in the United States during the 1800s.

> The right to vote was something important that men held in common. And, as class, geography, kinship, and community supplied less reliable sources of identification than they had at an earlier time, men could at least define themselves in reference to women. Parties were fraternal organizations that tied men together with others like themselves in their communities, and they brought men together as participants in the same partisan culture.[42]

Women began to be included in the activities of the national political parties when, in 1876, Sarah Jane Spencer of the National Woman's Suffrage Association was granted the opportunity to speak on the second day of the National Republican Convention by unanimous consent.[43] According to an account of the event in the *New York Times*:

> The scene was an exceedingly noteworthy one, and well deserving of a more detailed description than it is possible to give it at this time. The woman, a slight and delicate person, but full of nerve and courage, stood up before the 5,000 men present without displaying the slightest trepidation or alarm, and during the ten minutes allotted her she succeeded in making herself heard in all parts of the hall, and in this respect, too, was much more successful than many of the strong men who made speeches after her. She urged upon the Convention the policy of favorably considering the claims of women, and warning them that if they failed to do so they would lose the large and intelligent vote of the thoughtful women of the country, who were sure to be enfranchised sooner or later.[44]

In her ten-minute address she noted that suffrage had been granted to African Americans with ratification of the Fifteenth Amendment, but not to women.[45] The 1892 Republican national convention marked the first seating of women at a convention, Therese Jenkins and Cora Carleton, alternates from Wyoming, in that state's first delegation to attend a convention after gaining statehood.[46] In 1900 Elizabeth Cohen became the first woman to attend a Democratic National Convention, where she delivered a seconding speech for William Jennings Bryan.[47]

From 1892 until 1920, only a handful of women were seated as either delegates or alternates, numbering about 1 percent of either party's convention delegates in 1916. However, with the suffrage movement nearing success in 1920, both the Democratic and Republican parties responded to this potential new constituency by increasing the representation of women to their respective party conventions.[48] At the 1924 party conventions more than 10 percent of the delegates were women.[49] In addition, the Republican National Committee (RNC) established a Woman's Division in 1918. Two years later, "Republican women maintained active organizations under a woman director in each of the three [Harding] campaign headquarters in New York City, Chicago, and Marion, Ohio."[50] In the same year, the Democrats passed a rule requiring equal representation of men and women on the national party committee. The Republicans followed suit in 1924, although a proposal to have a man and woman from each state on the RNC had been introduced at the last Republican convention.[51]

In spite of the dramatic increase in representation of women between 1916 and 1924, the percentage of women delegates at the Republican and Democratic Party conventions remained less than 20 percent for the next four decades until the party reforms of the 1970s.[52] Yet even without formal representation, substantive concerns of women had received some attention from convention delegates since the late 1800s. For example, in 1896 with no women delegates, the Republican National Convention included an "Equal Rights for Women" plank in their platform, which stated: "The Republican Party is mindful of the rights and interests of women and believes that they should be accorded equal opportunities, equal pay for equal work, and protection to the home. We favor the admission of women to wider spheres of usefulness and welcome their co-operation in rescuing the country from Democratic and Populist mismanagement and misrule."[53] The platform did not, however, call for an ERA. Four years earlier, in 1892, the party had heard from Mrs. J. Ellen Foster, chairman of the Woman's Republican Association of the United States, who had told delegates and party leaders to "seek the cooperation of Republican women sympathizers in their communities."[54] A vote of the convention was unanimous in its endorsement of this volunteer group of Republican women to assist in campaigns.

Setting the Agenda: Party Platforms

With women nearly absent from national party activity, it is not surprising that the platforms of the Democratic and Republican parties would dance around the issues of suffrage and equal rights for decades. For many years the emphasis in the national party platforms would be on the role of states in changing laws or their own state constitutions to provide equal rights for women. Wyoming, which as a territory had granted suffrage to women in 1869, included such a provision in its state constitution when it joined the Union as the forty-fourth state in 1890.[55]

A plank in the 1876 Republican platform clearly noted the implications of a federal system on the rights of women:

> The Republican Party recognizes with approval the substantial advances recently made toward the establishment of equal rights for women, by the many important amendments effected by Republican legislatures in the laws which govern the personal and property relations of wives, mothers, and widows, and by the appointment and election of women to the superintendence of education, charities, and other public trusts. The honest demands of this class of citizens for additional rights, privileges and immunities should be treated with respectful consideration.[56]

In fact, in 1916, as the suffrage movement gained momentum, both the Democratic and Republican Party platforms emphasized that women's suffrage was an issue for the states, not the national government, and included the planks near the end of their platforms.[57] But as Sara Hunter Graham has noted, World War I and splits within the women's movement between the National American Woman Suffrage Association (NAWSA) and the National Woman's Party contributed to an intensified support for a constitutional amendment.[58] Even President Woodrow Wilson had changed his position from favoring state action to supporting an amendment by 1917. Wilson's support came in part from watching the growing "militancy of the NWP [National Woman's Party]; the pickets [of the White House and congressional office building], jail terms, and hunger strikes" suggesting the "inevitability of the reform."[59] He was also lobbied by Helen Hamilton Gardener, who was able to work through several White House contacts with direct access to the president.[60]

The Republican platform in 1920 was notable for its inclusion of provisions that would reflect the agenda throughout the next fifty years for federal involvement in the lives of women, especially working women, and demanded that presidents respond, including a call for "the permanent establishment of the Women's Bureau in the United States Department of Labor to serve as a source of information to the States and to Congress." Other planks in the platform included: equal pay for federal women employees; "federal aid for vocational training . . . [to] take into consideration the special attitudes and needs of women workers;" and limits on hours for women in "intensive industry."[61]

In time, after the Nineteenth Amendment had shifted some responsibility in securing and protecting the rights of women from the states to the federal government, momentum slowly began to build for greater protection of equal rights for women by the national government. In 1940, the Republican Party platform included a call for a *constitutional amendment* providing for equal rights for men and women, the first in either a Democratic or Republican Party platform. The plank read, "We favor submission by Congress to the States of an amendment to the Constitution providing for equal rights for men and women." In 1944, the Democrats joined the Republicans in this endorsement. And beginning in 1948, the Republican Party platform returned to the issue of "equal pay for equal work regardless of sex," first raised in 1896.

The Politics of Participation

Once suffrage was won, women became more visible in leadership roles and active in both the Democratic and Republican campaigns for president. For example, Sally Hert managed a women's campaign for Calvin Coolidge in 1924. Future First Lady Eleanor Roosevelt, who earlier had served an "apprenticeship" with the League of Women Voters, was in charge of Al Smith's New York Women's campaign in 1928.[62]

The 1944 election, in the middle of World War II, found an electorate that was more than 50 percent women.[63] Twenty years earlier when women first entered the national electorate, there were fears that a women's bloc could determine the outcome of a national election, and party leaders increased the formal representation of women in the party as convention delegates, but for only a few short years. Not surprisingly, given the composition of the electorate in 1944, a woman was once again heard from at one of the major two party conventions when Representative Clare Boothe Luce (R-CT) delivered a formal address to the delegates, enhancing the symbolic representation of women in the party.[64] And as noted above, both parties included support for an ERA in their respective platforms. Both parties had recognized the potential strength of women voters.

By 1960, the view that the party organization was the best way for women to be elected and appointed to public office was quite well accepted. In fact, in the report of the Subcommittee on Political Rights of President Kennedy's Commission on the Status of Women, issued in March, 1963, the conclusion was that "the role of women in the political parties is a major, if not principal determinant of their achievement of public position." The subcommittee specifically noted the representation of women and men on both the Democratic National Committee (DNC) and RNC, and the number of states which required a 50-50 equal distribution of women and men in party offices and committees.[65] However, at the same time a change was under way. Political parties would no longer be the focal point in bringing women into government service. As will be seen in the next chapter, the Kennedy and Johnson administrations brought personnel operations into the White House.

THE GROWING INFLUENCE OF WOMEN'S ORGANIZATIONS, 1920–60

A number of scholars identify the 1970s as the period in which women's organizations, such as the National Federation of Business and Professional Women's Clubs (NFBPWC or BPW), the National Council of Negro Women, and the American Association of University Women (AAUW), "began to address women's rights and problems."[66] Others have noted that "among educated, upper-status women, this change was taking place in the 50s and 60s, well before the women's liberation movement as such came into being."[67] Kristi Andersen has found that:

> During the 1950s and 1960s, the growing numbers of working women who entered more fully into the political sphere did so as individuals; there were no organizations which mobilized them as women, and perhaps even more important, there was little sense of shared problems which could motivate individual participation and which might form the basis for a new social and political movement as well. The rise of the women's "movement," despite its structural fragmentation, created the latter condition; and our data seem to indicate that in 1972, the Democratic party and the candidacy of George McGovern came close to providing the first— a political organization through which the interests of the women's movement could be expressed.[68]

Perhaps the role of women's organizations in contributing to the national agenda was not as visible in earlier periods, and so most scholars have focused on the groups which emerge in the late 1960s and early 1970s, united in support for an ERA, at a time when the ERA finally achieved a two-thirds vote in both the House and Senate, and was then submitted to the states. With an amendment drive being fought in fifty separate states, coordination of activities through a national organization became more apparent and important. However, unions had long been working on behalf of women, as had organizations such as the National Federation of Business and Professional Women.[69] There was, however, a tension between the interests of professional and business women and the interests of blue-collar workers, with an ERA viewed by the latter as a threat to the protective workplace legislation that had long been sought. In addition, many of the women's organizations had a history of non-partisanship. Some scholars may have interpreted that as apolitical, which was not the case. And the organizations themselves had to make conscious decisions as to what political role to play, in addition to lobbying for policy. For example, the NFBPWC had been active in moving issues of concern on to the national agenda through involvement in the Women's Joint-Congressional Committee beginning in the 1920s. But not until 1944 did the organization allow its member organizations to endorse candidates for appointive and elective office.[70] The change in position can clearly be observed in an address by Hazel Palmer, president of the National Federation of Business and Professional Women, who in September, 1956, urged her members to take an active role in the upcoming elections.

> We owe it to not only our communities, state and nation to participate in political activities—but to ourselves as well. While partisan politics has no place in our Federation activities, let us not fail to urge qualified women to seek elective and appointive offices and placement in policy-making posts, at every level of government. Let us support these women in such manner and to such extent as fairness and good ethics permit in a non-partisan organization.[71]

Furthermore, in looking at two studies of Democratic and Republican Party committeewomen, one published in 1933 and the second in 1944, there is an overlap of those women who are active in political parties with those women who are active in women's organizations. Sophonisba P. Breckinridge's 1933 study of Republican and Democratic Party national committeewomen, and Marguerite J. Fisher's and Betty Whitehead's follow-up study in 1944, both indicated that each woman party activist responding to their respective questionnaires belonged to at least one women's organization, among them the League of Women Voters, YWCA, General Federation of Women's Clubs, and the NFBPWC.[72]

However, as Breckinridge observed in her comprehensive study, there were in essence two groups of political women who emerged in the post-suffrage period, each with a different agenda and strategy. The Women's Joint-Congressional Committee was formed as an umbrella organization for groups whose leaders would, over the next four decades, come together on a regular basis and, in fact, set the agenda that the women's movement of the 1970s would address. And, while individual members of these groups were also active in party politics, the groups themselves would testify before the national party platform committees.[73] The other organization of women was the National Woman's Party, whose sole objective was passage of the ERA.[74]

Others have identified three groups of women: clubwomen; women born in the twentieth century with a college education, and the third group—social workers, such as Molly Dewson and Emma Guffey Miller.[75] Still others have noted the role of women in running for union office and serving as representatives to labor unions beginning in the 1800s, and in organizing the Women's Trade Union League, which eventually focused on protective labor legislation for women. Again there was an overlap between women in labor and professional women.[76] The number of groups, variety of groups, and competing interests all with their own respective agendas foreshadow the tension that arose within subsequent administrations in deciding national policy concerning women. For example, in the 1970s, the decade when the ERA would nearly meet with success, both Presidents Gerald R. Ford and Jimmy Carter decided to embrace a broad agenda—an ERA was one objective, but with so few amendment drives achieving success, these administrations also attempted to set policies which would clearly establish rights through statutes and presidential directives.[77] In the next chapter the history of this split between labor and supporters of the ERA with direct implications on the presidency will be more fully addressed.

BUILDING AN AGENDA, ESTABLISHING NETWORKS, AND CHANGING GOVERNMENT STRUCTURES

Women began to play a more influential role in defining issues for the national agenda as well as in shaping the structure of the national government to be responsive to those issues at the beginning of the twentieth century during Theodore Roosevelt's administration. From this point on, each administration would begin to include women in appointive positions and as advisors in both formal and informal ways and become more responsive to issues of concern to women.

For instance, in 1906, Mary McDowell and Jane Addams, both social reformers, met with a receptive President Theodore Roosevelt to request a government investigation of the work conditions for women and children in the workforce.[78] However, Roosevelt had already given attention to this issue. In his fourth Annual Message (December 6, 1904), Roosevelt had stated that the Department of Commerce and Labor should compile data on state labor laws, especially in regards to child labor.[79] Roosevelt repeated this request the following year.[80] Congress responded to Roosevelt's request and appropriated money to examine the conditions of children and women in the workforce.[81] Although women were included in the data, the emphasis at this period of time was on the protection of children, and specifically, the passage of legislation to outlaw child labor, at least in the District of Columbia.[82] In 1909, Roosevelt called the first White House Conference on Children.[83]

Responding to the recommendations of the conference, a Children's Bureau was established in the Department of Labor[84] during the last year of the Taft administration. Following lobbying by a number of individuals, including Susan B. Anthony, as well as First Lady Helen (Nellie) Taft, President Taft appointed Julia Lathrop to head the new Children's Bureau. Lathrop had been the only woman among the final four candidates. This marked the first time a woman was named to head a major bureau.[85] The report which emerged from the study of the conditions of women and children, and authorized in 1907, also led to the creation of a Women's Division of the Bureau of Labor Statistics in the Department of Commerce and Labor.[86]

Establishing Networks

During this time period, Franklin D. Roosevelt gained firsthand knowledge of the work of both Frances Perkins and Mary Anderson in the area of labor policy. Perkins became acquainted with Roosevelt while he was serving two terms in the New York State Senate. Roosevelt, Al Smith, and Robert E. Wagner all served in the state legislature at the same time, and all three worked on passage of the legislation creating the New York State Factory Investigation Commission. Wagner chaired the Factory Investigation Commission, and Perkins served as the commission's secretary during its four-year investigation.[87] Following the Triangle Shirtwaist Factory Fire in 1911, the technical information and analysis compiled helped the state pass factory safety legislation. Perkins would later serve in Roosevelt's cabinet as secretary of labor, the first woman appointed to a cabinet position.

During World War I, Mary Anderson, assistant director of Woman in Industry Service in the Department of Labor was able to attend meetings of the War Labor Policies Board, chaired by Felix Frankfurter.[88] At the time, Roosevelt, assistant secretary of the navy, represented the Navy Department on that board.[89] Later, in the Roosevelt administration, Mary Anderson served as director of the Women's Bureau in the Department of Labor.[90]

Working Together: The Federal Government and Women's Organizations
Women have long been organized in religious, cultural, and fraternal groups. However, once the United States had entered World War I, it became clear that there were no national organizations of women that could be called upon to fill manpower shortages arising from the entry of the United States into the war. The War Work Council, a part of the YWCA, received a grant of $65,000 from Secretary of War Newton Baker to conduct a survey and determine how best women could help in the war effort. The YWCA, with membership organizations in most states, invited "two representative business and professional women from each state east of the Rocky Mountains to meet for a two-day conference in the Ann Fulton Cafeteria of the YWCA in New York City on May 11 and 12, 1918."[91] The purpose was "to consider ways and means to allocate the business and professional women qualified by training and experience to take places of the men who were leaving the offices and business positions for service."[92] A committee, the National Business Women's Committee, was formed to work to broaden representation from all the states.

Before the committee could take much action, the armistice to end the war was signed on November 11, 1918. However, Secretary Baker allowed the group to continue to use the $65,000 as a post-war project to establish "a broad organization of women from all training, professions, and disciplines."[93] This organization paralleled the development of national organizations for men, including the American Legion, incorporated through an act of Congress in September, 1919.[94]

The first national meeting of the new organization for women, the NFBPWC, came just one month after the Senate had joined the House in passing the suffrage amendment.[95] This new organization had the potential to influence the national policy agenda once women gained the right to vote in all forty-eight states. From its very beginning, this organization had lobbied for the civil and political rights of women. It had "urged the open-ing of all Civil Service examinations to women as well as to men, and . . . asked that official rank be given to all nurses who had served in the World War."[96] In addition it set out to compile information on women in the workforce, especially their working conditions.

Also in 1919, the Women's Joint-Congressional Committee was formed as a clearinghouse for the twenty-two national organizations that had offices or representatives in Washington. The clearinghouse monitored legislation of concern to women.[97] This group included the NFBPWC, American As-sociation of University Women, American Nurses Association, Girl Scouts, National Council of Jewish Women, Inc., National Women's Trade Union League, and the YWCA.[98]

During the 1920s activity took place on a number of fronts to establish a working relationship between the White House and the various organiza-tions representing the different interests of women. The focus of legislative and regulatory action centered around the well-being and health of work-ing mothers and potential mothers. The working conditions of women in the workforce had now moved on to the national agenda.[99] World War I provided the impetus for the creation of a Women's Bureau. The Women's Bureau, created a decade before the emergence of the social welfare pro-grams of the New Deal, was to assist the states in setting workplace stan-dards and policies to "promote the welfare of wage-earning women, improve their working conditions, increase their efficiency, and advance their opportunities for profitable employment."[100] The Women's Bureau would not enforce laws, but rather gather data on labor legislation passed and share this information among the states. It would provide information on these laws, and on how to file a complaint, and initiate model programs to ben-efit women workers (e.g., minimum wage laws and hour laws). In addition, the bureau conducted investigations into the working conditions of women in various occupations in different states and assisted states that lacked the resources to do such investigations. The bureau also did studies on the demographics of women in the workforce, drawing on the academic com-munity, as well as groups such as the NFBPWC, for assistance.[101] In addi-tion, the bureau worked with, and published, a survey the NFBPWC had done of its own members. The Women's Bureau began gathering employ-ment data for women in every sector of society. The scope of these studies ranged from working conditions including "the installation and mainte-nance of toilet facilities in places of employment," to "changes in women's occupations."[102]

Limitations of Presidential Leadership

With an expansion of responsibilities for the federal government, the president's appointments would become more important in defining presidential leadership. Appointments could respond to symbolic needs for inclusion of a wide range of interests in society, whether Westerners, farmers, business, labor, women, or others, and appointments could also signify the importance of a particular department and policy area, or the role a secretary might assume given the expertise and interests of both the cabinet secretary and the president.

Yet appointments are but one tool of presidential leadership. The management style of a president will influence both where decisions are made and by whom. A president may make selective use of cabinet secretaries to more broadly encompass external ideas, or the president may turn to an inner circle of White House advisors in making decisions. Throughout the twentieth century, presidents have also made use of a wide range of external advisory structures, including commissions, advisory boards, and White House conferences. Cabinet secretaries and White House staff have also drawn on these bodies for advice and recommendations.

As the century wore on, and the modern presidency began to take form, presidents could more directly set a legislative agenda and influence the shape and direction of public policy.[103] Thus, presidential leadership can be defined by the president's involvement in directly shaping and implementing policy through budget decisions, legislative recommendations to Congress, enforcement of existing statutes, and the use of executive orders and directives to departments and agencies. And, as Theodore Roosevelt observed, "Much can be done by the Government in labor matters merely by giving publicity to certain conditions."[104]

One policy area that has always commanded the attention of the president, and in which there has been deference to the president by the other two branches of government, is in the area of war powers, stemming from the clear statement in the Constitution that "the President shall be Commander in Chief of the Army and Navy of the United States." A nation at war, therefore, has witnessed the president's leadership abilities through his administration's actions, often in ways that are particularly important for women. As Treasurer Spinner noted during the Civil War, in times of tight budgets and a manpower shortage, women were suitable federal employees. Times of war have also changed the attitudes of society, albeit temporarily at times, to more broadly allow and expect the equal participation of women in the workforce. With two world wars and the Korean and Vietnam

Wars within a sixty-year period, the same period of time in which the institutionalized presidency became firmly established, the wartime actions of
presidents and their administrations played a part in the form and direction of the women's movement throughout much of the twentieth century,
which will be demonstrated in subsequent chapters through a closer look
at each of five administrations.

A MOVEMENT FROM FORMAL TO SUBSTANTIVE
REPRESENTATION, 1920–61

While looking at actions taken by presidents and their administrations with
regard to women, it is also important to keep in mind both the legal and
political status of women during this same period of time. [See Box 1.1 for a
memo Ramsey Clark prepared outlining the Supreme Court's major decisions regarding women's rights as of 1963.]

BOX 1.1

Historic Supreme Court Decisions Regarding Women's Rights

Right to vote:
> *Miner* [sic] *v. Happersett*, 21 Wall, 162 (1874), (held that the State
> had the power to restrict to men the right to vote)

Right to practice Law:
> *Bradwell v. Illinois*, 16 Wall, 130, 138, 173 (1872)
> *In re Lockwood*, 154 U.S. 116 (1893)
> (Held that the State had the power to restrict to men the right to
> practice law)

Right to work on same conditions as men:
> *Muller v. Oregon*, 208 U.S. 412 (1908)
> *Miller v. Wilson*, 236 U.S. 373 (1915)
> *Bosley v. McLaughlin*, 236 U.S. 385 (1915)
> *Radice v. New York*, 264 U.S. 292 (1924)
> *West Coast Hotel Co. v. Parrish*, 300 U.S. 379 (1937)
> *Gossert* [sic] *v. Cleary*, 335 U.S. 464 (1948)
> (Held that the State had the power to regulate and limit hours,

---

wages and conditions of paid work by women as contrasted with paid work by men, and in many other respects to permit discriminations to continue.)

Right to Jury Service:
  Commonwealth v. Welosky, 276 Mass. 398 (1931)
  Certiorari denied. 284 U.S. 684 (1932)
  (Held that State statute completely excluding women from Jury service was not invalid)

  Hoyt v. Florida, 110 So. 2d, 261 U.S. Supreme Court (1961)
  (Held that State Statute providing different jury service law for women than for men was not contrary to 14ᵗʰ Amendment)

Right to Education:
  Heaton v. Bristol, 317 S.W. Reporter 2d 86 (1958)
  Certiorari denied April 20 (1959)
  Petition for rehearing denied May 18 (1959)

  Allred V. Heaton, 336 S.W. 2d 256 (1960)
  (Five women students denied admission to publicly supported college, solely on basis of sex.)

Source: "Memorandum With Regard to Recommendation in Report of the President's Commission on the Status of Women, 1963," "EX FG 737 Pres. Comm. On the Status of Women" folder, FG 737, Box 404, Lyndon Baines Johnson Library.

The movement from formal representation to substantive representation began with ratification of the Nineteenth Amendment. As noted, it was only in the late 1800s when women began to be included in national party activities. Substantive policy issues such as equal pay were symbolically added to platforms, yet the vote itself, and thus the gaining of formal representation, was an issue left to the states. With the Civil War a not too distant memory, Woodrow Wilson until 1917 held firm in his belief that the issue should be left to the states, even as the movement for suffrage accelerated.

When the Republicans regained control of both the House and Senate in 1918, the suffrage amendment was introduced and passed.[105] Arguments used to gain support included the fact that women were already enfranchised in a number of states. In fact, Wyoming had given women the right to vote in 1869 while still a territory and insisted that women's right to vote be included in its Constitution when admitted as a state in 1890. Pragmatic political considerations also influenced support. In the election of 1916, 91 electoral votes of 531 cast were from states where women had the right to vote. By 1917, with increasing numbers of states granting women suffrage, the total number of such electoral votes had risen to 193, or 36 percent.[106] In addition, the responsibilities placed on women in the national government to meet the country's workforce needs in time of war made suffrage a national issue according to the House Committee on Woman Suffrage in its favorable report of a suffrage amendment in January, 1918.[107]

Women as voters and constituents, rather than women in Congress or women as political appointees, seemed to be the catalyst in bringing about the most significant change for women.[108] And perhaps this is not unexpected, given that the responsiveness of government to the people has always been an important part of this democracy, and why formal representation in the electorate is essential.

The administrative state arises at a time when women come into the electorate. Not only will the federal government take on more responsibilities in responding to the substantive needs of constituents—be it unemployment insurance, social security, health care for the poor—in time the federal government also becomes an equal opportunity employer through an expanding civil service.[109]

Substantive Representation: Equal Pay and an Equal Rights Amendment

The advent of polling in the 1930s coincided with women becoming a part of the electorate, thus the major polling organizations[110] have included questions concerning the role of women in the workforce and civil and political rights of women from the very beginning of scientific polling. Hazel Erskine observes that during the 1930s "interest was focused on the rights of women to share scarce jobs with men during the Depression. Then came a short period of concentration on the need to recruit women for defense jobs."[111]

Over time there was a gradual shift in public opinion, with increasing support for a woman being appointed to or running for high federal office, including the presidency. At the same time, there was constant and overwhelming support for women serving on juries,[112] as well as support for equal pay for women for equal work (see Tables 1.2, 1.3, and 1.4).

The National Woman's Party and others pushed for a broad sweeping ERA, but not until 1944 did both the Republican and Democratic National Parties include support for the ERA in their respective platforms, and even then that support did not remain constant in following years.[113]

The war effort in the early 1940s facilitated acceptance of equal pay for equal work, but not acceptance of the broader ERA.[114] And even when support was called for in the platform, it did not necessarily translate into active support by the standard bearer for the party. For example, in 1956 both the Republican and Democratic Party platforms called for a constitutional amendment providing equal rights for women. Yet during the fall campaign, President Eisenhower voiced his support for equal rights for women, but not the ERA. "We shall seek, as we promised in our platform, to assure women everywhere in our land equality of rights."[115] And, following his second inaugural in 1957, Eisenhower became the first president to formally include mention of the ERA in a message to Congress, when in his annual budget message he identified the support an ERA had had in both parties' platforms. But his message also stated, "I believe that the Congress should make certain that women are not denied equal rights with men."[116] Again, he fell short of an outright endorsement of the amendment himself, and instead suggested that a legislative route ensuring equal rights be pursued.

TABLE 1.2
Support for a Woman President

"If your party nominated a woman for President, would you vote for her if she were qualified for the job?"

| | Percentage Who Would Vote for a Woman | |
	Men	Women
1937	27%	40%
1945	29%	37%
1949	45%	51%
1955	47%	57%
1963	58%	51%
1967	61%	53%
1969	58%	49%

Source: Gallup Poll, in Hazel Erskine, "The Polls: Women's Role," Public Opinion Quarterly, pp. 278–79.

TABLE 1.3
Support for Women in the Work Force

Gallup: October 31, 1945:

"If there is a limited number of jobs, do you approve or disapprove of a married woman holding a job in business or industry when her husband is able to support her?"

Favor women working: 10%
Oppose women working: 86%

Roper: August 1946:	*Percentage in agreement:*	
	Men	*Women*
"All women should have an equal chance with men for any job in business or industry regardless of whether they have to support themselves or not."	22%	29%
"Only women who have to support themselves should have an equal chance with men for jobs in business or industry."	46	49
"A man should have preference over all women for any job that he can fill satisfactorily."	28	17

Source: Hazel Erskine, "The Polls: Women's Role." *Public Opinion Quarterly,* pp. 274–90.

Also during the post-war years, a number of interest groups, including the Women's Joint Legislative Committee for Equal Rights, the National Association of Women Lawyers, the NFBPWC, and the National Woman's Party, worked to get all senators, including John F. Kennedy, a Democrat from Massachusetts, to sign a card pledging support for a Constitutional amendment. The leaders of the National Woman's Party proved time and again to be savvy lobbyists. For example, to pressure then-Senator Kennedy, an Irish Catholic, into a public endorsement of the ERA, they invoked the name of Pope Pius XII as a supporter of equal rights for men and women and obtained a letter written years earlier from Cardinal Dougherty of Philadelphia, supporting the ERA.[117] Kennedy refused. In responding, Lee C. White, a legislative assistant to Kennedy, noted that the senator was "in general sympathy with the intention underlying the proposed amendment, . . . [but had] had some reservations as to whether the amendment would not have a harmful effect upon women in certain regards."[118]

Kennedy was also being heavily lobbied by those opposed to the amendment, including many union organizations as well as the ACLU.[119] While Kennedy did not support the ERA, he was a supporter of equal pay legislation and had introduced legislation to provide "equal pay for equal work for women" while serving in the House of Representatives in 1951, namely, the "Women's Equal Pay Act of 1951."[120] He never would, however, support an ERA. His ties to labor were too strong.[121]

TABLE 1.4
Support for Equal Pay Legislation

Gallup:	Yes, paid the Same	No	No Opinion
"If women take the place of men in industry, should they be paid the same wages as men?" (February 13, 1942)	78%	14%	8%
"Do you think women should or should not receive the same rate of pay as men for the same work?" (September 19, 1945)	76	17	—
"If a young single woman is doing exactly the same kind of work as a married man with children, do you think she should receive the same rate of pay?" (September 19, 1945)	66	28	6
"Do you approve or disapprove of paying women the same salaries as men, if they are doing the same work?" (June 5, 1954)	87	—	—

Source: Hazel Erskine, "The Polls: Women's Role," *Public Opinion Quarterly*, pp. 274–90.

As the National Woman's Party pushed for an ERA, which would eliminate some of the protective legislation for women, the different objectives of the women's organizations became more visible. However, as later chapters will demonstrate, not until the 1970s would the momentum for an ERA take hold, forcing presidents to become more directly involved in this crusade.

The Strengthening of Women's Policy Networks, 1920–61

Groups such as the NFBPWC, which emerged early in the twentieth century, did not become instrumental in guiding items on to the national agenda until the 1940s. In part the organizations themselves were in their infancy, spending more time setting forth rules and procedures than in debating the issues of the day.[122] However, World War II helped serve as a catalyst to bring about a greater role for these and future organizations. The circumstances of a nation at war, with rationing, price control, war bonds, and civilian defense programs, provided opportunities for organizations such as the BPW to develop a working relationship with political leaders at the national level, as well as state and local levels.

In 1939 the BPW, with seven other women's organizations, joined to form the Group Action Council.[123] The council served as "a clearing house for information about the status of legislation affecting women."[124] Once the United States entered World War II following the bombing of Pearl Harbor in 1941, the focus of the council was on the contribution of women to the war effort. An objective of the council was

> The effective use of womanpower to win the war, including recruitment of all available women for essential war or civilian work; . . . effective training programs providing for upgrading and improvement of skills; and the breaking down of discrimination against women on the part of unions, management, and women themselves.[125]

Consistent with support for an ERA, these organizations also endorsed a draft of women for the war effort and continued opposition to protective legislation for women.[126]

During the war, women's organizations pushed for women in the armed services to gain equal status with men. By 1943, the army had incorporated the Women's Army Corps (WACS) "on an equal status with men," when FDR signed the Reynolds bill, and shortly thereafter the Women Accepted for Volunteer Emergency Service (WAVES) and Women's Reserve of the Coast Guard (SPARS) gained similar benefits and allowances.

Women's organizations would become far more important in setting the national policy agenda once the war was over. Yet these organizations were active during the war years. By 1942, as the White House planned for demobilization, sending legislation to Congress in the areas of vocational training, medical care for the disabled, and education,[127] the Group Action Council began the "study and discussion of post-war problems."[128] A "GI Bill of Rights" was prepared by the VFW and sent to Congress in 1944. At the same time, the Group Action Council worked to get post-war employment planks favorable to women in the party platforms for the 1944 election. The women's organizations were interested in setting up an infrastructure for veterans in terms of services, educational opportunities, and jobs and an economy to sustain full employment in order that women who had both chosen and been recruited to join the workforce could "seek equal opportunities in the postwar job market."[129]

The GI bill was an important political decision—i.e., what to do with millions of returning soldiers. The experience of the First World War, when a depression aggravated the plight of unemployed veterans, led to advance planning this time around for demobilization. In addition, women had been drawn into the labor pool, and many would want to retain their jobs. The GI bill became a way for women to retain their place in the workforce, as many men returning from the war took advantage of the education benefits and delayed their return to the workforce. The bill also provided for unemployment compensation for up to a year.

Two gatherings in particular shaped the political agenda for women in the post-war years as well as the response of each administration to women: the 1944 White House Conference, "How Women May Share in Post-War Policy Making," and in May, 1945, the "Conference on Postwar Career Problems of Service Women" organized by the NFBPWC in Washington, D.C. with the commanding officers of all the women's service organizations in attendance, including Col. Oveta Culp Hobby of the WACS, who was to later become the first secretary of health, education and welfare in 1953.[130] With potential power to influence the 1944 election outcome, there had come a realization in women's organizations that women in particular would also need to gain "political literacy" both on the platforms of candidates, as well as legislative agendas.[131] In addition to the discussion of policy matters, therefore, these organizations also began to take a more active role in influencing who the policy makers would be.

On May 11, 1944, Eleanor Roosevelt had invited the presidents of national women's organizations, many of which were also member organizations of the Group Action Council, "to a meeting at the White House . . . to discuss the need now for the appointment of qualified women to wartime and post-war policy-making posts at home and abroad."[132] Also included were "appointed observers from Government departments and agencies."[133] A month later, on June 14, two hundred women attended the conference held in the East Room of the White House,[134] including leaders from the National Education Association (NEA), AAUW, the National Women's Trade Union League, and the Associated Women of the American Farm Bureau Federation.[135] Participants "learned the utter futility when it comes to high government appointments, particularly federal ones, of simply recommending a woman." In her opening remarks, Eleanor Roosevelt summarized the purpose of the meeting:

> "the heads of government agencies, even when inspired by the best intentions often made poor selections of women for important posts simply because they did not know, and had no means of finding out, who the qualified women were. What the heads of such agencies need . . . were lists of names of qualified women to draw upon when selecting appointees for posts which can appropriately be held by women. It was for the purpose of interesting women's organizations in preparing such lists for the use of the heads of the various governmental departments that the conference had been called.[136]

Ellen Woodward, a conference participant and member of the Social Security Board, noted the need to distinguish "between those prepared to serve as technical experts and those qualified to contribute to policy determination."[137] Another participant identified a strategy to adopt: organizations needed to "get behind one woman that you think is qualified and to give them the name of the woman to appoint if you think she is of value."[138] The recommendation from these organizations of names for presidential appointments, especially for positions on boards, commissions, and post-war committees soon followed, even though there was very little news coverage of this conference.[139] (Unfortunately the conference was held one week after the D day invasion when wartime reports filled the pages of almost all newspapers.) A Committee on Women in World Affairs, headed by Emily Hickman, was organized to "get the women's organizations and the political organizations to work together on the talent discovery of women who would have competence . . . and . . . political acumen."[140] The committee was especially of use to the State Department in identifying women to represent the United States at international conferences.[141]

By the time Eisenhower took the oath of office in 1953, representatives of women's organizations had thus met in national forums on several occasions to consider how to increase the numbers of women appointed to high-level posts. Less than two months after Eisenhower's inauguration, the NFBPWC organized a "Conference on Women in Policy Making Posts." This conference marked the first of many attempts by women's organizations to *systematically influence and shape the decision-making process as well as the appointees resulting from that process*.[142] (Some of the organizations represented included the National Woman's Party, the YWCA, the National Association of Women Lawyers, the League of Women Voters, the American Medical Women's Association, the AAUW, the Council of Jewish Women, and the Associated Women of the American Farm Bureau Federation.) Even though Republicans had regained control of the White House, some boards statutorily required bipartisan membership, enabling Democratic women as well as Republican women to be considered for posts, although the DNC would not play much of a role in selection or clearance of nominees.[143]

Presentations were given on career opportunities in the federal civil service and on the appointments process for political positions. Bertha Adkins, assistant chairman of the RNC, and India Edwards, vice chair of the DNC, spoke on behalf of their respective parties. Adkins went over the procedural steps of the appointment process and outlined Republican Party policy on appointments in the new Eisenhower administration:

> The Executive Committee of the Republican National Committee has established the policy of having the assistant to the chairman and Head of the Women's Division, in consultation with the National Federation of Women's Republican Clubs . . . responsible for being alert to openings and promoting women who have complete endorsement from their states. . . . Lists of qualified women should start with state level endorsement.[144]

Some organizations had already been forwarding recommendations to departments, with a copy to Adkins at the RNC. Given the process by which appointments could come—e.g., directly from the White House, through political party recommendations, or through the recommendations of cabinet members and agency heads—organizations such as Women in World Affairs, Inc. had sent recommendations to both the RNC, as well as a department or agency head.[145] Adkins noted that "because of the long lean period of appointments for the Republican Party, political endorsement is essential."[146] Organizations were encouraged to do the leg work in getting the necessary political clearance by state party organizations before submitting a recommendation and to learn the clearance procedures in each state.

Adkins also noted that the Executive Committee of the National Republican Committee had recommended to each of the cabinet secretaries that a woman in each department serve as a liaison with the head of the Women's Division of the RNC to alert the RNC to appointive positions for women as vacancies arose. Both Adkins and Edwards noted that positions should be identified which have been held by women in the past, "at the same time avoiding the establishing of certain jobs as only for women."[147]

Given the significance of political parties in presidential elections up until this point in time, political parties were seen by some as the best avenue for obtaining a patronage position. Even when Eisenhower delegated responsibility to cabinet secretaries for selection of subcabinet members, and later, Schedule C appointments, these appointments were cleared through the RNC.[148]

The Women's Division of the Republican Party was quite active in monitoring the status of women in both elected and appointed posts, at the county, state, and national levels, during the Eisenhower administration. A series of surveys published by the Women's Division of the RNC, titled "Women in the Public Service," appear to be the first systematic efforts to collect such data nationwide, including positions held by both Democrats and Republicans.[149] Subsequent administrations, as well as outside organizations, would later build on these figures, in identifying the number of women appointed to high-level posts. The Eisenhower administration, through the RNC, proudly acknowledged its record number of women serving in appointed positions. For example, in a press release from September, 1959, Clare B. Williams, assistant chairman of the RNC, noted that "the record shows that during his two administrations, President Dwight D. Eisenhower has appointed 218 women to high level positions in government, the diplomatic service, on boards and commissions. . . . An additional 190 appointments by Cabinet officials and agency heads brings the total to 408 women so honored, a record of progress of which all women can be justly proud."[150] As will be more fully detailed in subsequent chapters, how an administration counts appointments and who is counted has been the subject of much dispute by those in the White House as well as those outside the White House.

Once women's organizations had begun to be involved in the appointment process in a formal way, beginning with the World War II conference called by Eleanor Roosevelt, they would remain involved, although the Republican Party took on a more activist role in the process during the 1950s. The Eisenhower administration would be the only administration in the latter half of the twentieth century in which the party organization appeared to play a more significant role than did non-partisan organizations. The active role of interest groups in recommending appointments and working closely with the party organization did not continue in the Kennedy and Johnson administrations, in part because political parties would begin to play less of a role in both electing a candidate and in organizing a government. However, the close collaborative work in both seeking out and promoting women for office between interest group organizations and an administration would resurface when the next Republican administration took office—that of Richard M. Nixon.

CONCLUSION

The Progressive movement in the early part of the twentieth century, which had both an emphasis on a merit-based system of hiring, as well as on the government taking an active role in responsibility for social policy, contributed to the entrance of women into executive branch positions, beginning with the appointment of Julia Lathrop. Subsequently, the Women's Bureau was established and suffrage for women was attained. In the 1930s, a New Deal coalition of women contributed to expansion of the government and the creation of a programmatic legacy which would shape the domestic policy agenda of administrations until the emergence of increasing budget deficits in the late 1970s. Once women in all states had gained formal representation with the granting of suffrage,[151] presidents and their administrations began to confront issues of symbolic as well as descriptive representation and, to a lesser extent, substantive representation of women. The appointment of Frances Perkins as secretary of labor by Franklin D. Roosevelt early in 1933, while important in that it was the first time a woman was named to serve in the president's cabinet (with the press noting the symbolic[152] virtue of the appointment perhaps even more than did the White House), was also significant in illustrating the role women would play as a link between government responsibilities for social policy emerging during the Progressive era, and the expansion of the federal government's role in social and economic policy beginning with the New Deal.

As of the early 1960s the view that the party organization was the best way for women to be elected and appointed to public office was quite well accepted. In fact, in the report of the Subcommittee on Political Rights of President Kennedy's Commission on the Status of Women issued in March, 1963, the conclusion was that "the role of women in the political parties is a major, if not principal, determinant of their achievement of public positions," noting the equal representation of women and men on both the DNC and RNC, and the number of states which required a 50-50 equal distribution of men and women in party offices and on committees.[153] During the transition period following the election of John F. Kennedy, Margaret Price, vice chairman, and director of Women's Activities, at the DNC, prepared a "Survey of Major Presidential Appointments of Women to Positions in Government."[154] The report, in addition to identifying women who had served in past administrations and in the current Eisenhower administration, also provided a blueprint for the issues soon to face Kennedy upon his inauguration, issues which would also face his successors in office.[155]

The role of the federal government in facilitating the formation of networks of women would be repeated on several occasions throughout the next forty years. These groups of women would, in essence, define the national policy agenda concerning women, once suffrage was granted.

The chapters that follow are organized around five administrations, from John F. Kennedy through Jimmy Carter, but the focus is more on the continuity between the administrations, and the role of the president and the presidency in a political system in which power is shared with Congress and the courts, and divided between a national government and the states. This will be most evident in looking at the movement of policy items on to the national agenda and the expansion of public policy to include equal opportunity for both men and women. Throughout the book the emphasis is on the policies of each administration and the shapers of that policy.

CHAPTER 2

The Kennedy Administration

Advocating for Women—

Esther Peterson and the President's

Commission on the Status of Women

JOHN F. KENNEDY'S term of office began just after noon on Friday, January 20, 1961, when the oath of office was administered by the chief justice on the East Capitol Plaza, in a Washington blanketed with six inches of fresh snow.[1] There was an air of anticipation, with a partisan transition ending eight years of Republican rule and a generational change in power. However, "a new President does not step into a policy vacuum on inauguration day. He enters a situation in which previous commitments have been made, legislative processes are in motion, and pressures are building up for decisions. Congress is already in session."[2] While the president sets the tone for an administration, selects which advisors to listen to, and sets forth a legislative agenda, the president also responds to a national agenda already in place and faces constraints by outside forces as part of a world community. As Charles O. Jones has so succinctly stated, "This nation has a government, not just a president."[3]

A new Congress may begin every two years, yet there is an institutional continuity in that branch, set forth in the Constitution, which allows turnover in but a third of the Senate. In addition, members of Congress are not saddled with the term limits imposed on a president since ratification of the Twenty-second Amendment. Seniority, a key determinant of power and influence in Congress in the 1960s, and a means for institutionalizing expertise, would contribute to congressional advantages in the policy process.

Also, at the time Kennedy took the oath of office, the Supreme Court was in the midst of the Warren Revolution, entering into the policy fray in an activist mode, using the Fourteenth Amendment to end segregation and broaden civil liberties. Rulings of the Court had forced his predecessor, President Dwight D. Eisenhower, to become involved in the battle over civil rights.

Within the executive branch, a new administration was being grafted on top of a bureaucracy that remains in place regardless of which party gains control of the White House. Each department and agency had programs already in place, with personnel to administer them. Although the president-elect had begun to structure his administration in the two months following the election, not all appointments could be made, nor any confirmed, until after the oath of office had been taken. It would take weeks, if not months, for the administration to be put in place.

The 1960s would also mark a period of social change. A women's movement that had been fragmented and class bound would begin to take on a popular form. In Washington, the nature of politics was undergoing a transformation. The formation and success of the Democratic Study Group would open the way to other institutional challenges to the power structure in Congress. Campaign finance reform affecting both congressional and presidential candidates, as well as election law reform opening up participation through primaries, would contribute to a political system shifting from institutionalized to individualized pluralism, as the role of political parties as institutions declined in importance. As Samuel Kernell has observed, "The declining influence of political parties on the electorate" would also lead to a rise in divided government.[4] The 1956 election had seen the Republicans retaining control of the White House and the Democrats winning Congress, resulting in divided government, a frequent pattern for the next half century.

In a number of ways, the presidential campaign and presidency of John F. Kennedy would contribute to the transformation already under way. In fact, an observer of the 1960 nomination and convention noted that the surprising success of the "Kennedy school" of campaigning—where "the nomination would go to the man who establishes the best claim to it by proving his vote-getting ability in the primaries as well as by his ability to negotiate effectively in the smoke-filled rooms. . . . in all probability will mean that the presidential nomination process will henceforth be more like that of 1960 than like most before 1960."[5] In fact, winning over voters in primary contests to capture the party's nomination would become the rule by the 1970s.

In addition, "routine use of the exclusive interview, cultivation of the press outside Washington, and live telecasts of news conferences," innovative in the 1960s, would soon become the model used by subsequent presidents.[6] Samuel Kernell's *Going Public: New Strategies of Presidential Leadership* focuses on how this transformation has affected the president's relationship with Congress in defining and moving a policy agenda. "Politicians can no longer depend on their party's performance for their personal success and have made a strategic turn to self-reliant individualism."[7] This transformation has also affected what goes on within an administration.

THE PRESIDENCY AND THE WOMEN'S MOVEMENT

The weakening of party ties, which contributed to major change in the presidency, did, in fact, result in a greater inclusion of women and consideration of issues of concern to women—issues long absent from the nation's policy agenda. In addition, the rebirth of the women's movement paralleled this transformation in the Washington community, forcing presidents to respond to this new constituency while at the same time influencing the direction of the movement.

The Kennedy administration, although not consciously aware of its role, would soon be a player in the direction of the women's movement. And the administration's role would be influenced by the changing nature of the presidency vis-à-vis the Washington community. A hint of this involvement was given during the course of the campaign, when presidential candidate John Kennedy, unbeknownst to him, was drawn into a controversy that had festered for years: Presidential support for a constitutional amendment guaranteeing equal rights for women. During the campaign, clandestine activity was undertaken to obtain the signature of Kennedy on a letter endorsing the ERA. Emma Guffey Miller, chair of the NWP, managed to get a draft letter crafted by campaign workers Myer Feldman and Esther Peterson at the campaign headquarters, which carefully stated that Kennedy "believed in equality of opportunity and was going to work toward that." There was no mention of the ERA, reflecting the Democratic platform's only statement on equality for women: "We support legislation [not an amendment] which will guarantee to women equality of rights under the law, including equal pay for equal work."[8] Acting on her own, Miller made a handwritten modification before the memo went to the typist, so that Kennedy would be "on the record" in stating support for the amendment. The new wording stated, "You have my assurance that I will interpret the Democratic platform . . . to bring about, through concrete actions including the adoption of the Equal Rights Amendment, the full equality for women which advocates of the equal rights amendment have always sought."[9]

However, support for the ERA was not that simple, especially for a Democrat who needed the strong support of labor. While Kennedy himself was not involved in this episode, which received little public notice, through his appointments and the use of a number of legislative devices available to a president and his administration he would soon play a major role in the consideration and inclusion of women by subsequent administrations. Women would find a place in the Oval Office.

A POLICY AGENDA FOR WOMEN

To understand the depth of sentiment over the ERA—which, as previously noted, led a Democratic campaign worker to jeopardize her own candidate's integrity in the race—one needs to look back to the beginning of the twentieth century, to a time when women were denied access to the ballot. For some women activists, the primary objective was suffrage; with the vote, women's interests would be represented. But at the same time, a movement was under way to seek passage of legislation to protect women in the workplace.

The "Women's Bureau Coalition"

Cynthia Harrison has identified a "Women's Bureau coalition," which grew out of "the settlement movement of the 1890s and the Progressive-era push for protective labor legislation for women. Middle-class women concerned about the welfare of their underclass sisters working in factories had formed organizations to improve conditions for industrial laborers."[10] These organizations, which included the Women's Trade Union League and the National Consumers League, persuaded the federal government to gather and disseminate data on working conditions. This information, in turn, was used to secure the passage of state laws setting "minimum wages, maximum hours, weight restrictions on lifting, and prohibitions against night work" for women workers.[11] By 1920, the Women's Bureau had been established in the Department of Labor to continue "the collection of information about women workers."[12] This time period corresponds with a second wave of unionization in American labor history emerging in the 1910s, "primarily in the clothing industry."[13]

Following the New York garment workers' strike in 1909–10, the ranks of the International Ladies' Garment Workers' Union (ILGWU) and the

Amalgamated Clothing Workers (ACW) swelled with the addition of many unskilled and semiskilled women workers.

> The definition of unionism [was broadened] to encompass not only economic but also social functions, pioneering in such areas as union-sponsored health care and educational programs. Yet the leaders of these unions still viewed women as an entirely different species of worker than men. ... Women's militant organizing efforts were centered not on economic demands for gender equality, but rather on moral appeals for better protection against management abuses. ... implicitly or explicitly invoking their special vulnerability as women.[14]

Until 1971, the courts would support such legislation. "The judicial approach to women was that their rights, responsibilities, opportunities, and obligations were essentially determined by their position in the family. ... as wives and mothers."[15] In *Muller v. Oregon* (1908) the Court upheld a law restricting the number of hours that a woman could work in a factory "on the grounds that women's 'physical structure and a proper discharge of her maternal functions—having in view not merely her own health but the well-being of the race—justify legislation to protect her. ... the limitations which this statute places upon her contractual power ... are not imposed solely for her benefit, but also largely for the benefit of all. ... The reason rests in the inherent difference between the two sexes, and in the different functions in life which they perform.'"[16] This approach was endorsed by labor organizers and women activists in the labor movement.

The NWP and the ERA

Even as the movement for the protection of women workers progressed throughout the first half of the twentieth century, after suffrage was obtained in 1920 the NWP, a militant feminist organization, focused their attention solely on passage of an ERA. In contrast to those who had worked to win legislation protecting women workers, the NWP "took the position that laws only for women did more harm than good."[17] The NWP attempted to reach a compromise, since it initially viewed the ERA as "aimed primarily at the plethora of laws which restricted women's property rights, disadvantaged them under state family laws, or barred them from holding office or serving on juries."[18] Eventually, however, the ERA debate became increasingly polarized and the amendment was perceived as eliminating all protective legislation.[19]

The split between support for and opposition to the ERA often broke down along class lines. Women working in or associated with blue-collar industry jobs (especially those in the trade unions) favored protective legislation, while professional and business women favored the ERA to compete fairly with men in their professions. Over time, this class division would lead to the Republican and Democratic Parties adopting different planks in their respective platforms. By 1940, Republicans had included endorsement of the ERA in their platform.[20] In 1944, both parties endorsed the ERA in their respective platforms. In essence, two arguments helped proponents win endorsement of the ERA in the Democratic platform in 1944: "Were Democrats less committed to equality for women?" and how could one "limit women's hours when men were dying on foreign battlefields?"[21]

In 1960, the Republican Party nominee, Richard Nixon, endorsed the ERA, and the Republicans continued the longstanding inclusion of support for the ERA in their platform, dating back to 1940. The Democrats, who had had more sporadic support for the ERA, did not endorse it.[22] This is what had prompted Emma Guffey Miller to take matters into her own hands during the fall campaign in seeing that her party's nominee was on record as endorsing the ERA.

The ERA would not receive the attention from the Kennedy administration that it would command in later administrations, yet the ERA and its long history would be the undercurrent shaping the administration's response to women. And the fact that John F. Kennedy turned to Esther Peterson as an advisor on issues of labor and about women would, not surprisingly, bring the administration down on the side of those opposed to an ERA yet sympathetic to the plight of women, especially working women.

Esther Peterson and Labor

Esther Peterson had known Kennedy for years. She had become acquainted with Kennedy in the late 1940s when she was assigned to get the support of the newly elected member in the House of Representatives for legislation increasing the minimum wage.[23] Kennedy was first elected to the House in 1946, and Peterson was then a legislative representative for Amalgamated Clothing Workers of America. Kennedy's service on the House Education and Labor Committee kept Peterson in touch with the young representative early in his career. In 1958, when Peterson worked as a legislative representative of the Industrial Union Department of the AFL-CIO, she again worked with then-Senator Kennedy, who was now serving on the Senate Labor and Public Welfare Committee. Peterson, through her work in the trade unions movement, also came to know several advisors to Kennedy—in particular Ralph Dungan—who worked as a staff assistant to Senator Kennedy in the late 1950s, and Myer Feldman, one of the three members of Kennedy's "personal Brain trust," who would later be a part of Kennedy's inner circle helping him to win the Democratic nomination in 1960. Both Dungan and Feldman would move on to posts in the White House in the new Kennedy administration.[24]

Peterson was asked by Robert Kennedy to join the campaign early on in its quest for the Democratic nomination. However, Peterson had to decline because of personal reasons (family illness).[25] Although Peterson was not a formal staff member on the campaign, John Kennedy did call on her for advice and recommendations concerning campaign strategy and a read on potential supporters around the country. It is important to note that Esther Peterson's role in the campaign stemmed from her long-time work with the labor union movement and not through the party hierarchy. Even though campaigns were undergoing a transition from being party driven to candidate-centered operations, the 1960s would continue to find some people arguing that the best way for women to gain a voice, and thus move into the ranks of the elected and appointed, was through party work. This was a path and model set by Molly Dewson earlier in the century, when she worked to "use patronage to reward women political leaders, and thereby build up the women's side of the Democratic party," as head of the Women's Division of the DNC.[26] Yet this was only one approach that Dewson used. She also drew on a network of women in politics and government in the 1930s—a "New Deal network"—to promote social justice and had "hoped that placing talented women in prominent government positions would demonstrate the value of women's contribution to the public sphere: 'I am a firm believer in progress for women coming through appointments here and there and a first class job by the women who are the lucky ones chosen to demonstrate.'"[27] This second approach would perhaps be the more appropriate model in the 1960s, when parties would lose their institutional role.

The 1960s marked a transition to a new era. The interests of labor women were positioned for inclusion in the new administration, by virtue of Esther Peterson's work with Kennedy outside of the party framework.

Peterson supported Kennedy's bid for the Democratic Party nomination early on. She declined offers from the other candidates, including Adlai Stevenson and Hubert Humphrey. She did not formally endorse Kennedy (labor was waiting through the primaries before giving any formal endorsements) but she did work on his behalf throughout the primaries.

For example, she gave suggestions to the Kennedy campaign as to who in labor to contact in the various states and worked the convention in 1960 to gain the support of several state delegations. After Kennedy had won the formal nomination from the party at its summer convention, Peterson worked for the DNC. She did not, however, work under the direction of Margaret B. Price, head of the Women's Division, but instead reported to Larry O'Brien and Ralph Dungan. She did organization work with the unions and served as a liaison from the party to labor unions, attending meetings and speaking on behalf of Kennedy as needed.[28]

In examining the inclusion of women in a president's administration, there are several distinct aspects of representation to consider—among them, symbolic, descriptive, and substantive representation. In the Kennedy administration, the focus was on issues of substantive policy. The symbolic importance associated with the appointment of women would not be ignored, but would not be of paramount importance. Esther Peterson, by virtue of her access to the president and key advisors, would play a major role in influencing how the administration structured its response to women.

Esther Peterson's Focus on Women in the Workforce

For Peterson, substantive policy directly affecting the lives of women workers was of utmost importance. She found that her long-time work with Kennedy gave her an advantage over those pushing for the ERA. According to Peterson,

> I think my advantage was that I worked with him not on women's questions; I worked with him on issues, of unemployment insurance, or minimum wage, and it wasn't a women's thing. And I really think because of that that I was able to make some progress with him on the others, when I talked to him about having the Commission on the Status of Women. But, you see, Margaret's [Price, head of the Women's Division in the Democratic Party] issue was women. And this is something I remember about the equal rights amendment, a feeling of, Oh, Why do we waste our time on those things when wages are important, security is important. And I really was quite disgusted with the women who spent all their time running around for women's rights. That doesn't mean that I didn't think a lot should be done about it, but I do think that my strength was that I worked with him on substantive issues, and I think the women who did work with him on substantive issues never had any trouble working with him.[29]

According to Peterson, who was appointed by Kennedy to head the Women's Bureau in the Department of Labor, "the labor people and the women in the labor movement felt so strongly that if the group . . . pressing for an [equal rights] amendment . . . got their way . . . we would lose the ground that we had in the minimum wage and in matters of this kind that protected both men and women. . . . [This] indicates the basic fight that we had on that question which led to the formation of the President's Commission on the Status of Women,"[30] which Peterson soon urged Kennedy to establish. Secretary of Labor Arthur Goldberg also agreed with the long-term views of the Department of Labor, which held that women needed to be protected to protect the interests of children.[31]

It was clear that the emphasis on women as the nation's primary homemakers—the view of those in the Women's Bureau and its allied organizations—would shape the work of the future President's Commission on the Status of Women (PCSW). The pervasiveness of this philosophy is demonstrated in the draft of a letter (which was not sent) turning down an applicant for a job with the PCSW:

> As you know, technical secretaries for the committees are key people who will provide the day to day continuity needed for full functioning of the committees. These are full-time positions which may require overtime work and occasional travel. In view of your family responsibilities, I believe that it would be extremely difficult for you to meet these requirements.
>
> We plan to keep your application on file. Should a need arise for a person with your background on a part-time basis, we shall certainly consider your application seriously.[32]

PRESIDENTIAL COMMISSIONS AND COMMITTEES

One institutional device available to presidents is the use of commissions and informal task forces and advisory committees. Presidents have made use of these devices in varying ways. While a commission is designed to act independently of any existing government structure, adding fresh insight, it is shaped by the administration responsible for its establishment. The president sets forth the mission and goals of the commission, and, in fact, shapes its final recommendations by selection of the commission's members.

An outside commission may be created to deal with the pathologies of bureaucracy and the problems of managing the government. When a new administration takes over, there is more to governing than initiating new programs and setting forth a new direction. A cabinet secretary may have been selected for reasons having more to do with the symbolic needs of representation than as the person best suited to carry out the administration's overall agenda.[33] The secretary may need to contend with an undersecretary or deputy secretary placed in the number two spot to keep a watchful eye on the direction of the new administration.[34] Not only does the president face pressure from those outside the administration, he also faces pressure from the competing interests of cabinet members and from the White House staff. Assistants to the president are often the closest to the president and begin to carve out their own territory by attempting to influence political appointments as well as policy. The careerists in the departments and agencies can also make their preferences known and push for one of their own to be elevated to a position as bureau chief.[35]

Presidents generally have broad powers to reorganize the executive branch, although Congress will need to authorize positions and appropriate funds. In the case of the Department of Labor, a reorganization plan was put forth by President Kennedy in 1961, which resulted in the addition of a new assistant secretary position. The Bureau of Labor Statistics (BLS) and the Women's Bureau were placed under the direction of this new assistant secretary of labor, Esther Peterson, elevated from her post as head of the Women's Bureau. A turf war broke out between these two bureaus, both wanting to do studies on women in the labor force. Peterson was caught in the middle of this bureaucratic turf war:

> In the Women's Bureau area, some of the women who were on my staff didn't want to give up doing their own studies. I felt BLS should do the studies. They had the competence and the expertise. But some of my people would get mad and say, 'We should do it.' And I didn't like all these little fiefdoms, you know. My theory was that we outline the study, we say what we want, but BLS should do it. They had the competence. We should have it done where that competence is. And it was the same awful fight between the Women's Bureau and Labor Standards, where they were duplicating work. But to get them to get together and do it was just hell.[36]

In fact, as noted later in this chapter, one of the reasons for the creation of the PCSW was to help resolve related turf issues. If outside pressure could be brought to bear on the department, the careerists in the department would be more likely to comply. And the political appointee might also be prodded into backing the administration's position vis-à-vis a recalcitrant agency bent on doing things as always done in the past.

The President's Commission on the Status of Women

The PCSW was a high-powered commission structured in such a way to ensure that it would fulfill both symbolic and substantive needs of the administration. The chair was former First Lady Eleanor Roosevelt, frequently at the top of "most admired women in America" lists.[37] (See Box 2.1 for a list of members of the PCSW.)

The commission of twenty-six members included both men and women (fifteen women and eleven men). Five cabinet members served on the commission, including the president's brother, Attorney General Robert F. Kennedy, as well as the secretaries of agriculture, commerce, labor, and health, education, and welfare (HEW). If the commission were to make recommendations that the president could implement as executive orders, it would be the departments and agencies that would carry them out. In addition, including these high-ranking officials on the commission would enable the commission to easily draw on the resources of these departments to do its work.

The PCSW was designed to force action. Some on the commission were pragmatic players in the political process, others were outsiders needing lessons on the structure of government. The membership of the commission included a strategic selection of cabinet secretaries, members of the House and Senate, and representatives of key constituent groups. Its members consequently included bipartisan and bicameral representation of men and women, from Congress, with Republicans George D. Aiken, a senator from Vermont, and Jessica M. Weis, a representative from New York, and Democrats Maurine B. Neuberger and Edith Green, a senator and representative, respectively, from Oregon. Senator Maurine Neuberger was also a member of the Senate Post Office and Civil Service Committee, which had jurisdiction over policies and benefits affecting federal workers. As a result, for example, the commission's recommendations on legislation concerning the insurance rates paid by federal employees for family coverage, which were then different for men and women, would come under the jurisdiction of a Senate Committee with a member already well informed on the need for this policy change.[38]

At least one member viewed women's role as one of passivity, and regularly suggested that women needed to observe the policy-making process before taking a place at the decision-making table.[39]

The commission also included university presidents and academics and representatives from labor unions and industry. These members added to the breadth and depth of interests represented, laying the foundation for a widespread positive reception to the final recommendations.

BOX 2.1

Members of the President's Commission on the Status of Women

Mrs. Eleanor Roosevelt, Chairman

Dr. Richard A. Lester, Professor of Economics, Princeton University, Vice Chairman

Mrs. Esther Peterson, Assistant Secretary of Labor, Executive Vice Chairman

Robert F. Kennedy, Attorney General

Orville L. Freeman, Secretary of Agriculture

Luther H. Hodges, Secretary of Commerce

Arthur J. Goldberg, Secretary of Labor

Abraham A. Ribicoff, Secretary of Health, Education, and Welfare

John W. Macy, Jr., Chairman, U.S. Civil Service Commission

Senator George D. Aiken (R-Vermont)

Senator Maurine B. Neuberger (D-Oregon)

Representative Edith Green (D-Oregon)

Representative Jessica M. Weis (R-New York)

Mrs. Ellen Boddy, civic leader and rancher, Henrietta, Texas

Dr. Mary I. Bunting, President, Radcliffe College

Mrs. Mary R. Callahan, Member, Executive Board, International Union of Electrical, Radio, and Machine Workers, AFL-CIO

Dr. Henry David, President, New School for Social Research

Miss Dorothy Height, President, National Council of Negro Women; Director, Leadership Training Services, Y.W.C.A.

Mrs. Margaret Hickey, lawyer, Contributing Editor, *Ladies' Home Journal*

Mrs. Viola H. Hymes, National President, National Council of Jewish Women

Edgar F. Kaiser, Industrialist

Miss Margaret J. Mealey, Executive Director, National Council of Catholic Women

Miss Marguerite Rawalt, lawyer, former President of National Federation of Business and Professional Women's Clubs; branch chief in Office of Chief Counsel, IRS

William F. Schnitzler, Secretary-Treasurer, AFL-CIO

Dr. Caroline Ware, Sociologist, Historian for UNESCO

Dr. Cynthia Wedel, psychologist, teacher, former Vice President, National Council of Churches; Member, National Board of Girl Scouts of America

Source: "Members of the President's Commission on the Status of Women," document 5, Feb. 8, 1962, "General Meetings, 2/12/62–2/13/62" folder, PCSW, Box 2, John F. Kennedy Library.

The Commission's Mission

While a commission is ostensibly established to give the president independent advice, it is the president and his advisors who structure the commission, setting the parameters for the depth and scope of its work. For instance, a commission is dependent on the administration for its inclusion in the annual budget requests sent to Congress. In the Kennedy era, this meant seeking the approval of the Bureau of the Budget for funds. Until appropriations are forthcoming, the commission may be dependent on staff detailed from sympathetic departments and agencies. And any recommendations from the commission will be implemented by the administration.

A dependence on existing governmental machinery for help regarding secretarial, technical, and data entry tasks, as well as for background reports, can compromise the judgment expected of commissions. Esther Peterson was named executive vice chairman of the PCSW, and, during its life, the work of the Women's Bureau and the PCSW were in close parallel. For example, in May, 1961, the Women's Bureau met with representatives of women's professional, civic, issues, and religious organizations. Those same representatives were invited to a meeting held by Esther Peterson as vice chairman of the PCSW in January, 1962, just weeks before the first meeting of the PCSW. These same representatives were also notified that they would soon be invited to meet with members of the PCSW.[40]

Just before President Kennedy's announcement of an executive order establishing the commission, a confidential background paper was circulated among several people in the administration "in order to explain the need for such a Commission and to invite comment on its proposed mandate."[41] While the memo notes that it "should not be construed as pre-judging the operations or decisions of the Commission," it clearly lays out the administration's intentions for the commission.[42] A similar set of materials, identified as "factual information" available "merely for your information," was delivered to commission members, and again defined the parameters of the commission's work.[43]

A number of reasons were given justifying the need for a commission. These included statements that "women, like men, have the right to life, liberty, and the pursuit of happiness. Each makes her own decision on dividing her energies among her family, earning a living, and other pursuits." But there also was a statement reflecting the interests of the labor unions which helped elect President Kennedy:[44] "Women's difficulties are intensified because prevailing institutions and work practices were largely shaped by and for men, motherhood involves special needs and responsibilities, and women's role outside the home is relatively new."[45] This statement reveals the influence of Esther Peterson in shaping the mission of the commission, and her interest in doing all that she could to protect women in the lowest rungs of the labor force, who often worked for low wages with no benefits. The background paper then provided data on the wage gap between men and women, with the annual average earnings of full-time working women only 3/5 of the salary paid to men working full-time, with African American women earning far less than their white counterparts; on the millions of working mothers with children under the age of three; and on the millions of women earning less than $1.00 per hour.[46]

The document lays out a policy agenda that in effect became a blueprint for the commission's work and served as an outline for policy considered or enacted by the federal government over the next three decades. In fact, the document was a reflection of issues that had been brewing for years, brought together as a cohesive package.

In shaping the agenda of the commission, the focus would be on the role of the federal government as an employer, since this was an area in which the president, as chief executive, could have the most sway. This had been most clearly demonstrated over two decades earlier, when the last Democratic president, Harry S. Truman, used an executive order to end segregation in the armed forces.

Esther Peterson saw an outside commission as a way of helping to put pressure on the departments and agencies to change their policies and programs to better meet the needs of women. According to Peterson, "We'd have to have an outside group [the commission] to say, 'Those are the things we must do.' So I would go to the various agencies and say, 'this idea is the result of a recommendation, the commission's. This isn't just Esther Peterson talking.' We needed so badly, in order to change the bureaucratic approach to things, to have a basis for the changes. And Kennedy recognized this point when we talked to him about having a commission."[47]

It was also clear that the commission would be building on the work of the Women's Bureau in the Department of Labor, with a clear focus on issues of equality in the workforce, especially issues of equal pay and benefits. The broader issue of political rights, which supporters of the ERA felt was paramount, was included on the commission's agenda as one of several items to consider, rather than the Holy Grail under which all other items would be subsumed. That the PCSW was also an effort to substitute for the ERA is suggested in remarks President Kennedy made several months before receiving the final report of the commission. At a ceremony in the Flower Garden at the White House, for the issuance of an Amelia Earhart Commemorative Stamp, Kennedy referred to the PCSW as the "Commission on Equal Rights for Women."[48]

From the very start, therefore, the commission's work was influenced and guided by the administration. At the first meeting of the PCSW, information papers were provided on:

— federal government contract employment and employment standards, an important area in looking at equality in the work force since it was "estimated that in 1960 the Government bought 20% of all goods and services produced in this country,"[49]

— federal and state laws governing employment of women,[50] and the

— civil and political rights of women

The bulk of information received by commission members focused on employment issues and the role of the federal government as employer. This was not unexpected given the clear demarcation of the role of the national government and state governments, and perhaps reflected a heightened sensitivity to the division of power between the national government and state government in an era when the issue of civil rights was clearly moving toward national resolution. President Kennedy himself frequently pointed out the limits of the national government throughout his term of office and the need for states to change their own policy. (No governors or mayors were among commission members.) Especially in the area of political and civil rights, the role of the national government in defining policy was quite limited. For example, while the Civil Rights Act of 1957 had included provisions barring the exclusion of women from federal juries, in practice, women continued to be excluded from juries in several states.[51] Not until 1964, a year after the PCSW finished its work, would major civil rights legislation be passed which would provide a means by which the Justice Department could enforce the law.

In the background material provided on the "civil and political rights of women," there was no mention of the history of the ERA. There was brief mention that "the middle of the nineteenth century . . . saw the beginning of an organized movement for equal political rights for men and women by amendment to state constitutions, and began the long task of winning suffrage state by state."[52] Even given the orientation of the administration in opposition to the ERA, it is surprising that the only reference to equal rights is made in terms of efforts to amend state constitutions—the issue of women's suffrage is put in terms of a state-by-state battle, rather than the battle for the Nineteenth Amendment. Rather, the discussion focuses on political rights such as jury service, property rights, and family relations.

The absence of consideration of the ERA also reflects political reality in that the role of a president is extremely limited when it comes to the process of amending the Constitution. Article V of the Constitution identifies a role for the Congress, the states, and the people, but not for the president.[53] In this instance as in many others, the president can use the bully pulpit and moral suasion, but has no formal role in the process of amending the Constitution.

The Commission Begins Its Work

By avoiding debate over the ERA, the commission was able to engage in a wide-ranging study of the status of women. In the process, the commission acquired data useful in educating the public and policy makers, as well as in changing longstanding practices and policies.

The work of the commission was done in seven committees, each of which made recommendations to the full commission.[54] The commission itself met eight times during 1962 and 1963.

In terms of bringing women into the ranks of the elected and appointed, some thought that the approach should be a gradual one, with women gaining experience in government at the local level (e.g., school board, city council, and town committees), and then naturally progressing to positions in state and federal government. Others saw inroads being made by women in the professions, thus gaining entry into judicial posts as the number of women lawyers increased, and in entering the pool of those considered for cabinet posts, as greater numbers of women held elective and appointive posts and as more became established in the business world.

The different perspectives brought to the work of the commission, while broadening discussion, did not appear to adversely limit the scope and depth of the recommendations emerging from its work. The commission worked through its seven committees, and membership on the committees was broadened to extend beyond solely the members of the commission to reach out to those in the academic community and interest groups not represented on the commission itself. Some committees further broadened the reach of the commission by making use of subcommittees.

THE STATUS OF WOMEN: THE ADMINISTRATION'S ACTIONS, 1961–63

The commission would be a catalyst and facilitator of the administration's consideration of women. However, other individuals and structures in the administration would also play important roles, and at times the commission would be responding to actions taken by those outside of the executive branch, especially in regards to legislation already on the national agenda. Within the executive branch, the actions of John W. Macy, Jr., and Attorney General Robert F. Kennedy were key. John Macy, as chairman of the Civil Service Commission, did much to advance the role of the Kennedy administration in changing longstanding policy and practice concerning the federal government as an equal opportunity employer.

Executive Orders and Presidential Prerogative

Presidents can influence national policy by setting federal policy in areas in which they have the most control, that is, directives to those in the executive branch they administer.[55] Given the sizeable federal workforce as well as the number of those working under federal government contracts, policy change at the federal level may lead to changes in policy at the state and local levels, and in the private sector. In 1961, the federal government was the nation's largest employer, employing 2,435,808 civilians as of June 30, 1961, "including about 29,000 in the legislative and judicial branches. Of the total number, 76 percent were men and 24 percent, or about 590,000 were women."[56] In addition, 86 percent of all federal government positions were in the competitive civil service, under the direction of John Macy.[57]

In looking at the differences between men and women in the competitive civil service, a 1959 survey revealed that for:

Nonprofessional White-collar Employees

—Most women employed in the Federal service are in the nonprofessional white-collar occupations. These occupations accounted for 1,239,000 employees, 803,000 of whom were men and 436,000 of whom were women.

—The median grade of men in these occupations was 3 General Schedule grades higher than that of women. Their average salary was 27 percent higher: $5,525, as compared with $4,340 for women.

—In "general office work," the largest single category of nonprofessional white-collar positions, there were 254,000 women and 90,000 men. The median grade of women in this category was one grade below that of men.

Professional Employees

—There were 219,000 professional employees. Of this number 40,000 or 18 percent, were women employees, one-half of whom were employed as nurses.

—The median grade of men holding professional positions was 4 grades higher than that of women.

—The average salaries of men in professional positions were 42 percent higher than that of women employees: $8,550, as compared with $6,000 for women.

Top Grades under the "General Schedule"

—There were 1,537 employees in the top three grades of the General Schedule. Of this number, 18 were women.[58]

At the time of the formation of the PCSW, John Macy had already begun work on changing the interpretation of an 1870 federal statute which had allowed departments and agencies to specify the sex preferred in posting job announcements for the civil service. In December, 1961, shortly following a directive from the president, Macy had sent out a memo to departments and agencies asking that they provide reasons as to why a certain sex was preferred when listing a job announcement. Given a 1934 ruling by Franklin D. Roosevelt's attorney general, Macy could not refuse any department or agency request for a stated sex preference for a job, regardless of the reason offered. However, Macy's *asking* for an explanation prompted a tremendous and immediate change in hiring practices throughout the federal bureaucracy. For example, in 1961, prior to Macy's request for an explanation, 67 percent of the job announcements listed a preferred sex; immediately after Macy's request, only 14 percent of the listings indicated a sex preference. The results were remarkable. According to Macy, his request for an explanation as to why a job required a certain sex greatly "reduce[d] the use of a request for men or women only. Further, there is evidence that at least some agencies are taking a fresh and searching look at their traditional practices of specifying a particular sex for certain types of positions."[59]

The efforts of Macy and the commission resulted in the removal of statements such as "for the majority of these positions the agency generally prefers men" in civil service exam announcements unless unusual circumstances justified such wording.[60] Macy realized that vigilance was needed. According to Macy, "Later statistical data will reveal the extent of actual growth in the employment of women. It is clear to us that we cannot relax, nor do we intend to do so. We plan to study very carefully the periodic reports that we will be receiving from all of our examining officers."[61]

Similarly, for the Federal Service Entrance Exam, which was the "chief avenue through which the Federal government hires young people of college caliber for its career professional and administrative careers," agency requests for certification in the Washington area in which a specific sex was specified fell from 52 percent of all requests to less than 2 percent within two months after Macy asked agencies to provide a reason why a certain sex was preferred[62] (see Table 2.1).

TABLE 2.1
Federal Service Entrance Exam
Agency Requests for Certification (Washington Area)

Requests for:	Nov. 13–Dec. 8, 1961 *Percentage of Total Requests*	Feb. 4–March 3, 1962 *Percentage of Total Requests*
Women	7.3%	.1%
Men	45.1	1.6
No sex specified	47.6	98.3
	100%	100%
Total positions covered	454	694

Source: Report, "Employment Policies and Practices of the Federal Government," April 9, 1962, "General Executive Letters #1–5" folder, PCSW, Box 1, John F. Kennedy Library.

The implementation of the president's executive order of December 15, 1961, was quite vigorous, as the data suggest. The president can issue directives, but it is up to those in appointive and career civil service posts to carry out those directives. John Macy was in full compliance with the president's wishes. He asked agencies to review personnel policies and submit copies of policy statements to indicate compliance. By April of 1962, forty-four agencies (a majority) had responded. In categorizing the policy statements received, Macy reported that twelve indicated minimal compliance; seven were defensive in nature, with such comments as "nothing new needed here; we have never discriminated;" seventeen were in perfunctory compliance; and eight demonstrated vigorous compliance, with such statements as "we will make certain that the President's interest becomes thoroughly effective within our organization, and we intend to pursue a program of internal audit to check."[63] Macy indicated his intent to follow up with letters "tailored to the response given" and "calling for a greater degree of consistency in the agency approach to this objective."[64] He observed that for many agencies "a particular sex [had been] . . . specified primarily because of habit and no thought was given to this limitation."[65]

Macy's action, in conjunction with the simultaneous creation of the PCSW, moved the bureaucracy to action, resulting in a dramatic policy change. As Macy observed in reporting to the commission, "It seems to me that here is further evidence of significant impact brought about by the establishment of this Commission and of broader opportunity for well qualified women graduates to compete on equal terms for federal careers."[66]

The commission acted quickly in those areas where the president and his administration had the most authority to effect a permanent change in policy. Macy's action prompted a change in practice, *yet because of the 1934 ruling by the Attorney General, he could not challenge any department or agency's insistence on the need for a sex preference in a job posting.* Therefore, while the Kennedy administration was quick to end this discriminatory behavior, it was no guarantee that subsequent administrations, with a change in personnel, would follow through with Macy's vigilance.

At the April 9, 1962, meeting of the commission, Margaret Hickey, chairman of the Committee on Federal Employment, made a motion that the Civil Service Commission seek a new opinion on the 1870 statute.[67] The commission adopted the recommendation, and, following the meeting, Eleanor Roosevelt sent a letter to Macy:

requesting that his agency seek a new interpretation from the Attorney General. The Civil Service Commission formally requested a new Department of Justice opinion, and, as . . . Hickey commented later, "the wheels of Justice did <u>not</u> grind slowly."

On June 14, Attorney General [and commission member] Robert F. Kennedy sent to the White House a new opinion, which said in essence that Federal appointing officials do not have final discretion regarding the hiring of "men only" or "women only" for Federal Civil Service positions and, therefore, the 1870 statute doesn't limit the authority of the President acting through the Civil Service Commission to regulate with respect to matters involving the efficiency of the Federal service and the fitness of candidates for Federal positions.

It is unusual for an Attorney General to reverse a finding of an earlier Attorney General, but, in this case, Robert Kennedy felt that his predecessor had not had his attention called to the fact that the phrase "in the discretion of the head of the department" was not in the original Act, but was added in a codification. Attorney General Kennedy also indicated that the legislative history of the 1870 statute showed clearly that no sex discrimination was intended.[68]

At the June, 1962, meeting of the PCSW, Deputy Attorney General Nicholas Katzenbach presented a letter from President Kennedy to Eleanor Roosevelt outlining the opinion of the attorney general, whose interpretation of federal statutes greatly opened up employment opportunities for women in the federal sector, and directed Macy to amend the civil service regulations. In the letter, President Kennedy summed up the actions his administration had taken, and noted the constitutional and statutory authority the president had to determine if a position could be classified as open to only men or only women. The chair of the Civil Service Commission would now review hiring and promotion policies to ensure selection of government workers on the basis of merit without regard to sex. Any agency requiring a single-sex position would need to justify that request.[69]

BROADENING THE LEGISLATIVE AGENDA
ON WOMEN'S ISSUES

Oftentimes the president is seen as a legislative leader, with the annual delivery of a State of the Union address before a joint session of Congress and a national television audience in which the president recaps the country's domestic and foreign policy stance while at the same time setting forth a policy agenda for the coming year. This is followed by the president's annual submission of a budget to Congress detailing the administration's priorities as measured by the spending commitment to each.

Yet the president's agenda is often fixed. Positions taken during the campaign or a remark at a press conference may constrain options. Issues may have been simmering for years in Congress, waiting for the right committee chair or configuration of committee members to move legislation to the floor.[70] Similarly, the president must contend with those who are already working in the departments and agencies, who will remain in the bureaucracy after the president's tenure in office is over. The civil servants have a mission to fulfill, and may have a policy agenda at odds with the administration, or at least contending with that of the president.

However, presidents do have a number of legislative tools to use at their discretion. As noted earlier, President Kennedy made use of commissions, including the PCSW, as a way to gather input, add legitimacy to policy recommendations, and shape the legislative activity ensuing in Congress and in the departments. He also made use of another tool favored by many presidents—executive orders—that allowed the president to bypass Congress and direct the departments and agencies to carry out an action without seeking congressional approval. As seen previously, an executive order, for example, directed the civil service to take actions to end sex discrimination.

A separate but related issue is that of "credit-claiming." Presidents may take credit or be given credit for legislation they take on as their own, even though it may be an issue which has been on the national agenda for years. Similarly, a recommendation from a task force or commission may reflect work that has been ongoing for years with a consensus building, yet the commission's imprimatur may supply the needed boost to gain public support compelling political leaders to act. The policy process is not cut and dried, and often not linear. The policy initiatives associated with any administration often have a long and convoluted history. This is very evident in the history of pay equity.

The PCSW is often given credit for passage of the Equal Pay Act in 1963. However, this was an issue that had been on the national agenda since the administration of President Harry S Truman and that had appeared as a plank in the Republican platform as early as 1896.

Equal Pay

At the first commission meeting, Mrs. Roosevelt expressed her thought that endorsement of the Equal Pay Act by the PCSW "would be a publicity thing that we could give out and say that the Commission had endorsed the principle."[71] For most on the commission, it was an issue that had been on the nation's agenda for years, and one they had worked on in the constituent organizations they were representing on the commission. Perhaps because the commission was just getting under way, other members, however, voiced concern over being a rubber stamp for a prearranged agenda, and felt that it was too early to make a decision, and so a heated discussion ensued.[72] Finally, after a much needed coffee break, Mrs. Roosevelt, who perhaps had grown impatient with the discussion and the inability to move forward, suggested the need for some type of statement for the press. "One thing I could say . . . is that the Commission as a whole considers that the present practice of paying lower wage rates to women workers for the same or comparable work as that performed by men workers is contrary to the concept of equality and justice in which we believe. . . . Or we could simply say that we are embarking on our work and have no real statements to make until we are beginning to get in the information and studies which we need."[73]

Mrs. Jacobson, sitting in for Secretary of Agriculture Orville Freeman, seemed to sense the plight Mrs. Roosevelt was in and urged the PCSW to take a stance, if there was at least consensus on a principle. "I believe that there is a public attitude toward Commissions often that they are set up to shove aside major questions. I think that in this particular case any postponement of any substantive comment—just saying we are working on how to proceed—would be unfortunate and would not represent the real nature of this Commission."[74] By the end of the meeting, Eleanor Roosevelt had been authorized to report to the press that the commission "feels that where the rates paid to women are lower than the rates paid to men performing the same work in the same installation, the concepts of equality and equity in which we all believe are violated."[75] The principle of equal pay would be endorsed, without endorsing any particular piece of legislation.[76]

The White House and the Department of Labor let the Women's Bureau take the lead legislative role for the administration in lobbying efforts for the Equal Pay Act. In retrospect, the Equal Pay Act has been viewed by scholars as one of the most important measures to be passed in 1963, along with ratification of the Nuclear Test Ban Treaty and several education bills.[77] Larry O'Brien, special assistant to the president for congressional relations, would look back at 1963 and view the year as a legislative success, with thirty-five of the administration's fifty-eight "must bills" being signed into law. On this list, O'Brien included:

> approval of the Nuclear Test Ban Treaty, expansion of the Peace Corps, the Clean Air Act, Water Pollution Control, extension of the Juvenile Delinquency Act, the District of Columbia Cultural Center (which became the Kennedy Center for the Performing Arts), a higher education bill, education bills to train teachers of retarded children and to provide aid to medical schools and vocational schools, an equal-pay-for-women bill, the mental-health and mental retardation act, a child-health bill, an increased authorization for housing programs for the elderly, increased benefits for the families of veterans, a $450-million appropriation for accelerated public works, establishment of a Commission on Science and Technology, and a permanent increase in the size of the House Rules Committee.[78]

However, a contemporaneous "confidential listing of the standing of White House legislative proposals omitted equal pay legislation under both 'major' and 'minor' headings."[79] John F. Kennedy, as chair of the Senate Labor Subcommittee, had co-sponsored an equal pay bill in 1957, and yet had never held hearings on the bill. He was a supporter of equal pay measures, given his long-term interest in labor issues, "but without vigor." Within the administration, while the Women's Bureau was an ardent supporter, there was outright opposition from the undersecretary of labor, W. Willard Wirtz, who wrote Labor Secretary Arthur Goldberg in May, 1961, "'Arthur: I am not in favor of this proposal. I think it is utterly unrealistic and that if such a bill were adopted it would be the worst failure since the 18th Amendment.'"[80]

A president has limited political capital and must use it wisely. In 1962, the administration was seeking statutory authority to change the President's Committee on Equal Employment Opportunity to be the Equal Opportunity Commission, which would be "empowered to eliminate discrimination in employment practices."[81] The focus was on race. The groundwork was being laid in 1962 and 1963 for legislation that would finally emerge during the Johnson administration—major civil rights and voting rights laws, as well as Medicare and other social programs. Esther Peterson was also well known to O'Brien, having worked under him during the 1960 campaign, and so had the political acumen and skills, and the interest, to be the lead lobbyist for the administration on equal pay.

Peterson had some discussion with President Kennedy regarding equal pay, and later observed that "he gave us some good statements and we'd write something and he'd say it. . . . We had verbal help. I think that was typical of all of them. But you know equal pay was never top priority. Well, they helped me at certain times, but I've literally carried that bill up."[82] Peterson had the support of the secretary of labor and the solicitor's office, but she and her staff did their own legislative lobbying. The White House "didn't interfere" since the bill was "not on O'Brien's list. We were given the responsibility and we lobbied it through. . . . We got the bill through ourselves."[83] Peterson was involved in planning the testimony for the 1962 hearings[84] as well as in orchestrating the support of interest groups to lobby their members of Congress. She made use of the PCSW to help with these efforts.[85]

Although equal pay "was well on its way before the Commission acted," the PCSW also did its part to move equal pay forward. The PCSW got Secretary Goldberg to add equal pay to his list of legislative priorities. In Peterson's words, we "had to convince . . . [the legislative people in Labor] that it was a good political issue, that they had to do something for women and that this would be one of the best things they could do," and "we got Mrs. Roosevelt to testify for it." In addition, Richard Lester, vice chairman of the PCSW, also testified on behalf of the commission before Congress.[86]

Congress failed to pass equal pay legislation in 1962, since different versions were passed by each chamber, and time ran out before procedural and substantive matters could be resolved. According to Peterson, "In those last frantic days of an extended Congressional session, equal pay—in company with some other administration bills—failed of enactment. But for the first time in American history, equal pay bills passed both Houses of Congress. And with that achievement behind us, we've nowhere to go but ahead to passage of equal pay legislation."[87] The bill was easily passed in the new Congress, which began in January, 1963.[88] Peterson was disappointed in the final bill, having wanted stronger legislation, but "you take one good giant step and it establishes the principle, then you've got to build on that. You never get the whole piece anyway. It never happens."[89] One of the issues for Peterson was that to get passage, wording was changed from "equal pay for comparable work" to "equal pay for equal work."[90]

Women and the Military

In a number of areas in which the administration was already proposing or considering legislation, the PCSW recommended how the legislation could be broadened to include agenda items of special concern to women. In all cases, study reports were done and appropriate departments and agencies were consulted early in the process to be sure their voices were heard. For example, the Commission's Committee on Federal Employment Policies and Practices set as a priority the issue of women in the military. This was in response to the legislative agenda of the Defense Department, which was at work on a bill regarding the career management of officer personnel. The committee was reinforcing the work already done by the Defense Advisory Committee on Women in the Military Services, which had made similar recommendations in both 1960 and 1961.[91]

At the June, 1962, meetings, the PCSW recommended to the Department of Defense that restrictions on the number of women in the highest officer ranks be eliminated, "with the number of such officers . . . left to the discretion of the Secretary of each service within the over-all limitations provided for all officers."[92] Within a month the administration had adopted the commission's recommendation. Secretary of Defense Robert McNamara assured Roosevelt that the bill submitted to Congress on the career management of officer personnel would not include separate restrictions on the numbers of women officers.[93] While a change in policy would not come during the Kennedy administration, the issue was receiving the attention of key policy makers, as was the case for other issues such as child care.[94]

Tax Law

At the October, 1962, meeting of the PCSW, the Committee on Social Insurance and Taxes presented a background paper on federal income tax deductions for child care and disabled dependents. While no motion was presented, there was discussion of current law as well as a discussion of proposed changes in the deductions. A representative from the Treasury Department was present for the discussions given the department's jurisdiction over tax reform legislation. These discussions helped to lay the foundation for recommendations that became part of a tax reform package sent to Congress in 1963.[95]

Richard Lester testified on behalf of the commission before the House Ways and Means Committee during hearings on proposed changes in the tax law, in support of child care deductions.[96]

As a whole, the members of the PCSW were an astute group. They were action oriented and always interested in how to implement policy. They were well aware of the need for appropriations as well as authorizations to effect a successful policy change. For instance, at the fourth meeting of the commission, in October, 1962, "the Commission empowered the officers to find some effective means of hastening favorable action on appropriations for day care service for children authorized as a part of Public Law 87-543."[97]

Employee Benefits

The Committee on Federal Employment reviewed laws which required married women in the federal workforce to pay more than married men for health insurance for "self and family" and recommended that the law be changed. During 1963, when Congress was considering changes to the federal Health Insurance Act, the issue was raised in hearings before the Senate Health Benefits and Life Insurance Subcommittee. John Macy, commission member and chairman of the Civil Service Commission, testified that "the Civil Service Commission would not oppose legislation to equalize the Government contributions for married women and married men." The Senate Committee on Post Office and Civil Service didn't finish work on this legislation, but its committee member, Senator Neuberger, also a commission member, could communicate the commission's interest to the full committee. However, the House committee would not consider such an amendment during this presidential administration.[98]

POLITICAL PARTICIPATION

The interests of the PCSW extended beyond just policy items. As demonstrated in Chapter 1, the interests of women's organizations included having women appointed to policy-making positions. The precedent for appointing a woman to the cabinet had been established by President Franklin D. Roosevelt, with his appointment of Frances Perkins to be secretary of labor in 1933. While President Truman appointed no women to the cabinet, Eisenhower followed Roosevelt's lead with the elevation of Oveta Culp Hobby from the post of federal security administrator to HEW secretary. However, the Kennedy administration did not emphasize the appointment of women for either symbolic or descriptive representation needs. The inclusion of women was not yet viewed in terms of the strategic electoral calculations, which would be made in subsequent administrations (e.g., the "gender gap" in voting; "soccer moms" in the 1996 election). This may reflect the lack of support from women in the 1960 election, where only 49 percent of women voted for Kennedy, in contrast to 52 percent of men who supported Kennedy.[99] In fact, no women were appointed to the cabinet or held cabinet rank in the Kennedy administration. The lack of interest in the representation of women as a constituency is clearly illustrated in a memo from Dan H. Fenn, Jr., to Ralph A. Dungan, outlining the pros and cons of candidates under consideration for the post of commissioner of education.[100] The only woman on the list, Mary Bunting, was described as follows: "President, Radcliffe College since 1960. Intellectually keen but major drawback (in addition to sex) is lack of experience or association with public education field."[101]

That Mary Bunting's sex would be viewed as a drawback in 1962, at a time when the work of the PCSW was already under way, is quite telling. It is even more surprising that being a woman would be viewed in a negative light for the post of commissioner of education, since editorials had long ago predicted that a likely post for a woman, if one were ever to be appointed to a cabinet post, would be to head a new Department of Education.

While representation has been an important consideration in looking at the formation of a president's cabinet—i.e., whether the cabinet is representative of certain constituent areas, such as farmers, labor, business—it also is an important consideration in the president's appointments to lower-level posts.[102] The push to include women qua women on a sustained basis came with later administrations. However, there was still a push to include women in the Kennedy administration. The effort came primarily from within the organizational structure of the Democratic Party, as well as some interest groups. The administration's response would be minimal.

In the Democratic Party, the Women's Division, headed by Margaret Price, submitted names of women, active in the party, for consideration as presidential appointees. However, Price did not have Peterson's long-time working relationship with President Kennedy and some of his advisors. The Kennedy campaign organization was a forerunner to the campaign organizations that would emerge a decade later, with the growth in the number of primary elections—i.e., presidential candidates run independent of the party organization, developing their own personalized basis of support. The party organization provides organizational support, but the candidate and the candidate's campaign organization run the campaign. The party becomes one part of the organizational structures contributing to the candidate's success, along with interest groups, labor unions, corporate America, and so forth.

Ralph Dungan would turn, therefore, to Esther Peterson—who had been active in the Kennedy campaign organization—for advice on the list of names sent over.[103] Peterson did meet with Price to go over the list of names. However, the role Peterson could play in recommending these names was limited in that her experience, networks, and associates had come out of the trade union movement, not out of the Democratic Party organization.

Although she had worked in campaigns and on behalf of candidates, she had not "been part of the formal party structure."[104]

She was being asked to pass judgment on individuals she did not know very well, a problem facing any incoming administration. "We did collect an awful lot of names . . . our problem . . . was that you get a lot of names of people who worked in the political campaigns, but you didn't know exactly what Ella Grasso did, for example. You didn't know the practical experience of the women. You see, you had women who ran things, and then you'd come up with the business of their needing an appointment, but where do you put them and what is their experience and what is their background to get them well placed?"[105] Peterson did not view this effort as successful, and this was another reason why she would urge President Kennedy to establish a commission on women. A more systematic approach was needed to both bring women in to government positions, and address substantive policy issues. From her prior work with Kennedy, she thought the president would be responsive to such an approach.[106] During Kennedy's Senate years, whenever Esther was in meetings with Kennedy and other committee members and labor leaders, Kennedy sought out her opinion the same as from others in the meeting. Kennedy would say, "'I'd like to know what Esther thinks about this, too.' There was always, I think, a respect, and I liked that. It meant a great deal to me because very frequently, as a woman, you learned that if all your points were made by others, you let them be made, and hurrah. But I always felt he respected me as a person who had some ability."[107]

Outside groups were also lobbying on behalf of women appointments throughout the administration. For example, the Women's Bar Association of the District of Columbia endorsed a resolution in April, 1962, which they forwarded to Eleanor Roosevelt as chair of the PCSW: "Be it resolved that the Corresponding Secretary address a letter to the President of the United States respectfully urging that consideration be given to the appointment of a qualified woman to fill the next vacancy occurring in his Cabinet."[108] But perhaps the women's organizations were playing the largest role in pushing for women as representatives of the United States at international conferences. Margaret Hickey, a member of the PCSW, noted that "the women's organizations can take a great deal of credit for pushing on this" (i.e., the appointment of women as delegates and representatives to international organizations).[109] The problem with this approach was that it provided an opportunity for a number of women to be appointed, therefore increasing descriptive representation, but mostly became a way of enhancing symbolic representation. These women had no power to set policy.

The symbolic aspects of appointments were clearly a consideration in the discussions of the PCSW. In discussing the appointments of Presidents Eisenhower and Kennedy, Hickey observed, " . . . when you look at the unusual and very high level of appointments, keep in mind that in any analysis of this situation you will see that a political convention tends to advertise the prestige for appointments, so that we know a great deal about the women who were appointed, say, by the Eisenhower administration and they were unusual and very high level appointments. They had the women . . . to decorate their platform. . . . They are very brilliant and able women. Now the Democrats come along. . . . Mary McGuire, Commissioner of Public Housing and Administration . . . [is] a very important appointment, because this is a big agency. . . . It is not a traditional place. . . . Much more should be made of that."[110]

Esther Peterson's nomination to be director of the Women's Bureau in the Department of Labor was heavily promoted by women active in the trade unions, who asked if she would let them suggest her name for the post in a letter to Kennedy. However, Esther Peterson did not feel that she was appointed to the post in response to this pressure, and that the work on behalf of her nomination by the trade union women was not necessary for her to secure the post.

> I'd met Kennedy [after the election], and I remember him saying to me, "What do you want?" And Ralph [Dungan] mentioned a number of possibilities. And I think I said the Women's Bureau, partly because I know that area, have some competence in that area, and partly because I was interested in women's employment . . . wanted to really see if I couldn't do something to help the women in the low wage jobs. . . . And then I didn't like the feminist, equal rights approach. I thought maybe we could elevate some of the tactics being used. But I really think I could have had some different appointment if I'd wanted.[111]

The presence of an individualized pluralistic model is most evident in that some objected to Peterson's appointment, asking what she had "ever done for the party?"[112] She had, however, been involved in the election of Democratic candidates for years, working outside of the organized party structure. Esther Peterson also did work with the Women's Division at the Democratic National Party headquarters and had Jackie Kennedy assist her in the launching of "Labor Women for Kennedy."[113]

The appointment of Peterson could certainly be justified in terms of issues of descriptive representation, since it was labor women who "did one of the most effective jobs in the country" in getting Kennedy elected.[114] In fact, Esther Peterson tried to get the substantive interests of labor women included in the work of the Women's Division of the Democratic Party. Peterson wanted these women to be able to "discuss the content rather than just the frills or run around doing the dirty work,"[115] and the campaign made its appeal to women as consumers and as workers.

Although the issue of the appointment of women to high-level posts in the administration was not a major agenda item for the PCSW, given the structure of the seven committees that corresponded to the agenda President Kennedy outlined when establishing the commission, it did receive the attention of several of the commission's committees. For instance, the Committee on Civil and Political Rights noted the barriers to women's participation in the highest levels of elective and appointive office. Women were not always a part of the eligibility pool for certain posts, given state laws in the early 1960s. In some states, women could not own property and as a result never became business owners or business executives, thus precluding their consideration for certain posts.

In the discussions of the PCSW, there was an emphasis on the role of political parties as a vehicle for increasing participation among women in elective and appointive posts. Margaret Hickey, chairman of the Committee on Federal Employment Policies and Practices, which developed several recommendations for the commission to consider on the issue of women in appointive posts, observed that "women have become increasingly active in party work in recent years." She noted that Molly Dewson's "approach . . . was to equate party activity . . . with political leadership."[116] What Hickey and the commission failed to note was that the ongoing change in campaigning was already diminishing the role of party. What worked in the 1930s might not be successful in the latter half of the twentieth century. And even Dewson's success came from her involvement in a network of women involved in social issues and labor, politics, and policy, and government, and she also promoted the appointment of women from that network.[117]

Working within the party structures was seen by some as the path for inclusion of women. However, if women relied on this institutional structure, they would soon be sitting on the outside with the rise of individualized candidate–centered approaches to politics in the Washington community.

Throughout the discussions of the commission on the need for women to move into top executive branch posts, either through career routes or political patronage routes, the discussion centered more on issues of symbolic representation of women than substantive representation of their policy interests. For example, Hickey observed that

> it was the feeling of the committee [on Federal Employment Policies and Practices] that we could not avoid taking a strong position on this leadership area because of its symbolic importance in the whole leadership structure within the federal government, and that until we get more women into these top political executive positions we are not really doing the job that needs to get done.... The status of women in the federal service will be improved by the appointment of more women to these symbolic visible posts of leadership.[118]

Hickey wanted the PCSW to "develop positive, affirmative steps which will help bring this about," and develop a "strategy on how best to implement such a recommendation." Mary Bunting also wanted the commission to recognize the "sensitivity of these appointments and the absolute importance of having very able women in them." Peterson added, "[T]here is so much talk of having a woman because she is a woman, having a Negro because she is a Negro, that we want to lift this on a merit basis as rapidly as we can."[119] And yet "merit" remained a point of contention.

It was quite difficult for the commission to reach a consensus on the issue of appointments. For instance, there were discussions over whether appointments would be made with "ability" and "merit" in mind. If the recommendations stated women "with political acumen and experience" should be considered, would this preclude consideration of women who had gained experience in non-partisan organizations, the traditional routes women had used for years to gain political influence? The following passages provide some of the flavor of the debate:

> **Senator Maurine Neuberger:** "I just object to making too tight a statement that suggests that 'by golly, the President has got to appoint a woman to the Cabinet.'"[120]
>
> **Esther Peterson:** "I think we have no right to be stepping into the political area where the Executive of whatever party is in power has the right to determine the Executive appointments ... this is a prerogative under our political system. However, as a Commission considering this, we can have in the report sometime the importance of the political activity as part of the whole role of women."[121]

Miss Pauli Murray [a member of the Committee on Civil and Political Rights]: "One of the ways in which you might de-emphasize or avoid the charge of politics is the principle that I think all of us agree that today that there is a great need for wide representation of all people on all levels, and that probably none would disagree that there is a need for women in important positions."[122]

At the October, 1962, meetings of the commission, Margaret Hickey worked to get the commission to agree to a "positive, affirmative statement recommending the appointment of more women of talent and competence in the field of the political executive."[123] After much discussion, the commission finally reached agreement on a resolution, concluding "that increasing and continuing consideration should be given to the *desirability* [author's emphasis] of appointment of women of demonstrated ability and political sensitivity to policy-making posts." The commission members were quite concerned that they not appear to be attacking the record of appointments of the prior administration or the current administration. Hickey summed up the main points of the discussion, explaining the reasons for this resolution: (1) High-level positions for women would be of "symbolic value," inspiring young women to consider careers in government service; (2) women elected or appointed at the state and local levels would, in time, provide a pool of candidates for high-level appointments by the president, and therefore women should be encouraged to pursue state and local posts; (3) in making appointments consideration was needed of the alternative career paths which have been more accessible to women, providing experience in business or as leaders in women's organizations, or local or state government service.[124]

Public release of this recommendation was to be deferred until after it had been discussed and reviewed by the White House. However, the press of outside events delayed this discussion: On October 14, 1962, Soviet offensive missiles were discovered in Cuba, following a series of diplomatic "moves and countermoves" on the part of Soviet and American officials concerning the placement of missiles in Cuba.[125] As Graham T. Allison noted, "the Cuban missile crisis was a seminal event. History offers no parallel to those thirteen days of October 1962, when the United States and the Soviet Union paused at the nuclear precipice. Never before had there been such a high probability that so many lives would end suddenly."[126] As a result of this foreign policy crisis, consultation with the White House over the commission's recommendations was postponed.[127] Shortly thereafter, early in November, 1962, Eleanor Roosevelt, the chairman of the PCSW, passed away and so the attention turned to issues of leadership of the commission in its remaining months.

However, Margaret Hickey was able to meet with Dan Fenn, staff assistant to the president responsible for presidential appointments, before the next meeting of the commission in February, 1963, and her Committee on Federal Employment Policies and Practices came up with a series of recommendations for the commission to consider at that meeting based on her conversations with Fenn. The recommendations included: (1) The establishment of a White House office to "give continuing, systematic, and expert attention to a positive search for talent" to increase consideration of women for appointive posts; (2) "designation of a small committee to be attached to the Commission to cooperate with the Staff Assistant to the President in locating talented women for political executive posts," and (3) "that learned societies, women's organizations and associations, and the national political committees be urged to establish continuing arrangements for locating and recommending talented women for political executive positions."[128]

The White House did "set up a small unit to seek able candidates qualified for political executive positions," and it was hoped that the presence of such a unit would lead to the recognition of talented women.[129] The second recommendation was adopted by the commission and a small committee was established, under Esther Peterson's direction, to help suggest women for positions. Fenn said he "would welcome the help of such a committee"; however, he did not want it to be a "public committee," and did not want it to be "the type of committee that would start bringing pressures on him for appointment of particular people. He want[ed] to just have a contact whereby he can begin to make appointments."[130] With only nine months left in the administration, the impact of this new effort would be minimal, especially with no public acknowledgment of these efforts until October, 1963.

At the February meeting of the commission, the Committee on Government Contracts also recommended "the establishment and maintenance of a roster of women qualified for appointment to high level positions in various types of public and private activities."[131] However, the idea of a roster met with greater opposition than support among commission members and it failed to win endorsement by the commission. The committee created to advise the president's special assistant on possible women appointees was given the task of exploring the idea of a roster, and the Committee on Federal Employment Policies and Practices also issued a report on the subject later in the spring, which served as the basis for the commission's final recommendations on this matter.[132] The arguments were summed up in the final committee report:

> The advantage of a roster as a means of securing greater consideration of women should be weighed carefully. On the positive side it would be an answer for those who are willing to consider women for policymaking posts but who have no source of well-qualified women to call on. There would unquestionably be some placement made from a roster that would otherwise not be made. On the negative side is cost, difficulties of keeping a roster current, and the need for study and creative effort to work out methods of evaluation and categorizing volunteer experience.[133]

The February, 1963, meeting of the PCSW, where the structural mechanisms to routinize the inclusion of women for consideration in appointive posts were considered, had run into problems, shortening debate and discussion. A snow and ice storm began to shut down Washington, D.C., and the commission soon lost a quorum of its members as people tried to hurry to get home. This circumstance exacerbated the problems following the end of the October, 1962, meetings when first the Cuban missile crisis, and then the death of Eleanor Roosevelt, had limited the administration's response and follow-up on the issue of appointments. Cumulatively, then, the vicissitudes of life postponed action on any kind of infrastructure for the consideration of women appointments. It would take years to move in all of the directions which the PCSW committees recommended in 1963, and these political developments will be considered more fully in the following chapters.

CONCLUSION

The commission did everything it could to garner the support of the permanent government—the departments and agencies—and in selling the work of the commission to interested parties and the constituents of the various departments. Cabinet officers and department staff participated in the meetings and work of the commission and, near the end of the commission's work, as the final report was being printed, Esther Peterson wrote to the cabinet secretaries to again keep them informed and ensure their support:

Copies of our report, "American Women" have just arrived from the printer and I want you to have one right away. I feel sure you will agree it is a document in which the Commission can take great pride and, as we all hope, a fitting memorial to Mrs. Roosevelt.

Of course the report is not to be given any public distribution before the presentation ceremony at the White House on October 11. After that its real success will depend on its receiving widespread publicity and public support. We are hard at work at this moment developing a public relations program and anything you can do to help bring our report and recommendations to the attention of interested people and groups will be most important.

At this time—when the report is actually in hand—I do want to express my deep personal appreciation for the contribution you have made in the work of the Commission.[134]

Some commission members felt that a permanent structure should be created to continue the work after final recommendations had been submitted to the president. However, John Macy was quick to point out that Kennedy's management style was to not create new governmental entities. Also, any new governmental structure would require the support of Congress in the form of authorizations and appropriations. As a practical matter, presidents are given a good deal of leeway in reorganizing existing departments, but not in creating new posts or offices. According to Macy, Kennedy preferred to place the cabinet secretaries in charge, and as a result, made use of interdepartmental advisory groups and advisory committees to cabinet secretaries. This was the way in which Kennedy had worked in the past. According to Macy,

It has been President Kennedy's position in virtually all of the new programs that have come along to tie them into some existing government institution and to designate a responsible organization head to follow through and accomplish the job and report to the president.

... [For example:] The area redevelopment administration. The President recommended and the Congress enacted assignment of that function to the Department of Commerce.

The Department of Commerce, however, is not the only Federal agency concerned. There are half a dozen or so other agencies, but the President looks to the Secretary of Commerce to see to it that that particular program is carried forward.

In the area of the ageing the President by Executive Order has designated the Secretary of HEW to serve as the responsible monitor and coordinator for the Federal Government in all its various programs that relate to the older citizen.

And under the Secretary of HEW there is an interdepartmental committee that is used to bring together all of the action on this front ... [and a panel of consultants] ... and ... an effort to contact the various citizen groups that are interested in this program.[135]

Macy's recommendation was followed. Shortly after receiving the commission's report in October, 1963, President Kennedy issued an executive order establishing two continuing federal bodies (an Interdepartmental Committee and a Citizens' Advisory Committee) to "evaluate progress made, provide counsel, and serve as a means for suggesting and stimulating action." The role of these committees in the Johnson administration in building on the work of the commission will be explored more fully in Chapter 3.

The president sets the tone for the administration. And this was an administration that was receptive to change. The president was interested in the work of the commission, and members found that "the prompt response of executive agencies to its early recommendations, result[ed] ... in major, broadening of women's opportunities even before the final report was rendered."[136]

The recommendations of the PCSW came to the president only shortly before his assassination, leaving the Johnson administration with the task of responding to the recommendations and formulating and implementing policy. However, in the short time of the administration, just two years and nine months, much was accomplished. Posts were opened up to women in the civil service, setting the federal government as a role model for state and local government and the private sector. Equal pay legislation was passed, a quota which had greatly limited the number and kinds of women officers in the military would soon be abolished, and a link was made between the use of the Fourteenth Amendment to rid discrimination on the basis of race with the ridding of discrimination on the basis of sex (an alternative approach to an ERA). In essence, the federal government had become involved in issues of women's rights, and in the policy concerns of women, in a systematic and ongoing fashion, fostering dialogue as well as action in new areas.

Much more could have been done. In March, 1963, President Kennedy had sent Congress "The Manpower Report of the President." In the report,

Kennedy described a "hidden underemployment" where women, among other groups, want to work, but are denied job opportunities. Kennedy observed that "racial, religious, sex, and age discrimination must be eradicated to keep faith with our ideals and to strengthen our resources and speed our growth," noting how his administration had been moving to eliminate discrimination in the federal government as well as with the contractors to the federal government.[137]

In spite of Kennedy's inclusion of "sex" in discussing discrimination, the Johnson administration would not work to include "sex" the following year as the civil rights bill made its way through Congress. While Kennedy included sex in language that would become part of the 1964 Civil Rights Act, this would not be a priority of the administration that African Americans were.

It would take nine years until one of the national parties would adopt the recommendation of the commission's Committee on Political and Civil Rights encouraging a 50-50 split in the participation of women as delegates to the national conventions. Not until 1980, however, would women achieve that goal, when nearly 50 percent of the delegates to the Democratic National Convention were women. The goal was met only after Democratic Party rules were changed requiring that "state delegation[s] be equally divided between the sexes."[138]

No woman would serve in the cabinet as head of a department during the Kennedy, Johnson, or Nixon administrations.

The courts would become a vehicle for change, in the meantime, as cases were presented to test the use of the Fourteenth Amendment as a way to gain and guarantee equal rights for women. This followed the strategy suggested by committee member Pauli Murray as an alternative to a constitutional amendment guaranteeing equal rights.

Legislative approaches would also become more popular in the next two decades, especially following the inadvertent (but successful) inclusion of "women" in the 1964 Civil Rights Act. An agenda was in place for the Johnson administration to move forward on.

CHAPTER 3

◉

The Johnson Administration
A Different Agenda—Inclusive Appointments

THE NATION WAS IN a period of mourning following the assassination of the thirty-fifth president on November 22, 1963. President Johnson and his family let the young widow and the two small children of the slain president continue to live in the White House, not moving in until December 7. Aware of the awesome responsibilities that make the life of the president so very different from the life of the vice president, Johnson addressed the nation the night before Thanksgiving, two days after much of a stunned nation had spent a somber Monday transfixed by the black and white television images of the funeral cortege that carried the body of President Kennedy from the Capitol to St. Matthew's Cathedral and then to its final resting place in Arlington National Cemetery. While many could remember the death of President Franklin D. Roosevelt, few were alive who could recall the death of William McKinley in 1901, the last president to have died in office from an assassin's bullet.

This would be only the first in a series of political assassinations that would add to the violence and political turmoil of the 1960s. It would also mark the beginning of a greater intimacy between the American public and its political leaders greatly facilitated by television, as the public awaited word of Kennedy's status after he was taken to Parkland Hospital, saw the accused assassin gunned down, and then watched the funeral procession.

However, there would also be continuity with the past. In this inherited presidency, as in same party electoral transitions, staff and executive branch personnel already in place continued the day-to-day functionings of the government. An agenda was already in place, as the first session of the 88th Congress was winding down. President Kennedy's legislative priorities of civil rights legislation, tax cuts, a health care program for the aged, and general school aid remained.[1]

JOHNSON AND THE ERA: THE LEGACY OF THE PRESIDENT'S COMMISSION ON THE STATUS OF WOMEN

As black crepe still hung in the East Room, and even before the newly sworn in president had moved into the White House, supporters of the ERA hastened to obtain Johnson's support for their crusade. Jane Grant, president of the Lucy Stone League, Inc., and a leading supporter of the ERA, sent a letter to Johnson less than two weeks after he had taken the oath of office. Inquiring "What is your present stand on the Equal Rights Amendment which is before Congress?" she noted, "We are aware of your sometime support of the measure while you were in the Senate and your approval of the principle in the Democratic platform. But your recent marked exclusion of women's organizations when you invited important factions to the White House for consultation, may indicate a re-appraisal of your policy."[2]

Just as she had in the last administration, Esther Peterson helped define the administration's response and position on this issue. In drafting a reply for Myer Feldman, deputy special counsel to the president, to send to Grant, as well as to others who might write on this question, Peterson emphasized the importance of continuity in that the president "hold[s] to the position taken by the President's Commission on the Status of Women."[3] The suggested wording for administration replies was closely followed:

> The President's Commission on the Status of Women gave very careful consideration to this question and reached the unanimous conclusion that "the U.S. Constitution now embodies equality of rights for men and women" and that "a constitutional amendment need not now be sought in order to establish this principle." The President is impressed by the Commission's position and believes that this approach should be fully explored before considering a new constitutional amendment on this subject.[4]

There had been hope among ERA supporters that Johnson's support would be stronger than that of Kennedy. But given that Johnson kept the Kennedy staff pretty much intact until he had won election in 1964, and even after in some cases, the *administration's* consistency in policy is not surprising, even if *Johnson's* own position had appeared to change. Even after the Kennedy people had left the White House, the Bureau of the Budget, which provided legislative histories for the Executive Office of the President and maintained files detailing the administration's past responses to inquiries on legislation under consideration by Congress, continued to provide White House personnel with the recommendations of the PCSW, which would serve as the basis for the administration's response.[5]

In her letter to the president, Grant also asked whether the issue of "civil rights" and "equal rights" "appl[ied] now to the Negro problem exclusively." Feldman's response to Grant, while highlighting the work of the PCSW, also linked the issues of civil rights for African Americans to equal rights for women. Feldman noted:

> It is to be regretted that your organization has the impression that concern over civil rights is limited to the Negro problem. Although great efforts are being expanded to assure that these basic Constitutional freedoms will not be denied our Negro citizens, who, as you know, have suffered the greatest denial in this area, we are still acutely aware that basic Constitutional rights are for everyone; we are working toward removing prejudice from our national life whether such prejudice be on the basis of sex, race, age, physical handicap, religion, previous condition of servitude or national origin.[6]

This was not, however, the thrust of subsequent administration efforts. Indeed, these policies would not be linked until the 1970s when the women's movement gained form and acceptance.[7]

The PCSW had recommended that existing governmental institutions be used to effect change: Congress and state legislatures to pass statutes; court cases to allow for judicial clarification of existing constitutional provisions; and the presidency, to use the power of executive orders. An ERA was not deemed necessary.[8]

Letters would be received periodically from the NWP, as well as from other advocates of the ERA, throughout the course of the administration. The NWP noted how, in a series of cases since the addition of the Fourteenth Amendment to the Constitution, the Supreme Court had rejected the use of the Fifth and Fourteenth Amendments to provide equal rights for women.[9] Others pointed out that the commission's recommendations urging interested parties to pursue rights for women through the judicial process had failed to take note of the costs of such litigation. For example, the costs of the *Brown* court challenge were more than $200,000, and any litigation, in addition to monetary burdens, also took many years to fight.[10]

As the 1964 presidential campaign neared its closing days, Emma Guffey Miller was again seeking the support of the nominee of the Democratic Party for endorsement of an ERA, to no avail.[11] The National Federation of Business and Professional Women also wrote to the president urging his support for the ERA.[12] The issue was not one that received much attention in the White House, except for the exchange of letters among staff in order to update draft responses to these inquiries.

In time, with the staff that had worked in both shaping and facilitating the work of the PCSW moving on to other posts in the administration or the private sector, the ERA fell far below the White House radar. Proof of this claim is found in a communication sent between two White House staffers preparing a draft response from the president to Emma Guffey Miller, late in 1967. "Can you have someone prepare a statement on the Equal Rights Amendment *(about women)* [emphasis added] for submission to the President with the attached?"[13] Thus, a lasting legacy of Kennedy's Commission on the Status of Women would be its influence in shaping the direction of White House policy concerning women—and its insistence that an amendment was not necessary.

A NEW ADMINISTRATION: ESTABLISHING STRUCTURES FOR WOMEN'S ISSUES

Johnson faced a delicate balancing act. He wanted to provide the continuity necessary for the nation and his own presidency, having not yet won a mandate to govern in his own right, yet he also wanted to move forward on his own agenda. According to a close friend, once President Johnson "began thinking about the points at which he could distinguish himself from his predecessor without criticizing, which he obviously was not going to do ... it must have occurred to him or been suggested to him ... that one point on which Kennedy had been rather weak was on his recognition of women, as governmental figures."[14]

Esther Peterson had originally wanted the PCSW to come to an end after the issuance of its report. She thought that the Women's Bureau, which she headed and which had been intimately involved in the work of the commission, would guide the administration in carrying out the recommendations of the commission and issue periodic progress reports.[15] However, the commission members, who had invested a great deal of time and energy in their work, felt that they should have some oversight role in following the administration's implementation of their recommendations. As a result, shortly before turning in their final report, the commission recommended to President Kennedy that (1) an advisory council be set up to meet two or three times a year to review the progress being made, and (2) an interdepartmental committee be created to implement the commission recommendations. Two structures were soon in place—a Citizens' Advisory Council on the Status of Women (CACSW), and an Interdepartmental Committee on the Status of Women (ICSW)—as called for in one of the final executive orders of the Kennedy presidency.[16]

Johnson himself had taken an active interest in the work of the PCSW while serving as vice president. As vice president, shortly after Kennedy's Commission on the Status of Women began its work, Johnson urged Democratic Party women to go beyond precinct work:

> . . . there are twoo [sic] few willing to push beyond the precincts.
>
> I understand there are reasons for that—and one of them is men—but there is also an unwillingness on the part of women to take the risks.
>
> A wise man in our party once said, when referring to politics, "If you can't stand the heat, stay out of the kitchen."
>
> But it has been my experience that when the going gets tough, it is the women who can take it. Here, in this "kitchen" setting tonight, I urge you not to run from the competition. Qualify yourselves to run for public office yourselves or to help someone who is running.
>
> The political life of this country needs you, not only as doorbell ringers, but as conference table thinkers.
>
> Somehow, in your own political organizations back home, you must pave the way: through voluntary service, or part-time paid employment, to be the exciting training ground for young women who are on the diaper circuit today, but could be on the stump-speaking circuit tomorrow.[17]

Johnson's interest gave added impetus to the work begun by the commission. In fact, the Johnson administration summary of "What the Administration has Done for Women" early in 1964 highlighted the work of Kennedy's Committee on Equal Employment Opportunity. The document stated that the committee, which Vice President Johnson had chaired, along with the administration's "campaign for equal opportunity carried out by the United States Employment Service at the suggestion of the President

[had] stimulated similar campaigns and committees at the State level across the Nation."[18]

Kennedy's designation of Johnson as chair, with advice to "keep an eye on the deliberations" of the PCSW, had placed the future president in direct contact with John Macy, chair of the Civil Service Commission and a member of the PCSW. This provided an institutional and structural means for Johnson to become involved in the issue of equal employment opportunities for women.[19]

A close working relationship developed between Macy and Johnson. According to Macy, "This was where I first became really closely acquainted with Lyndon Johnson, because he saw very quickly that where we could make the greatest progress in equal opportunity for Negroes and Mexican-Americans was in the Civil Service, because here it was the government as the employer."[20] Macy observed that Johnson's role as chair of the President's Committee on Equal Employment Opportunity was important in that "in the Kennedy years the Civil Service Commission was really mobilized for the first time to carry out its responsibility on equal employment opportunity. . . . Johnson was a decided inspiration in making that possible. He recognized progress; he kept a prod on us; he was always available to give us support. And although neither of us would feel that we went as far as we hoped we would be able to, I think it really turned the government service around during those periods."[21]

Johnson eventually brought Macy into the White House to run his personnel shop. In addition, as a friend of Johnson's later observed, "he sincerely believed in giving more recognition [to women]. . . . I know John Macy said they just searched and searched for women. And the President kept after him all the time. So it was a genuine thing. But I really think, though I've never seen it suggested by any commentator, that it was part of his effort to distinguish himself from Kennedy."[22] While Kennedy had established a PCSW, and was thought to have given the endorsement to an ERA sought by a number of women's groups, he had not appointed a woman to the cabinet as had his predecessor, Dwight Eisenhower, and had virtually ignored the Women's Division in the Democratic Party.

Interdepartmental Committee on the Status of Women, and the Citizens' Advisory Council on the Status of Women

As previously noted, two structures emerging from the recommendations of the PCSW were the ICSW and the CACSW. The ICSW consisted of those cabinet secretaries who had served on the president's commission, as well as the secretary of state and secretary of defense, and the chairman of the Civil Service Commission.[23] Since most of the departments represented had participated in the work of the PCSW, this cabinet-level committee was well-informed of its responsibilities, and, according to Mary D. Keyserling, the next director of the Women's Bureau, ready to get to the business at hand.[24]

Secretary of Labor W. Willard Wirtz, chair of the committee, called for its first meeting to be held on January 20, 1964, with a meeting of the CACSW, the second structure emerging from Executive Order No. 11126, to be held the month after. The membership of the advisory council was in essence the members of the PCSW who were not in the executive branch departments or agencies, plus a few additional members. President Johnson named Margaret Hickey as chairman of the CACSW. Hickey, an active member of the commission, had served as chairman of the Committee on Federal Employment Politics and Practices.[25] Wirtz picked February 12 as the meeting date for the CACSW. This was the anniversary of the first meeting of the PCSW with President Kennedy and of the reception then-Vice President Johnson and his wife had held for the commission at their home.

Early in January, Johnson had "made it very clear [to his cabinet] that he expected that employment and advancement in the Federal Service will be solely on the basis of Merit. . . . top jobs will no longer be reserved for men and . . . the head of every Department and agency [should] . . . take immediate steps to see that the brain-power of American women is more fully put to the task of government than it is today."[26] At the meeting of the ICSW, reports on the status of women throughout the executive branch were given. John Macy observed that "where we have a problem . . . is in an apparent lack of clear communication in many instances throughout all administrative levels of agencies, particularly in the field services, with respect to the new program of non-discrimination on the basis of sex. This has resulted in a wide range of degrees of compliance with the program from complete and enthusiastic cooperation to token acceptance."[27] According to Macy, one of the biggest problems was in changing "conventional assumptions concerning the employment characteristics of women workers as compared to men, and the generally widespread negative attitude of men with respect to the abilities of women to handle more responsible job assignments."[28]

As part of its work, therefore, the ICSW eventually created three task forces to work on improving employment opportunities for women. One task force worked on employment issues in the federal sector, the second on the implementation of Title VII provisions regarding sex discrimination once the Civil Rights Act became law, and the third task force worked on the training and education of women in order to increase their numbers in professional and technical careers. In addition, all agencies were to begin the systematic collection of data on the number of women working at each grade level.[29]

In spite of these reviews and close monitoring by the White House, change was slow in coming, especially in the field offices throughout the country. In August, 1964, given the press of international events demanding the president's attention,[30] a formal meeting between the ICSW and the president was canceled, but the president did send a strong letter that could be used as a prod to get a better "agency follow-through" especially in the field offices. The president wrote,

> I appreciate the progress report of the Interdepartmental Committee on the Status of Women . . . which while it offers some encouragement, also indicates the distance we have to go before equality of employment opportunity is a reality.
>
> [H]owever, many of the out-moded customs and prejudices which have historically barred women from consideration for such appointments still remain and must be destroyed before further progress can be made.
>
> Therefore, I expect those agency and department heads which have not yet done so to instruct their officials here in Washington and throughout the field to recruit, hire and consider for advancement qualified women on all levels on an equal basis with men. I also expect those agency and department heads which have established enlightened employment programs for women to make sure that the work which has been so well begun at their headquarters will be effectively implemented and continued outside of as well as in Washington. And I especially want the appropriate field officials to know how much we are all depending on their daily decisions on appointments and promotions for the ultimate success of this program—nationwide and at every level of Government.[31]

Within a year, the ICSW and the CACSW were able to report the following accomplishments to the president, which extended beyond just the opening of higher ranks in the civil service to women: an increase in allowable tax deductions for child care, job training for women as well as funds for higher education, and a slight increase in the percentage of women beginning training in the foreign service.[32]

Both the council and the task force remained in place throughout the rest of the Johnson administration. However, bureaucratic politics soon came into play as the administration worked to implement the recommendations of the commission.

The Women's Bureau

Esther Peterson, who continued on as assistant secretary for the Bureau of Labor Standards and had also become special assistant to the president for consumer affairs and chairman of the President's Committee on Consumer Interests, was finally relieved of one of her many responsibilities when Mary Keyserling was named director of the Women's Bureau. However, according to Peterson, she and Keyserling had opposing views. Peterson visualized "turning the Women's Bureau into the staff arm of this commission [the PCSW] . . . and making it the operating group and the staff group to see that the recommendations were carried out."[33] Esther had wanted the directorship of the Women's Bureau to become a career civil servant post, removed from politics, following the pattern of Mary Anderson, the first director of the bureau who served in both Democratic and Republican administrations from 1920 to 1945. However, as Paul Light has observed, given the thickening of government, it would be far more likely for a government position to be converted into a political appointment for a president to make and Senate to confirm than for a political post to be removed.[34]

Moreover, Peterson correctly observed that the position of director of the Women's Bureau was becoming identified in terms of "here's a job for a woman." With women slowly being added to the ranks of presidential appointees, and an increasing demand for women's representation in government, there were strong arguments against removing this position from the list of presidential appointments. In fact, the statute establishing the Women's Bureau required that a woman be the director.[35] The tensions which Esther Peterson had identified earlier between the different bureaus continued. For instance, the Bureau of Labor Standards and the Women's Bureau both wanted to produce data needed to monitor and assess the status of women and to sponsor conferences.

In spite of these conflicts, the Women's Bureau helped facilitate the implementation of the recommendations of the PCSW. For instance, while the federal government is usually viewed solely in terms of Washington, in fact the federal government has long had a presence throughout the United States. In the 1960s the percentage of federal employees working in Washington was only 9.4 percent.[36] This decentralization of federal departments and agencies facilitated the work of the Women's Bureau in pushing for the creation of state commissions on the status of women. The Women's Bureau had five regional offices and, according to Keyserling, the bureau's director, "we set, as one of our highest priorities, the job through our regional directors of reaching out to friends in each of the States to move toward the establishment of State Commissions."[37] The field office directors contacted governors and state legislators and worked through the local chapters of national interest groups, such as the National Council of Negro Women and the National Council of Jewish Women, and labor unions to help in these lobbying efforts. In addition, Virginia Allan, vice president of the BPW at the time, had offered the assistance of the BPW's national and state constituent groups to "push the idea" of state commissions to change restrictive state laws. (This organization had been working to establish state commissions since 1962.)[38]

By 1967, all fifty states had established State Commissions on the Status of Women. Notwithstanding the limited role of the federal government in influencing state statutes, especially in the early 1960s, the Women's Bureau had implemented a significant state-based recommendation of the PCSW.[39] Conferences of the state commissions were held in Washington each year beginning in 1964, and top White House officials and cabinet secretaries met with these members as did President Johnson on several occasions.[40] The result was the passage of hundreds of state statutes which gave women the civil and political rights they had not had.[41]

Johnson and the National Organization of Women

In 1966, members of the State Commissions on the Status of Women gathered in Washington for their third national conference. Several women, who all had had prior experience with national organizations, met with Betty Friedan and, from this meeting, NOW, the National Organization for Women, emerged.[42] With most states now having formed a state commission to review statutes, attention could be turned to a broader national agenda. And NOW's activist founding members wanted an acceleration of that agenda.[43] They immediately sought a meeting with the president to discuss their concerns, which ranged from intervention by the attorney general to enforce implementation of Title VII, to equal treatment for men and women in all federal pensions and retirement programs, to more women in high-level posts in the administration and more women appointed to the federal judiciary.[44] They met with members of the Equal Employment Opportunity Commission (EEOC), but given that NOW was in its infancy and not viewed as representing the interests of all women, and especially given Johnson's recovery from recent surgery, they were denied an appointment with the president. However, if NOW's membership grew, as its officers claimed it would in the coming year, they could again seek a meeting with the president once they had "achieved a status worthy of Presidential attention."[45]

A year later, Betty Friedan again tried to get an appointment for the officers of NOW with the president. This time, Harry McPherson wrote to a staff member, "It is all right to regret. These women are 'inconsolable,'— nothing you can say will satisfy them."[46] NOW's membership remained small throughout the remainder of the Johnson administration, with only three hundred charter members during its first year and fifteen thousand members by 1973. In contrast, BPW had more than 178,000 members in 1967.[47]

WOMEN AND CIVIL RIGHTS IN THE JOHNSON ADMINISTRATION

The primary focus of the Johnson administration concerning women was in opening up the government to women—both career positions in the civil service as well as in appointive positions. But Johnson clearly had his own domestic policy agenda: civil rights, with an emphasis on securing rights for African Americans; the budget, in order to first pay for his War on Poverty and then later the war in Vietnam; and the War on Poverty itself. Charles Jones has noted "the President becomes part of a continuous though changing government" and "under most circumstances, the agenda is full to overflowing."[48] As a result, a successful president "designates" which issues he will focus on and set as a priority. In the area of civil rights, Johnson's priority was black Americans.

Shortly after assuming the presidency, when Johnson let it be known that civil rights was a top priority, some staff members "in heated debates" tried to persuade Johnson "not to push for the civil rights bill." One advisor went so far as telling the new president "you should not lay the prestige of the Presidency on the line" to which Johnson replied, "What's it for if it's not to be laid on the line?"[49]

The administration's focus on civil rights—for African Americans—was in accordance with the recommendations of the PCSW in that the commission had clearly stated that the push for equal rights for women would come second to the push for equal rights for African Americans. Moreover, the programs of the "Great Society" addressed structural aspects of society that had worked to perpetuate discrimination against African Americans. However, these programs would also benefit women.[50] For instance, the Higher Education Act, passed in 1965, created federal undergraduate scholarships ("educational opportunity grants") for needy students from low-income families and also established a guaranteed student loan program which would now open up college opportunities to women in middle-income homes in the same way the G.I. bills of the past two decades had provided the opportunity for a college education to many men following military service.[51] Representative Edith Green (D-OR), a strong supporter of federally subsidized loan programs for students from middle-income families, noted that the federal financial aid programs in the 1965 Higher Education Act, and Title IX legislation, passed as an amendment to that act during the Nixon administration, "allowed women for the first time to have equal opportunities in going to college.... Traditionally in the United States, a middle income family, if they have two sons and two daughters, who's going to get the money to go on to college? The sons, because, quote, 'They are going to have to be the breadwinners of the family.'... The girls in the family stayed home."[52] And in fact, Congress, more than the White House, was responsible for the creation of programs targeted at women. For example, in establishing the Job Corps, the push to include women came from Congress rather than the White House. Representative Green, a member of the House Education and Labor Committee, later noted that although the Johnson administration had opposed the amendment she had offered, which opened up the Job Corps for women, the administration did claim this as one of its legislative achievements when it passed. Some of the women's groups which had been represented on the PCSW, such as the National Council of Negro Women and the National Council of Catholic Women, joined forces with other women's groups in forming "Women in Community Service," which became a vehicle for federal money to be used to meet the needs of poor young women. The infrastructure already provided by these organizations via their community-based social services facilitated the inclusion of women in some of the Great Society programs. For example, Women in Community Service "contracted to screen girls for Job Corps Centers and later assumed responsibility for providing continuing community service for girls who had expressed an interest in the Job Corps."[53] Thus, while the programmatic focus of Johnson's Great Society addressed longstanding issues of systemic discrimination against African Americans, women also benefitted from some of these same programs. Policy would change, but slowly.

Equal Pay and Title VII

After the Equal Pay Act was passed in 1963, the Labor Department worked to develop policies for the successful administration and interpretation of the act. The 1963 act prohibited wage discrimination on the basis of sex and applied to "every employer having employees . . . subject to the minimum wage requirements of the Fair Labor Standards Act."[54] The Equal Pay Act of 1963, however, was limited in scope, in that it only "applie[d] to workers covered by the minimum wage provisions of the Fair Labor Standards Act."[55]

In 1964, Representative Howard Smith, a Democrat from Virginia, chairman of the House Rules Committee, and one of the strongest opponents of civil rights legislation, added "sex" to the provisions in Title VII of the Civil Rights Act of 1964, with the intention of slowing down passage of the bill.[56] There was little debate of the amendment, which was added on the floor, never having been brought up in committee hearings. Once "sex" was included, it was never removed.[57]

According to Keyserling, the Kennedy Commission on the Status of Women had not recommended the addition of "sex" since it "did not want to introduce any issue which might impede the progress of the civil rights legislation. It was a deliberate hold-back on that ground. . . . The hope was that once the 1964 Civil Rights Act was passed, it could then be amended to include a prohibition of discrimination on the basis of sex." But Keyserling wanted "sex" to be in from the start. Keyserling "felt that if we had deliberately included in the first draft all of the grounds on which discrimination must be prohibited, that it would not have weakened its cause and might have strengthened it. And so that did prove to be the case. What congressman is going to say, 'Take sex discrimination—that clause—out,' and risk the hostility of the women voters."[58]

In contrast, Esther Peterson did not want to jeopardize the administration's chances for passage of a civil rights bill. In the following letter to a constituent Peterson outlines the reasons for her position:

> The President has asked me to reply to your telegram urging that amendments to the civil rights bill be introduced to prohibit discrimination on the basis of sex in all sections of the bill. I think the position of the President and this Administration on the importance of equal opportunity for women is well established. As you know, Title VII of the civil rights bill relating to employment now included a prohibition of discrimination in employment on the basis of sex.

Enactment of the civil rights bill is of paramount importance in insuring basic civil rights to the citizens of this country. Hearings were held both in the House and in the Senate and the bill which passed the House and is now pending before the Senate has been developed in light of those hearings. I do not believe it is practical to suggest the introduction of additional amendments at this time which were not considered and agreed on at the time the hearings were held. The discriminations which this bill seeks to prohibit would apply equally to men and to women and I believe that passage of it in its present form would be a great step forward for the women of this country.[59]

Within the 1964 Civil Rights Act, Title VII provisions broadened the scope of coverage of equal pay protection by adding employees working in "industries affecting commerce and unions having 25 or more employees or members."[60] Passage of the Civil Rights Act of 1964, however, revived the old dilemma of protective labor legislation for women versus the end of discrimination in employment on the basis of sex, issues which had split the women's movement in the past, with the Women's Bureau in the Department of Labor championing protective labor legislation for women and opposing the ERA. The longstanding position of the Women's Bureau was evident in that the administrative history of the Department of Labor reported that "efforts were intensified to achieve the kind of administrative flexibility in protective labor laws which would reconcile the intent of the Civil Rights Act with sound labor standards concepts."[61]

Workshops were held by the Women's Bureau in cooperation with the National Committee for Equal Pay for state labor commissions, labor unions, management groups, and women's organizations. The Department of Labor assisted state commissions on the status of women or state departments of labor in working on equal pay protection legislation by providing technical information and assistance.

Undoubtedly problems would arise where compliance with Title VII provisions led to violation of state laws. The courts began to deal with "the question of whether or not it was the intent of Congress that Title VII supersede State protective labor laws in those instances when they in fact limit equality of employment opportunity."[62] By the end of the Johnson administration the Supreme Court had yet to resolve this issue.

INFLUENTIAL WOMEN IN THE JOHNSON ADMINISTRATION

During the Johnson administration three women had roles in the Executive Office of the President—Esther Peterson, Liz Carpenter, and Betty Furness. Structurally, Esther Peterson and Betty Furness should have had the most influence, but in fact Liz Carpenter, as a trusted aide, would have the more influential role. Peterson's influence would be the strongest in her role outside of the White House office as assistant secretary of labor, while Furness was more of a showcase appointment, with little substantive input.

Esther Peterson

Throughout the abbreviated Kennedy administration, efforts were under way to reach out to women by focusing attention on consumer issues, an issue Kennedy noted had been of interest to women during his 1960 election campaign. The Council of Economic Advisors became the vehicle by which this was done, and a Consumer Advisory Council had been established, reporting to the Council of Economic Advisors.[63]

In October, 1963, Ralph Dungan approached Peterson to see if she would consider a position as special assistant to President Kennedy to work on consumer issues. However, Kennedy never had time to follow through on this plan. This is an area where Johnson, once president, moved quickly, continuing a program already under way during the Kennedy administration. According to Peterson, "The basis was . . . built, just like the basis for the status of women was built, with Kennedy, although a lot of the activity followed with Johnson."[64]

The plan that had begun under the Kennedy administration might have worked better under the staff arrangement then in place, since Esther Peterson had long worked with Myer Feldman, Ralph Dungan, Larry O'Brien, and the president himself. And Peterson had endorsed Kennedy in the 1960 campaign, not Lyndon Johnson.

Although given the title special assistant to the president, Peterson was never viewed as one of the "special assistants to the president" in the same way as Bundy, Moyers, Busby, and so forth. This is most evident in records of staff attending cabinet meetings; staff attending White House staff meetings; and listings of White House organization charts outlining the responsibilities of each of the special assistants to the president. Peterson is conspicuously omitted.[65] In addition, Peterson was given an office in the Executive Office Building, not in the White House, with only one secretary and no budget.[66] Even when "consumers" were placed specifically on the agenda for a cabinet meeting, Esther Peterson was not necessarily in attendance.[67]

In announcing the appointment of Esther Peterson as his special assistant for consumer affairs, President Johnson said that "for the first time in history, the American consumer's interest—so closely identified with the public interest—will be directly represented in the White House."[68] But Peterson's role was left ambiguous. While serving in the White House, she remained an assistant secretary of labor. After the 1964 election when plans were under way for a Domestic Planning Council in the White House to coordinate domestic priorities and programs, Peterson was not among the White House staff listed to serve on the council. In looking at the responsibilities of staff, the unofficial role that Peterson played in the Kennedy White House, as a consultant on women considered for administration posts, is another area where she was overlooked in the Johnson White House. John Macy's personnel recommendations went to Bill Moyers and Jack Valenti for review, and depending on the area, to Bundy.[69] Peterson also had to go through Moyers or Valenti to see the president, although she had a title and position which structurally should have included her in the decision making at the highest levels. This was especially true given her long work on women's issues, and her service as executive vice chairman of the PCSW. Yet, at a time when Johnson was prioritizing the inclusion of women in his administration, White House operations precluded Peterson from participating in the highest levels of domestic policy making or personnel decision making.[70]

In the Johnson White House, the cabinet was not used as a forum for policy debates, but as a means of sharing information to keep all informed as to the goals and direction of the administration. In contrast with the meetings of the Kennedy cabinet, where few members of the president's staff attended, the Johnson cabinet meetings had a comparatively large number of staff in attendance. The Johnson special assistants regularly attended the cabinet meetings. With their focus on coordinating legislative pushes, restraining spending, and monitoring hiring—all tasks usually thought of as centralized in the White House—the attendance of White House staff at cabinet meetings was entirely appropriate.[71]

Unlike all of the other special assistants, Peterson rarely attended cabinet meetings. When she was invited she was listed with other "visitors," not as a White House staff member.[72] Especially in 1966 and 1967, the cabinet meetings were widely attended by staff and often by other guests, including senators and even the prime minister of Italy at one meeting. Yet, when the issue of "consumers" was on the agenda in March, 1965, Peterson was not present. Peterson's plight was clear, yet effective action to resolve the situation was not forthcoming.

In March, 1966, Peterson talked with Bill Moyers about resigning as special assistant to the president for consumer affairs, while staying on as assistant secretary of labor. Moyers sent a memo to the president, outlining the situation.

> Bill Wirtz had already called me on this. He concurs in Esther's choice. He not only needs her full time but believes the frustrations of the Consumer's job have left her ready to leave it behind. After talking to Esther, I am sure both are right.
>
> This leaves us—if you approve this step—with the question of what to do about the Consumer role. For political reasons I doubt the wisdom of leaving it unfilled. While it does little substantively, it does fill a political need. For the President to be concerned with consumer affairs is important. With your concurrence, I will talk to John Macy and Joe Califano about this problem.
>
> Esther, by the way, had wanted to make this effective soon. I told her I needed to talk to you, but that I personally felt we should wait two months or so to make certain no one felt she is resigning out of dissatisfaction with the consumer's message or any other aspect of the situation. She saw this and agrees."[73]

Over time, with the loss of Kennedy staffers such as Ralph Dungan and Myer Feldman who had been involved with the creation and work of the PCSW and had worked closely with Esther Peterson in a number of different settings and on a number of different issues, the sensitivity of the Executive Office of the President to issues concerning women seemed to diminish.

Peterson's departure from the ranks of the special assistants was timed to coincide with the broadening of her responsibilities at the Department of Labor. Appointed assistant secretary of labor in 1961 by President Kennedy, Peterson had been responsible for the Women's Bureau, the Bureau of Employees Compensation, and the Bureau of Labor Standards. In March, 1967, her responsibilities at the Department of Labor were expanded to also include a new Wage and Hour Division and the Public Contracts Division. This gave her the responsibility for enforcement of the Equal Pay Act, the

Fair Labor Standards Act, and the Public Services Contract Act.[74] These were all areas Peterson had been deeply involved with, drafting the legislation and lobbying on its behalf for many years. The area of consumer policy, in contrast, was one that President Kennedy had been interested in, drawn to this area during the 1960 presidential campaign. By the time Betty Furness was named special assistant to the president for consumer affairs in 1967, the supportive environment in the White House that once might have been there was gone.

The Appointment of Betty Furness

With Esther Peterson's departure from the White House imminent, discussion focused on who should replace Peterson and what post should this person hold. In sending President Johnson a list of potential replacements, John Macy identified the credentials (or more accurately, the characteristics) necessary for this position: "I have discovered in my search several ladies who appear to have the necessary affinity to the Nation's housewives, who are articulate, persuasive and loyal, and who would have the political sensitivity to be successful."[75]

Macy described Betty Furness as a:

former television personality for Westinghouse, [who] seems to have been bitten by the "public service bug." In addition to conducting a radio show, Miss Furness has been working as a VISTA volunteer, drumming up support for Headstart projects throughout the country, according to published reports. The same reports credit the First Lady's talk at a White House meeting with being a large inspiration to Miss Furness' efforts. If she were available for this assignment, Miss Furness would bring to the job the advantages of a well-known name, physical attractiveness, much poise and presence in public, and persuasiveness. Her political sensitivity and abilities to survive the bureaucracy should be the subject of further checking.[76]

Macy also consulted with Margaret Price and learned that Furness was an active Democrat, involved in the 1964 Democratic campaign, and in the 1966 congressional elections had "conducted a political telecast on which Mrs. Johnson and Mrs. Humphrey appeared on behalf of the Democratic candidates."[77]

In forwarding Macy's recommendations to President Johnson, Califano noted that "the person who takes this job would be Special Assistant to the

Secretary of Health, Education and Welfare for Consumer Affairs, Chairman of the Interdepartmental Consumer Committee and Executive Secretary of the President's Committee on Consumer Affairs, which would be chaired by John Gardner. The job is largely a public relations job and may be important in Congressional and Presidential campaigning in 1968."[78] Califano's memo placed the new appointment in a department and out of the Executive Office of the President. Earlier in the administration, Betty Furness had been recommended to the president by Liz Carpenter to fill a vacancy in the post of U.S. Treasurer.[79] Peterson herself included Betty Furness's name on a list of those who could take over her consumer responsibilities.[80] By the time Betty Furness was sworn into office on May 1, 1967, the White House had begun a public relations campaign to repair damage caused by a perception that the Johnson administration had a "Showcase Operation," in the words of one anonymous presidential appointee, where there was a "lack of follow-through on the much-publicized effort" to place more women in top-level positions throughout the administration.[81] The White House focused on winning acceptance for Furness, who some viewed as a broadcast personality, lacking consumer expertise. The public relations effort included statements from the secretary of labor explaining why Peterson was needed full-time at the Department of Labor and stating that Peterson had asked that she be relieved of her White House duties. Staff from the Departments of Health, Education and Welfare; Commerce; and Treasury were detailed to the White House to assist Furness, and she was given extensive background material in the area of consumer policy.[82] In addition, the White House undertook a campaign to highlight the volunteer work Furness had done at VISTA and the issues she had covered in her television program, soliciting testimonials from those at public and private welfare agencies, labor unions, and federal agencies.[83] A citizen's advisory consumer council was to be created, to help solidify support for Furness. President Johnson, ever sensitive to political winds, agreed to swear Furness into office.

Johnson's White House staff, again viewing women in more traditional roles, recommended that Johnson include in his remarks at the swearing in ceremony that "the Furness appointment has precedents and indeed is typical. For most women who start working in the adult years—and there are millions—will have to switch from one career (housewife) to another career."[84] Instead of the emphasis suggested by his staff, Johnson focused on the *number* of posts that Furness would hold. In his remarks, the president noted the number of "Easter bonnets" Furness would be wearing—

special assistant for Consumer Affairs to the President, chairman of the President's Committee on Consumer Interests, and executive secretary of the Consumer Advisory Council[85]—and noted the challenges facing Furness with her three different "bonnets." This was a means of increasing the statistics relating to the number of posts held by women in the administration. Johnson also noted that he had issued executive orders which would "strengthen the Committee on Consumer Interests, including on it for the first time the principal officers of the Cabinet of the President of the United States, and the principal agency heads of this Government. This will give the Committee increased authority in carrying out the consumer programs. It will strengthen the voice of the consumer in the councils of Government."[86] With the executive order, eight cabinet members as well as several agency heads would serve on the newly elevated committee.[87] Prior to this, under the chairmanship of Esther Peterson, members of the Committee on Consumer Interests had been at the rank of assistant secretary.[88]

Esther Peterson missed Furness's swearing-in-ceremony, and since this would be duly recorded in news coverage of the event, Califano reported to the president that it did not appear as if Peterson had missed the "swearing in" ceremony to register dismay.[89] In fact, shortly after she left her post as assistant to the president, Peterson had held a small reception in her office for Furness. Liz Carpenter, press secretary and staff director for the First Lady, always working to keep the president in the best light, noted that Peterson's gesture might "stop some of the ridiculous jibes at Betty, . . . from some of the organized women." Carpenter, with acute political sensitivity, suggested that the president "call and chat with both during the party. . . . The guests will be some people from govt., but also the 'consumer press.'"[90]

The East Wing of the White House: Lady Bird and Elizabeth Carpenter

Although no women served in Johnson's cabinet, and only two women served briefly, and with limited influence, in the highest levels of the White House staff, Lyndon Johnson's personal life had found him surrounded by strong women whose abilities he clearly recognized. Mary Keyserling noted that Johnson's mother and his wife Lady Bird were "both . . . influences when he talks of his awareness of the talents of women that our society can more fully draw on."[91] Johnson dedicated his autobiography, *The Vantage Point*, to four women important in his life: his mother, Rebekah Baines Johnson; his wife, Lady Bird; and his two daughters, Lynda and Luci.[92] While the overt political partnership seen between future Presidents Jimmy Carter and Bill Clinton with First Ladies Rosalynn and Hillary, respectively, is not present, it is clear that Lady Bird had influence, which Johnson himself acknowledged and respected.[93] For instance, when Johnson met with members of state commissions on the status of women in 1965, he mentioned that you can discuss issues with Lady Bird and Liz Carpenter, and "if you don't get the proper response from me, take it up with Lady Bird because she and Liz Carpenter mount that door all the time."[94]

Elizabeth Carpenter, a Texan and long-time reporter in Washington, had met the Johnsons when she first came to Washington in 1942. Shortly after the 1960 Democratic National Convention, Carpenter began work for the Johnsons as executive assistant to the vice president. Carpenter was with the Johnsons on the fateful campaign trip to Dallas, November 22, 1963. It was Carpenter who dashed off the fifty-eight words Johnson delivered at Andrews Air Force Base, his first communication to the Washington community and outside world as president. In December, 1963, Carpenter was appointed press secretary and staff director for the First Lady. According to Lewis L. Gould, "The appointment represented a key development in the institutional history of the position of the first lady: No previous presidential wife had appointed a professional journalist to serve as press secretary. The title of staff director was also an innovation. It recognized that a successful first lady needed more than the services of the social secretaries who had been a White House fixture since the turn of the century."[95]

Liz Carpenter's close personal relationship to both Lady Bird and the president gave her access to the president in a way that, especially for the Kennedy holdovers, could be viewed as threatening. One particularly revealing memo from Horace Busby to the president shortly after his election in 1964, focusing on the White House press and its attitudes toward the White House, noted that "the newsmen, in my judgment, have their knives out for Liz Carpenter . . . and some of them are trying to compromise her position or George's [Reedy, the press secretary] by promoting her speculatively for press secretary. No one actually believes she will be appointed press secretary, so I am uncertain what the motive of this story actually may be."[96] At this point in history, women reporters continued to be excluded from the National Press Club.[97]

Throughout his presidency, Liz Carpenter constantly nudged the president to appoint women by sending him lists of possible women appointees every time there was a vacancy or forthcoming vacancy.[98]

Shortly after Johnson took over the presidency, Liz Carpenter was pushing for a change in the directorship of Women's Activities for the DNC. She recommended that India Edwards be named director, with the assistance of a board composed of Lindy Boggs, Roz Wyman, and a few other women Democrats. According to Carpenter, "The Margaret Price situation needs either bolstering or correcting. She really is more ceremonial than workhorse and Esther Peterson, India, and I all agree that something must be done soon for the campaign."[99] Liz Carpenter attended cabinet meetings and was included in weekly staff meetings with Moyers, Reedy, Busby, Carter, and Valenti.[100] Liz understood the need for loyalty to the president and the administration's programs, and at the meeting of senior White House staff, she suggested that more use should be made "of the Cabinet as agents and spokesmen for the President" by having them "serve as the President's eyes and ears—reporting on public opinion regarding our strengths and weaknesses—and our programs and ideas."[101] Carpenter herself often served in the role she envisioned for members of the cabinet, constantly funneling him political information in a wide range of areas. That Carpenter was regularly included in cabinet and staff meetings suggests that others were aware of the role she played as an advisor to the president.

Carpenter kept the president informed of the pulse of women in response to actions taken by the administration. According to Carpenter, her "usual method of operation with the President was to write memos filled with candid suggestions—more than anyone could say grace over. At the day's end, I would slip quietly into his empty room and leave my memos conspicuously on the President's bedside table—then stay out of range until an answer came by phone or note."[102] In one brief memo sent to the president, Carpenter wrote, "Thought you would like to know the reaction to the Isabelle Shelton story today that you were planning to put 50 women in top U.S. jobs within the next month. Dudley Harmon, CBS executive here in Washington, telephoned the moment she saw the story and said, 'I would vote for President Johnson just on the basis of this important announcement. I wouldn't consider voting for a Republican now.'"[103] Carpenter would often put her recommendations to Johnson in the form of election critiques. Carpenter understood Johnson's avid interest in the pulse of election politics, and framed her memos to the president in terms of the language to which he would be most responsive.

While Carpenter appeared to get along with the Texans, she did not hit it off too well with the Kennedy holdovers. During the 1964 campaign, she came up with an idea of using Mrs. Johnson's talents on a whistlestop tour of the South.

I tried and tried to meet with Kenny O'Donnell [a Kennedy special assistant and political advisor, and now a Johnson campaign advisor] about this campaign. Kenny O'Donnell had no respect for any women in politics whatsoever. The whole attitude of the Kennedy men who worked in this operation was to keep women barefooted and have them on their feet, preferably pregnant, on election day—but nothing beyond that. Kenny O'Donnell wouldn't even meet with Bess [Abell, White House social secretary] and me to talk about this until I laid the whole plan in front of the President. The President yanked him up there on the second floor of the White House and we got out maps and the President was obviously so enthusiastic about what Mrs. Johnson could do on a train trip that we sat there and planned it. I enjoyed watching Kenny O'Donnell being brought around by the President of the United States on the value of women, and he had to suffer three of them—Mrs. Johnson, Bess, and me, for that period.[104]

Ralph Dungan, special assistant to the president, who had always appeared supportive of the work of Esther Peterson during the Kennedy administration, did not have a particular fondness for Liz Carpenter. In an interview at the end of the Johnson administration, Dungan recalled Carpenter "with the greatest distaste . . . who always used to call up and have 50 women. . . . I used to tell her to go to hell, and told her if she wanted to run appointments she could come on over and do it, 'Well, the President said to me he wants more women,' and I said, 'Well, bullshit.'"[105] According to Dungan, Johnson "was very strong on the women's side and I used to have to keep a tabulation of how many women he had appointed and how many of this, and that, and the other thing."[106]

Liz appeared to be more comfortable in giving suggestions to Jack Valenti and other Johnson loyalists than to the Kennedy holdovers. Shortly after the 1964 election, she wrote to Valenti:

A good group to bring in for a ranch appointment would be three or four young people to talk about their ideas. . . . It would be nice fresh look picture-wise and pick up the enthusiasm engendered during the campaign which has not yet been picked up.

. . . I think you ought to make Shriver bring some of his "poverty" thinkers including some women—they get broke, too—along.

The Job Corps for Girls got a good launching with Mrs. Johnson here in a seminar on the South Lawn, but the President could pick it up and find out what has happened. Are residence halls to be established in the big cities? It is a dramatic story and just up his alley.

The President is such a good brain picker that any sessions of him engaged in this at the ranch and discussing the State of the Union speech would be a plus. Women help to get pictures on page 1 so get some.[107]

Carpenter even had recommendations for the president concerning Vietnam, suggesting that there were women in the military willing to serve in Vietnam, yet not being sent (with certain exceptions, e.g. nurses), who could help meet the needs of the Agency for International Development (AID), which was trying to find either men or women willing to go and work with the civilian Vietnamese population in refugee camps, filling medical, social welfare, and community development needs. Women in the military specializing in communications and public relations could also be of service to the military.[108]

THE CALL FOR CHANGE

Earlier in the chapter the structures for dealing with women's issues that were put into place early in the Johnson administration were identified. This section will examine how effectively Johnson used these structures and other means to fulfill his desire to change the demographic composition of the federal government. In recognizing the talents of women, Johnson insisted that affirmative steps be taken by his administration to change the demographic composition of the federal government. While no women were appointed to the Johnson cabinet, he worked to change both perceptions and law. According to Mary Keyserling, director of the Women's Bureau, there was a change from "mere declaration of rights to the actual opening of the doors of opportunity. There was still much door-opening to be done, and it was done through law. But it was also—'Let's find out *why* people aren't going through those doors and if there are barriers that are keeping them from realizing the opportunities now released through change in law.'"[109] However, Johnson's preparation for his Great Society legislation also began in earnest during 1964. Changing the demographic composition of the federal government would not be easy since he introduced cost-cutting measures and a freeze on federal hiring as a means of freeing up monies which he wanted to direct to his Great Society programs.

One of the problems in complying with the president's request was that at the same time that the president was asking department and agency heads to change the composition of their departments to be more inclusive of women (and African Americans and Hispanics and other under-represented groups in society), he was also asking administrators to hold the line in spending. To gear up for his War on Poverty program, which would be introduced in the next Congress, after winning election in his own right, he began to change the shape of the federal government with a waste reduction program and trimming of programs. With a down-sizing of programs, not all vacancies could be filled, and so the process of changing the composition of the federal workforce would be slow in coming.[110] And, a "virtual freeze on Federal civilian employment" was planned for fiscal year 1967, according to directives coming from the Bureau of the Budget to departments and agencies at the request of the president.[111]

Yet Johnson, and his administration, began work toward this goal shortly after he took office. At a meeting with his cabinet in January, 1964, Johnson had set a target of appointing fifty women in fifty days. Shortly thereafter, Ralph Dungan, special assistant to the president, sent a directive to the heads of all departments, agencies, commissions, and any other federal governmental structure, in which he strongly communicated the president's interest in seeing to it that more women were appointed to top-level positions.[112]

Departments barely had a chance to respond to this request when another call went out to the departments and several agencies two weeks later, asking them to report on the number of women who had been hired or promoted to jobs at the GS-14 level and above since January 1, 1964. Of the ten departments, three had not hired any women. A total of sixty-three women had either been promoted or appointed at this level (including foreign service appointments) in the remaining departments and agencies. In addition, President Johnson had appointed ten women, and fourteen women had been invited to join the Defense Advisory Committee on Women in the Service. A staff assistant, in compiling the data penned the following note: "Not much of a showing. Demonstrates that results require Presidential action on pending top level vacancies and White House pressure on agencies for lower level actions."[113]

Liz Carpenter followed with a memo to "Anyone Interested in Women," suggesting:

> There is wide and increasing interest by the press in the upgrading and appointment of women and I would urge the following procedure to get it going. . . . That immediately any cabinet member or agency head who has an appointment of a woman to make—or the advancement of any

woman from a Grade 13 up—announce it with a little more fanfare than usual—a picture of the agency head with the woman appointment, and the statement that the appointment "emanates because of President Johnson's call for the Federal government to make greater use of qualified women in executive appointments."[114]

Carpenter went on to offer a number of other suggestions: "Whenever the President has any to announce, he might want to do so with a little more fanfare—pictures with them (let the newswomen come in during the picture taking time.)"; "Save one or two to announce at the Women's National Press Club speech on March 4."

Following up on the president's initiative, the chair of the ICSW, Secretary Wirtz, pressured departments and agencies, as well as staff in the Executive Office of the President, to submit reports on the number of women appointed, as well as on the actions to advance and maintain equal opportunity for women. Bill Moyers, special assistant to the president, placed more calls to departments in the middle of February, this time wanting reports on the hiring of women in GS-12 positions and higher.[115] The high-level nature of the request, from the president, prompted a high-level response in some departments. In reporting on the status of women in the Department of Health, Education, and Welfare, Secretary Celebrezze noted that he had "personally re-emphasized to the heads of our agencies both orally and in the form of written policy the necessity for making sure that both the spirit and the letter of your request for full and equal consideration of women in filling all vacancies is faithfully adhered to."[116]

Affirmative actions were taken in some departments to actively seek out women in order to comply with the president's request. Not surprisingly, given the role of its Women's Bureau, the Labor Department began an extensive search process. A list was compiled of women outside of government for consideration when vacancies arose. Bureaus were asked to review hiring currently under way to see if women were being considered for posts, and officials in the department were using personal contacts to seek out potential women candidates, and were informally contacting women's organizations to see if there might be possible candidates.[117]

Secretary of Commerce, Luther H. Hodges, who had been a member of the PCSW, and who was serving on the ICSW, also responded to the request coming from Bill Moyers, reporting on the numbers of women in each of the grade levels at grade 12 and above, but also explained why the percentages might be so low.

There is no doubt that our Department [Commerce] can make a greater effort to find and use the talents and abilities of many more qualified women in positions at these grade levels. However, it is not only many years of a lack of definite policy that has created the situation we now face, for in this Department specifically there exist many operations that are beyond the usual capabilities or training of women. Many functions in the Maritime Administration, Weather Bureau, National Bureau of Standards, Coast and Geodetic Survey, or Bureau of Public Roads for example, do not attract nor could they be filled by women.[118]

The high-level attention given to the appointment of women is reflected in the fact that Special Assistants Walter Jenkins and Ralph A. Dungan, Liz Carpenter, Katie Louchheim, deputy assistant secretary of state, and Esther Peterson met near the end of February, 1964, to review the status of women in the administration. In that meeting, a list of agency vacancies and potential women candidates were discussed, with follow-up action assigned, either in investigating the candidate further or in making an offer of a position. In addition, weekly status reports from agencies on the employment of women were distributed to Liz Carpenter, Walter Jenkins, Ralph A. Dungan, and Esther Peterson.[119]

For an example of a directive sent by a cabinet secretary to carry out the president's command, see Box 3.1.

BOX 3.1
Carrying out the President's Orders

February 19, 1964

To: Heads of Bureaus and Offices
     Treasury Department
Subject: <u>Nondiscrimination on the Basis of Sex</u>

President Johnson has made clear his determination that there shall be no discrimination in his administration on the basis of sex with respect to employment. This has been and will, of course, continue to be the policy of this Department.

I believe that we in the Treasury Department have already made a good record in this field. In a recent address to the Interdepartmental

Committee on the Status of Women, Mr. John Macy, Chairman of the U.S. Civil Service Commission, said:

> The Treasury Department is especially noteworthy for opening up greater areas of work in which the employment of women was previously unknown or exceptional. Offering career opportunities in fiscal, economic and enforcement work can be of long-term significance as young women plan their educational and career training. The Treasury has also been a leader in advancing women to new career heights.

Despite Mr. Macy's kind words, I believe that additional progress can be made and must be made if we are to meet the President's objectives. I therefore, ask you to lead the way in your respective organizations with affirmative actions that will insure that women are afforded opportunity for appointment, advancement, and training equal to that accorded to men. Such action is essential if the full potential of the Department's available skill is to be realized in performing the tasks that lay ahead.

I shall, therefore, appreciate your personal efforts in further encouraging the type of atmosphere in your organization which assures equal employment opportunity to employees of both sexes. Also, it is requested that in all instances of appointments and promotions to positions GS-13 or higher in your organization, you especially assure yourself that available qualified women have been sought out and have been given full consideration. I request that the Director of Personnel report to me periodically on the progress you achieve in developing your program and on specific personnel actions resulting therefrom.

Source: "EX PE 2 2/15/64–3/9/64" folder, WHCF, PE 2, Box 7, Lyndon Baines Johnson Library.

Johnson's repeated public statements on the appointment of women kept the issue as an initial focus of his administration. In welcoming the six recipients of the 1964 Federal Woman's Awards to the White House, in his remarks Johnson stated the now familiar phrase, "I believe a woman's place is not only in the home, but in the House and the Senate and throughout the Government service."[120] The Johnson "Famous Fifty," while designed as a presidential tool, soon became the bane of the administration. How do we count the fifty, which fifty? Ralph Dungan, acutely aware of the problem, wrote to Salinger, Carpenter, Jenkins, and Valenti:

> I am attaching an up-to-date recapitulation of female appointments since January 1, 1964. This list contains the names of women who are accurately described as "Presidential appointees" but it also includes some (e.g., Rose McKee) [information director, Small Business Administration] who are not strictly speaking Presidential appointments.
>
> I circulate this list so that we can all, in any contacts we may have with the press or otherwise, speak from the same list and list the same numbers. If you have any additions or deletions which you want to make, let me know. Otherwise, let's consider this the standard list for the White House.[121]

At the presentation of the Eleanor Roosevelt Award at the Women's National Press Club, Johnson announced the appointment of ten women, including Mary Keyserling to head the Women's Bureau. Like a number of Johnson appointees, Keyserling had not known that her appointment was to be announced that night.[122]

The effort to identify women and announce their appointment in dramatic fashion continued for several months. In late March, the president had a "surprise press conference" at his ranch home to announce the appointment of five more women to high-level posts, including the appointment of Mary Ingraham Bunting, president of Radcliffe College, as the first woman to serve on the Atomic Energy Commission. After giving the statistics on women appointments and promotions, Johnson observed, "I'd say the girls are doing right well these days."[123]

By the end of February, 1964, only two departments and ten agencies had not yet reported the appointment or promotion of women at the highest levels in the civil service.[124] By June, the count of women who had been appointed or promoted to positions in Grades GS-12 and above was nearing one thousand.[125]

Most departments and agencies designated an individual responsible for their program's efforts to increase the utilization of women, in effect an affirmative action officer, responsible for reports on the levels of women employed, as well as for seeking out qualified women candidates for vacancies as they may arise. It was clear that affirmative action guidelines were being put in place because of the personal interest taken by the president in this matter.

Where the New Women Came From

Given Johnson's long-time familiarity with the Washington community, and his work with Macy during the Kennedy administration on issues of civil rights, Johnson's selection of John Macy to run his personnel shop in the White House, in addition to chairing the Civil Service Commission, made a good deal of sense.[126] Macy organized an elaborate "talent search," to provide President Johnson with several recommendations for each vacancy that occurred. The talent search drew on three different sources for potential candidates: an "Executive Inventory" of those in "the top levels of the career services . . . both civil service and Foreign Service;" a "talent bank maintained on a computerized basis from names secured through the White House from a broad variety of backgrounds . . . [with] 30,000 names at the peak of this operation;" and from "a network of about 400 advisors from across the country and in all of the professions. . . . men and women . . . selected on the basis of their interest in the appointment process and their capability to provide objective evaluations of the qualifications of candidates for Presidential appointment."[127]

In time, a "talent search for womanpower" was instituted, and women were urged to write to the Civil Service Commission to "Womanpower" to gain information or apply for positions in the civil service.[128]

Johnson was a believer in merit. A public school teacher, he prized education as a visible commodity and credential. Johnson often included the academic qualifications in announcing an appointment. Johnson thus concluded, if the civil service system was a merit-based system, why not select those from the federal sector for political appointive posts?

Thus, the president was not content to let the ICSW be the sole source of oversight of the federal government's employment practices concerning women. As the ICSW was beginning its work, departments were also having to respond to requests from staff in the Executive Office of the President for detailed statements concerning the employment of women in their departments.

Yet even if a department, such as Justice, had been involved in the work of the PCSW, longstanding conventions as to what jobs were appropriate for women remained.[129] While the department noted it would comply with the president's expressed wish of a nondiscriminatory hiring policy, Assistant Deputy Attorney Gen. William A. Geoghegan wanted the White House to take note that "although the Department of Justice employs approximately 32,000 persons, 26,000 serve in the F.B.I. Bureau of Prisons and the Immigration and Naturalization Service. The nature of the work of these agencies obviously limits opportunities for the employment of women except in secretarial or clerical positions. Even in these agencies, however, there are women employed at the higher grade levels," and there was one presidential appointee, Eva Bowring, who served on the Board of Parole and "whose term expires on September 30, 1964. I presume the President may be interested in replacing her with another woman and I shall appreciate hearing from someone on the White House staff about this."[130]

Each department reported on its recruitment and promotion of women in grades GS-12 and above, and these results, along with presidential appointments of women to full-time positions, as well as to advisory committees, were sent to the president each week, and included in his weekend reading materials.[131]

It was clear that the president's leadership in this area resulted in a change in behavior on the part of the administration. As an example, Katherine Louchheim, in charge of the dinner honoring Women Federal Award winners, observed that for the first time ever, *every* cabinet member "promptly accepted her invitation" to the dinner, the result of Johnson making the "government woman-conscious."[132]

The Politics of Demographic Change

The political motivations of President Johnson cannot be overlooked. There are presidential seasons to consider, and in looking at the work of any administration, one must always consider the temporal dimension to the presidency—a presidential election every four years, as well as congressional elections every two years.

For instance, on January 27, 1964, Senator Margaret Chase Smith (R-ME), Johnson's former House and Senate colleague, announced her bid for the Republican Party nomination for president. The White House kept close tabs on Smith's announcement and the reaction of the media, especially as it related to Johnson's endeavors concerning women. Smith's announcement received front-page coverage in the *New York Times*.[133]

A month before, Johnson had written the following letter to Senator Smith:

I am delighted to have your letter of December 15th with its reference to your 75% support rating on legislation in the last session of Congress, as compiled by Congressional Quarterly. This confirms what I have known all along.

I suppose there will always be a little of the fire hose in me after my years as Majority Leader, because I am still fascinated by head counts and results. Now, as then, I appreciate fully the consistent support you have given me. I have not forgotten the promise to review the results of agency policies and practices in the area of congressional relations.[134]

In 1960, the Republican party ticket of Nixon-Lodge had won 51 percent of the women's vote whereas the Kennedy-Johnson ticket had won only 49 percent of the women's vote. While the Democratic ticket had narrowed the gap, the Republican ticket had been favored by women in each election since 1952.[135] In addition, while the voter turnout of women had traditionally been less than that of men, in the 1964 election the actual number of eligible women voters would surpass that of men.[136] Both of these circumstances recommended that Johnson pay close attention to Smith's candidacy as a barometer for women in the electorate, as his re-election campaign got under way.[137]

The president's interest in equal opportunities for all is apparent, yet, given his mastery of politics and persuasion, it is also clear that Johnson was well aware of the symbolic values and resulting political benefits that could accrue from the cultivation of women. Johnson himself did much to stage manage coverage by the Washington press corps.

And those in the departments and agencies below him also contributed to these efforts. For example, the Commerce Department distributed a news story, "Women in a Man's World," which profiled professional and career women working in high-level positions in the Department of Commerce. One of the individuals profiled in the article, Hazel Tatro, a meteorologist in charge of a Commerce Department Weather Bureau Station, who had worked for the department since 1945, noted, "The attitude of government agencies has changed radically," and "women's chances for advancement in government are better now than they ever were before." The change was attributed to President Johnson, whose efforts to increase the employment and promotion of women in the federal government matched his words that "a woman's place is not only in the home, but in the House, the Senate and throughout our government service."[138] This material was also included in the president's nightly reading material, since Johnson craved data of all sorts, and his staff diligently provided him with the material.

A sustained push for the appointment of women both from within and from outside of the White House would not develop fully until the Nixon administration. However, there were still concerted efforts made to see that women were considered for posts. The Office of Women's Activities in the DNC offered assistance, but with the lack of influence in the White House during most of the Johnson administration, the Democratic Party would not play a strong role in this process. While a number of women were appointed to part-time positions on boards, on commissions, and as members of advisory panels, few were appointed to full-time positions. In addition, not all of those in the administration viewed the efforts to recruit women *as a part* of the administration's "talent search" to find the best person for each appointive post.

For example, Frank Mankiewicz sent Bill Moyers several recommendations of individuals to keep in mind if vacancies were to arise, writing, "Although I didn't mention her yesterday morning, if you are still looking for top women in government, I think you should pay some attention to our old friend Gretchen Handwerger."[139] No specific position was identified.

While Johnson worked to include women in his administration, a related strategy of turning to the federal service for appointees, however, diminished the pool of women available. As noted in Chapter 2, not until 1962 does one begin to see the end of sex classifications for civil service jobs. In the 1960s, there is a wide discrepancy between the grades reached by men and women. Thus, there are limitations on career advancement for women in the federal services.

In announcing the formation of a Study Group when presenting the Federal Woman's Awards in 1966, Johnson emphasized a career path for women not dissimilar to that of men, with the need for women to perform the same jobs as men in the workforce.

> The under-utilization of American women continues to be the most tragic and the most senseless waste of this country. It is a waste that we can no longer afford. Our economy is crying out for their services. In the next decade alone we will need 900,000 additional school teachers and college instructors; 1 million additional specialists in the health services; 800,000 additional science and engineering technicians; 700,000 additional scientists and engineers; and 4-1/2 million additional State and local employees, exclusive of our teachers.
>
> The requirements in these fields alone will be 110,000 additional trained specialists, every month for the next 10 years. That requirement cannot be met by men alone.[140]

The Study Group picked up on Johnson's charge to the group, as well as the president's own words to help focus and clarify its agenda. A year after their appointment, they gave a progress report to the president in which they outlined several recommendations, including the need for the collection of systematic data by the civil service, since the status of women could not be assessed without comparative data.[141]

The Study Group also called for a new executive order. Their review of existing statutes and executive orders revealed that Title VII of the 1964 Civil Rights Act set "a national policy of equal opportunity in private employment, without discrimination because of race, color, religion, sex, or national origin," but did not apply to the federal government in its hiring practices.[142] In addition, Johnson's Executive Order 11246 of September 24, 1965, extended prohibitions against discrimination in employment because of race, creed, color, or national origin, but not sex.[143]

Shortly after the report was given to President Johnson, a new Executive Order was issued, Number 11375, which extended the policy of equal opportunity and non-discrimination in federal employment to include sex.[144]

Assessing Progress

Throughout his administration, the role of women and African Americans was constantly on the president's agenda, as seen through the work of the president's staff and the reports demanded by the president. A combination of a changing social climate in which affirmative action would begin to guide and influence hiring and promotion decisions, as well as Johnson's penchant for mastering details and gathering of evidence to overwhelm any opponent, led to the use of quantitative measures to assess the progress being made in the area of equal opportunities for women as well as for members of minority groups. Cabinet meetings and staff meetings became a way for the gathering and dissemination of the data that Johnson craved. Broader policy debates, such as the course of the Vietnam War, were not as susceptible to easy measure, and so the agenda of both cabinet meetings and high-level staff meetings became dominated with personnel reports and quantitative analysis of hiring and promotion activities.[145] However, other than Liz Carpenter and Juanita Roberts, Johnson's personal secretary, it was rare to find another woman invited to these meetings.[146]

Early in the administration, when Johnson exhibited a constant concern over comparisons of his administration with that of his predecessor, John Kennedy, attention was given to the recruitment of women and minorities. However, two years later, when the subject of appointments was placed on the agenda, attention was focused on identifying the best candidates for vacancies, people who were "creative and experienced," with "devotion to . . . [the] foreign, social, and political objectives" of the administration.[147]

In a 1966 report prepared for the president on the background of his appointees to executive branch positions, the categories by which the appointees were discussed included: education and awards, publications, and work experience (e.g., past governmental service, work in business or law). There is no mention of race or sex.[148]

CONCLUSION

Johnson drew from the ranks of those in government in making appointments, but with few women in high-level posts in the civil service, few women were available for high-level appointive posts. By 1968, the Johnson administration had established an impressive record, both in terms of women working in the government and in policies of concern to women, through legislation and through executive orders, yet surprisingly little was made of that record once the campaign for "Fifty Women" was over. However, this was an era in which there still was blatant discrimination against women. For instance, early in 1968, the three women who were White House Fellows were not allowed onto the floor of the House of Representatives to hear the president's State of the Union message, although the men in the White House Fellowship Program were allowed. It "was inappropriate" for the women to be on the floor, although there were ten women serving in the House at the time.[149]

The significance of Johnson's record regarding women and women's issues remained unrecognized, even to some of those in the administration. For example, in preparation for a cabinet meeting in May of 1968, a thick binder was prepared by Joe Califano listing the domestic achievements of the administration. The intent was to have this material available for cabinet secretaries to use in their speeches around the country and for the National Committee to use in the coming elections. While the record of the administration in terms of women is impressive, there is no mention of women in the material included in the binder. Instead, the topics were: economic prosperity, jobs, education, health, housing, cities, civil rights for minorities, children and youth, older Americans, new opportunities for the poor, the rural poor, crime, the American worker, consumers, national heritage, American farmers, veterans, and American business.[150]

According to Patricia Roberts Harris, who would later serve in the Carter administration as secretary of HUD and then HEW (Health and Human Services [HHS]), Johnson helped change the way issues were talked about.[151] Similarly, Johnson made it known, both inside and outside of the government, that women and others long lacking representation in government would be included. This was a major change from preceding administrations. With no women serving in the Johnson cabinet, Patricia Roberts Harris noted that some found the Johnson cabinet "wanting because there was no woman on it. . . . I'm not quite as critical as most people because on this issue nobody has done very well since President Eisenhower with Mrs. Hobby. . . . Nonetheless, he did articulate a position with respect to women, incidentally, that made everybody very conscious of the fact that something ought to be done to be sure that women were present. . . . It was Johnson that dealt with women."[152]

Throughout the Johnson administration, attention was given to the "effective use of womanpower." To a large measure, Johnson continued the work begun by Kennedy's Commission on the Status of Women and kept the focus on issues of assessment. In the next administration, that of Richard Nixon, efforts to systematically implement affirmative action would begin. Johnson came into office with some institutional structures in place to move forward on an agenda for women, and he was also more committed to getting women into government. His choice of Macy to serve as a recruiter of personnel for both the civil service and political appointees provided continuity as well to the work begun under the PCSW. However, his most important contributions came in his first two years in office. As Secretary Harris has stated, Johnson made all aware "that something ought to be done to be sure that women were present," especially before his focus turned to the Vietnam War and domestic battles over issues of civil rights for African Americans, a time when consciousness-raising would no longer come from the White House.

CHAPTER 4

◉

The Nixon Administration

Women Establish a Lasting Presence

in the White House Office

BY THE TIME Richard Milhous Nixon took the oath of office on January 20, 1969, a number of federal laws had been passed prohibiting discrimination against women. However, as history has so vividly demonstrated, the passage of landmark legislation or the ratification of constitutional amendments does not result in immediate change. Action taken by one branch of government does not necessarily lead to action by another branch of government. For example, fifteen years earlier, Chief Justice Earl Warren had been sensitive to the inability of the Supreme Court to enforce its rulings, therefore delaying the decision on the landmark school desegregation case, *Brown v. Board of Education of Topeka Kansas,* until the Court could achieve unanimity in its decision, to help lead to public acceptance and executive branch enforcement. The Court followed its ruling in *Brown,* on May 17, 1954, with a ruling a year later, urging enforcement "with all deliberate speed," yet schools remained segregated.

In a different setting, in an unsuccessful effort to block the passage of civil rights legislation, "sex" was added to Title VII of the 1964 Civil Rights Act. Five years later, as the Nixon administration came into power, the Justice Department had yet to initiate a *sex* discrimination case, while at the same time the department had prosecuted at least forty-five cases in the area of *racial* discrimination.[1] In part, this reflected the longstanding involvement of the executive branch in the issue of civil rights for African Americans, from President Lincoln's Emancipation Proclamation issued on

January 1, 1863,[2] to President Truman's Executive Order directing the end to a segregated armed forces in the summer of 1948.[3] It also reflected the fact that an institutional structure was already in place for the executive branch to implement racial discrimination laws passed by Congress. There was no similar structure for enforcement of sexual discrimination laws.

During the 1930s, President Franklin D. Roosevelt used an important tool of the presidency in issuing an order establishing a civil rights section in the Justice Department. Roosevelt's establishment of that unit allowed for the "building [of] a skilled bureaucracy of lawyers and other trained professionals to further the cause of black civil rights in the United States." In time, "the Civil Rights Section became an ally of the NAACP in filing suits to bring about school integration and in lobbying Congress to pass civil rights laws."[4] The infrastructure needed for the executive branch to move forward in enforcing the provisions of the 1964 Civil Rights Act was in place for racial bias, but not yet for sex discrimination.

The new president inherited legislative authority to move forward in implementing sex discrimination legislation but needed to structure his own administration to gain control over a bureaucracy primarily established during the Democratic administrations of Roosevelt and Johnson and to advance his own priorities.[5]

WOMEN'S ISSUES ON THE AGENDA AT THE BEGINNING OF THE NIXON ADMINISTRATION

While statutes may outline the structures in the Executive Office of the President, the advising and decision-making apparatus in the White House is left to each president's discretion, although scholars have recently identified the evolution of a complex organizational structure within the White House office itself. That evolution moved more rapidly beginning with the Nixon administration.[6] A more fluid advising and decision-making process which can either enhance or hinder the administration's response to outside groups has resulted.[7]

In addition, issues remain on the national agenda from prior administrations or that were added during a campaign full of promises and often recorded in the party's platform. Two issues in particular which surfaced during the 1968 campaign were the appointment of women to high-level positions in the administration, an issue President Johnson had clearly made a part of his agenda, and the addition of an ERA to the Constitution, which the Republican Party had long endorsed (see the Appendix).

Nixon and the Appointment of Women

Shortly before the 1968 election that pitted former Vice President Nixon against Hubert H. Humphrey, the sitting vice president, the RNC released a statement by Nixon, in which he recounted the record of the Eisenhower-Nixon administration in including women in the administration, contrasting it with the record of the Johnson-Humphrey administration:

> The present Administration [Johnson] began with glowing promises about appointing women to top government positions.
>
> But our present leaders must think that it is an administration's prerogative to change its mind completely: compared to the eight years of the Eisenhower-Nixon Administration, the past eight years have seen an eclipse of women in the upper levels of government.
>
> In the Eisenhower years, Mrs. Oveta Culp Hobby became the first Secretary of Health, Education and Welfare; in the past eight years, no woman was appointed to a post of Cabinet rank.
>
> During our term of office, Mrs. Clare Boothe Luce was appointed Ambassador to Italy; and Mrs. Frances Willis was the first woman career diplomat to be elevated to ambassador. Since that time, no women have been ambassadors to major countries.
>
> I do not believe in quota systems for any group or sex; but certainly since 1960 there has been a reversal of the trend we set in motion for the proper recognition of the contribution that women can make to the leadership of this nation.
>
> This Administration, in its put-down of women, has sent a bad example to industry, to labor, and to the professions.
>
> A Nixon administration will not be as blind as this Administration has been to the contribution that women can make to the leadership of this nation.[8]

The appointment of women to high-level posts within the administration would remain an issue throughout the Nixon administration. By the time of Nixon's run for re-election, the White House Office would begin to establish a structural mechanism for the inclusion of women, which becomes an institutionalized feature of subsequent White House offices.

An Equal Rights Amendment

In 1940 the Republican Party became the first party to include support for an ERA to the Constitution in its platform. By the time Richard Nixon took the oath of office in 1969, the House and Senate had yet to pass an ERA, with the same language within the same Congress, with the constitutionally mandated two-thirds vote in each house.

During the summer of 1968, while campaigning, candidate Richard Nixon issued a statement outlining his position on the amendment (see Box 4.1). Throughout the course of his administration, the language used by Nixon in this statement would prove problematic for his staff in that some would take the words "It is my hope that there will be widespread support for the Equal Rights for Women Amendment to our Constitution . . ." as an indication of Nixon's full endorsement of the amendment, while others took the words literally to mean that Nixon hoped others (i.e., Congress and the states) would support the amendment.

The ambiguity surrounding the president's (and administration's) position can be illustrated in a number of ways. For instance, William H. Rehnquist, then an assistant attorney general in the Office of Legal Counsel in the Justice Department, who opposed the amendment, provided testimony at House Judiciary Subcommittee hearings in 1971 that was so "am-

---

BOX 4.1

Statement by Former Vice President Richard M. Nixon on
the Equal Rights for Women Amendment

JULY, 1968

Forty-eight years ago, American women were given the Constitutional right to vote. Today it is accepted as a matter of course that men and women have an equal electoral franchise in this country and that American men and women will have an equal voice in choosing a new President, a Congress and state and local governing officials and bodies.

But the task of achieving Constitutional equality between the sexes still is not completed. All Republican National Conventions since 1940 have supported the long-time movement for such equality.

It is my hope that there will be widespread support for the Equal rights for Women Amendment to our Constitution, which would add equality between the sexes to the freedoms and liberties guaranteed to all Americans.

Source: Statement of Richard M. Nixon, July, 1968, "ERA [3 of 3]" folder, WHCF, SMOF, ALA, Box 7, Nixon Presidential Materials.

bivalent" that outside women's organizations wrote Nixon to get clarification on his position.[9] These groups were concerned because the Office of Legal Counsel had "a very special function in the Department of Justice, serving as the chief interpreter, for the whole government of the Constitution and the Statutes of the United States . . . in effect, the President's lawyer's lawyer."[10] As such, Rehnquist might be more likely to be accurately reflecting the president's views.[11] Shortly thereafter, Helen Delich Bentley, a Republican and chairman of the Federal Maritime Commission, organized a letter to be sent to the president, signed by the Republican women in the House and by Republican women in appointive positions in the executive branch. The letter noted the upcoming election in 1972 and the need for the president to "reaffirm" the position he took in 1968 regarding the ERA.[12]

Even after the ERA was successfully passed in both the House and Senate in 1972, Nixon's support was ambiguously worded, with no statement urging ratification by the states. Instead, Nixon's statement was as follows: "On this occasion, I wish to join with you in saluting this significant advance in the long drive to achieve equal rights for the women of America. It is crucial that no group of people be denied the free rights they deserve, and I assure you that this Administration will continue in its determined efforts to ensure that equal opportunity for women is translated from ideal into reality."[13] Throughout the life of an administration, administrative structures as well as White House staff personnel change. The policy goals and priorities of an administration also become modified in response to the press of outside events, and so each year in a four-year term presents different opportunities as well as constraints. This will easily be seen throughout this chapter as the ERA, while not a central focus of this administration, remains simmering on the back burner.[14]

Agenda Setting and Task Forces

After the Republican national convention in 1968, Nixon's campaign staff organized a series of task forces, covering a range of issues such as tax policy and welfare reform, which would eventually help to shape the direction of the Nixon administration during its first year in office. The use of task forces continued throughout the president's first term, and Arthur Burns, counselor to the president, was given the responsibility for their administration.

Pressures on the new administration were already being applied. Representative Florence P. Dwyer (R-NJ) and other Republican women in the House pushed President Nixon to establish an office of Women's Rights and Responsibilities headed by a special assistant to the president, shortly after his inauguration.[15] Dwyer's proposal was quickly made known to a number of women's organizations, and the president soon received letters in support of Dwyer's proposal from a number of organizations. Elizabeth Boyer, president of the Women's Equity Action League (WEAL), in a letter of support, suggested that the special assistant

> preferably [be] a woman, who has a personal history of interest and activity in this area. The working women in America are becoming more sophisticated in distinguishing palliatives from actual constructive efforts. If I assess their attitudes correctly, a groundswell of feeling is developing, on a highly responsible level, which will not brook very much delay or circumlocution. The burgeoning membership in our organization, which has expanded into nearly twenty states by word-of-mouth alone, certainly testifies to this.[16]

The first set of task forces established in 1969 included one on Women's Rights and Responsibilities, which was given the following charge: "The task force will review the present status of women in our society and recommend what might be done in the future to further advance their opportunities."[17]

Like presidential commissions, task forces can "give access to the President to thinking outside of the governmental establishment."[18] However, in contrast to presidential commissions, Burns noted that "a task force will function over a brief period and ordinarily will not undertake new research." The task forces appeared to serve as blueprints for administration action, both for departments and agencies as well as within the White House.[19] The task forces were designed to sum up findings from studies already available, sifting through, synthesizing material, and deciding plans for executive or legislative action. The Task Force on Women's Rights and Responsibilities, unlike Kennedy's Commission on the Status of Women, would be done with its work in just a few months.

Virginia Allan, a former president of the NFBPWC, was named chair of the Task Force on Women's Rights and Responsibilities on October 1, 1969 (see Box 4.2 for task force membership).

While the task force was being organized, Assistant to the President Daniel Patrick Moynihan noted the emergence of a women's liberation movement in a memo to the president and suggested that the president take advantage of it through his "appointments (as you have begun to do), but perhaps especially in your pronouncements. This is a subject ripe for creative policy leadership and initiative."[20]

BOX 4.2

Task Force Membership

Virginia R. Allan, Chairman; Executive Vice President, Cahalan Drug
Stores, Inc.

Elizabeth Athanasakos, Judge

Ann R. Blackham, President of Ann R. Blackham Company

P. Dee Boersma, graduate student, Ohio State University

Evelyn Cunningham, Director, Women's Unit, Office of the Governor, New York

Ann Ida Gannon, President, Mundelein College

Vera R. Glaser, Newspaper correspondent, Knight Newspaper

Dorothy Haener, Women's Department, UAW

Laddie F. Hutar, President, Public Affairs Service Associates, Inc.

Katherine B. Massenburg, Chairman, Maryland Commission on the
Status of Women

William C. Mercer, Vice President, Personnel Relations, American Telephone and Telegraph Co.

Alan Simpson, President, Vassar College

Evelyn E. Whitlow, attorney

*Source: Arthur F. Burns to President Nixon, memorandum, Sept. 30, 1969, "EX FG
221-40 Women's Rights and Responsibilities [1969–1970]" folder, WHCF, Subject
Files, FG 221, Task Forces, Box 7, Nixon Presidential Materials.*

John Ehrlichman, counsel to the president, forwarded Moynihan's memo
to the president, with the subject identified as "Female Equality," and noted
that since "female equality will be a major cultural/political force in the
1970's . . . [Moynihan] recommends that you take advantage of this in your
appointments and pronouncements."[21] Other staff assistants were in agreement that announcement of appointments would "politically" present "a
golden opportunity and that we should whenever possible, champion female equality."[22] A slightly different response came from Staff Assistant Peter Flanigan who observed that "as a member of the staff who has borne the
brunt of women's attack, I am well aware of the increasing use of violence."[23]

In 1969, at the height of protests against the Vietnam War, news publications prominently featured articles on and photographs of women members of such radical groups as the Weathermen faction of Students for a

Democratic Society, giving rise to Flanigan's comments on "the increasing use of violence" on the part of women seeking equal rights.[24] Following the circulation of the Moynihan memo, there appeared to be a brief effort to identify and congratulate women for prominent achievements, a consciousness-raising exercise within the White House, lasting but a few months.[25]

The Report of the Task Force on Women's Rights and Responsibilities

On December 15, 1969, just two-and-a-half months after the membership of the task force had been announced, its report was sent to the president, offering a number of recommendations. Prominent among the recommendations was a call for the establishment of an Office of Women's Rights and Responsibilities in the White House, to be headed by a special assistant to the president, reporting directly to the president. In addition, the task force asked the president to call for a White House Conference on Women's Rights and Responsibilities to mark the fiftieth anniversary of women securing the right to vote and the creation of a Women's Bureau in the Department of Labor.

A legislative agenda was also outlined in the task force report, including an ERA and modifications in the landmark 1964 Civil Rights Act to include women under additional Titles[26] and strengthen the hand of the executive branch in enforcement of civil rights statutes prohibiting discrimination because of sex.[27] Other legislative items included child care provisions, equalization of fringe benefits for men and women federal workers, and equal pay to a greater range of workers, issues President Kennedy's Commission on the Status of Women had identified earlier. In addition, the task force outlined actions the president and his administration could take on their own to end sex discrimination, including implementation of Executive Order 11246 concerning federal contractors[28] by the secretary of labor; initiatives by the attorney general to file *amicus curiae* briefs in cases before the Supreme Court challenging the validity of laws involving sex discrimination under the Fifth and Fourteenth Amendments; the appointment of women in all departments; and ensuring that "qualified women receive equal consideration in hiring and promotions."[29]

While the agenda reflected a number of issues raised and positions taken by Kennedy's Commission on the Status of Women, the strong call for an ERA marked a change in emphasis in the quest for women's rights. Even the name of the task force reflected the language being used to garner support for the ERA—"rights," and "responsibilities" (which accompany rights), as a way to ward off amendment critics: the ERA would result in equity for women regarding standards for enrollment in college, prison sentences, and so forth; yet men would also gain equity in such areas as alimony and child custody, and both men and women would share responsibility for military service.

The report of the task force, submitted in December, 1969, and printed in April, 1970, was not, however, released until June 9, 1970. This was but one of a number of task forces organized during the Nixon administration's first year in office, with others focusing on air pollution, aging, highway safety, model cities, oceanography, and prisoner rehabilitation. Several of these reports, including aging, economic growth, and prisoner rehabilitation, had also been submitted and printed during April, languishing in the White House while they awaited release.[30]

Following receipt of the task force's report, several members of the White House staff attempted a response to the recommendations included in the report, with a focus on the failure of the administration to appoint women to high-level positions and the addition of a special assistant for women's rights to the White House staff. The highest ranking woman in the administration at this point in time was Patricia Hitt. Hitt served as an intermediary between the White House and women's groups, a role which was rather unusual given that she was an assistant secretary in the Department of HEW, and had no formal or official role in the White House. However, she was a friend of Pat Nixon, and was also national co-chair of Nixon's 1968 campaign.[31] With her position's similarity to the jack-of-all-trades role played by Esther Peterson in the Kennedy administration, Hitt was perceived by some in the administration as the representative as well as the individual responsible for any policy, action, or appointments concerning women.[32]

Hitt found herself under fire early in the administration when she stated: "[I] cannot name a single woman qualified for a Cabinet position."[33] She later explained that her "reference had to do with the number of qualified women available for Cabinet level positions. Qualifications and availability, ... are two very different things. There is absolutely no doubt that we have a sufficient supply of woman-power well suited for Cabinet membership—unfortunately these ladies are extremely busy helping carry on the work of the world in other areas."[34] The words chosen, however, would continue to haunt her throughout her tenure in the administration. Hitt was assigned responsibilities as the Nixon administration's link to women's groups, and also took on her own initiatives in this area. While Hitt served as the administration's surrogate for women, her influence in the Nixon administration was minimal.[35]

In April, 1970, Hitt sent a strongly worded memo to John Ehrlichman urging that the report be released. She also pointed out how votes for the Republican presidential candidate from women had been eroding from 51 percent of women voting Republican in 1960 to only 38 percent of women voting Republican in 1964, and then rebounding to support from 43 percent in 1968. Hitt observed that "with the rising popularity of the women's 'liberation' groups, and the increasing feminine interest in politics, . . . it bothers me to see the Democrats taking the lead on the Equal Rights Amendment." She went on to suggest that

> it would certainly take the ball away from the Democrats and be a plus for the Administration if the President would follow former President Eisenhower's lead and send a message to Congress urging action on the amendment. According to the Executive Director of the Citizen's Advisory Committee on the Status of Women, Ike was the only president to send a message to Congress during his term in office. It makes good campaign talk, but unless you follow through it's just so much "oratory."[36]

However, Hitt's words fell on deaf ears as several more months passed without the release of the report. She was not in a position to speak for the president or to be privy to high-level decision making.

Pressure began to build from outside the White House for a response from the president, first from the Republican women members of Congress and then from the National Federation of Business and Professional Women and other organizations. Lucille Shriver, federation director, wanted to have an off-the-record meeting with John Ehrlichman, who forwarded the request on to Charles Colson, special counsel to the president.[37] Colson met with Shriver, along with representatives from B'nai B'rith, Women United, the National Association of Women Lawyers, and the RNC.[38] In spite of the fact that a former president of the NFBPWC had chaired the task force appointed by President Nixon, Colson, following his meeting, described the leadership of the NFBPWC as a "very militant group, . . . on the question of women's rights, the appointment of women, . . . amendment of civil rights legislation to include women and a host of other things."[39] However, based on his past contact with the organization, Colson thought that in spite of their leadership "their membership by and large would be very much in our corner. They tend to be the better educated, career oriented women and are generally conservative."[40] Colson told the women that given President Nixon's efforts to reduce the size of the White House staff, adding a new special assistant was highly unlikely. Colson did suggest to Haldemen, however, that "someone on the White House Staff" could take on liaison to women's groups "as an additional responsibility." Colson noted "this need not involve any substantive realignment but would be largely cosmetic. It would let the organized women's groups know that we are concerned with their problems and would give them a point of contact. . . . I think they would like to feel that there was someone who had the specific assignment for handling questions of women's rights."[41]

Cosmetics aside, Colson's meeting with these women leaders began a productive working relationship between women's groups such as the NFBPWC and the White House, which would continue throughout the Nixon presidency. As a result of these contacts, some of the recommendations of the task force would be addressed, albeit indirectly, throughout the remaining years of the Nixon administration.

The Administration's Response
to the Task Force Report

The report of the task force, delivered to the president in December, 1969, was finally released to the public in June, 1970. In the intervening months, it is clear that the idea of such an Office of Women in Government was under consideration. For instance, a memo circulated among the president's staff identifying an "ideal" candidate for this new post, Frances Knight, "because of her truly outstanding record at the Passport Office." However, there were other motivations at work as well, as the memo went on to note that it was

> important that Miss Knight and her husband, Wayne Parrish, are long-time Republicans who have consistently supported President Nixon. The appointment of Miss Knight could give real leadership in a field that is most important in obtaining and regaining a proper political posture with regard to equal rights for women. Also, . . . placing Miss Knight in this position and on leave from her present job as director of the Passport Office might provide a means of eliminating the crisis condition that exists in connection with the Passport Office and its dealings with the Chairman of the House Appropriations Subcommittee.[42]

Knight, director since 1955, had job security through civil service protection.[43] Elevating her to a White House position would remove her from this post, but in a voluntary way. Peter Flanigan contacted Haldeman and noted, "I know Frances Knight quite well and have discussed in some detail parts of the problems of the upcoming survey of passports. . . . Before deciding that we should make her Special Assistant to the President and Director of the Office of Women in Government, we should determine whether we want the office. For operational purposes, I would doubt that it would be an effective addition. It may be that for cosmetic purposes we need it," a point with which Haldeman agreed.[44] Haldeman sent the matter to Len Garment, who oversaw this area, and this is where the issue remained for months. Haldeman also suggested having a woman already on the White House staff or in the departments and agencies take on the task—e.g., Special Assistant to the President for Consumer Affairs Virginia Knauer, Assistant Secretary of HEW Pat Hitt, or Ethel Bent Walsh in the Small Business Administration.[45]

The creation of an Office of Women's Rights and Responsibilities headed by a special assistant to the president had been one of the recommendations made to President Nixon by Republican women members of the House of Representatives shortly after his inauguration. That the consideration of such an office was under discussion among the White House staff early in 1970 might have contributed to the delay in the White House's response to the task force's report.

The final nudge to get the White House to release the task force report may have come from Elizabeth Duncan Koontz, director of the Women's Bureau. She had pleaded with John Ehrlichman to have the task force report released in time for a national conference, hosted by the Women's Bureau, celebrating the fiftieth anniversary of the bureau's founding. With more than seven hundred participants, including representatives of women's organizations, members of state and local commissions on the status of women, members of Congress, and other leaders in attendance, Koontz pointed out the embarrassment to be faced by the administration if the report were not soon released. The conference, "American Women at the Crossroads: Directions for the Future," was scheduled to begin June 11, prompting Koontz to write Ehrlichman on June 1: "We know that the participants will raise questions about the status of the Report. . . . Although not released officially, the report has had wide circulation . . . and questions will be raised concerning it. . . . Since the conference date is a little more than a week away, time is of the essence. I feel that it would be most advantageous to the Administration . . . to have the report released by the President."[46]

Since the past president of the National Federation of Business and Professional Women had chaired the task force, copies of the report had been available to Federation Women since December, 1969, when the report was given to the president. The report was finally released to the public on the morning of June 9, 1970. However, Koontz, who was not a member of the White House staff, was left to come to the White House to explain the "administration's response" to the report to the press. In doing so, she announced new guidelines to bar sex discrimination on government contract work and require affirmative action. Unfortunately, Koontz, who did not even hold subcabinet rank, encountered a hostile White House press corps, as the following exchange illustrates:.

> **Q:** Mrs. Koontz, have you discussed the Task Force itself with President Nixon? Has he given you any indication of what future action you may plan on it?
>
> **Koontz:** No, I am sorry there has not been that. It has been, in segments, referred to various agencies and departments for discussions and evaluation and I am sure that those departments will be the ones that will have conversations with the President before anything else is done.
>
> **Q:** Has the President read the Task Force report . . . ?
>
> **Koontz:** I would assume that the President has read it or has at least put into the works the process.
>
> **Q:** Does anyone on the President's staff here know whether he has read it? I see Mr. Garment here. Do you happen to know whether the President has read it?
>
> **Garment:** Mr. Warren can answer that.
>
> **Warren:** The President has read it and as Mrs. Koontz said, it has been sent out in segments to the various departments which are concerned for study and evaluation and those reports will be sent back to the President's staff.
>
> **Q:** Why in segments?
>
> **Warren:** I think it is because various departments have interest in various parts of the Task Force report.
>
> **Q:** They can't read the whole thing?
>
> **Warren:** Every department read the whole thing?
>
> **Q:** It is only 34 pages.
>
> **Warren:** Of course they can, but each department has a responsibility for different parts of the recommendation in the report.[47]

Given the strong emphasis in the report for support of an ERA (the task force lists the ERA first in its list of legislative recommendations that the president should make to the Congress), the reporters pressed Koontz and

Warren as to why the administration, and in particular the Justice Department, had not yet testified before Congress as to its endorsement.

> **Mrs. Koontz:** The President is on record since 1960 and 1968 in support of the Equal Rights Amendment and the Labor Department's position is in support of the Equal Rights Amendment. The Women's Bureau is in support of the Equal Rights amendment. There are reservations about some of the implications, but we feel that these are the kinds of things that will be studied.
>
> **Q:** Are you speaking of the Labor Department or the White House?
>
> **Koontz:** Both.[48]

The report of the task force was thus released, but without any action taken. Staff Assistant to the President George T. Bell was one of the few in the White House pushing for action. In a memo to Haldeman, Bell noted that he had been "staunchly in favor" of creating a new position—special assistant to the president for Women's Rights and Responsibilities. Bell noted, "It could be substantively useful in getting qualified women into Government in responsible positions, in dealing with women's organizations; and it would be politically valuable in signaling the President's concern for professional and working women."[49] Bell suggested that the president meet with women attending the upcoming Congress of Career Women Leaders in Washington, organized by the NFBPWC, and announce the appointment at that time.

However, Len Garment, whose office had jurisdiction over the administration's response to the report, was not in favor. In spite of growing pressure from women's groups, Garment remained steadfast in his opposition (e.g., see the letter Garment sent to Margaret E. Walsh, National League for Nursing, Box 4.3).

The president himself had not read the report, and the members of the task force never met with the president.[51] Just as the formation of the task force had received perfunctory listing in the White House Daily Digest of Events, the release of the task force's report, "A Matter of Simple Justice," was also routine, without direct presidential involvement.[52]

The confusion in the administration as to the role of all task force reports was evident in the response of various offices. While John Ehrlichman might have viewed the task forces as a means to internally coordinate and focus domestic policy initiatives, some staff members viewed the external political environment as the target. For instance, one member of the White House staff sent a letter to different women's organizations noting that with

BOX 4.3

The Administration's Response to the Task Force Report

Dear Mrs. Walsh:

The President has asked me to thank you for your telegram . . . recommending the creating of a Special Assistant to the President for Women's Rights and Responsibilities.

The President is . . . intensely interested in attacking all forms of demeaning discrimination which are supported by governmental power at any level.

The question . . . is whether the appointment . . . would be an effective step.

. . . in the years since the Brownlow Report of 1936[50] first recommended the creating of general assistants to the President, there has been a boom in requests for "special" Special Assistants in that Office. "Woman", "Black Affairs", "Mexican-Americans", "Spanish-Speaking Americans", "Indians", "Consumers", "Social Policy", "Poverty", "Youth", "The Aged", "Physical Fitness" and a goodly number of others have been named as candidate-areas for formally-delineated White House Staff monitorship. . . .

Yet it is my belief that over a third of a century—under six Presidents—several sound principles of public administration have emerged with respect to the Presidential staff:

—The creation of any one Specialist area is precedent for others, but the demarcation of several or a lot of such jurisdictions would leave Presidential staff areas hopelessly overlapping, e.g., to which White House ombudsman would a young, poor, Indian woman consumer appeal?

—Comprehensive staff work for the President defies boundary lines: it requires, rather, pursuit of an issue across any, and often many, "jurisdictional specialties."

—The President is best served, in his immediate Office, by high-brainpower people working in a low-publicity mode. . . . Yet the "special" Special Assistants of the kind you recommend are inevitably high-visibility officers.

—Assistants piled upon Assistants overlapping with Assistants would derogate from the Presidency and would tend to hide the President as if at the remote end of a labyrinth of liaison. . . . just as there can be no one "representative" of the 103,000,000 women in America.

Different Presidents have made one or more exceptions to these principles and some have worked well. . . . But it is my personal opinion, speaking to you more as a public administrator than as a politician, that each exception made weakens the defense against the flood of others and if a President in the future found himself with the whole panoply, he would simply withdraw from all of them and build a staff of inner circle intimates which White House history since 1936 shows are the kind Presidents need.

I repeat: President Nixon is going to continue to use the powers of his office, together with that of the Courts, to take out after any institutional or governmental discrimination which he can constitutionally reach, specifically including demeaning discrimination on the basis of sex. . . . You and your colleagues should hold our feet to the fire if we do less than our best. But with respect to the organization of the President's immediate staff, I hope you will join with a generation of public administrators in upholding the principles of anonymity, generality and flexibility.

Sincerely yours,

Leonard Garment

Source: Leonard Garment to Margaret E. Walsh, Oct. 6, 1970, "[GEN] HU 2-5 Women, 1/1/70–12/31/70" folder, WHCF, Subject Files HU, Box 22, Nixon Presidential Materials.

the release of the report and publication of new guidelines on sex discrimination, which were to apply to government contractors, "we . . . have done something tangible."[53]

Thus, some in the White House viewed the document as serving political needs—responding to an important constituency group, women, prior to the 1972 election. In contrast, others in the White House saw the report as a means for developing a cohesive policy agenda concerning women.

While there was ambivalence within the administration as to a response to the task force report, and what action to take, the president himself appeared to take interest in the issues raised. Several months after the release of the task force report, H. R. Haldeman communicated to Robert H. Finch, counselor to the president, that the president was anxious that we make some progress in working with women and feels we haven't done an adequate job in this area. He would like as one step, for you to talk to Helen Bentley[54] and get her advice as to what we should do in the way of bringing women into the Administration or in working with women to see where we can make some political hay.

As another step, he is considering again, the idea of designating Pat Hitt or someone else as Special Assistant to the President for dealing with women and their interests.

He feels that we have failed to grab the ball on the whole women's business and that we need to do some things to see that women are properly recognized and that we get credit for the things we do carry out with women.

We also need to see that our programs are properly oriented toward women.

We also need to work out a way of working with the wives of the Labor Leaders, the VFW Auxiliaries, etc., especially in the volunteer area. I know that he's going to be looking hard for recommendations on this and we should be ready as soon as we can.[55]

With Nixon's campaign promise in October, 1968, that "a Nixon administration will not be as blind as [the Johnson] . . . Administration has been to the contribution that women can make to the leadership of this nation," the focus of the administration's efforts during 1969 and 1970 turned to the appointment of women in the administration and the establishment of an affirmative action policy in the government.[56] However, the agenda of women's groups was far broader, and as a result the administration's efforts in the area of affirmative action were overshadowed, and to some, appeared non-responsive. For instance, consider the agenda items presented to the president by the delegation of four Republican women in the House of Representatives who met with President Nixon in July, 1969, to discuss "matters of direct and immediate concern to women generally."[57] Each woman held a significant position in the House, and Assistant to the President Bryce Harlow made note of this in briefing the president: "Flo Dwyer is ranking Republican on the Government Operations Committee which handles your reorganization bills; Cathy May is an important member of the Agriculture Committee and introduced your food stamp program; Peggy Heckler is a member of the Banking and Currency and Veterans Affairs Committee; Charlotte Reid is a member of the Appropriations Committee." In spite of a detailing of the positions of each in regards to how they might help the movement of the president's legislative agenda through the House, their *policy* interests were ignored. Harlow observed that "undoubtedly the group will dwell on the need for more Federal appointments for women."[58]

While the four women had an agenda that covered a wide range of issues, the administration only saw their interest in terms of issues of descriptive representation (see Box 4.4).

The focus on appointments is not surprising, given the emphasis on women in government in the preceding administrations, both in appointive positions and in the higher ranks of the career civil service. And, in spite of a broader agenda, women's organizations had also emphasized the appointment of women, and taken a number of steps to build on the work done by women's organizations and within the Democratic and Republican Parties in the past few decades.

The NFBPWC would soon pass a resolution at their convention that laid out the origins of a talent bank, with provision for participation by a number of women's organizations. The action taken by the NFBPWC would have a long-lasting impact. For the first time, there would be a systematic effort to identify and consider women for appointive posts. While the idea was not new, having been discussed and proposed on numerous occasions for nearly a quarter century, this was the first time that systematic action would be taken involving both the White House and outside groups.

During Nixon's meeting in July, 1969, with the four women Representatives, the president stated that he "was interested in more women appointments, particularly in areas where they had not previously served . . . . [and] urged that women be considered for regulatory agencies and for the judiciary."[59] Nixon "agreed that Congresswoman Reed be appointed to the FCC after her current term in Congress expires. He also urged the ladies to look for the kind of women who could be groomed through service in the lower levels of the judiciary to eventual appointment to the Supreme Court."[60]

Nixon's focus on appointments, however, was broadened to include the education of women. Nixon voiced concern over the educational opportunities available to women, which would provide women the stepping stones needed to gain entry into professional positions. One of the areas explored by Kennedy's Commission on the Status of Women had been that of educational opportunities for women, and for women gaining the training and experience needed for career advancement. Nixon kept sight of that point, and later in the year when he met with members of the President's Advisory Council on the Status of Women in the Cabinet Room of the White House, he "talked . . . of the importance of the education of women, linking the

BOX 4.4
*Meeting of Republican Women Members of Congress
with the President*

Representative Dwyer presented the President with a series of recommendations outlining the "positive steps" which the Administration could take:

1. "A major speech by the President—preferably a message to Congress—outlining the disabilities faced by women, proposing specific remedies, and calling Congress and the country to act accordingly."

2. "Establish a governmental structure necessary for the protection of women's rights and responsibilities and the advancement of women's opportunities to consist of (a) a Special Assistant to the President for Women's Rights and Responsibilities; (b) an Office of Women's Rights and Responsibilities within the Executive Office of the President, headed by the Special Assistant, to provide the needed policy direction and the evaluation of the Government's performance; (c) an interdepartmental committee to ensure coordination and follow-through; and (d) an independent, bi-partisan commission to make necessary studies and investigations, provide legal information to the public, make recommendations for executive and legislative action, and stimulate complementary action in the private sphere."

3. "Issue a Presidential directive to the White House staff, Cabinet officers and agency heads, informing them of his active interest in women's rights and opportunities and soliciting their cooperation in promoting such rights and opportunities in their respective jurisdictions."

4. "Inform all departments and agency heads that, wherever possible, women be specifically considered—on their merits alone—in filling all remaining Presidential and Schedule C appointments."

5. "In view of the agency's special significance to women and its major responsibilities in the field of sex discrimination, appoint a woman (Commission [*sic*] Kuck) to the vice chairmanship of the Equal Employment Opportunity Commission."

6. "From existing personnel recruiting files in the White House, departments and agencies, and the Republican National Committee, provide for a comprehensive inventory of women whose abilities and availability indicate their fitness for appointment to responsible positions; and supplement such an inventory by actively soliciting recommendations of and applications from other similarly well qualified women."

7. "Provide for greater recognition of outstanding women through such means as (a) a series of women's luncheons in the White House or with Mrs. Nixon; (b) special ceremonies honoring women for particular achievements, and (c) the inclusion of more women at official White House dinners and other functions."

8. "Assure that all Federal offices responsible for the enforcement of laws prohibiting sex discrimination and for programs aimed at enhancing women's opportunities are adequately staffed and funded and are performing effectively."

9. "Recommend enactment of, and urge early hearings on, the proposed Equal Rights Amendment to the Constitution as a means of invalidating State laws discriminating against women."

10. "Recommend that Congress provide 'cease and desist' powers for the Equal Employment Opportunity Commission so as to enable it to enforce its decisions."

11. "Recommend that Congress authorize the Civil Rights Commission to enlarge its jurisdiction to include discrimination based on sex."

12. "Recommend to Congress that Title VI of the Civil Rights Act be amended to prohibit discrimination in education based on sex."

13. "Propose to Congress expanded programs for the construction of multi-purpose day care centers for the children of working mothers and for job training for mothers of dependent children in order to reduce the number of women on welfare."

14. "Expedite the issuance by the Secretary of Labor of effective guidelines to eliminate sex bias by Federal contractors."

15. "Direct the Department of Justice to file suites [*sic*] under Title VII in sex bias cases in the same manner now in effect in the field of racial bias."

16. "Utilize more frequently the opportunity of appearance before business and academic groups to emphasize the need for more equitable policies regarding women and be able to cite Federal leadership in this area."

17. "Order a comprehensive survey of current practices, in and out of Government, to identify and correct sex discrimination in the areas of compensation, pensions, retirement, promotion, management training, taxes, and Social Security."

Source: Rep. Florence Dwyer to President Nixon, memorandum, July 6, 1969, "[GEN] HU 2-5 Women 1/1/70–12/31/70" folder, WHCF, Subject Files, HU, Box 22, Nixon Presidential Materials.

development of the improvement of the status of women since the time of the Civil War. The President pointed out that in our society it was more and more important that able, well-educated and trained individuals join in the productive segment of the society."[61] The administration began counting the number of women it had appointed in 1969, including in its counts women appointed to part-time positions, advisory boards, and commissions and as White House Fellows.[62]

The focus on appointments resulted in nearly simultaneous efforts, by White House personnel and interest groups, to create structural mechanisms to facilitate the consideration of women for high-level governmental posts. The ideas that had been kicking around for years took on lasting structural form as a result of these efforts.

BRINGING WOMEN INTO THE NIXON ADMINISTRATION

In 1969, Nixon issued an executive order laying out an affirmative action policy that would be implemented later on in the administration, with first the addition of Barbara Franklin to the White House staff as a recruiter of women, and especially with the addition of Anne L. Armstrong as counselor to the president following Nixon's landslide re-election.[63]

However, the effort to include women began before either Franklin or Armstrong came into the White House. Just as John F. Kennedy and Lyndon B. Johnson had been questioned early in their administrations regarding women appointments, Nixon, at one of his first press conferences, was asked why only three appointments had gone to women of the two hundred appointments named so far. Nixon's response that he "had not known that only three had gone to women," and would "see that we correct that imbalance very promptly," may have nudged those at the highest levels in the White House to include consideration of women as positions in the new administration were filled.[64]

Thus, early in the administration, efforts were made at the highest levels to include women.[65] The women under consideration underwent the same review process as other candidates—with the RNC first reviewing each woman's political affiliation, even noting precinct work.[66] There was pressure to appoint individuals who were conservative, southern, or women, with care given that no liberal Democrats were appointed.[67] At times sex was not a criterion for a job; other times sex placed restraints on those considered.[68] In addition, like its predecessors, the Nixon administration added a responsibility for its women appointees to serve as liaisons to the nascent women's movement.[69]

The use of a talent bank, created by the NFBPWC, created some problems for the White House.[70] The three goals of implementing affirmative action plans *and* appointing those most loyal to the president, *and* appointing those loyal to the party, could not always be reconciled. In fact, the White House drew more heavily on the recommendations of the talent bank than of the party faithful, in a manner not too different from the Kennedy and Johnson administrations, which had also bypassed the party organization in filling positions.[71]

However, when active Republican Party women learned of the talent bank, they became alarmed that the party faithful would not find a place in the administration. With the next presidential election in two years, these women were an important core constituency of the Republican Party. Charles Colson worked to alleviate that fear, and in a letter sent to a party chair, Colson wrote:

> Let me first assure you that women who have worked for, or been endorsed by, the Republican Party are given preference for presidential appointments. The activities of the National Federation of Business and Professional Women is by no means a substitute for the regular political organizations. The Business and Professional Women decided on their own to sponsor a "Talent Bank" and we told them, as we would any organization, that we would be glad to receive recommendations that they might have from around the country for various Federal appointments.[72]

The president's opportunity to fill Supreme Court vacancies also resulted in controversy. In particular, the president's appointments of Lewis F. Powell, Jr., and William H. Rehnquist upon vacancies caused by the departures of Justices Harlan and Black in October, 1971, led to strongly worded attacks from women's organizations who were shocked at the president's failure to nominate a woman.[73] For years, a number of women leaders had been pushing for a strategy of using the Fifth and Fourteenth Amendments in ending sex discrimination, in cases brought before the Supreme Court, rather than a strategy of adding an ERA to the Constitution. The absence of women on the Supreme Court, as well as the paucity of women serving as federal judges, was viewed as particularly egregious, especially in light of the Court's unwillingness to address issues of sex discrimination.[74]

POLITICS, PUBLIC RELATIONS, AND PROGRESS:
THE ADMINISTRATION GEARS UP FOR THE 1972 ELECTION

As the Nixon administration reached the halfway mark of the first term, attention began to focus on the president's re-election campaign. As Herb Asher has noted, "Throughout 1971 and even into 1972, it appeared that Nixon would face a tough battle for reelection because of the nation's economic difficulties and the continued American involvement in Vietnam, albeit at a sharply reduced level. For example, in a trial run between Nixon, Muskie, and Wallace in February of 1972, Gallup found that Nixon held a scant 43-42 percent advantage over Muskie among registered voters with 10 percent for Wallace and 5 percent undecided."[75] Where John Kennedy and Lyndon Johnson seemed to pay particular attention to the vicissitudes of an electoral college strategy in their campaigns, the Committee to Re-elect the President, Nixon's campaign organization, gave special attention to different groups. Constituencies were identified and responded to as such through the use of "surrogate candidates with something in common with each group."[76] Women, as constituents, received attention, and in particular the White House wanted to know whether the "women's liberation movement" had public support.

Both Gallup Polls as well as private polls were consulted.[77] In Nixon's previous run for the White House in 1960 he had had greater support from women than from men. Given the relative loss in support from 1960 through 1968 women were a constituent group that could not be ignored in 1972.[78] Hauser, a lawyer who had worked on Nixon's 1968 campaign and would become co-chair of the 1972 Committee to Re-Elect the President, had earlier identified women as an important voting bloc, with the women's movement a major catalyst in bringing women and a different set of issues for the national agenda into the Oval Office.

By the time of the 1972 election, there was a rallying cry from a number of women's organizations that not only did women need to run for office, but they needed to vote.[79] This cry may have been less noticed as the election also marked the first time that eighteen year olds could vote, a result of ratification of the Twenty-sixth Amendment.

While Hauser as co-chair of the 1972 re-election campaign tried to integrate women into the campaign, and not have a separate women's organization in the campaign, others felt that women, while a voting bloc, should be viewed differently.[80] For example, in one campaign memo, it was suggested that "surrogate speakers" be used "before female audiences." As far as topics, it was noted that "among women there is a profound lack of understanding of the concept of revenue sharing. . . . The philosophic underpinnings of revenue sharing dovetail neatly with the female expectation that, governmental power should, in many instances, be focused at the local level. . . . The process of edification may necessarily be more detailed but must not fail to correct the obvious dichotomy of male/female understanding." In addition, "women also express a significantly lower understanding of issues related to foreign affairs."[81]

Rita Hauser had tried before to educate the White House staff as to this potentially powerful constituency. In the spring of 1971, Hauser had submitted a memorandum to the president on "Emergent Responsible Feminism—Why We Are Missing the Boat for 1972." Hauser's memo had provoked a great deal of discussion in the White House. Hauser recommended that the president hold a "rap session" with "women of different walks of life" to "learn why they feel as they do on key issues" such as "sex discrimination in employment, housing and public places," tax laws, abortion, and federally sponsored day care centers.[82] While the idea of a "rap session" was soundly rejected by the president's all-male inner circle of advisors, the memo did create a dialogue.

Harry S. Dent, special counsel to the president, suggested that if there is a meeting that

> we lean toward . . . average women in America—Mrs. Middle America, Mrs. Housewife, Mrs. Secretary, Mrs. Nurse, Mrs. Teacher. We would want to include . . . some key women leaders in the country, but . . . if we get too far out front with this matter we may wind up with another long list of demands being made to liberate all the women in the country. . . . It would be good to have some women come out of that meeting saying we don't favor the women's lib movement and that we think the Nixon administration is doing a great job for all the people and that's how we wanted to be treated, just like anybody else.[83]

The suggestion of a "rap session" prompted Fred Malek to respond: "We're put into a 'can't win' position. On the one hand, a truly representative sample of today's women should probably include some of the more vocal and militant ones, but if they are involved, I think we run the risk of embarrassing the President. On the other hand, if we put together a 'safe' group, it will look contrived and would be interpreted by the press and others as a public relations gimmick."[84]

Malek, regarded as a trouble-shooter in the White House, was right on target when he identified the problem of the administration in responding to women.[85]

> [W]hat we really need is a well thought out, well coordinated and well executed program to deal with the major issues of concern to women. Currently, we appear to be dealing with these issues in a piecemeal fashion—the White House is spearheading the top-level recruiting effort, Justice is handling the Equal Rights Amendment, HEW is dealing with day care programs, and the Women's Bureau at Labor disseminates information, etc. It's time—given the growing concern and restlessness of women across the country, plus the upcoming 1972 election—to deal with these issues in an integrated way.[86]

Charles Colson tried to give support to Hauser's second point, which recommended the creation of a White House office for women's affairs. This office would have helped fill the needs suggested by Malek. Colson observed that he had been trying for the past eighteen months to have a special assistant to the president for women's affairs be designated. The position, he argued, could be established merely by defining a set of responsibilities for an existing appointee. He noted that in 1970 "we were about to name a woman to this position but the idea was killed at the last moment."[87]

Director of Communications Herb Klein outlined for the president the potential impact of the vote of women in 1972, stating that since "more women than men vote in Presidential elections, it becomes especially important that we zero in on the issues of particular interest to women voters this year."[88] Klein noted the skepticism that greeted the administration's announcement of its efforts to recruit women, and he also endorsed the suggestion of a White House advisor on women's affairs:

> [I]t is essential that we pinpoint responsibility and coordinate our efforts on the women's issues. As far as I know, there is no one at the White House assigned to think in terms of issues of special relevance to women.
>
> At the very least, someone on the domestic staff perhaps, should be specializing in this general area. My personal recommendation would be that Pat Hitt be brought to the White House as Counselor to the President. She is probably more familiar with issues involving women than anyone in the Administration. The President knows and respects her and this is widely known so it would appear less political.

.... The key is ... coordination of administration activities on issues of interest to women. ... my office would work closely with whomever is designated to handle the substantive issues to ensure that we get maximum mileage in the press.[89]

The administration's efforts regarding women, however, continued to focus on appointments. For instance, Robert H. Finch and H. R. Haldeman, a former advertising executive, presented a plan to the president for "Enhancing the Role of Women in the Administration." According to Finch, "To really make a difference in the minds of women voters, we must do much better and will need to focus on high level, visible appointments."[90] Fred Malek was given the task of doubling the number of women in high-level posts, from twenty-six to fifty-two. Barbara Franklin was brought into the White House in April, 1971, as staff assistant for executive manpower, to work full time on recruiting women and to provide "visible leadership to the effort."[91] The president sent a directive to the heads of executive departments and agencies to develop and implement action plans, i.e., "affirmative action," to bring more women into high-level positions in the government and report monthly to Finch or Donald Rumsfeld on the progress made. In addition to a publicity campaign to promote the achievement of these goals, Finch also planned to have the Civil Service Commission establish a program whereby professional women could work part time.[92] Nixon found the plan to be "excellent," but he "seriously doubt[ed] if jobs in government for women make many votes from women"(see Box 4.5).[93]

A timetable was set outlining a plan of action for the administration to take in promoting women. First, Nixon would sign the memo with "no direct White House publicity at this point," followed by a press briefing by Franklin several days later, with Franklin then working on outreach to women's groups. Anne Armstrong, co-chair of the RNC, was then to follow up with mailings to women's publications, with announcements made of women appointments.

Promoting Women

In carrying out this public relations campaign, the president, with a press pool and photographers present, appeared with four women in the Oval Office on April 29 to announce their respective appointments to high-level posts in the administration. Jayne B. Spain was nominated as commissioner and vice chairman of the Civil Service Commission; a career civil servant, Dr. Valerija Raulinaitis was named director of a veterans' administration

BOX 4.5
Affirmative Action

In this Administration we have firmly espoused the rights of women, and we must now clearly demonstrate our recognition of the equality of women by making greater use of their skills in high level positions.
. . .

To this end, I am now directing that you take the following actions:
— Develop and put into action a plan for attracting more qualified women to top appointive positions (GS-16 and up through Presidential appointees) in your Department or Agency by the end of this calendar year. This plan should be submitted to me by May 15.

— Develop and put into action by May 15 a plan for significantly increasing the number of women, career and appointive, in mid-level positions (GS-13 to 15). This plan should directly involve your top personnel official.

— Ensure that substantial numbers of the vacancies on your Advisory Boards and Committees are filled with well-qualified women.

— Designate an overall coordinator who will be held responsible for the success of this project. Please provide this name to me by May 15.

I have asked my Special Assistant, Fred Malek, to meet with each of you individually to review further the requirements of this project and to offer his assistance in locating highly qualified women candidates for top positions.

Source: *"Memorandum About Women in Government," April 21, 1971, pp. 580–81, Public Papers of Nixon.*

hospital, the first woman to hold such a post; and Vicki Keller and Sallyanne Payton were appointed associates on the Domestic Council. With the press present, Nixon "told the women he was impressed with their backgrounds, and said it was clear they had been chosen because of their qualifications and not because they were women." After the press had left, the president told the women that "a woman should retain her femininity at the same time she demonstrates her competence on the job. . . . [and] hoped the group would attract other women to serve in government posts and would help keep his Administration sensitive and responsive to issues of concern to women."[94]

President Nixon regularly held an "Open Door Hour" in which he met briefly with individuals for the purpose of a photo op and a brief exchange of pleasantries, making a presentation of bow pins, tie clips, or paperweights. These sessions became an additional way to publicize the women in his administration. For instance, following his directive to departments and agencies, the president met with Ann Ucello, director of consumer affairs in the Department of Transportation and Mary Lou Grier, a member of the National Advisory Council of the Small Business Administration. Even though these women were not presidential appointees, the president's staff arranged for them to meet with the president since his "greeting of the two women will serve to show . . . your interest in involving women at the high levels of the Administration."[95] Although the posts held by these women could hardly be considered "high-level positions," the five-minute meeting in the Oval Office served its purpose.[96] Nixon deftly ended the meeting by ushering the women into the Rose Garden for a special tour, which left a favorable impression on the women.[97]

With department and agency compliance, the White House was able to gather data on appointments of women at the GS-16 level and above. Lists of those women serving in the administration were then released to the press, along with comparison data of how the Nixon administration had surpassed the Kennedy and Johnson administrations in its inclusion of women in high-level posts (see Table 4.1).[98]

The White House public relations campaign got off to a good start. However, as often seemed to be the case in this administration with its large staff, there soon were conflicting priorities and a change in emphasis. For in-

TABLE 4.1
Comparisons between Administrations

Women in high level Executive branch positions (GS 16 and above):		
Nixon Administration	*Johnson Administration*	*Kennedy Administration*
2 1/4 years	6 years	2 1/2 years
27	27	18

Women appointed to Presidential Advisory Boards and Committees:		
Nixon Administration	*Johnson Administration*	*Kennedy Administration*
223	238	145

Source: "Notice to the President," April 21, 1971, "April 22" folder, White House Press Releases 4/21/71–5/31/71, Box 19, Nixon Presidential Materials.

stance, during the summer of 1971, Nixon decided on a new direction for his campaign. He now directed his personnel recruiters "to place the highest priority on Blacks and Chicanos."[99] Both groups were among those targeted by the president's re-election campaign.[100] This shift in priority is reflected in a speech given by Barbara Franklin, shortly thereafter, to members of the NFBPWC who were attending their July, 1971, convention in Cleveland. In the original draft of the speech, Franklin outlined recent prominent appointments of women made by the president, including Catherine May Bedell, first woman to chair the U.S. Tariff Commission; Charlotte Reid, first woman commissioner of the FCC since 1948; Dr. Valerija Raullinaitis; and Jayne B. Spain, all of whom had met with the president. With the president's sudden emphasis on the recruitment of African Americans and Hispanics, Franklin penciled in several additional names that not only identified women, but *black* women in the administration.[101] In addition, where the text in the speech previously had read "women," insertions were made to refer to "black women," or "women—all women, be they *black* or white," or "women, *whatever their color*" (emphasis added). Where the original text acknowledged the work of the NFBPWC in organizing a "talent bank committee" and its source "of potential candidates," and asked for them to continue to add names to the talent bank and let her know of "outstanding women," the revised text asked for help of a more specific nature: "I have come here to ask you—directly and specifically—for your help in recruiting black women. You can help me by doing three things: (1) get as many names of outstanding black women you know into the talent bank as soon as possible; (2) be on the lookout for outstanding black women, and let me know who they are as soon as you spot them; and (3) suggest to me as soon as possible any other sources of outstanding black women I could tap."[102]

The Talent Bank

By 1971 the White House had so completely embraced use of the talent bank established by the NFBPWC that Barbara Franklin, who had only been in the White House for three months, claimed it as her own project. Given the complaints from Republican Party women the year before, usurpation of the name and function was one way of taking advantage of the talent bank without alienating Republican women, especially given the upcoming election.

In her speech to the NFBPWC, Franklin described her approach to the recruitment of women as follows:

I have divided the country into ten regions. I am going into each one, setting up a network of source contacts—women's groups, community leaders—who can lead me to outstanding women. . . . At the same time, I am building a talent bank of top women in my office. It is my hope that as high-level vacancies occur, I can search my talent bank and my source network, and come up with a number of qualified women very quickly. Then, I'll make sure those women are considered for the positions—and hopefully, that they are placed.

Needless to say, I cannot do this alone. And I haven't been. I know you are part of the Talent Bank Committee organized by the National Federation of Business and Professional Women's Clubs. You deserve a great deal of credit for your support of these good efforts.[103]

In the fall of 1971, Franklin aggressively sought out the names of women to include in "her" talent bank. She reached out to the academic community and wrote to representatives of various organizations and associations, such as the National Association of Manufacturers, seeking out names.[104] Given the talent bank operation begun by the NFBPWC, the use of the term "talent bank" was confusing to others in the administration and to those outside government.[105]

Franklin also tried to enhance the public's awareness of the administration's efforts regarding the inclusion of women by making the most of the president's speeches and public appearances. She recommended that the president's 1972 State of the Union Address include a passage addressing equal opportunity for women, including endorsement of the ERA, a statement on the progress made by the administration in appointing women, and action taken by departments and agencies to force compliance with equal opportunity regulations.[106] The speech the president delivered before the Joint Session of Congress, however, made no mention of women. The expanded written text sent to Congress included a section on "Equal Rights for Women," but not a section endorsing the ERA (which would soon be approved by Congress). The text, however, included Nixon's interest in expanding the jurisdiction of the Civil Rights Commission to have "strong enforcement of equal employment opportunity for women under Title VII of the Civil Rights Act."

During 1972, an election year, Franklin had wanted to mark the one-year anniversary of two actions Nixon had taken in 1971 to advance the role of women in the federal government: (1) his issuing of a directive to department and agency heads to move forward in implementing his affirmative action directive of 1969, and (2) the appointments he had made of Barbara Franklin to recruit women political appointees and of Jayne Spain to guarantee equal employment opportunity for career women in the civil service.[107] Instead of an Oval Office meeting with the president, which she had sought, the White House press secretary issued a statement outlining these accomplishments. Franklin was, furthermore, directed to "find a way to get this out without the President's involvement."[108] As a result, Franklin had a "Fact Sheet: Women in the Federal Government" released[109]; and she and Spain, joined by other women in the administration, held a press conference at the White House.[110] The president and his advisors had the opportunity to take credit, but the issue of women was not of such priority to move the issue to the active agenda.

Changing the National Policy Agenda

As had become the pattern in the 1960s, the administration kept a close count on the number of women appointed by the president and in high-level positions in the civil service. Here, as in other instances, Franklin identified the number of appointments her office could take credit for.[111]

While the administration's public relations efforts focused on the numbers of women appointed, the substantive policy changes with direct impact on women received little attention, either in administration efforts to promote the president's actions regarding women, or by the press. For example, the following are among the achievements of the Nixon administration which have had a lasting impact, yet rarely are associated with this administration:

1. Nixon's executive order issued in 1969 to prohibit discrimination on the basis of sex in the federal government
2. The secretary of labor's guidelines issued in December, 1971, which required all federal government contractors to have affirmative action plans to hire and promote women
3. The Equal Opportunity Act signed by Nixon in March, 1972, which gave the EEOC the power to use the courts to enforce civil rights laws prohibiting discrimination against women; in addition the jurisdiction of the Civil Rights Commission was expanded to include sex discrimination.
4. The "Higher Education Amendments of 1972" (PL 92-318) signed by Nixon on June 23, 1972, which included in Title IX, provisions to end federal funding to any educational institution discriminating on the basis of sex

5. Provisions in the 1971 Revenue Act signed into law by Nixon, allowing for tax deductions for child care.[112]

While the administration could not take credit for all of these changes, they all had the support of the administration. Sorting out the extent of support and White House involvement vis-à-vis Congress and outside interests, as well as departments and agencies, remains a task for other scholars to pursue. At this point in time, in the area of civil rights the focus of the administration was on desegregation of schools and the use of busing to achieve that goal.[113] In addition, the ERA dominated the women's agenda, and so actions taken to enforce existing statutes received far less attention, both in the administration, and by women's organizations.

Interest in "women's rights" was just emerging on the national agenda. Between 1969 and 1972 there was a dramatic jump in the percentage of women willing to vote for a woman for president.[114] Although NOW had been organized in 1966, it took several years before its membership grew substantially; the organization lacked the numbers and thus the authority and legitimacy to gain immediate sustained media attention. The term "women's liberation" did not become widely used until 1971. However, the issue of women's rights was nonpartisan at this point in time as well, thus women's rights was becoming an important issue, but not one that divided the parties as of yet, or had been claimed by either party.[115]

Little noticed were the administration's efforts to increase the number of women in the military, which also began in 1971. For the all-volunteer service Nixon envisioned to be viable, women would need to be a significant part of the armed services. When the right wing of the Republican Party led by Phyllis Schlafly began to fight the ERA, invoking fears of women being drafted, the administration's silence perhaps inadvertently let both the drive for the ERA and expansion of the numbers and role of women in the armed forces move forward.

While the identification of women appointed in the administration received prompt attention from the departments and agencies, with the White House publishing these figures and promoting media coverage of these women, the "action plans to attract and place more women in top and middle management positions in the Federal Government" were more slow in coming, with little to show by the end of 1971.[116] In fact, the White House staff appeared to take a united, but defensive stance, in regard to the action taken to implement affirmative action within the federal government (see Box 4.6 for two administration letters).

Administration Women and the 1972 Campaign

Many of Franklin's activities were directed toward the president's gaining the support of women in the electorate in 1972. For instance, Franklin assisted the campaign by compiling a briefing book on "women's issues," which was given to Julie Eisenhower, the president's daughter, for use in preparation for campaign appearances.[117] In the networking that has been a hallmark of women's growing inclusion in administrations over time, Franklin sent letters of congratulation to newly elected presidents of women organizations.[118] Throughout 1972 she sent mailings to various women's organizations updating the number of women appointed in the Nixon administration. However, Franklin's role was more that of support staff than decision maker. For instance, in January, 1972, departments and agencies had "to set goals for the placement of women in high-level positions during 1972" and report back to the president's key advisors. Franklin was not involved in this process, although she volunteered her services.[119]

BOX 4.6

The Administration's Response to Affirmative Action

HERBERT G. KLEIN, DIRECTOR OF COMMUNICATIONS, TO LIANNE B. RIDENOUR, *THE FAYETTEVILLE OBSERVER*, NOV. 10, 1971

I am aware of the request for copies of the "plans" directed by the President and want to assure you that these will be made available. The problem is one of the definition of the word "plans." These have been in the form of working files—exchanges of memoranda, notes, telephone conversations, and so forth which are meaningful to the persons working on them but not necessarily self-explanatory. This is a result of the President's commitment to a strong program and the fact that some of the preliminary departmental plans have been supplemented and made more effective through White House pressure.

. . . You may be sure we have your hope that soon the names of women in high-level government positions will be so commonplace as not to make special news. This is certainly the President's goal.

Source: "[GEN] HU 2-5 Women 10/1/71–12/31/71" folder, WHCF, Subject Files, HU, Box 22, Nixon Presidential Materials.

BOX 4.6, *continued*
FREDERIC V. MALEK TO PAUL FISHER, FREEDOM OF INFORMATION CENTER, NOV. 15, 1971

As you know, the plans mentioned in the President's memorandum [April 21, 1971] fall into two categories. First, proposed plans for attracting more qualified women to top appointive positions ... were to be submitted to the President so that programs could be developed and put into action by the end of the year. . . . However, these plans and recommendations are not yet final, and my office is now in the process of formulating a final plan with representatives of the Departments and Agencies involved.

Since all the materials so submitted are working papers and preliminary exchanges of ideas within the Executive Branch, and are not yet final programs to be implemented, it would be inappropriate for them to be released at this time. Additionally, as you are aware, the Departments and Agencies involved are not required to release such recommendations and proposals, by virtue of the fifth exemption of the Freedom of Information Act (5 USC 552(b)(5)).

However, when finalized, these plans will, of course, be made available.

The other plans which you have requested are those to be formulated to significantly increase the number of women, career and appointive, in mid-level position. . . . The Civil Service Commission is monitoring this aspect ... and Ms. Spain will respond in a separate letter.

Source: "[GEN] HU 2-5 Women 10/1/71–12/31/71" folder, WHCF, Subject Files, HU, Box 22, Nixon Presidential Materials.

As a part of the 1972 campaign effort, "The Women's Surrogate Program" was created.[120] Teams of administration women campaigned across the country, generating favorable press coverage. The "Surrogates" included the wives of key White House advisors, such as Jeanne Ehrlichman and Joyce Rumsfeld; the wives of cabinet secretaries, such as Mary E. Butz, Anne Richardson, Lenore Romney, Marie Hodgson, and Marnie Kleindienst; as well as women appointees in the administration, such as Pat Reilly Hitt, Helen D. Bentley, Barbara Franklin, and Virginia Knauer.[121] All the women in the administration were evaluated for their efforts in the campaign, with regular notes

BOX 4.7

The Women's Surrogate Program

Evaluation:

Helen Bentley, Chair, Federal Maritime Commission: "Outstanding Effort. Scheduled heavily and participated in the flying squad—she has worked hard for months to get the administration's story to the people."

Virginia Allan, Deputy Assistant Secretary for Public Affairs, State Department: "Adequate effort. Had little staff or Department support and is relatively new to the job at Department of State. Is most effective with women's groups which limited her scope."

Elizabeth Hanford, Deputy Director, Office of Consumer Affairs, White House: "Outstanding effort. Was heavily scheduled and was always looking for more events. If an appearance fell through she worked on getting another. Made a strong contribution while assuming a major portion of the responsibility for the day to day operations of the Office of Consumer Affairs in Virginia Knauer's absence."

Nancy Hanks, Chair, National Endowment for the Arts: "showed no interest in participating."

Jayne Baker Spain, Vice Chair, Civil Service Commission: "Disappointing effort. Spent 5 days in Australia in September and 14 days in Europe in October."

Ethel Bent Walsh, EEOC Commissioner: "Adequate effort. Wanted to do more but demands of her job kept her busy a good deal of the time."[123]

made of their contributions, level of participation, and consequent media coverage. By the end of the campaign a detailed report noted that in the ten weeks before the election, "27 women surrogates made 373 appearances in 39 states" (see Box 4.7).[122]

In his landslide win Nixon had nearly equal support from women and men.

A PLACE IN THE WHITE HOUSE

After the elections, the battle for ratification of the ERA slowly gained intensity. The president, whose own party would eventually lead the fight against the amendment, could, however, stay above the fray. The president has no role in the amendment process, except the use of the bully pulpit in a campaign of moral suasion. The same had been true more than fifty years earlier when the Nineteenth Amendment for women's suffrage was submitted to the states during the Wilson administration. And the issue was ratification of the amendment—a decision to be made by each state. Given Nixon's programs of "new federalism" he would let the states decide. This strategy avoided the internecine battles that would plague his own party in the next two decades.

By December, 1972, a wide range of interest groups had begun lobbying on behalf of candidates for the new administration, both male and female and of various ethnic and racial backgrounds. Included in this deluge of requests were telegrams sent by women's organizations urging the appointment of a woman to the cabinet in the new administration.[124]

During the 1972 campaign Anne Armstrong had served as co-chair of the RNC with Senator Bob Dole and in that role began her work with the Nixon administration.[125] Armstrong's major focus as party co-chair was on the newly enfranchised 18–20 year olds and on women, primarily in increasing the number of women in high-level posts in the administration. Therefore, Armstrong worked with the White House Personnel Office on a daily basis.[126]

Counsellor to the President

After the election, Nixon named Anne Armstrong a counsellor to the president with cabinet rank.[127] Armstrong also received an office in the West Wing, between the offices of John Ehrlichman and Roy Ash (director of Office of Management and Budget or OMB).[128] Although Armstrong referred to herself as a member of President Nixon's cabinet in some correspondence as she was settling into her post,[129] cabinet rank did not give her a salary equal that of the other cabinet members.[130]

Armstrong had begun her political career working for Harry S Truman's election while a student at Vassar. By 1952, she had joined the Republican Party and campaigned for Eisenhower in the first election in Texas carried by a Republican presidential candidate. Armstrong's political career took the path of a number of Republican women in the 1950s and 1960s. She began work in the party at the precinct level, moved into the state party leadership, was selected as a Republican National Committeewoman, and then became co-chair of the RNC in 1971.

Armstrong has cited the role of Republican Party leaders in Texas such as George Bush and John Tower in opening up opportunities for women.

She has recounted how the Democratic and Republican Parties differed in Texas. The Republican Party was

in striking contrast to the Democratic party in Texas where women were and, I think still are shut out from policy-making roles. I will never forget a debate I had back in 1964 with Sissy Farenthold when she pointed out that we were both treated differently in our respective parties. At that time I was a delegate and had served on the platform committee at the Republican National Convention. Sissy had been manning telephones for the Democrats that year. Sissy remarked that as long as she had worked in the Democratic Party she never really had access to it. She has since said that she was nominated for Vice President last year not because of her work in the party but because of her leadership of the National Women's Political Caucus.[131]

Just as Esther Peterson had a number of posts, Anne Armstrong also was given a number of responsibilities: she was a member of the White House Domestic Council; was a member of the Committee on the Economic Role of Women; was in charge of the nation's bicentennial celebration planning, the New Federalism initiative, and the status of the ratification process of the ERA; and was the White House representative to Spanish-speaking Americans.[132] Armstrong's role as a member of the president's cabinet enabled Nixon to cite the record of the two Republican administrations, Eisenhower and Nixon, and their respective appointments of Oveta Culp Hobby and Anne Armstrong, in contrast to the Democratic administrations of Kennedy and Johnson, in which no women served in the cabinet. While Armstrong was showcased as a symbol of the representation of women in the administration, she did not see her role in that manner. This is most evident, for example, in the list of potential speech topics for the president that she prepared when requested to do so. The topics she outlined were: the bicentennial, the economy, energy, equal opportunity for minorities, housing, youth, and senior citizens. There was no mention of women.[133] As counsellor to the president, Armstrong's correspondence thus reflected a wide range of issues. In addition, as a Texan with significant interests in ranching, she also fielded constituent queries from her home state and congressional correspondence about such issues as the beef industry.

Armstrong brought a new perspective to White House deliberations, which was important both in terms of ensuring that names of women were included on lists of candidates for vacant positions in the administration and that issues of concern to women were brought to the table. Armstrong's role in shaping administration policy was, therefore, particularly important in moving new issues onto the national agenda. For example, when Caspar Weinberger, secretary of HEW, outlined a national health insurance proposal, Armstrong worked to ensure that yearly physical exams for women be included, since yearly pap smears and breast examination for cancer had become a standard recommendation of the health community.[134]

Early in Nixon's second term, Armstrong aggressively pushed for the consideration and appointment of women to high-level posts in the administration. For example, she pressed Ron Ziegler to consider the promotion of Virginia Allan, deputy assistant secretary for public affairs at the State Department for the post of assistant secretary for public affairs. In urging her appointment, Armstrong noted she was "highly respected by the solid national women's organizations,"[135] and, moreover, she had chaired the president's task force on women's rights and responsibilities early in Nixon's first term. Armstrong and Franklin developed a network by and for women. Franklin would send a name to the appropriate office for consideration, and then Armstrong would contact that office and say she learned of the recommendation and urged that it be acted upon.

The addition of Armstrong to the president's White House staff strengthened the attention given to women and women's issues. In his 1974 annual message to Congress on the state of the union, a considerable passage was devoted to "the Rights of Women," addressing issues of discrimination, ratification of the ERA, and enforcement of equal employment laws. In addition, the president noted the role of his administration in "leading by example—by insisting on equal employment and promotion opportunities within the Federal service, by promoting more women into the professionally critical areas of middle management and by continuing our special recruiting drive to bring more women into the highest levels of government."[136] While noting the firsts of his administration concerning women—the first woman counsellor to the president, creating a new Office of Women's Programs (OWP) in the EOP, the increased number of women heading agencies—Nixon also added to his legislative agenda support for legislation that would end discrimination which "denies women equal access to credit."[137] And, in the president's annual economic report to the Congress, Nixon noted, "We must push forward, as we have been doing, to remove barriers against the entry of women and minorities into any occupation and against their maximum training and advancement. The men and women of the country are its greatest economic resource. To fail to use any of this resource to its full potential is a serious loss to us all."[138]

Armstrong also had access to the president and was able to meet with him to review candidates for positions and update him on her work.[139] The impact of Watergate on the staff structure of the White House and thus the influence of any one advisor to the president in setting domestic policy is an area needing closer examination. Whether Armstrong's presence and influence would have been as strong or perhaps stronger, without the dismantling of the White House organization and president's distraction from domestic policy as events of the Watergate investigation unfolded, is a question for others to address.

One other change that came about when Armstrong came on board was that women who worked in the White House Executive Office Building Complex finally gained access to the White House gym and health facility when then-Chief of Staff Alexander Haig approved the change in September, 1973. Once some modifications were made in the facilities, the women were allowed to work out between the hours of 8:00 A.M. and 11:30 A.M. Armstrong noted in a memo to Haig's assistant that "we will probably have to divide the week so that women members could use the facility on certain days according to the first letter of their last names," pointedly noting that the two-and-a-half-hour time slot, during normal working hours, would not be sufficient![140]

Armstrong outright refused to have her office take on extra administrative tasks in order for women to gain access to the gym, and she let Haig's office know this in no uncertain terms:

In talking to Chuck Wardell last week a member of my staff, Mrs. Vera Hirschberg, learned that you were not inclined to administer the women's health unit membership fund in the same way that you administer the male membership fund. I would like to recommend that you administer the women's health unit in the same way that you handle those arrangements for men. I feel strongly that what we are talking about is really not just a question of separate but equal status for women—i.e. the gift of unused time—but the principle of true equal opportunity and equal rights for women.

Women could very well have their own separate organization with officers, as I understand the men have, but the administration of the women's group should be done as is the men's group—through your office.

Waddell said the facility could be ready for women in a little over a month. When this announcement is finally made, it could result in some amusing and favorable media publicity. But as you know, the press will very likely discover quickly any cases of unequal treatment.[141]

White House Office of Women's Programs

Shortly after Armstrong was appointed counsellor to the president, she established the first White House OWP. Barbara Franklin was appointed to the new Consumer Products Safety Commission (CPSC), and left the White House.[142] The ad hoc nature by which women had been a part of the White House Office was soon to change, and Armstrong, with cabinet rank, was able to expedite that process. Rather than having an intermediary between the White House recruiter for women and the president, as had been the case with Franklin, Armstrong herself had more direct access to Nixon.[143]

Jill Ruckelshaus was appointed Assistant to the Counsellor to the President for Women's Programs and Vera Hirschberg was named Director of Women's Programs. The office initially had six tasks:

1. Consulting and cooperating with federal departments and agencies on their plans for the advancement of women
2. Providing information and counseling to the public on matters of discrimination on the basis of sex and information on the laws that aim to eliminate such discrimination
3. Acting as a liaison with national women's groups on matters of mutual concern
4. Communicating to the public the programs of the federal government to advance women in the economy
5. Channeling individuals' and groups' sex discrimination complaints and suggestions on how to deal with them to the proper government agencies
6. Providing information to Mrs. Armstrong as a spokeswoman for issues of concern to women[144]

One of the first tasks given this new office was to compile a list of all major federal laws and regulations in effect regarding sex discrimination, including executive orders, directives, and statutes. This list was updated as needed, and became a way for the president and White House staff to begin to monitor enforcement of sex discrimination laws already on the books and take action and be responsive to the concerns of women, at a time when the ratification process for the ERA was well under way.[145]

Some of the accomplishments claimed by the OWP during President Nixon's truncated second term included:

- the provision of "information, advice, and clarification to individuals and groups on such issues as the Equal Rights Amendment, day care, Federal aid for grants, and affirmative action plans";
- monitoring the "progress Federal Government agencies are making in their affirmative action plans in hiring, training, and promoting more women," [required in the 1972 Equal Employment Opportunity Act]; [and]
- Anne Armstrong and Jayne Spain, Vice Chairman of the Civil Service Commission visiting the heads of agencies to "check first hand on progress within the government on the hiring and promotion of women," and "to urge them to appoint more women to top and mid-level government jobs."[146]

As the Nixon administration was inexorably coming to its premature end, Armstrong's office was preparing for the work that lay ahead. Jill Ruckelshaus had left the office in March, 1974. In June Pat Lindh was appointed Special Assistant to Anne Armstrong for Women's Programs.

The midterm elections were just months away. Early in August, Armstrong was given summaries of public opinion data showing approval levels for Congress and the embittered president as the impeachment proceedings moved forward. She also received information on women running for office compiled from the RNC, National Women's Political Caucus (NWPC), and also Congressional Quarterly. And, as part of the political activities of her office, it was expected that the month of August would see "increased involvement in the fall campaigns including the development of detailed background information for the dozen states . . . [with] primaries during the next five weeks. Increased contact with state party officials and RNC personnel and . . . identification of contests where . . . [Armstrong's] personal involvement . . . [was] desirable and advantageous."[147]

While action in the White House would be briefly interrupted by Nixon's resignation on August 9, 1974, the work of the presidency would go forward.

Institutionalizing Change

While the Nixon administration would both respond to the growing women's movement and help shape the direction of that movement, vestiges of the past would remain. For instance, in his *Public Papers*, President Nixon is listed as giving "Remarks at a Reception for the Association of American Foreign Service Women" on March 13, 1973.[148] He appeared at the reception to show his appreciation for the

> many unsung heroines. They are the wives of our Foreign Service at all levels who do the job of the entertaining and all that sort of thing, which, to me, would be the most difficult of all—you may have to eat with somebody you don't particularly care for . . . but in addition to that, who go out and engage in these volunteer activities, volunteer activities working with the local people, communicating with them in a way that sometimes their husbands really can't do. And for this we are very grateful.[149]

Rather than women foreign service officers, of which there were only a handful at the time, spouses, always "wives," would be singled out for special recognition.[150] It would take another decade or two for any appreciable numbers of administration "spouses" to consistently include both husbands and wives, and for career couples to come to Washington, with both partners serving in government.[151]

The pace of change in government mirrors a slow and evolving movement in society to broaden the role of women. The 1960s marked the first in a series of decades that would slowly see the transformation of women's role in society and in government. By 1969 organized efforts by outside groups began to exert pressure on the White House for the appointment of women to high-level positions in the administration. In the Nixon administration, since there were few women appointed, the civil service continued to be a focus of administration efforts, as it had been during the Kennedy and Johnson administrations.[152] In fact, this followed the recommendations of the PCSW, and reflected earlier reports on the subject. Once women were in government they would become part of a pool from which presidents could draw on for appointments. Not until 1972 did data on the numbers of women and men by grade level in the civil service begin to be systematically recorded, now required by statute, thus providing a mechanism by which to monitor affirmative action efforts.

One area that had received extensive consideration by Kennedy's Commission on the Status of Women was the socialization and education of women. In 1972, when Jayne Spain was asked in a press conference, "Will the Civil Service Commission inform high school counselors and colleges of the types of jobs and skills there is most demand in government for so that young people who are interested in a government career can take the training that will help the most?" Spain replied, yes,

> but we have to go all the way back to grade school. This is where girls are conditioned that you don't go into this field or that field because that is a man's field.
>
> In fact, you have to go back to the mothers and fathers of girls and boys who brainwash them from the time they are infants in saying, "No, Mary, you don't play with this nasty boy's toy." It starts there. We have to stop the brainwashing and say, "you should do whatever you most like to do because wherever you have the best aptitude that is the field you ought to go into."[153]

Spain was sensitive to budget cuts in the administration that reduced the number of training programs for career civil servants, thus limiting opportunities for career advancement and upward mobility in the civil service. She suggested that women also had to seek out other avenues, if training courses were not available. For example, "If your agency doesn't give you what you would like to have, women in the private sector get it on their own. You go out and get it on your own. There are all kinds of evening courses you can take to better yourselves."[154] Kennedy's Commission on the Status of Women had also considered the alternative career paths taken by women. In the early 1970s, some women viewed their credentials in terms of volunteer activities, others in terms of degrees earned and jobs held. Armstrong, for example, forwarded the resume of a woman who was seeking a position in the administration to the White House Personnel Office that did not list education; rather, the resume consisted of volunteer work done for various community boards and fundraising activities for both community and Republican Party events.[155] (In fact, the questionnaire for the "Talent Bank" asked for marital status, political affiliation, "areas of expertise," and "brief summary of background and experience" in this order. There were no specific spaces for education or occupation.)

The 1970s marked a period of societal transformation. Although the phenomena of women turning down appointments in Washington if it meant uprooting a husband and children to move to Washington remained, women who accepted a position in Washington could begin to find other women to help them in their search for an appropriate position for a husband.[156] For instance, Armstrong pushed the White House Personnel Office to find a position for Assistant Secretary of Commerce Betsy Ancker-Johnson's husband.[157]

CONCLUSION

The Nixon presidency spans the years when the women's movement becomes a powerful force to reckon with. Throughout his presidency, Richard Nixon would be influenced by a changing society in which the role of women would be forever altered. And so the Nixon presidency would be a series of contradictions. One would see John Ehrlichman giving an overview of the president's domestic program to a gathering where the wives of subcabinet members, the wives of White House staff personnel, and the women presidential appointees were all brought together.[158] But one would also see the establishment of affirmative action programs, with a concerted effort to see that women were being hired and promoted. Sometimes the motivation was politics, sometimes public relations, sometimes a sincere effort to utilize the talents of women, but the striking thing is that the Nixon administration felt the need to stay consistently involved with the question of the role of women in government.

The shape of the Executive Office of the President would take on new form with the addition of an office for women's issues. This office would remain a part of the White House organizational apparatus throughout the 1970s. Several other structural devices were put into effect to carry out the administration's program concerning women. For example, Women's Action Programs were established in the departments. In the case of the Department of HEW, early in 1972 an advisory committee on the rights and responsibilities of women was established.[159] John Ehrlichman received status reports from cabinet secretaries, and reports were also sent to Secretary of Labor Hodgson, who chaired the ICSW.

The Nixon administration would also mark the end of an era in which women were absent from the cabinet. The administrations of the 1960s—Kennedy, Johnson, and Nixon—had all failed to appoint a woman to head a department. However, the Nixon administration and Republican Party would provide job opportunities for three women who would later serve in cabinet positions in subsequent Republican administrations: Elizabeth Hanford Dole, Barbara Franklin, and Ann Dore McLaughlin.[160]

CHAPTER 5

The Ford Administration
The ERA Takes Center Stage

THE STABILITY OF THE American political system is most vividly seen in the transition from one administration to the next. This has been true regardless of whether a president has come into office through a landslide win in the electoral college, a win in the electoral college but a loss in the popular vote, succession upon the death of a sitting president, or through the use of the Twenty-fifth Amendment by which an unelected vice president succeeded to the presidency.[1]

At noon on August 9, 1974, Gerald Ford took the oath of office in a ceremony in the East Room of the White House, before a crowd of several hundred people. A decade had passed since a new president, Lyndon Johnson, had taken the oath of office in an unanticipated circumstance. This transfer of power was different. The nation and Ford had been bracing for the impeachment of a president, a rare event in the nation's history.[2] Instead, Richard Nixon had chosen to resign, leading to a smooth, though sudden, transfer of power to his vice president.

Gerald Ford, who said his "life's ambition was to be Speaker of the House," had never sought the highest political office in the nation, instead moving up the leadership ranks in the House of Representatives to the post of minority leader.[3] Ford was the first vice president to be selected under the provisions of the newly ratified Twenty-fifth amendment, when he was named to the post on October 12, 1973, to fill the vacancy caused by Spiro Agnew's resignation. The announcement had been elaborately staged in the East Room, before a national television audience. Ford's "honesty, integrity and candor" won him overwhelming approval in both the House and Senate.[4] That is not to say that Ford's finances, voting record, and especially his views on the powers of the president were not carefully scrutinized by both the House and Senate.

Ford would be the last president in the twentieth century to have had an extensive congressional career before serving in the White House. His immediate predecessors had all served in Congress: Kennedy for six years in the House and eight years in the Senate; Johnson for twelve years in the House and twelve in the Senate; and Nixon for four years in the House and two years in the Senate.

However, unlike Johnson, who had had experience serving as both his party's minority leader and majority leader, Ford had only served as minority leader. In fact, having first been elected in 1948, Ford, in his twenty-five years in the House, had only served for two years under a Republican majority. As a result, this new president would be more used to responding to an agenda than defining an agenda.

A DIFFERENT KIND OF TRANSITION

The White House apparatus had been anticipating a change, with a number of resignations preceding that of President Nixon. Some projects were on hold, awaiting the inevitable transfer of power, but much of government continued. Throughout the month of August, 1974, Anne Armstrong, as counsellor to the president, continued in her efforts to end discrimination against women being hired for the federal workforce. Agencies reported to her on the obstacles faced in hiring women (e.g., Veterans preference worked against women being selected for civil service jobs; the patterns of work experience of many women differed from their male cohorts, and thus were viewed as problematic in the assessment of qualifications).[5]

Without the flexibility of creating a new administration, as a number of Nixon appointees remained in their posts, Ford had decided initially to keep Nixon's cabinet and White House staff pretty much intact.[6] However, while a new president elevated to this high office without an election may leave much of an inherited government in place, change will soon begin to occur in the White House staff and at the cabinet level. In the case of the Ford administration, the "transition [was] officially over," by February 9, 1975, six months after Ford had taken the presidential oath of office. By this time many members of the Nixon White House were gone, replaced with Ford's own people.[7]

With few opportunities initially for women to move into high-level appointive posts, Anne Armstrong and her staff turned attention away from appointments and to the president's policy agenda and legislative initiatives. This is illustrated by the attention given to policy at both the president's meetings with political appointees in August and September, 1974, and the president's meetings with leaders of women's organizations early in September. In fact, at the meeting with women political appointees, Armstrong deflected discussion away from the solicitation of resumes of women, in spite of the president's invitation to those appointees present that they "help him get more women in top positions in government," joking "it's the best way to keep [me] . . . out of the doghouse with Betty [First Lady Betty Ford]."[8] But there were few vacancies to fill. Instead, attention at the meeting centered primarily on the International Women's Year (IWY), veterans' preference in the civil service, and resume writing for women applicants in the civil service (e.g., how to include volunteer experience on the application).

Armstrong seemed to be keenly aware of the political problems which could arise if expectations were set too high that the administration would shortly begin appointing women to high-level positions.[9] Even as she had tried to temper the enthusiasm of the women appointees who had met with Ford with the realities of the situation, she similarly tried to let the president know that creating expectations that cannot be met is a strategy fraught with difficulty.

That same week, Pat Lindh, who had replaced Jill Ruckelshaus earlier that year, also noted in correspondence regarding statistics on women in the administration:

> I wish I could say that they are terrific, but they really aren't, however we aren't pushing statistics so much as round figures.
>
> Our total count, give or take a dozen, for women appointees is about 150. The top appointees number around 50. I believe the percentage is 1.4% or 1.8% of all appointees. Now you can see why we don't talk about the percentages.
>
> The President is really trying to put women in top level positions, but . . . there aren't that many top level women unfortunately, however, he has given us a commitment and we are trying our darndest to fulfill it.[10]

Given the president's invitation to the women in his administration to recommend more women for positions, the push for the recruitment of women was not only followed up by Armstrong's office, but by others in the administration as well.[11] Ford's emphasis prompted members of the cabinet to forward the names and resumes of women for consideration to top-level posts in the administration.[12]

The transition team responded to Ford's interests in seeing that women who ran for office were brought into higher-level positions. The team acquired a list of names of the women running for statewide office in the November elections and identified "some of the unsuccessful candidates" who would be potential "prospects." The emphasis was on women activists in the Republican Party (i.e., those who ran for office, as opposed to the "club women"). The focus on women actively involved in the political process—e.g., as candidates—followed the pattern seen in the early 1960s where those who helped elect the president gained roles in the administration, not those women coming out of the party organization or in national campaign organizations. The changing role of party is a phenomenon most often associated with the growth in the number and importance of primaries in the 1970s. For women, though, this movement to the "doers" as opposed to the "club" party members, to women who sought political office or were active in the campaigns, or were working in Washington, pre-dates the changes usually associated with the reforms of the 1969 McGovern-Fraser Commission, which opened up the party nomination process. But the RNC also provided a career route for women, which was not the case for Democratic women.

The Opportunities for Republican Party Women

In the 1970s the Republican Party provided an opportunity structure for women, which was not the same for Democratic Party women. In the Kennedy and Johnson administrations, the party apparatus had not provided women with a career path into the White House. Rather, the women in the administration had professional careers independent of the party. In contrast, the Republican takeover in 1968 had led to direct opportunities in the White House for women who had been active in the RNC, as was the case with Armstrong, who had not known Nixon prior to her work for the RNC.

Ann Dore McLaughlin, a future secretary of labor in the Reagan administration, began her political career working on Nixon's 1972 re-election campaign and second term inaugural committee. Pat Lindh had begun her party work as Parish (County) chairman of the Republican Party. Later she became vice president of the Louisiana Federation of Republican Women from 1970 to 1974, and vice chairman of the Louisiana State Republican Party. She also served as chairman of the Southern Association of State Vice Chairmen and then served as a Republican National Committeewoman from Louisiana when she moved to the White House in 1974 to begin serving as a special assistant to Armstrong, who was counsellor to the president for women's programs.[13]

When Armstrong left, Lindh then moved to the post of special assistant to the president for women's programs, serving until 1976.[14] However, Lindh did not hold the same rank as Armstrong, or the same rank as a number of others on the White House staff. Lindh would thus not be as successful in promoting the interests of women.[15] Yet, the continuing expansion of the Executive Office of the President throughout the 1970s contributed to an advancement of the role of women in the White House in accordance with the agenda set out by Armstrong and outside organizations.[16]

High-level women in the administration continued to be given more than one role in the administration, following the pattern set by both Esther Peterson in the Kennedy and Johnson administrations and Pat Hitt in the Nixon administration. Peterson had served as both assistant secretary of labor and more broadly as an advisor on women's issues and appointments; Pat Hitt, as assistant secretary of HEW in the Nixon administration played a similar role as advisor. Women in the Ford administration also took on dual roles. For example, Susan Gordon, while serving as assistant secretary for public affairs in the Department of HEW, was asked by the Ford White House to write responses to questions asked of Ford and posed by *The Single Parent* magazine. She was given four days to complete this task, including work over a weekend. She also drafted articles under the by-line of "Jerry Ford" regarding goals and programs for older Americans.

The OWP became institutionalized in the Ford White House, building on the foundation laid by Armstrong and her work in the Nixon White House. In her correspondence, Armstrong routinely explained the White House OWP:

> This office is not a separate bureau or agency—it is a small office staffed by Patricia Lindh, her assistant Karen Keesling, and one secretary.
>
> The purpose of this office is to act as an advocate for progress and change, both in the government and in the private sector; to provide liaison with national women's organizations, and to disseminate information about statutes and regulations dealing with issues of sex discrimination. This office is also responsible for bringing to the attention of the proper authorities highly qualified women candidates for top-level positions in government.[17]

Yet women were but one constituent group. In time, the Ford administration would establish the White House Office of Public Liaison as an outreach to various constituencies, including women.[18]

Counsellor to the President Anne L. Armstrong

Within a week of Ford's taking the oath of office, Armstrong was seeking out his support for a proclamation for Women's Equality Day, August 26 (the fifty-fourth anniversary of women's suffrage). As the proclamation included an endorsement of the ERA, Armstrong was directed by David Gergen, whose office had given editorial clearance to the proclamation, to have the proclamation reviewed by Robert T. (Bob) Hartmann, who was most familiar with the new president's past policy positions.[19] (Hartmann would not only serve as the president's watchdog over policy positions, but would also be a top screener for appointments, weighing each individual's political and professional qualifications.)[20] The proclamation was issued, and Ford called for "states who have not ratified the Equal Rights Amendment to give serious consideration to its ratification and the upholding of our Nation's heritage."[21]

As with others serving in the White House at the time of Nixon's resignation, Armstrong stayed on in her post in the White House as the Ford administration began. The stability of the U.S. political system is often a puzzle to many foreign observers, especially those from the emerging democracies in eastern and central Europe. In 1974, even as the impeachment hearings were proceeding and the country was faced with a potential constitutional crisis, those on the president's staff continued to schedule events. The Nixon presidency moved forward.

As previously noted, early in the Ford administration, Armstrong took the initiative to have women considered for posts that might become vacant in the new administration, although she was keenly aware of the few vacancies available, and to bring together groups of women in the White House. Less than a month after taking the oath of office, President Ford met with representatives of a number of women's organizations including the Interstate Commissions on the Status of Women (ICSW), Federally Employed Women, the NFBPWC, NOW, and the NWPC, as well as the Women's Equity Action League.[22]

In addition, Armstrong organized a series of meetings for the president to meet with the women members of Congress, the top women appointees in his administration, and leaders of the major women's organizations, all within his first month in office.[23] In these meetings Ford affirmed his support for the ERA, the IWY, and the inclusion of more women in high-level posts in his administration. The organizations responded in-kind with follow-up letters suggesting names of women for consideration to high-level posts.[24] In these meetings, Ford also identified legislation concerning women that he had supported.[25] By 1974, there were sufficient numbers of women throughout the executive branch that gatherings of women in government began to be tailored to reflect the women's varying positions and constituent interests, for instance, political appointees or top career civil servants would have separate meetings.

Shortly after the transition, the White House Conference on Women, scheduled for December, 1974, dropped in priority, as meetings with women appointees, other women in government, and women's organizations soon became routinized. Armstrong formed a Women's Advisory Committee to assist her and her office "to obtain guidance and advice from a small group of women leaders in order to set priorities for the Office of Women's Programs from the many ideas exchanged during meetings of women appointees and women's organizations."[26] The members of the advisory committee included the highest-ranking political appointees, including Gwen Anderson, assistant to Counsellor Dean Burch.[27]

These meetings, with both large and small groups of women, centered around efforts to set legislative priorities for the OWP, identify priorities regarding federal regulations and administrative action, set priorities for the IWY Commission, and increase the numbers of women political appointees.[28]

From the meetings organized by Armstrong throughout 1974, the following agenda emerged:

Administrative Action
I. International Women's Year
    A. President's Commission
    B. Activities throughout year
II. Appointment of Women
    A. Full-time Jobs-Cabinet, OMB, Agriculture
    B. Boards, Commissions
    C. Advisory Committees and Delegations
        *Citizens' Advisory Council on the Status of Women
    D. Military Academies
III. Employment of Women
    A. Upward Mobility for Women in Department

B. Task Force to study EEO

C. Awareness Program for Managers
   *Inter-Departmental Committee on Women

D. Presidential Directive to Department Heads

E. Affirmative Action Plans

E. [There are two E's.] Emphasize Mid-Level Positions

F. Revise Standard Form 171 [to include guidelines for women listing volunteer experiences in applying for civil service positions]

G. Veterans Preference

IV. *White House Conference on Women

V. Enforcement of Laws

A. Equal Employment Opportunity for Women

B. Office of Federal Contract Compliance

C. Title IX of the Education Amendments

Legislation and Regulations

I. Abortion

II. Child Abuse

III. Credit

IV. Day Care

V. ERA

VI. Military Academies—Admittance of Women

VII. Sex-role Stereotyping in Education

VIII. Title IX Regulations

IX. Veterans Preference[29]

Many of the efforts made in the policy arena were devoted to enforcing existing statutes and issuing guidelines (e.g., to implement Title IX) and to reviewing existing federal laws to identify those which discriminated on the basis of sex. In addition, the ERA, in the hands of the states, remained on the president's agenda. It was an issue on which Ford made known his support while he served as a member of Congress, and the ERA received public attention not given to other issues on the agenda, although as previously noted, in the amendment and ratification process the president's only role is that of persuasion.

While not all of these issues were addressed during the Ford administration, the administration was relatively successful in increasing the number of women in high-level positions. A greater percentage of appointments had gone to women than ever before, 6 percent, double the percentage of the Nixon administration.[30] In addition, the appointment of Carla Hills to be Ford's secretary of housing and urban development (HUD) marked the first time in twenty years that a woman had been named a cabinet department head.

As counsellor to the president, Armstrong solicited and received a considerable number of names of those women holding at least a GS-16 status in the departments and agencies. In addition, she solicited vacancy notices in the departments and agencies, and among regulatory boards and commissions, to be certain that the names of women, when available, would be considered for these posts, and she was successful in receiving such notices, which she then forwarded to the White House Personnel Office for follow-up.[31]

The Women's Action Organization representing women in the foreign affairs agencies—State, USIA, and AID—used Armstrong's office to intercede on their behalf in getting career foreign affairs agency women included as representatives on U.S. delegations to international conferences and on the staffs of permanent U.S. missions to international agencies. The State Department was under fire from both women and from blacks because of their near absence on U.S. missions to international organizations.[32] Also in 1974, efforts were made by White House aide Stanley Scott to make the EEO office in the State Department an effective organization in identifying and eliminating barriers facing women and minorities in career advancement in the State Department.[33]

The absence of women from international delegations had produced, for example, the ironic situation of having no women from the foreign affairs agencies in attendance at a U.N. conference in Ottawa, which "was charged with drafting a background paper on ending discrimination against women in preparation for the International Women's Year Conference in 1975."[34] The case of Armstrong was emblematic of the concern of the career women in the foreign affairs agencies, i.e., that prominent *women from outside of government service or in other non-foreign affairs* agencies were selected for such delegations, overlooking the professional women in the State Department. Armstrong, who did not serve in the State Department, but rather in the White House, was selected as one of the U.S. delegates to the World Food Conference.[35] Once again, a non-foreign affairs woman was on the delegation.

In spite of Secretary of State Henry Kissinger's expressed concerns to representatives of the Women's Action Organization earlier in the year, "that the Department utilize opportunities to name women to delegations and staffs of international organizations,"[36] and President Ford's own words upon

elevation to the presidency, there had been little progress in advancing toward a greater inclusion of women in international delegations, "but some
actual retrogression in the name of budgeting."[37] At the time, L. Dean Brown,
deputy undersecretary for management, was responsible for both EEO and
budgeting in the State Department.[38] Given conflicting directives from Secretary Henry Kissinger to reduce the size of delegations to save costs, while
increasing the numbers of women on delegations, the latter objective was
sacrificed to the former.[39]

Armstrong's Departure from the White House

While Lyndon Johnson, having come to office so abruptly and in such a
tragic manner, was slow to bring about a change in the advising structure,
waiting until after his winning of the presidency in his own right in a landslide election in 1964, under Ford the White House structure soon began to
evolve into one better suited to his needs. As a part of that reorganization,
Ford accepted the resignation of Armstrong as counsellor to the president
on November 27, 1974.[40] At the time this was perceived as a major loss to the
representation of women's interests in the Ford administration. With the
departure of Armstrong, the Ford administration had no women with cabinet rank. This would be the case for several months until Carla Hills was
named secretary of HUD in February, 1975.

Armstrong had begun a series of White House programs during the Nixon
administration that brought together high-level women in the career civil
service and in politically appointed posts, providing a means to network, as
well as a forum to discuss issues of concern, and an opportunity to hear
from high-level officials in the administration. Two such gatherings took
place before Nixon resigned from office, and the third was scheduled for
December, 1974.[41] Given that this gathering took place just two weeks after
Ford had accepted Armstrong's resignation, the event was perceived as a
farewell to Armstrong. Many of those attending the meeting felt that this
signaled the loss of commitment to issues of concern to women. According
to one of those attending the event, the message from the White House was
that since "'the status of women was only one of about eight special areas
Mrs. Armstrong was involved in, . . . in losing her we were not losing our
only advocate.'" However, "This did not 'jibe with my understanding that
Anne Armstrong was the person at the White House whose primary concern was upgrading women in government.'"[42] The White House itself had
fostered that impression given Armstrong's supervision of Lindh and the
OWP, which had been created under Armstrong's direction.

In fact, when the White House issued a press release in January, 1976, announcing Armstrong's appointment as ambassador to the United Kingdom of Great Britain and Northern Ireland, her work as a liaison to women came near the end of the paragraph summing up her responsibilities in the Ford administration:

> Mrs. Armstrong was named Counsellor to the President in 1973, with Cabinet rank, and served in that capacity until December 1974. She was the first woman to hold that position. As Counsellor to the President, she served as a member of the Domestic Council, the Council on Wage and Price Stability, the Commission on the Organization of Government for the Conduct of Foreign Policy, and as Chairman of the Federal Property Council. She also served as the President's liaison to women, young people, Hispanic Americans, and the American Revolution Bicentennial Administration. Under her direction, the first Office of Women's Programs in the White House was established.[43]

The fears expressed by many attending that meeting, however, were not realized.

The work that Armstrong had begun in creating an OWP under President Nixon became an institutionalized part of the White House apparatus, which would continue through the end of the century, albeit in different forms for different administrations. In the Ford administration, this office established a far greater presence in promoting the interests of women than Armstrong herself could have done, given that women were but one area of responsibility. Lindh, special assistant to the president for women, and Karen Keesling, director of the White House OWP, provided the infrastructure that would allow the work begun under Armstrong to be carried forward. No longer would one woman have the responsibility of being the sole representative of women in the administration, the role that had been played by Esther Peterson, Liz Carpenter, and Pat Hitt, respectively, in the Kennedy, Johnson, and Nixon administrations.

PRESIDENTIAL APPOINTMENTS

The administration was interested in cutting government spending and President Ford had unveiled a plan to attack inflation. With a planned reduction in the size of government, it would be difficult to increase the percentage of women in the administration, yet Ford did make this an early promise in his administration. Armstrong continued on in this area during the three months she remained on the White House payroll.

However, with the transition, the White House Office files concerning resumes of women in the Nixon "Talent Bank" were carted off to the National Archives. The Ford personnel operation had to begin again, and re-solicit resumes to re-create the "Talent Bank."[44] Given the outreach efforts of Armstrong's office in organizing meetings with top women appointees, including brief appearances by the president, the White House soon had a "Women's Talent Search" under way, identifying women leaders in business, education, the corporate world, judicial posts, and other government jobs for possible appointments.[45]

Beverly Splane, who was replacing Barbara Franklin as the administration's recruiter for women, soon began to get the names of women to consider for vacancies throughout the administration from labor and business organizations, the American Bar Association (ABA), and women's groups and from women already working in government. In addition, names were recommended from members of Congress and their spouses. Lindh sent letters to newly appointed women in high-level posts in the administration, and by doing so helped build a network of the women appointed in the administration, while also informing these women of the work of the OWP.[46] The efforts to create a Ford talent bank were well under way.[47]

While the Justice Department's push for civil rights enforcement began in the 1960s for blacks, the department's push for sex discrimination cases would not begin until the 1970s. In contrast, efforts in the White House to identify and recruit women for high-level posts was well under way for women during the Nixon administration, but it is not until 1975 that such a talent search is considered for African Americans.[48] The Nixon and Johnson administrations kept lists of minorities and women appointed in their respective administrations, but the emphasis in these administrations was on counting, rather than on recruiting and seeking out candidates, and having their names and professions readily available when vacancies occur. In the Ford administration, an institutionalized search process to identify and seek out women and minority candidates was well under way within a few months.

Robert T. Hartmann, Counsellor to the President and Ford's closest advisor, served as a clearinghouse for appointments, at least in the first few months of the administration.[49] He wanted to add women and minorities to the administration, but his major concern was in terms of the political benefits that might accrue from an appointment, especially to positions on boards and commissions. For Hartmann, the most exciting candidates under consideration were loyal Republicans.

For example, when a Democratic slot became vacant on the bipartisan Civil Rights Commission, Representative William Hudnut, a Republican from Indiana, recommended Murray Saltzman since the Civil Rights Commission already had two African Americans, one woman, and one Spanish-speaking member. Arthur Fleming, the chair of the commission, had also wanted someone of the Jewish faith since

> one of the areas of Commission concern is religious discrimination [and] no Commission member represents the religious minorities. . . . Congressman Hudnut is particularly interested in this appointment since he has been re-districted into an area with a high Jewish concentration and Saltzman's appointment would serve to neutralize this constituency in Hudnut's favor. . . . While we all feel it would be advantageous to appoint a woman to the Civil Rights Commission, Anne Armstrong, Bill Timmons and I feel that Hudnut deserves our strong help at this time and that Saltzman is an excellent appointment on the religious grounds.[50] Hartmann replied, "I concur if it can be done in time to do Hudnut any good—otherwise I'd favor a woman."[51]

Election Defeat and Political Appointments

While the role of Congress in the presidential appointment process is usually discussed in terms of the "Advice and Consent" role of the Senate,[52] another role for both the House and Senate is as a potential pool from which the president can select appointees to fill his administration. This is particularly true following election defeat of those members of Congress of the same party as the president. As a longtime member and party leader in the House of Representatives who knew many of those defeated in the November elections just three months after his taking the oath of office, Ford had a special interest in finding jobs for his former colleagues. In December, 1974, following the landslide Democratic congressional win in November, Jack Marsh wrote to Bill Walker, noting that "we have need of an 'inventory and status report' on the job placement efforts made by this Administration with regard to defeated and retiring Members of Congress."[53] Given the paucity of women in Congress—only Republican men were defeated—an additional constraint was placed on available slots for women.

As of April, 1975, eleven of the fifty-eight Republican senators and representatives who had either retired or been defeated in the 1974 elections had

been appointed by President Ford "or by officers of the respective Departments" to executive branch positions. In addition the House minority leader
had also appointed a defeated Republican to the Federal Elections Commission.[54]

While lists identifying possible women for appointments were being circulated, on the actual short lists of those being considered for top posts in
the departments few women were identified. Among the exceptions were
two Democrats, Martha Griffiths and Edith Green. Griffiths, recommended
for secretary of HUD, had just retired from a long career in the House and
had been a member of the Michigan congressional delegation with Gerald
Ford. Green had also left Congress of her own volition. Green was a twenty-
year veteran of the House and a conservative Democrat and was interested
in education. The Ford administration considered her for the post of director of the Office of Education or for the position of secretary of HEW, but
the appointment was not made.[55] However, in 1976 Green co-chaired "Democrats for Ford." [56]

Congressional Wives

Another aspect of congressional involvement, perhaps more important at
this particular juncture in history, was the role of congressional spouses.
Given that the Senate was all male, and the House had only nineteen women
in 1975, this discussion will focus on congressional wives. Soon after taking
office, Ford was confronted with the issue of "part-time advisory appointments for congressional wives." Shortly before Ford was inaugurated, the
White House Congressional Relations staff had made a commitment to
Senator Carl Curtis, a Republican from Nebraska with more than forty years
of combined service in the House and Senate, that his wife would be appointed to the National Advisory Council on Education Professions Development. This was in spite of a policy the Nixon administration had had in
place since 1969 that no congressional wives be appointed to part-time advisory positions, "the rationale being that once one such appointment is
made, you would be besieged with requests from the Hill to appoint Congressional wives to one Council or another."[57] In fact, the Congressional
Relations Office was soon "under pressure to appoint Mrs. Hugh Scott and
Mrs. Jacob Javits to advisory positions."[58] Not only did Ford need to decide
whether to support a decision already made by his Congressional Relations
Office, but he also needed to decide on the overall policy position of the
administration in this regard. While the issue was minor, it had serious
implications, with a number of trade-offs:

Congressional wives will give us great patronage with which to obtain votes on the Hill for critical legislation, and . . . there are many Congressional wives who could contribute valuably to appropriate boards and commissions. However . . . by appointing Congressional wives [we are left] . . . open to severe criticism for using such appointments as political tools . . . we run a risk of personally insulting a Member of Congress when we question the qualifications of his wife or refuse her appointment on the basis of qualifications. . . . Most uncomfortable will be choosing between one or more wives requesting the same appointment. There is also the strong likelihood of conflict of interest if a Congressional wife is appointed to a council that must report to or is funded by a legislative committee on which her husband serves or has cast a vote, apart from the general principle of separation of powers between the executive and legislative branches of government.[59]

In this case Ford avoided the recommendation of his congressional relations staff and appointed Mildred M. Curtis to the Advisory Council on Education Professions Development in October, 1974, fulfilling a promise made to a senator.[60]

The Politics of Appointments

In looking at the appointment process, there was a careful accounting in the Ford administration's summary data identifying home states of appointees. Maps of the United States were marked to indicate which states were represented, especially for memberships on large boards and commissions— geographical balance was of some importance. For example, in expanding the membership of the IWY Commission, a map of the United States that listed the current membership of the commission by state went so far as to place members by cities and towns within each state. While presidents, scholars, and journalists have often discussed cabinet appointments in terms of geographic balance, it is not common for a president to discuss appointments made to lower-level positions in the same manner. However, given the limited number of appointments to make with a government already in place, attention was directed to the overall geographic composition of the appointed government. This may also have reflected a strategic concern given that Ford had yet to run in any national election contest. The 1976 election, a contest for states, was near.

However, intra-party factions seemed to be more important regarding appointments made to cabinet and subcabinet posts. That party was more important than other variables, and party was viewed in terms of electoral strategies, is illustrated by Carla Hills. The first woman in the cabinet in almost twenty years (and through three administrations), Hills was identified as a member of the "Finch wing of the California Republican Party," in a listing of characteristics of those individuals under consideration for top positions in the Ford administration.

Appointments also provided an opportunity to cultivate congressional relations as nominees were cleared with representatives and senators in their home state. This was true even in the case of White House interns—courtesy letters were sent to senators and relevant Republican Party officials,[61] after the selection process, to inform them of those interns from their state.

INSTITUTIONALIZING AN OWP IN THE EOP AND THE GROWING INFLUENCE OF WOMEN'S NETWORKS

Following Anne Armstrong's resignation in November, 1974, the OWP was moved under the newly formed Office of Public Liaison, and Pat Lindh had a dual role as both director of a program and staff member under William J. Baroody, Jr., assistant to the president for public liaison.[62]

The outreach activities of the OWP became routinized. Lindh viewed her job as "enhanc[ing] the two-way communication between the Federal Government and the some 300 national women's organizations in the country."[63] She sent a letter to all of those individuals responsible for communications and public affairs in the departments and agencies, asking that an advance copy of any "press release which is of special interest to women, or which has an impact on issues of concern to" women, be given to her office. She noted "this would be of great benefit to me in my efforts to keep the dialogue moving between the Administration and its constituency."[64]

More generally, in mid-1975 Lindh summarized the activities of the OWP as follows:

1. To act as a liaison between the Administration and women and women's organizations in the U.S.

2. To assist in the development of Administration programs and policies for International Women's Year.

3. To facilitate the entry of women into all meetings with non-governmental and governmental groups, i.e., Economic Summit.

4. To reflect the Administration's responsiveness to the elimination of all forms of discrimination on the basis of sex.

5. To work with Departments and Agencies in the formulation of regulations to avoid any semblance of discrimination on the basis of sex.

6. To encourage qualified women to seek top level jobs within the Federal Government.

7. To assist in the preparation of an agenda of needed legislation of interest to women and this Administration.[65]

While legislation had been put in place to end discrimination and provide equal opportunity for women, the enforcement of such provisions took years. During the Nixon administration, the first court cases brought by the Justice Department in the area of sex discrimination began to wend their way through the legal system. Although "sex" had been added to the 1964 Civil Rights Act, the focus of the Justice Department had been in enforcing civil rights in cases involving racial discrimination. The same delay in response would be true once the Education Amendments of 1972 and 1974 were passed. The 1972 amendments (often erroneously referred to as the "Amendments to the 1972 Civil Rights Act") in time would become known as Title IX.

Early in her tenure as director of the OWP, Karen Keesling—a participant herself in women's athletics at Arizona State University—identified the "issuance of the final set of regulations for Title IX of the 'Education Amendments of 1972'" as an area in which the OWP would "eventually become actively involved."[66]

Among the other policy items of concern to the OWP were the following: ratification of the ERA; enforcement of affirmative action plans for educational institutions and private sector employers; the impact of a seniority system versus affirmative action in the workforce; child care; equitable distribution of social security benefits; equitable pension benefits; admittance of women to the service academies; and abortion policies.[67]

Lindh established links to a wide range of women's groups, broader than seen in previous outreach efforts by this or prior administrations. For instance, a newly formed National Women's Advisory Committee, consisting of women elected from each of fifteen locals of the American Federation of Government Employees (an AFL-CIO affiliated union), met with Lindh in the Old Executive Office Building "to open a dialogue between the women of this union" and the OWP.[68] Lindh not only responded to groups contacting the White House, but sought out information on groups which came to her attention. For instance, in a letter to Martha Roundtree, founder of the Leadership Foundation, Inc., Lindh wrote, "As Special Assistant to the

President for Women, I try to maintain a close working relationship with national women's organizations. Could you send me information on the Foundation including a list of officers, convention dates, and resolutions or policy positions passed by members of the Foundation?"[69] Additionally, the NFBPWC helped facilitate the outreach efforts of the OWP by helping to coordinate a meeting between representatives of a number of women's organizations in business (e.g., National Association of Women in Construction, Credit Women International, Future Business Leaders of America, and the American Society of Women Accountants) and representatives from the Departments of Commerce, Labor, HEW, the Small Business Administration, and OMB.[70]

Lindh urged other White House aides to alert her office whenever Ford named a woman to a high-level post in the administration. In a memo to Doug Bennett, director of Presidential Personnel, Lindh noted that

[o]ften some of our most concerned women in the press miss the announcement of the appointment by the President of women to high level positions in his Administration. We attempt to alert them, but our lead-in-time is normally ½ an hour so it is an uphill job to reach all of them in time. Would it be possible to let us know—2 or 3 hours or more before an announcement is made so that we can alert the press women and have them here for Ron's [Nessen] briefing? It would certainly win us some points with the press and serve to publicize the President's commitment to the appointment of women.[71]

Until the Ford administration, it had been a simple task to list all the women in high-level posts, both career and political appointees. By the fall of 1974, the number of women at the rank of GS-16, and located in Washington, D.C., had grown to about 250. Yet the OWP did not have a readily available list of those women when Representative Margaret Heckler asked the White House for one.[72] Lists were soon compiled, however, and efforts began in 1975 to introduce computer technology to help in their compilation. The introduction of such technology helped facilitate the tracking of women and mailing of information to women both in the administration and in outside groups. By the time the Carter administration came into power, mailing labels would be in place to assist in this task.[73]

Under Lindh the OWP also sought to keep "an open and direct line of communication . . . [with] our women appointees."[74] In a most interesting statement, Lindh describes the women appointees as "one of our main constituent groups."[75] Ford sought out greater contact with the departments, but there was never a direct liaison to each department or group of appointees, other than the women appointees. The women were thus perceived as having an additional role—and one distinct from their department responsibilities. As part of the effort to develop political ties between the White House and women appointees, Lindh arranged a meeting of the women appointees in March, 1975, to celebrate the nomination of Carla Hills to be secretary of HUD and provide an opportunity for the senior women in the administration to be briefed by the president's top advisors, especially regarding the White House organizational structure.[76] According to Lindh, this was an effort designed "to encourage further understanding between the White House and the President's appointees and to foster a real team spirit among our most traveled spokespersons," to cultivate these women appointees as liaisons to other women and women's organizations.[77]

A White House Talent Bank

The Ford administration was the first to have a systematic, inclusive method for soliciting input from women's organizations. The OWP, under the direction of Lindh, continued to both gather resumes of women for posts in the administration and prod others throughout the Executive Office of the President to consider women as vacancies occurred.[78] The time was ripe for such inclusion. The women's movement was becoming a movement of organizations of women, most of which came into existence in the late 1960s and early 1970s. Whereas President Kennedy mainly had to contend with the NWP, with its single focus on an ERA, by the mid-1970s there was no one group that would be the dominant political player. A number of single issue groups emerged, each with a focus on a different agenda item; a number of groups emerged to represent a particular set of issues; and a number of groups emerged to focus more broadly on the status of women.[79]

One of the groups submitting names was the Clearinghouse on Women's Issues, "a non-partisan effort to see that qualified women are appointed to federal posts in the new administration."[80] The NWPC suggested several candidates for positions as they became vacant.[81] This was an effective strategy, and one that followed the approach taken by the NFBPWC during the Nixon administration as they launched their talent search.

And the administration was under scrutiny by the Citizens' Advisory Council on the Status of Women. For example, Maxine R. Hacke, coordinator of Women's Programs at Gulf Oil Corporation and a member of the

Citizens' Advisory Council on the Status of Women, in a letter to Bennett, director of Presidential Personnel, in 1975, wrote:

> The nomination of Ms. Marjorie Ward Lynch to be Under Secretary of Health, Education, and Welfare, is good news. Indeed, each time the President announces appointments of women to substantial posts in the government it's absolutely great. Those of us who support him and desire to be of service are encouraged by such appointments.
>
> My records for the period September 8 to October 6 reveal that there have been 70 appointments to such posts, and to councils and boards. Of these, 8 were women—less than ¼. I'm curious to know how the number of women appointees can be increased. . . . Is there any assistance your office needs to expand your "inventory" of women in the country on whom you can draw for appointments?[82]

A good example of how the voices of women were beginning to be heard was in the drafting of a list of candidates for Supreme Court vacancies. While Gerald Ford did not appoint a woman to the bench, instead naming John Paul Stevens, his administration was the first where women were seriously identified as candidates for a seat on the court.[83] When Justice William O. Douglas stepped down from the bench, Attorney General Edward H. Levi used the ABA's Standing Committee on the Judiciary as a "confidential adviser." The first list of potential nominees submitted by Levi included eleven judges and lawyers, all men.[84] Lindh's office funneled incoming comments from women's organizations to the president objecting to the absence of women from the initial lists. In addition, several of those on Levi's original list were opposed to the ERA.[85] Intensive lobbying, both from within and outside the White House, prompted Levi to send an additional five names, including those of Carla A. Hills, secretary of HUD, and U.S. District Court Judge Cornelia G. Kennedy.[86] In a memo to the president, Douglas P. Bennett listed comments "received by Phil Buchen or myself concerning the nomination to the Supreme Court." The influence of outside women's organizations as well as Lindh's office is reflected both in the names presented as well as the order in which the recommendations were listed.[87] The first recommendation on the list came from "Jill Ruckelshaus, Audrey Colom (Chairman of the National Woman's Political Caucus) and the National Federation of Business and Professional Women's Clubs [who] strongly urge[d] the appointment of a woman to the Supreme Court."[88] The comments of Harry Dent, Roger Blough, Representative Grassley

(R-Iowa), and Representative Bob Michel (R-Ill) then follow. Table 5.1 summarizes a list of those federal and state court judges recommended by a wide range of individuals and organizations (see Table 5.1).

At this time, only a small percentage of women were on the bench and it was a rare occurrence for any of these women judges to be recommended for the Supreme Court, except when the recommender was a woman. Quite

TABLE 5.1
Recommendations for the Supreme Court

Recommender	Judge	Court
Multiple (all male): Hugh Scott, Frank McGlinn, William Scranton	Arlin Adams	Third Circuit Court of Appeals
Pat Lindh	Sylvia Bacon	D.C. Superior Court
	Julia Cooper	Federal District (South Carolina)
	Cynthia Holcomb Hall	U.S. Tax Court
	Margaret Haywood	Superior Court of D.C.
	Normalie Holloway Johnson	Superior Court of D.C.
	Florence Kelley	District Court— Eastern Michigan
	Elizabeth Kovachevich	Judicial Circuit Court of Florida
	Sandra Day O'Connor	Court of Maricopa, Arizona
Senator Thurmond	Robert Chapman	Federal District— South Carolina
	Charles E. Simmons	District Court-South Carolina
	Emery Widener	Fourth Circuit Court of Appeals
James O. Eastland	Charles Clark	Fifth Circuit Court of Appeals
Mixed: (men and women) Pat Lindh, Paul Harvey, John Byrnes	Mary Colemen	Supreme Court of Michigan

TABLE 5.1, *continued*

Recommender	Judge	Court
Thomas Munson	John Feikens	U.S. Dist Court-Michigan
Mark Hatfield	Alfred T. Goodwin	Ninth Circuit Court of Appeals
John Byrnes	Smith Henley	Eighth Circuit Court of Appeals
All women: Pat Lindh, Bobbie Kilberg, NWPC	Shirley Hufstedler	Ninth Circuit Court of Appeals
Alabama Bar Association	Frank M. Johnson	U.S. District Court—Middle Alabama
Roger Blough	Irving R. Kaufman	Second Circuit Court of Appeals
Mixed (Pat Lindh, NWPC, Richard Van Dusen)	Cornelia Kennedy	U.S. District Court-Michigan
NWPC	Constance Baker Motley	U.S. District Court-New York
Mixed (Pat Lindh, L. H. Fountain, North Carolina Delegation)	Susie Sharp	Supreme Court of North Carolina
Bob Goldwin	Philip Tone	Seventh Circuit Court of Appeals
Terry Slease	Joseph Weis	Third Circuit Court of Appeals

Sources: See memoranda and correspondence in "Supreme Ct. Nominations—Background on Recommended Candidates" folder, White House Operations—Richard Cheney Files, Box 11, Gerald R. Ford Library.

noteworthy in the list of approximately fifty candidates, is that nearly all the women recommended (about half the names on the list) had been recommended by a woman. For example, Lindh, Bobbie Kilberg and the NWPC recommended Shirley Hufstedler, a judge on the Ninth Circuit Court of Appeals (who would later serve as the first secretary of education under President Jimmy Carter). Lindh also recommended Sandra Day O'Connor, who at the time was a judge on the Superior Court of Maricopa, Arizona, and would be the first woman appointed to the Supreme Court in 1981 by President Ronald Reagan.

In looking at legal scholars under consideration for the Court, the NWPC identified Ruth Bader Ginsburg, a professor at Columbia Law School; Herma Hill Kay, a professor at the University of California Law School; and Ellen Peters, a professor at Yale University Law School. Lindh recommended Harriet Rabb, a professor of law at Columbia, and joined with Kilberg and the NWPC in recommending Soia Mentschifkoff, dean of the University of Miami Law School, and with Judy Hope in recommending Dorothy Nelson, dean of the USC Law School, and Jean Kettleson, professor at Harvard Law School.[89]

In looking at prominent attorneys, either in private practice or in elective or appointive political office, again the same pattern occurs, with women putting forward the names of women. Bella Abzug, Yvonne B. Burke, Martha Griffiths, Rita Hauser, Margaret Heckler, Elizabeth Holtzman, Barbara Jordan, Patsy Mink, Betty Southard Murphy, and Pat Schroeder are all identified by either Lindh, the NWPC, or Kilberg. In contrast, David Belia, Robert Bork, Philip Buchen, Edwin Cohen, Len Garment, Edward Levi, Harold R. Tyler, Jr., Casper Weinberger, and Charles Wiggins were all recommended by men. Only Hugh Scott recommends a woman (Carla Hills), and she was identified as his second choice.[90]

Networks of Women and Women's Organizations

It is in the administration of Franklin D. Roosevelt that an identifiable network of women working to promote the concerns of women, and movement of women into positions in government, is first identified.[91] The First Lady was a part of this network. Eleanor Roosevelt hosted garden parties at the White House during the late 1930s for women executives working in government, as well as wives of high-level officials in Washington, providing an opportunity for networking among the professional women living in Washington.[92] While it is clear that a network of women is working together, and promoting women and women's issues throughout the administrations from Roosevelt to Nixon, the Ford administration presents a significant change in routines. During the 1970s, the growth in the number of organizations representing the interests of women, as well as the growth in the number of networks that link the members of these groups, reaches such an extent that the networking activities begin to be reflected in the appointments of women.

While the formal structure of an OWP did much to facilitate communication from and among women in the administration, as well as women in a variety of organizations across the country, the informal network of women that had long been recognized as contributing to the inclusion of and promotion of women remained an invaluable resource. When Lindh left the OWP to become deputy assistant secretary of state for educational and cultural affairs, her farewell letter to women in the administration recapped the accomplishments of the Ford administration in its appointment of women and noted recent government reports on the status of women in business and in the workforce. Lindh concluded her letter, writing that her "association will surely continue via Executive Women in Government and, of course, our own unofficial grapevine."[93]

THE OFFICE OF WOMEN'S PROGRAMS—JEANNE HOLM

Jeanne Holm replaced Lindh in the White House. Holm served in the Women's Army Corps from 1948–49 and then in the U.S. Air Force from 1949 through 1975, achieving the rank of major general. Upon her retirement from the service she worked as a consultant to the Defense Manpower Commission and then was named special assistant to the president for OWP in March, 1976.[94]

In looking for a replacement for Lindh, the White House considered the ramifications of their choice to fill this position. A memo from Jim Connor to Dick Cheney outlined the possible approaches the White House could take in naming a successor for Lindh:

> 1. Replace Pat Lindh with a woman who would essentially continue in a relatively limited role as Special Assistant for Women. Her duties would be primarily ceremonial. She would spend most of her time as a liaison with interest groups. The advantages of this approach are that it would not be perceived as a dramatic change in an election year and would not alter any operations at the White House. The disadvantages are that it would probably be perceived by the press and

sophisticated women's groups as simply a token appointment and might open us to some criticism. In addition, it would probably waste a valuable spot.

2. A second option would be similar to the first but would entail appointing Karen Keesling to Pat Lindh's slot. The major advantage is that it would stress continuity since Karen worked closely with Pat and knows the women's interest groups quite well and is apparently relatively popular with them. The major disadvantages are similar to those outlined above, and in addition, Karen's relatively low grade and low level previous position would clearly signal to any sophisticated observer that the position of Special Assistant for Women is a very low level at the White House.

3. A third option is to select a woman with credentials above and beyond those of being a women [sic] and active in women's interest groups. For example, we might look for a lawyer, an economist, or perhaps even someone with really significant political experience and involvement. This kind of woman could be placed at a relatively senior level within the White House apparatus and her talents and skills used to enhance our chances in '76. In addition, she could be designated the Special Assistant for Women, which would solve the question of whether we actually filled the slot.[95]

A number of names were proposed, including Jill Ruckelshaus; Isabelle Sawhill of the Urban Institute; Catherine Cleary of the First Wisconsin Trust Company; Rita Hauser; Jewel LaFontant, former deputy solicitor general; and Marina Whitman, former member of the Council of Economic Advisors. Bobbie Kilberg also recommended herself, as well as Margita White and Judy Hope, assuming that the person selected would have a "change of responsibilities and a title change."[96]

Ford selected the search option that would give the position a high degree of recognition, and so the White House went with option three when Jeanne Holm was named special assistant to the president for women. The first female general in the U.S. military, Holm had resigned from the air force the previous June. In announcing her appointment, Ford noted that he would be giving Holm his full support. "'You can rest assured I'll back you 100 per cent,' Ford told Jeanne M. Holm in his Oval Office. 'If I don't, I'll hear from home.' The President laughed and added, 'I do now.'"[97]

Similar in stature to Anne Armstrong in the Nixon and Ford White House, Holm was more influential than was Lindh, even though both Lindh and

Holm had the same title. As the first woman general in the U.S. armed forces, Holm had an established record that helped her to command action on the part of others in the White House, although structurally her role and position were no different than that of Lindh, with both reporting to Baroody. However, Holm was able to get others in the White House to respond in a far quicker fashion.

Under Holm, those in the administration were again prodded to consider issues of concern to women. At a meeting with top women appointees in the administration, questions were raised about recent news items noting the growing earnings gap between men and women. Secretary of Transportation William T. Coleman had noted the same news item in a brief letter to President Ford. Coleman was also aware of the First Lady's interest in the subject and noted as much.[98] Holm, who had been given a copy of Coleman's letter, also forwarded it to William Grog, deputy assistant to the president for economic affairs, to identify the problems of noncompliance with the 1963 Equal Pay Act and with Executive Order 11246.[99] As noted in the following list, Holm pursued the matter. In a listing of proposed initiatives for the president prepared for Baroody, Holm identified the following:

1. Announcement of a woman deputy campaign director at the President Ford Committee.

2. Announcement of a cabinet or subcabinet appointment of a woman in addition to the upcoming announcement of Rosemary Ginn.

3. Presidential initiative on transfer of property between spouse and the elimination of the inheritance tax should be espoused by all Presidential advocates as well as the President.

4. Announce the convening of a White House Conference similar to the Economic Summit to discuss the widening earnings gap between women and men. The President could direct the Secretary of Labor and the Council of Economic Advisors or the Economic Policy Board to call the meeting. Secretary Coleman's letter to the President has precipitated an interest, in addition to the release of, a recent Census study.

5. Direct the Justice Department to establish a Task Force which would initiate a program of systematic review of all Federal statutes for the purpose of identifying those which discriminate without justification on the basis of sex and to initiate remedial legislation. We are

currently working with Justice on such an initiative, originally shoot-
ing for a June 30 date. We could move it up.

6. Propose legislation requiring that all persons retiring or after a
certain date under the terms of an employee retirement plan providing
periodic benefits, receive periodic payments which do not reflect a
differentiation based on sex. This has been recommended to the
President by the EEOC and is now being staffed by the Domestic
Council.[100]

As the preceding list indicates, Holm pursued a political as well as a policy
agenda. For instance, Holm identified events that the president could attend during the primary season [May 14–15: BPW Clubs State conventions
in Michigan, Ohio, and New Jersey; May 21–23: BPW's California State Convention; June 6: National Convention of the American Nurses Association
in New Jersey] as well as after the primary season had come to a close [June
11: National Association of Commissions for Women in California; June 28:
American Home Economics Association in Minnesota; June 30–July 1: IWY
Commission meeting and reception]. Holm also identified problem areas
to watch including: "GSA regulations on the use of Federal space for child
care . . . selection of White House Fellows (1/3 of the finalists are women)
. . . the appropriations bill to fund the National Women's Conference."[101] In
a carefully staged event, Ford followed Holm's recommendation and met
with the IWY's Commission on July 1, 1976, to receive their report.

By the fall of 1976, the OWP was geared toward the campaign and the
promotion of Gerald Ford's record. The following summary of Ford's outreach activities to women was prepared by Holm to be used in the campaign:

1) July 1, 1976 International Women's Year Ceremony, attended by
approximately 900 people . . .
    a) President's remarks were mailed to all attendees, and invitees,
which included 36 women's magazines, 60 women members of the
press, and 160 women's organizations . . .
    b) Photos and press releases of the new Commission members with
the President were sent to the hometown papers, women's organization magazines, black editors, Chinese media, Greek media, and
Hispanic press . . .
2) President's Bicentennial Speeches
    a) mailed to 160 women's organizations
    b) mailed to 115 women appointees

3) Summary of President's Record on Women's issues

    a) sent to 580 women's editors, 36 women's magazines, and 43 women members of the press

4) Women's Equality Day Proclamation (August 26, 1976)

    a) sent to July 1 list . . .

    b) sent to 580 women's editors

5) Spoken of the President's programs on . . . 45 occasions to groups ranging from 15 to 3000.

    . . . In most instances, outside of the Washington area, we have television and printed media coverage.[102]

Holm tried to maximize coverage of any event concerning women and inform women's organizations and women in the press corps as a way to target women and make a connection between activities in Washington and interests outside the beltway.

THE 1976 CAMPAIGN AND THE ROOTS OF THE GENDER GAP

The NWPC, with an emphasis on pragmatic politics, and with its workshops emphasizing the "how to's of campaigning," reflected the changing nature of presidential campaigns from party-centered to candidate-centered activities emerging in the 1960s and early 1970s. The campaign transformation would allow for an increased role for women in the campaign.

Republican Party Coalition

Even as Gerald Ford was taking the oath of office on August 9, 1974, Jimmy Carter's campaign for the Democratic nomination was beginning to get under way. Carter announced his candidacy for president on December 12, 1974.[103] The candidates of both parties would need to seek the party nomination by competing in a series of primary election contests to win support from a majority of delegates.[104]

Although Ford himself said he did not think he would have a challenge for the Republican nomination, it was clear that others in his administration took the potential for a challenge seriously.[105] Ford's congressional voting record was conservative, and he had voted against a number of civil rights bills. However, by the time he had become minority leader some of his longtime colleagues in the House noted that Ford had "shown more of a mellowness in accepting differences of opinion within the party." The "growth of Ford's tolerance for differing opinions" was noted by Speaker

Carl Albert (D-OK), who once informed President Nixon that Ford would be easily confirmed [as vice president] by the House and Senate.[106] However, Ford's becoming more accepting of the differences within his own party did not preclude a fractious battle for the nomination. In addition, Ford had no national election constituency to draw on. He had not run as Nixon's running mate in 1972; Spiro Agnew did. Ford had instead represented the people of Grand Rapids, Michigan, for twenty-five years as the representative of Michigan's fifth district. Ford had been chosen as Nixon's vice president, following the resignation of Spiro Agnew, as someone who could easily win confirmation and work with both the Republicans on the Hill, and with the Democrats who controlled both houses of Congress. In testifying before the Senate Rules and Administration Committee in his confirmation hearings for vice president, Ford described his "political philosophy as 'moderate in domestic affairs, conservative in fiscal affairs, and dyed-in-the-wool internationalist in foreign affairs.'"[107] The 1976 campaign would highlight the factions within the Republican Party.

The Ford campaign compared and contrasted the president's position with that of his challenger for the Republican nomination, Ronald Reagan, and with Jimmy Carter, the presumed nominee for the Democrats, who had amassed more than one thousand votes (of the 1130 votes needed to win) by the start of the Democratic Party convention (see Table 5.2).

Reagan remained a potential threat right up to the Republican convention. For many issues long on the agenda for women, Ronald Reagan had no position of record, in spite of two years as governor of California and a run for the Republican nomination in 1968. Whereas Ford and Carter both had taken similar positions on issues of concern to women, Reagan had either not taken a position or opposed the position held by Ford and Carter.[108]

Given that Reagan would be the standard bearer for the Republican Party in 1980 and 1984, the absence of either a record or a position on these issues by Reagan in the 1976 contest contributed to an erosion of support from women for Republican Party candidates—a gender gap—which would plague the party for the next two decades.[109] Two of the areas identified by Holm would come into play throughout the next four years. The Ford administration repeatedly stated that "14 percent of the President's appointments have been women." This would be a figure that the Carter administration would have to wrestle with. With Carter's pledge to increase the number of women in the administration and appoint women to cabinet positions and other high-level posts, his administration would have to explain that Ford's 14 percent included all appointments, both full and part

TABLE 5.2
Candidates' Positions on Key Issues as Identified
by the Ford Campaign in 1976

	Ford	Reagan	Carter
ERA	For	Supported as governor; has since changed position	For
Enforce Anti-Discrimination Laws	For	—	For
Economic Justice	Tax laws	—	Tax laws
Earnings Gap	Will address	—	—
Part-time; flex-time	For	—	—
Appointment of Women	"14 percent of the President's appointments have been women."	"In his November 20, 1975 press conference, he said he felt that women had a place in the federal government."	"To appoint women to Cabinet."

Sources: Jeanne Holm to Mike Duval, memorandum, Aug. 3, 1976, "Campaign of 1976—Republican Platform Reagrding Women's Concerns" folder, WH Staff File—Patricia Lindh and Jeanne Holm Files, Box 7, GRFL.

time. On the issue of equality of rights under federal statutes, Ford's campaign noted Reagan's statements at the press conference on November 20, 1975, where Reagan had announced his bid for the presidency, "'If there are any injustices, if there are still any inequities with regard to differences in treatment of men and women, they should be corrected by statute.'" With the growing strength of women's political organizations, and greater recognition of the areas in which there was discrimination against women, Reagan's statement reflected an absence of knowledge about this issue.

Thus, the 1976 election marked the beginning of a series of elections in which issues of diversity, especially in regards to the inclusion of women in the administration, played a prominent role in the rhetoric of the campaign. Perhaps it is not surprising then that four years later the 1980 elec-

tion would mark the identification of a stable gender gap in the voting behavior, party identification, and attitudes toward public policies of men
when compared with women.[110]

A Vice Presidential Running Mate

In a surprise move, Reagan had broken with tradition and named his vice
presidential running mate, Senator Richard Schweiker of Pennsylvania, three
weeks before the convention. As the convention drew near, Ford was repeatedly asked about his vice presidential running mate. Ford himself raised
the possibility of a woman joining him on the ticket, albeit in a joking manner, which was typical of the type of response given by Ford when asked
about women or women's issues.

In an appearance at Bowling Green State University, Ford was asked,
"What kind of person are you looking for Vice President?" Ford replied,
"Well, Betty tells me I ought to have a gal. To be serious, I want—and this is
the absolute criteria—the person that I select to be my Vice-Presidential
running mate has to be fully capable, totally qualified to be President of the
United States. That is number one. After that, we have a whole range of
things to be put into the formula. I think it is premature to make a final
selection. We have lots of good Republican talent, and we will pick a good
one, but that person, I can assure you, will be qualified to be President of
the United States. And that is the only basic criteria that has to come."[111]

That the Ford campaign was seriously considering the implications of a
woman on the Republican ticket is reflected in the polls conducted by Robert
Teeter for the Ford campaign throughout the summer of 1976. However,
internal campaign memos seemed to preclude the inclusion of a woman on
the final ticket, even though Ford listed Anne Armstrong and African American Senator Edward Brooke of Massachusetts among the dozen candidates
still under consideration a week before the convention.[112] The campaign
felt it judicious to make a symbolic gesture, "we'll float some names," but
were not seriously considering Armstrong at that time.

Early in August, 1976, a memo outlining the "Best Chance Strategy to
Win," from Robert Teeter's "National Surveys-Strategy Book," included the
following:

Select Vice Presidential running mate with following characteristics:
- able to carry a key state or region
- aggressive campaigner who can take the lead implementing the
attack Carter Plan
- a man who is perceived as an Independent, or at least moderate

Republican, without a strong party identification. Must have a <u>strong image of freshness and non-Washington establishment</u>. Honest - a man who has good credibility with the press.[113]

Given the selection of Senator Robert Dole, who was a Washington insider from the state of Kansas, and former co-chair of the RNC, the "aggressive campaigner who can take the lead implementing the attack Carter plan" seemed to have been the primary criterion for Dole's selection as the vice presidential running mate.

The memo also included a strategy for how the public was to be informed of the vice presidential selection process. In announcing this process, Ford would "show the President (not external forces generated by the Reagan challenge) as being firmly in control." The following actions were recommended:

- President adopts a strategy of revealing that he has a specific and disciplined <u>process</u> for selecting his running mate, but he will <u>not</u> reveal names.
- Advisors (Morton-Cheney) will let it be known that only the President knows who is on the list.
- The President could reveal the following about the list:
    - About a dozen names
    - He personally knows everyone
    - Women are included[114]

By August, Armstrong had been dropped from consideration, as the polling done by Teeter focused on the following vice presidential possibilities: Howard Baker, John B. Connally, Nelson Rockefeller, Ronald Reagan, William Ruckelshaus, and William W. Scranton.[115]

The results of an earlier survey, done by Teeter in June, 1976, may have been the most important factor in eliminating Armstrong from the list of potential vice presidential running mates. As Tables 5.3 and 5.4 illustrate, it was the core Republicans who objected the most to a woman on the ticket. One of the cardinal rules of any political campaign is that one needs to maintain one's political base—from there you move outward. That Armstrong was dropped from the final list of vice presidential running mates is therefore not surprising. As Table 5.4 illustrates, there was a marked lack of support, with 42 percent of Republicans reporting they would "be less likely to vote for a ticket that had a woman running as a vice president of the United States."

After winning the nomination, Ford met with his opponent, Ronald Reagan, and reviewed a final list of vice presidential candidates: Dole; Senator Howard Baker of Tennessee; William E. Simon, secretary of the treasury; William Ruckelshaus; and John B. Connally, former treasury secretary.[116] Dole had the support of Reagan and was selected as the Republican vice presidential nominee, upon ratification by the convention.

Campaign Politics

By the 1976 campaign, the "Talent Bank," originally an initiative implemented under Republican President Richard M. Nixon, appeared to have been lost to institutional memory. Holm lamented the Carter "Talent Bank," while none existed in the White House. In writing to a member of the White House staff concerning "Talent Bank 77," Holm observed,

> Mr. Carter is getting a lot of mileage out of this with women. He is probably doing a similar project with minorities.
>
> On the other hand, we are getting a lot of flak from women and the press about the President's record of appointments. The 14% figure we use if [sic] not going over very well, especially when I'm asked about full-time versus part-time positions. The figure is getting too slippery. Do we have any more recent data I can use? If so, is it better or worse? I fear the latter.[117]

The institutional structure for identifying women for appointive posts was not yet firmly rooted in the White House, but the campaign activity of Jimmy

TABLE 5.3
Support for a Woman on the Ticket

Percentage agreeing with the statement:
"I'd be more likely to vote for a ticket that had a woman running as Vice-President of the United States."

	Strongly Agree/ Moderately Agree	*Moderately Disagree/ Strongly Disagree*
Republicans	19%	50%
Ticket-Splitters	24	42
Democrats	31	38
18–24 year olds	32	30
Total	27	39

Sources: U.S. National Field Survey (June 11–28, 1976), Questions 45G and 45H; "U.S. National Study August 1976 Ford-Report-Data (5)," Robert Teeter Papers, Box 54, Gerald R. Ford Library.

TABLE 5.4
Lack of Support for a Woman on the Ticket

Percentage agreeing with statement:
"I'd be less likely to vote for a ticket that had a woman running as vice-president of the United States."

	Strongly Agree/ Moderately Agree	Moderately Disagree/ Strongly Disagree
Republicans	42%	34%
Ticket-Splitters	28	52
Democrats	26	56
18–24 year olds	15	63
Total	28	50

Sources: U.S. National Field Survey (June 11–28, 1976), Questions 45G and 45H; "U.S. National Study August 1976 Ford-Report-Data (5)," Robert Teeter Papers, Box 54, Gerald R. Ford Library.

Carter ensured that a talent bank of some sort would be a part of a Carter administration's appointment process. The rhetoric concerning the inclusion of women in the administration firmly takes hold during the 1976 campaign. For instance, Armstrong was among the Nixon holdovers who left within months of Ford taking office. Yet, two years later, as part of the "Campaign Issues Book on Women's Issues," Armstrong is prominently identified as having been a member of the Ford cabinet.[118]

Early in the summer of 1976, in another effort to gain the support of women, Jeanne Holm outlined a plan of action for the Justice Department to "develop, in consultation with affected Federal agencies, a comprehensive plan for accomplishing a review of the United States Code to determine need for revision of sex-based provisions that are not justified in law. . . ." Holm went on to note the political advantages of such an initiative, with little harm to support from the conservative base of the Republican Party in the upcoming presidential election. With the added support of his attorney general Edward H. Levi, Buchen, and Cannon, Ford sent such a directive to his attorney general on June 30, 1976.[119] Hartmann had also approved of this initiative to review federal statutes in terms of equality of rights, but suggested that the "action should be held for eve of GOP Convention."[120] Instead, Ford made the announcement the next day, July 1, 1976, at the ceremony honoring the work of the National Commission on the Observance of International Women's Year, 1976, acknowledging receipt of their report.[121]

President Ford won the support of women, but with a lower turnout rate for women than for men, he lost the election, since more men supported Carter than supported Ford. Jimmy Carter won the electoral college vote and 50.1 percent of the popular vote.

CONCLUSION

The Ford administration would be brief, yet by the time Jimmy Carter took the oath of office on January 20, 1977, "women's issues" were clearly on the national agenda. In an inventory prepared for Congress, the Ford administration outlined the legislation of concern to women which had thus far been passed by Congress: Title IX, affirmative action, civil service reform; establishment of an IWY Commission; and, for the first time in history, an ERA had passed both the House of Representatives and the Senate and was awaiting ratification by the states. Thirty-four states had approved the amendment, only four short of the number needed for ratification.[122]

In addition, an OWP, which had been established in a piecemeal way during the Nixon administration, had come into its own as an office in the EOP. While it is during the Nixon administration that the EOP begins to undertake and direct liaison activities to various groups, it is during the Ford administration that a systematic effort to reach out to a variety of constituent groups is fully developed.[123] Lindh even refers to the women appointees as "her constituents."[124]

Richard Nixon had set the course of action that would lay the foundation for significant change regarding the inclusion of women in both the Republican Party and in governing. Gerald Ford had come to the presidency from Congress at a time when both institutions were undergoing change. Ford had served in the House of Representatives for twenty-five years, leaving at a time when constituent service was expanding in response to the growth in government. A parallel growth in White House outreach activities came naturally to this longtime member of Congress, already in the midst of institutional change in Congress.

The Ford administration also marked a transitional era. Gerald Ford was fundamentally a caretaker. At a time when forceful leadership was needed in expanding and protecting the rights of women through legislation, executive orders, and enforcement, the Ford administration would not provide it. The Republican Party, which had long championed the rights of women, would, after Ford, drive women from that party at a critical juncture.

The pace of change that had begun during the 1960s culminating in the institutionalization of a structure for the inclusion of women and issues of concern to women would slow down, and even decline in the 1980s. While the institutional structures would thrive during the Carter administration, the *momentum* of the 1960s and early 1970s in changing discriminatory statutes and actions would be lost as the issue of an ERA took center stage. The Republican takeover of the presidency in 1980, along with the Senate, would result in little progress until the 1990s. At the 1980 Democratic Convention women made up 49 percent of the delegates; at the Republican Convention women comprised 29 percent of all delegates.[125] Although not the result of any Ford action, his lack of forceful leadership in using the powers of his office helped to allow a clear gender gap to emerge, which would help the Democrats reclaim the White House in 1992.

CHAPTER 6

The Carter Administration

Politics and Policy—A Turning Point for Women

THE 1976 ELECTION led to a
change in party control of the White House. Unlike his predecessor, Jimmy
Carter had time to plan for a transition, although, as all new administrations have found, that time slipped away quickly. Carter came into the White
House at a time when American political institutions were in transition,
and Carter himself ushered in a new model of presidential candidate when
he captured the party's nomination through a popularly based nominating
system. His presidency marked the beginning of an era where former governors rather than former senators again dominated the White House—a
pattern uninterrupted into the twenty-first century with George W. Bush's
presidency.[1]

The 1976 election also marked another turning point. It was the last election in which a greater percentage of men than women voted Democratic
and in which men had a higher turnout rate than did women in the twentieth century. Beginning in 1976, there is a noticeable gap in the voting behavior
of men and women, and by 1980 women support Democratic candidates to
a greater extent than do men.[2] During the 1976 campaign, both Democrat
Jimmy Carter and Republican Gerald Ford established clear policy stands
on such issues as the ERA, abortion, and the inclusion of women. While
both parties' platforms had included support for equal rights and for an
ERA in the past, this is the first campaign where rhetoric of the inclusion of
women is heard. Yet in spite of the focus given to the ERA, both by activists
in the 1970s and by scholars looking back at the women's movement, there
were other issues receiving the president's attention. The struggle for progress

women had been making in the civil service, toward equal pay, toward ending discrimination, and as presidential appointees would continue on into the next century.

WOMEN AND THE FORMATION
OF THE CARTER ADMINISTRATION

With a presidential election again bringing in a new party in control of the White House, the focus was on appointments. A strong push was made by a number of women's groups to have the incoming Carter administration fulfill its pledge that "for each major job . . . we have at least one qualified woman and one black."[3] A number of women's organizations, including the NWPC, the NFBPWC, NOW, the AAUW, and representatives from an ad hoc group of women in government, joined forces in an "Ad Hoc Coalition of Women's Groups" to push the newly forming administration to include women in cabinet and subcabinet positions and to set forth an agenda that would include issues of concern to women that had yet to gain staying power on the national agenda—for example, the elimination of discrimination against women and the enforcement of existing statutes outlawing discrimination practices. Each organization also pushed the administration on these same issues in separate communications.[4]

For the most part, the push for women was directed at the following cabinet departments: Labor, HEW, and Interior.[5] And while no woman was appointed to head these departments, Juanita Kreps was named secretary of commerce a week after the NWPC sent a mailgram in support. The NWPC also provided the Carter-Mondale transition staff with the names and brief records of women within departments and agencies who could be tapped for appointive posts. This was part of their effort to do "a constant talent search for women . . . qualified to be Assistant Secretaries and Deputy Assistant Secretaries."[6]

Two principles of the Carter search process, while not in conflict, would prove troublesome to meet: (1) inclusion of women and minorities in the administration and (2) delegation of responsibility for appointments in subcabinet positions to cabinet members. As a way of broadening the pool of those considered for posts in the new administration, a "Talent Inventory Program" was begun by which hundreds of resumes were both solicited and gathered. However, a smaller group, the Talent Advisory Group, used the more traditional approach, drawing on friends, business associates, and acquaintances in making recommendations to the president-elect and his vice president–elect Walter Mondale. The focus of the Talent Advisory Group was in identifying candidates for cabinet-level jobs.[7] The expectation was that these new members of the cabinet would identify and recruit those individuals to serve in lower-level posts within their respective departments.

In December, following the election, Mary King, who was on the transition staff, met with a small group of women in government, and kept Hamilton Jordan abreast of her activities in reaching out to women. She outlined in a memo for Jordan that "this is an excellent resource group of women already in government. I have worked with most of them in the past—they are positive, eager to help. I assured them of your interest in retaining and promoting women in government. Jimmy knows I am doing this to assuage some fears that had arisen."[8] Women present included those on congressional staffs, in federal departments and agencies, both career civil servants and political appointees, as well as members of interest groups. These women were aware that President-elect Carter had delegated responsibility for subcabinet posts to his cabinet secretaries, and they reached consensus on the following two points:

> 1. A recommendation that President-elect Carter make a strong personal request of his Cabinet and independent and regulatory agency's appointees to appoint women as Asst. Secretaries, Deputy Asst. Secretaries, Executive and Special Assistants, and to Federal Executive Programs.
> 2. The recognition that many women in government have been there long before Executive Orders established the legal means of placing women in government. These women can provide a resource of qualified and experienced women for President-elect Carter.[9]

These women very much saw a pipeline effect—if women were appointed as special and executive assistants, they could learn the system, especially if "given key managerial responsibilities with supergrade men reporting to them."[10] The president should "ask his Cabinet appointees either in writing or in public statement to appoint women to major decision and policy making positions."[11] They also noted that women had long held government posts and "promotion from within is important for women in government, to the Deputy and Assistant Secretary slots."[12] They also urged that newly appointed cabinet members meet with the women in their respective departments "as a beginning for their talent search for women."[13]

Among those on the transition staff advising the president on cabinet appointments was Anne Wexler, with responsibility for commerce. A week after King's meeting with these women, Juanita Kreps was named secretary of commerce on December 20, 1976, and the following day Patricia Roberts Harris joined the cabinet as secretary of HUD.

At the same time, President-elect Carter sent a memo to his cabinet designees on the subject of the "Appointment of Women and Minority Males to High Level Positions" (see Box 6.1).

The informal group of women from government continued to meet and worked to tie into the existing structures in departments and agencies—the Federal Women's Program Coordinators, as well as the Federal Executive Woman's Group—and to create informal networks among women within each agency or department. This ad hoc group sought the help of Carter-Mondale transition staff members Barbara Blum, Hamilton Jordan, and Mary King in arranging meetings with cabinet appointees as well as with women working in each department or agency.[14]

THE DIFFUSION OF APPOINTMENT RESPONSIBILITY, 1976–78

If one is seeking to identify structures that might lead to substantive change regarding the inclusion of women in high-level appointive posts and consideration of women's issues, the appointment of a special assistant to the president, or an assistant to the president for women, will not necessarily result in substantive change. On the other hand, a White House that centralizes its personnel operation, and not only monitors the appointment of women but also controls the appointment of individuals to the subcabinet, can have a greater substantive impact on the inclusion of women.

With President Carter delegating responsibility to his cabinet for sub-cabinet appointments, the White House efforts to increase the consideration of women and minorities for top-level posts was not as important as it might have been, since departments and independent agencies conducted their own searches.[15] For example, Arvonne Fraser, who served as a regional coordinator for the Carter-Mondale campaign in three Midwestern states (Minnesota, Wisconsin, and Iowa), actively sought the post of director of the Women's Bureau in the Department of Labor.[16] The NWPC endorsed her appointment. Ronnie Feit, deputy assistant to the president, tried to get

BOX 6.1
President-Elect Carter's Appointments

Carter's memo to his Cabinet Designees on the subject of "Appointment of Women and Minority Males to High Level Positions:"

    Women and minorities continue to be under represented in the
top levels in every department of the Federal government.

    When Judge Frank Johnson desegregated the Alabama State
Troopers in early 1972, he told the State: "Qualified blacks are out
there. I want you to find them." That should be your attitude for
women and minorities as you go about filling subcabinet posts
within your agencies.

    The particular selection scheme employed is less important than
the results achieved. Attention to certain considerations, however,
should prove helpful:

    1. <u>Number and Type of Openings</u>

Canvass both the number and the type of openings in the agency.
The initial commitment must be to place a substantial number of
women and minorities in non-traditional jobs and not restrict
them to positions that they have traditionally held.

    2. <u>Recruitment</u>

The Talent Inventory Program in the Transition Office has as-
sembled resumes of scores of minorities and females who are both
qualified for and interested in serving at the Assistant or Deputy
Assistant Secretary levels. This data should be utilized. In addition,
civil rights and women's groups can be contacted. (Note: Individuals who worked on the campaign or on the Transition staff, many of
whom are well qualified, should also be considered.)

    The goal of the recruitment program is to produce qualified
applicants. If qualified minorities and females are not forthcoming
through one channel, then another should be tried.

    3. <u>Screening</u>

Many competent women and minorities will have had career
patterns which differ from those of non-minority males; e.g.,
minorities or women may have achieved less corporate experience
but excelled in other equally indicative areas. To some extent,

BOX 6.1, *continued*

differing career and salary patterns are attributable to societal discrimination and for that reason the differences should not be given decisive influence in selection. In this vein, remember that a specific type of experience is not a prerequisite for most subcabinet positions, whereas the ability to manage and/or build solid management teams is essential.

The post-Christmas designee meeting will address the question of subcabinet appointments. At that time you will have access to data maintained by the Talent Inventory Program, if that has not previously been made available. Hiring commitments should not be made until all affirmative action avenues have been fully explored. Equal opportunity employment is the law.

Source: President-elect Carter to Cabinet Designees, memorandum, Dec. 22, 1976, "PE 2 1/20/77–2/10/77" folder, WHCF, Subject File-Executive, Box PE-5, Jimmy Carter Library.

others on the White House staff to block Secretary of Labor Ray Marshall's choice of Alexis Herman for the same post. Feit noted that a number of women's groups had supported Fraser and that there was substantial opposition to Herman's appointment.[17] However, President Carter had already signed off on Secretary Marshall's appointment of Herman.

As was the case with each of the prior administrations, the White House prepared tallies of the number of women in Senate-confirmed posts and of women "firsts" (e.g., first administration to have two women assistant secretaries in the Department of Agriculture; first administration to have a woman chair the EEOC.)[18] In part, the Presidential Personnel Office had to respond to inquiries from outside groups as to the status of women and minorities in appointive positions in the administration. The 1976 campaign, which featured President Ford stating his record in appointing women to 14 percent of the available positions and Carter promising to consider "at least one qualified woman" for each position, resulted in close scrutiny of the Carter appointments by outside groups.[19] For example, the Whittier/Southeast L.A. Chapter of NOW wrote to the president at the end of his first year in office: "We would like to express our disappointment with the lack of women appointees to top governmental jobs in your administration. You secured our votes in November, 1976 by the campaign promise that you would increase the number of women in government positions. However, as of December 1977, 552 top level positions had been filled, but only 64 or 12% of these had been filled by women. Ford's record was 14%."[20]

James F. Gammill, Jr., director of the Presidential Personnel Office, replied, "Our records reflect that women represented only 4.7% of all full-time positions appointed by Ford, whereas thus far in this Administration, 13.3% of all full-time appointees are women."[21] Once a president makes an invitation for the press and public to scrutinize appointments for a commitment to diversity, the "bean counting" begins.[22] Jimmy Carter's was the first administration to so blatantly promise a greater inclusion of women and minorities during the transition phase. As soon as Carter had begun to make cabinet appointments without a woman named among the early nominees, media scrutiny began that lasted throughout the administration.[23]

The counting of women continued throughout the Carter administration, with Sarah Weddington, special assistant to the president, periodically identifying women appointed to the highest-level posts and the "firsts" regarding women appointments (e.g., the first time a majority of commissioners on the Consumer Product Safety Commission are women). The counts included full-time as well as part-time posts. After two years in office, Carter had appointed 268 women, or 18 percent of the 1484 appointments to full- and part-time positions. This compared favorably to the Ford overall record of 12.9 percent (according to the Carter administration's count of the Ford appointments) of full- and part-time appointments.[24] By the end of 1979, 22 percent of all appointments in the administration were held by women.[25]

The bean counting that President Clinton would decry twenty years later had much of its origins in the Executive Office of the President, with presidents closely monitoring their appointments for the ethnic, racial, religious, and educational composition, in addition to sex.

In spite of Carter's admonition to his cabinet early in his administration, not all cabinet secretaries were in compliance. The office in the White House with jurisdiction over affirmative action was the Presidential Personnel Office. However, Margaret (Midge) Costanza, assistant to the president for public liaison, pursued complaints her office received from women and women's groups concerning the lack of affirmative action activities in certain departments. For instance, in a memo to Carter she identified the complaints her office had received from women and women's groups concerning the hiring practices in the Department of Energy:

The record of appointments already made shows a gross shortage of women, minorities—and even democrats.

My understanding is that there is a potential of 44 Presidential and Secretarial appointments at Department of Energy. Of these top level positions, 26 have been filled; 3 of these are held by women, 1 of whom is a minority woman. There is, in addition, 1 appointive position held by a minority man. . . .

Over and above the problem of hiring women and minorities is the problem of the Department's treatment of them once they are hired. My office has had confidential meetings with Department of Energy women, at their request, and learned of alleged charges of harassment and unequal pay.

At conferences with interest group representatives, I am told that Department of Energy, unlike any of the other agencies, has failed to consult interest groups or make any other real effort to develop and draw from a talent bank which includes women and minorities.

This will be among the topics raised by the Administration women when they meet with you next week to discuss the International Women's Year Conference in Houston.[26]

While the cabinet was given the responsibility for its own subcabinet appointments, the White House worked to influence the process, especially as time wore on.[27]

CENTRALIZATION OF APPOINTMENT
RESPONSIBILITY, 1978–81

In 1978, the White House sought to reclaim control over the administration's appointments, yet the president and two of his senior advisors, Hamilton Jordan and Jack Watson, still struggled to sort out cabinet-EOP relations. Jordan's efforts to develop closer ties between the White House senior staff and the cabinet, which resulted in weekly meetings between representatives of each department and the senior staff, provided one means for the White House to reclaim its appointive power. Anne Wexler, assistant to the president, suggested to Jordan that to achieve greater White House scrutiny and involvement in the appointment process, "gently urge the participants to bring with them to each meeting a list of Schedule C vacancies, telling them that we may be able to help them with problems they have on the one hand or we might be able to give suggestions of qualified people we would like for them to consider. For this first meeting this does not have to be hard line. Our indication that we would like to review their vacancies will be enough of a hint for them to understand what we are talking about."[28]

In 1979, the Carter White House moved to centralize control over the direction of the administration back in the White House, including over appointments.[29] The cabinet officers would no longer have the same degree of control in their selection of subcabinet personnel. It would be easier for the president to meet his goals of a diversified government if the White House more directly controlled the appointment process. The president could then look across departments and agencies to improve the mix of women and racial minorities in the administration.

Carter's advisors noted the benefits of "moving White House staffers to positions of line responsibility in the agencies."[30] The White House, however, prodded carefully. Nixon's legacy of centralized control in the White House remained.[31]

In June, 1979, President Carter sent notes to cabinet officers and agency heads instructing them that "before recommending appointees to me, first discuss the proposed appointment with Tim Kraft in the White House Personnel Office."[32] A month later, the White House Personnel Office forwarded a list of "good candidates for key sub-cabinet positions" to Jordan for administration posts. The lists were organized by departments, along with a "list of generalists who could serve well in a number of capacities."[33] Of 135 names, thirty-six or more than a fourth of the recommended names, were women.[34]

As an indication also of the tension between the cabinet and the White House that persists in any administration, the swearing-in ceremony of Shirley Hufstedler to head the newly created Department of Education is illustrative. Sarah Weddington, whose job as special assistant to the president was to provide outreach to women's groups, tried to elicit the support of President Carter in pressuring Hufstedler to recognize the overall goals and objectives of the administration in regards to women.[35] Accordingly, lists were prepared of constituent groups to be invited: Weddington identified women's groups, Anne Wexler identified education groups, and Frank Moore had identified members of Congress, to add to Hufstedler's own list of family and friends.

Weddington informed Carter that "it was only through White House insistence that she [Hufstedler] agreed to have a ceremony inviting people beyond a few of her family and personal friends. Now she is constantly telling us that she won't have anyone who is political, she doesn't want the leaders of women's groups who aren't directly and primarily involved in education, etc. She is questioning many of the names on other lists."[36]

The clash between the EOP and Hufstedler concerning her swearing-in ceremony as a new member of the cabinet also illustrates the additional demands that have historically been placed on women and minority members of the cabinet, when their appointment was a rarity. Weddington wanted President Carter to emphasize to Hufstedler "the need for her to give White House staff members flexibility in including a broad spectrum of people [i.e., a wide number of different constituent groups] and cooperating with us."[37]

Later, in making subcabinet recommendations to Hufstedler, Weddington sensed the dilemma Hufstedler faced and identified candidates for subcabinet posts who had strong backgrounds and interest in education policy. Still, mindful of her goals in the White House Office, she pushed the candidacy of Terry Saario, who was also "a leader in the women's movement in education," and enlisted the help of Liz Carpenter and Donna Shalala in lobbying for her appointment.[38]

Secretary of HUD Patricia Harris, an African American woman, offered to push for the appointment of blacks and was called upon to do so. She moved between what the White House perceived as two constituencies, African Americans and women, two worlds she well knew. Speaking at the NWPC convention, Harris acknowledged the impact of a woman heading the Department of HUD. When Carter had initially given to each secretary the responsibility of naming lower-level appointments in their respective departments, Harris had been able to increase the percentage of women in appointive posts to 49 percent of the department. The changed composition of the department resulted in "a notable effect on our policy and program development. . . . women at the top and in the middle makes a real difference."[39] As Harris stated,

HUD is becoming increasingly sensitive to the fact that housing is a "women's issue." . . . HUD is engaging in major initiatives specifically designed to help women and their housing needs. . . . the Women and Mortgage Credit Project is a two-year program which will provide technical assistance to women on the advantages and disadvantages of home ownership and on the process of purchasing a home. . . . HUD's message to the lending institutions is simple: Women are good credit. . . . HUD is responding to the terrifying increase of violence occurring in American homes. . . . shelters for battered women are now eligible for community development block grant funds. To date, HUD has funded approximately 20 battered women's shelters. We would like to triple that number in the coming fiscal year. More significantly, a government-wide effort to combat this problem has been initiated, and the President has established an Interdepartmental Committee on Domestic Violence. Economic Independence ... is especially important to those who are victims of domestic violence. . . . Clearly we woman are beginning to gain some victories and more of our needs are being considered. But we are not deceived. Our goal of full equality is still well ahead of us.[40]

The third woman in the Carter cabinet, and the first nominated, was Juanita Kreps, secretary of commerce. Kreps followed up on her promise to the president at the time of her appointment to identify women for posts, in response to Carter's claims of the difficulties in finding qualified women willing to relocate to Washington, D.C.[41] Shortly after being confirmed she sent the president a list of women to consider for various posts, urging Carter to "make a special effort in the near future to select several women for senior posts ... [with] a press conference ... [to] personally announce your choices."[42] As is often the case in an administration, Wexler's ties to the White House were stronger than those of Kreps's, and Kreps's choices were given to Wexler for comment.[43] (As previously mentioned, Wexler served on the Transition Talent Group, with responsibility for appointments in the Department of Commerce, especially the secretary.)

The Commerce Department, under the leadership of Kreps and Wexler, set up two of the new structures established by the administration to address the concerns of women: the Interdepartmental Task Force on Women Business Owners and the Office of Statistical Policy. While Wexler was in the Commerce Department, she chaired the Interdepartmental Task Force. Isabel Hyde, executive assistant to the secretary, assumed responsibilities as chair of the task force when Wexler left the Commerce Department for the White House. As executive assistant, Hyde would have close access to Kreps.[44]

PRESIDENTIAL LEADERSHIP

The initiatives begun during the 1960s to monitor, assess, and improve the status of women and minorities in the federal government continued through each succeeding administration. In part, the actions of each administration helped generate an institutional framework for its successor. For example, preceding administrations had begun the practice of using

August 26, the anniversary of the ratification of the Nineteenth Amendment (women's suffrage), as a means of expressing the administration's support for equal rights for women. Civil Service Chairman Alan K. Campbell alerted President Carter to this precedent. On August 26, 1977, a memorandum was sent to the heads of executive departments and agencies, in which Carter outlined the role of the attorney general and Justice Department "in eliminating sex discrimination from the laws and policies of the United States." He requested that each department and agency "initiate a comprehensive review of all programs which they administer in order to identify any regulations, guidelines, programs, or policies which result in unequal treatment based on sex." Carter went on to note the commitment of his administration to use executive action when possible, or recommend legislative action to Congress to end sex discrimination, and make "federal law . . . a model of non-discrimination for every state and for the rest of the world."[45] However, this ritualized gesture did not substitute for substantive action.

President Carter set the tone and direction for the inclusion of women in his administration and the consideration of women in the formulating of public policy, through memos, directives, and executive orders to department and agency heads. Even before a special assistant focusing on women was added to the Carter White House staff, Carter had sent a memo to the heads of departments and agencies, urging them to include women in their appointments. Once Weddington came on board as a special assistant to the president, Carter would pen "See Sarah," on the corner of a memo recommending appointments to a committee or commission if an insufficient percentage of women were included in the list of recommendations.[46] According to Weddington, "There were several instances . . . where he picked up on the fact that women were missing from a recommendation made to him and sent it to me and it was something I hadn't even known that was going on. So that he was very good about that and very conscious of it."[47]

Managing the Government and Affirmative Action

Under Carter, there was "a consolidation of equal employment functions under the EEOC with about a 40 percent increase in their budget and a thousand new positions." The reorganization resulted in the Departments of Justice and Labor, the EEOC, and the Civil Service Commission being better able to deal with problems, while avoiding jurisdictional conflicts and duplication of efforts. Over the previous two decades, these different

agencies had issued conflicting guidelines regarding the hiring of employees.[48] According to Weddington, this consolidation of enforcement powers
enabled the EEOC "to wipe out much of the backlog on complaints and
. . . be far more responsive to women in enforcing equal opportunity guidelines."[49]

The Carter White House also built upon the precedent that had been set
by its Republican predecessor when Ford sent a directive to heads of departments and agencies outlining an affirmative action policy. Ford observed
that if the percentages of women and minorities in the civil service in positions at the rank of GS-13 and above were to increase, "more is required
than non-discrimination and prohibition of discriminatory practices. What
is needed are strong affirmative actions . . . [including] recruitment activities designed to reach all segments of our society, fair selection procedures,
and effective programs of upward mobility. . . . Equal employment opportunity doesn't just happen; it comes about because managers make it happen."[50] This was a policy Carter would continue.

Carter and Civil Service Reform

Civil service reform was one of the top domestic priorities of the Carter
administration in 1978.[51] In the civil service, the aggressive action taken by
John Macy during the Kennedy-Johnson administrations to ensure the hiring and promotion of women and minorities was once again seen. There
was vigorous enforcement of equal employment opportunity practices, review and enforcement of federal statutes, and implementation of affirmative action programs.

Early in his administration, President Carter had also been alerted by
Chairman Campbell of the ten-year anniversary of President Johnson's EO
11375, issued October 13, 1967, "prohibit[ing] discrimination on the basis of
sex in Federal employment," and some advisors noted the extra political
capital to be gained by noting the anniversary.[52] Carter responded with a
statement to the heads of departments and agencies reaffirming Johnson's
executive order and the need for affirmative steps to meet the goals of a
"truly equal opportunity employer." The conference planned by the IWY
Commission was to begin in Houston in just a few weeks, and Press Secretary Jody Powell pushed to get the memo released.[53] Others in the White
House supported this move since in order for Carter to get civil service
reform he needed the support of women's groups. These organizations were
especially eager to modify veterans' preferences that limited the opportunities for women applying for civil service positions.[54]

The reform of the civil service system and creation of the Senior Executive Service (SES) during the Carter administration provided a structural means to enhance the inclusion of women in the highest levels of government service. Data from the first year indicated that this affirmative action effort did produce the intended results.[55]

By relying on past work experience and education as criteria for positions in the civil service, the composition of the federal workforce could be changed. The Sugerman Plan provided an alternative to traditional civil service testing procedures as a further means of bringing women and minorities into the federal government in higher grades to reflect their percentages in similar jobs in the private sector and in the pools of eligible candidates based on advanced degrees. With the advantages given to veterans, almost all men, in the civil service, women had been at a disadvantage in gaining entry into the federal government. Women who came from academic positions rarely had the administrative and managerial experience in supervising employees comparable to positions in the private sector. This was similar to the issues raised by the PCSW in that the work experiences of many women were different than those of men (e.g., organizer of a charity event). For instance, see a sample application form for the "Talent Bank" for women during the Nixon administration in Box 6.2.

In time, the Carter administration established a tripartite structure to address issues of diversity in the administration: Louis Martin, special assistant to the president, was to represent African Americans; Rick Hernandez, deputy assistant for political liaison was to represent Hispanics; and Sarah Weddington was to represent women.

Each of the three aides conducted outreach programs with their respective constituent groups.[56] This tripartite structure would be repeated during the Bush administration to aid in the search process for political appointees.[57]

Given the representation of Blacks, Hispanics, and women in the White House, other groups sought similar representation. While the administration considered an affirmative action plan and talent bank for the handicapped, other members of the administration were singled out as representatives of an ethnic or racial group by members of that group, with the expectation being that this high-level appointee would serve as their advocate as well as advance their career prospects. For example, National Security Advisor Zbigniew Brzezinski received inquiries from Polish Americans about job opportunities.[58]

However, as had been the case for the past two decades, positions were still being identified as appropriate for a "woman" or for an "ethnic" or a "minor-

---

BOX 6.2
Example of the "Talent Bank" Form of the BPW

Questionnaire for
Promotion of Women in Policy-Making Positions

Name:_____

Home Address:_____

Business Address:_____

   Business Telephone:_____

Date and Place of Birth:_____

Marital Status:_____ Political Affiliation:_____

Area of Expertise:_____

Brief Summary of Background and Experience:_____

Available for Full-Time Position:_____

                 Part-Time Position:_____

Source: Nixon Presidential Materials Project

---

ity." Once a woman had held a particular post, it then became a post for women. For instance, once Weddington was the first woman general counsel in the Department of Agriculture, the post was then identified as appropriate for women. Similarly, at the highest level, once Oveta Culp Hobby had served as the first secretary of HEW, subsequent heads included Patricia Harris, Margaret Heckler, and Donna Shalala.[59] And just as budget concerns had reduced opportunities to expand the federal workforce during the Johnson administration, inflation and the growing deficit was of constant concern to Carter.

Affirmative Steps in the White House

President Carter, known for his meticulous and at times excessive attention to detail, carefully reviewed data sent by Alan K. Campbell, director of the new Office of Personnel Management, on the employment of women and minorities in the federal service in August, 1979. Carter highlighted the following passage for his press secretary, Jody Powell, which noted:

> The lack of overall growth in Federal employment makes it difficult to improve its representativeness. There has a been a decline of about 2,000

in the full-time permanent employment in the Federal Government from November 1976 to November 1978. Against this decline I think it impressive that there has been an absolute increase of 22,000 in the number of women in full-time permanent employment while the comparable increase for minorities has been 17,000. In percentage terms this constitutes an increase from 34 to 35.3 for women and from 20 to 21.4 for minorities which is not that impressive. Nonetheless, the increase in absolute numbers and the lack of overall growth demonstrates the strenuous efforts which are being made by your departments and agencies to improve their employment profile.[60]

But Carter was also quick to note that even though the percentage of women serving in non-career executive appointments, while increasing from 6.6 percent (N=438) in December, 1976, to 13.3 percent (N=497) by December, 1977, and increasing again to 14.1 percent (N=575) by December, 1978, was "still not good."[61]

Early in his administration, Carter had decided that the White House should not be exempt from Title VII of the Civil Rights Act of 1964, as amended to apply to the federal government in 1972, which prohibits discrimination in employment. This reversed a decision that had been made by the Ford administration and defended by the Justice Department.[62] While it took a Republican revolution, the 104th Congress (1995–96), before Congress finally made most federal statutes applicable to Congress, Jimmy Carter moved the White House into compliance over two decades earlier by establishing a White House Equal Employment Opportunity Office.[63]

In accordance with Title VII, the White House prepared and submitted an EEO statement to the Civil Service Commission that "commits the White House Office and the Office of the Vice President to EEO and designates the Counsel to the President and Counsel to the Vice President as the officials responsible for implementing this commitment." Jimmy Carter and Walter F. Mondale both signed the EEO statement. In so doing, they committed themselves to a recruitment and hiring process. The senior staff "responsible for making employment decisions for the staff of the White House Office or the Office of the Vice President shall take all steps necessary to recruit and hire qualified individuals from groups which have historically suffered discrimination. The senior staff shall work with the EEO directors to insure that other employment decisions, including determinations as to promotions, also further the goal of equal employment opportunity."[64]

The senior staff would also be held accountable for reporting on the success and failure of affirmative action in White House employment throughout the Carter administration, either orally in senior staff meetings or in written reports to the president. Thus all sectors of the executive branch—political appointees, career civil servants, and White House staff—would be subject to the same affirmative action guidelines.[65]

DECISION MAKING AND THE CARTER WHITE HOUSE STAFF

The structure of the White House changes from one administration to the next, reflecting the differing needs and interests of each president. Even within a four-year term, the White House Office is subjected to a great deal of change. By the late 1970s, the White House Office had begun to establish a structure that would more closely resemble succeeding administrations than prior administrations. In part, this would be due to Congressional action in 1978.

In 1978 Congress approved legislation authorizing a specific limit on high-level (GS-18) White House staff, thus removing "[a] legislative cloud that hovered over most of the White House staff since 1939."[66] While the size of the White House staff had grown to more than 580 during the Nixon administration, falling to about 380 by 1978, the law had only allowed fourteen White House staff.[67] Congress had been regularly providing appropriations for a larger staff over the years, but a restive Congress had let it be known that future appropriations might cease without proper authorization.[68] Additionally, "[e]xplicit authorization . . . was given for staffs and support services for the vice president and the spouses of the president and vice president."[69]

The First Lady

Important to the evolution of the role of women in the White House was institutional recognition of the role played by presidential wives. The prominent (although not always visible) role played by First Ladies such as Nellie Taft, Eleanor Roosevelt, Lady Bird Johnson, Lou Hoover, and Bess Truman foreshadowed the continuing role of First Ladies, and especially the significant role assigned Hillary Clinton in 1993 by the president in leading health care reform.[70]

In the Carter administration, the First Lady played an influential role in the inner circle of presidential advisors. Along with senior staff, Mrs. Carter was kept informed of the status of appointments going to women in the administration as well as the response of the administration to the National Women's Conference.[71]

In fact, the president made certain that Stuart Eizenstat's report on the status of the administration's action in response to the areas identified in the National Plan of Action was reviewed by Rosalynn Carter before it was submitted to Congress.[72] Additionally, in 1978 when Hamilton Jordan proposed an ad hoc group of advisors to the president drawn from those outside of the administration, whom Carter could "trust and ... [feel] comfortable with and have the collective experience to provide ... advice on foreign policy, domestic issues ... image and the politics of the Presidency," the list included only one woman, Rosalynn Carter.[73]

Several women, in addition to Rosalynn Carter, played important roles in the Carter White House, including Midge Costanza, Esther Peterson, Anne Wexler, and Sarah Weddington, some from the very first days of the administration.

Midge Costanza

Midge Costanza, assistant to the president for public liaison, followed the career path of women in recent Democratic administrations who had come to work in the White House following work in the campaign. Costanza had been co-chair of the New York State Carter campaign. More generally, Costanza was a part of the feminist movement that emerged in the 1960s, an outgrowth of the writings and activism of Betty Friedan, Gloria Steinem and NOW, and the NWPC. In an interview conducted while she was heading the Office of Public Liaison, Costanza was quoted as saying about her position in the White House: "'I never would be here if it weren't for Bella [Abzug] and Gloria [Steinem]. They made it possible for the rest of us and I know it.'"[74] Perhaps Costanza's own foray into politics was influenced by Abzug and Steinem. But her Office of Public Liaison was an out-growth of the Nixon presidency, which had a similar outreach to women. And much had been done by organizations such as the BPW to bring women into high-level posts, establishing the concept of a talent bank and systematic efforts to consider women for political appointments as early as 1944 in the White House Conference called by Eleanor Roosevelt, and then again in the Kennedy and Nixon administrations.

However, because the links between Costanza and the more radical feminist groups were so strong, and the numbers of women's groups increased throughout the 1970s, the influence of the NWPC and NOW becomes more prominent, often overshadowing the work done by earlier generations of women's organizations.

Costanza performed an outreach service for the White House, however, which went beyond women's concerns, visiting natural disaster sites; meeting with groups; responding to a large number of speaking engagements for all sorts of organizations, groups, and fairs; attending Democratic Party functions; making recommendations for political appointments, and so forth.

Hamilton Jordan claimed that Midge held a policy post and a number of women's organizations, which were proliferating throughout the 1970s, viewed her role as a policy advisor to the newly elected president.[75] For example, Janice K. Mendenhall, director of the Federal Women's Program, congratulated Costanza on her "appointment as one of the top six people on the White House staff," and noted how "enthused [she was] about having an outstanding feminist like yourself at a policy making level."[76] However, one should note that hers was not a policy post but a political position.[77] Consider that the subunits of her office included "Troubleshooting." The showcasing aspect of appointments continued. In fact, women had served at higher levels as presidential advisors in preceding administrations. And Costanza was not included in regular senior staff meetings.[78]

Costanza's role was in facilitating communication between policy makers and constituent interests, rather than in active participation in policy making. In part, this was a function of Carter's wanting policy making pushed out of the White House and into the departments, and in part it was a function of her job. While Costanza herself appeared to recognize this distinction, part of the dismay of women's groups upon her departure from the White House may have arisen due to a mistaken sense that she was a policy intimate to Carter.

For example, in a letter explaining her job, she writes, "The Office of Public Liaison tries to bring into the White House women who are experts in their fields to discuss with policy persons on the presidential policy makers staff various issues. The office has started a series of briefings for women leaders at which time administration representatives present major initiatives. We also have on-going debates with women's groups representatives on a variety of so-called women's issues."[79]

Yet Costanza would, in fact, work to influence the policy position of the president in a number of cases. For instance, she disagreed with the president when he failed to take a stronger stance against the Hyde Amendment (on abortion),[80] and let Carter know her position, as well as the position of the women appointees in his administration.[81] Her office also investigated claims of patterns of discrimination in the way federal agencies administered programs and awarded federal grants or contracts, and in the compliance of those receiving federal funding with EEOC guidelines.[82]

Costanza's tenure in the White House, however, was brief. Shortly before Costanza's resignation on July 31, 1978, President Carter had sent a memo to the heads of departments and agencies, in which he announced a reformulation of her duties. Costanza was now only responsible for White House efforts regarding ratification of the ERA, implementation of the IWY Plan of Action, and monitoring of the status of women in the administration. She also was to provide input and recommendations regarding domestic policy affecting women.[83] Rather than continue on in an administration where she clashed with others on the senior staff, and had lost power and responsibilities, Costanza resigned.[84]

Esther Peterson

Consumer affairs was an issue President John F. Kennedy had latched onto during the 1960 presidential campaign, in noting the response of women to the issue as he campaigned across the country. Early in the Johnson administration, Kennedy's plan to add a special assistant to the president was realized when Johnson named Esther Peterson special assistant to the president for consumer affairs. Again in the Carter administration, Esther Peterson was named special assistant to the president for consumer affairs. With the title "assistant to the president" now the highest-ranking title for White House staff, Peterson's title was the same as it had been in the Johnson administration, but she was now in a second tier of White House staff assistants, the same as Costanza.

While Esther Peterson was not a part of the inner circle of advisors in the Carter White House, she does represent a continuity in service for three successive Democratic administrations, and her role as a special assistant for consumer affairs lasted the four years of the Carter administration. In her efforts to establish a Consumer Protection Agency the breadth and depth of her Washington experience is clearly exhibited. She established links to the public and community to win support for the president's legislative initiative, congratulated members of Congress on election victories, worked to get legislation through committee and on the floor, and did vote counts in Congress for the White House.[85]

Anne Wexler

Anne Wexler's role was different from that of Costanza in that she was brought into the White House in 1978 in a high-level policy position, with the title assistant to the president. Even when an OWP was later carved out under Sarah Weddington, Wexler played a more active role in sending policy recommendations to the president than did Weddington, and was a participant in high-level staff briefings in a way that Weddington was not. Hamilton Jordan outlined the new position created for Wexler, citing Jack Germond's description of Wexler as "'the best woman in Democratic politics.' She understands the nuts and bolts of politics and the art of communications."[86] Wexler, Jordan added, did not want it to "appear that she is being brought in simply to replace Midge." Instead, she insisted that she "'be part of the team' with access to the decision making process" and to President Carter. While Wexler would "deal with some of the more substantial groups and organizations that Midge dealt with," she would also work with, for example, Stu Eizenstat, in the development of a major policy initiative of the administration, providing political input and reaction. In addition, she would then "mobilize political and public support for the program."[87]

From the very start of her tenure, her role was as a policy advisor as well as a political advisor. Wexler's responsibilities included the areas of labor (Comprehensive Employment and Training Act programs [CETA]), inflation, tax policy, transportation, urban affairs, the interior, and small business. When weekly meetings were organized to develop closer ties between the White House senior staff and cabinet, Wexler was the only woman to participate, joining Jordan, Eizenstat, Powell, Kraft, and Moore in those meetings with department representatives.[88] The meetings, which continued for several months, addressed the administration's inflation and energy programs, budget priorities, and liaison with Congress.[89]

Wexler did, however, also take an aggressive stance in pushing for the inclusion of women. For example, when the president of the Chamber of Commerce of the United States of America sent Carter a list of twelve candidates for consideration in the president's reconstituted Export Council, Wexler responded with a letter to the president of the chamber noting the list was "impressive." Yet Wexler was "amazed that you could not think of one qualified woman in the entire United States to recommend. Want to try again?"[90]

One set of issues facing women in high-level posts was that their job did not necessarily involve "women's issues" although many outside the White

House assumed this to be a focus of any woman in the administration. Press reports surrounding the move of Wexler from the Commerce Department to the White House incorrectly noted her overlap with Costanza's office. Wexler herself was quick to correct false reports: "Many people were confused by the Press accounts of my appointment. My function at the White House is an entirely new one and in no way overlaps with Ms. Costanza's duties. Briefly put, my assignment is to generate public support for administration priority programs, and although I am sincerely interested in and committed to the ERA, I have no responsibility at the White House for the ERA or for women's issues in general, which remain under Ms. Costanza's purview."[91] Wexler also passed along speaking engagements to Weddington when the focus was on women.[92] Wexler's role as assistant to the president would make her the most prominent woman advisor to the president.

Sarah Weddington

Rosalynn Carter made the call to Sarah Weddington that brought her to the White House where Rosalynn, Jordan, and others interviewed her for the post of special assistant following Costanza's resignation.[93] Weddington, a lawyer, and former Texas legislator, had worked in the Texas legislature for ratification of the ERA and had gained prominence for her work in *Roe v. Wade.*

While the White House was soon to add special assistants for other targeted constituent groups—i.e., "Ethnics," and Hispanics, Weddington's position had a broader definition. While she would be replacing Costanza, her position was left open for her to help design and she wrote a position paper for President Carter shortly after taking office that outlined how she viewed the goals of her position. In essence her task was to be "sure that women were included in every aspect of the administration."[94] Later on in the administration, she would take on the political liaison work Kraft had been responsible for when he left in August, 1979, to be Clinton's campaign manager, and Weddington became an assistant to the president at the same salary ($56,000) Jordan and other top aides received.[95]

Like Costanza, Weddington assumed more of a political than a policy role. This corresponded with an increased politicization of the White House offices beginning in 1979, and increased efforts to control and direct the departments via personnel appointments. In November, 1979, Weddington's office gained a staff assistant, Bill Albers, detailed from the Appalachian Regional Council, first on a part-time basis and then full time in January,

1980.[96] Albers served as political deputy and headed the Political Matters section. His responsibilities included political correspondence—trouble-shooting—as well as outside communications and public relations. Earlier that fall, Linda Tarr-Whelan had been added to Weddington's staff as deputy assistant to the president. She was responsible for the ERA and the Interde-partmental Task Force on Women and was a liaison to women's groups.[97] Weddington also had Barbara Haugen on her staff working on communi-cations—with a focus on speeches, public information, and publications, and Tom Beard, who had previously worked on politics in a number of offices, including Jordan's.[98] On Weddington's staff Beard's responsibilities included work on political appointments, especially ambassadorial appoint-ments, another indication of the increased centralization of the Personnel Operation in the White House in the last two years of the Carter presi-dency, and the emerging political role of Weddington.

Weddington found her legal training most helpful in her position at the White House.[99] Soon after she was appointed special assistant to the presi-dent, Weddington met for lunch with the Capitol Hill Women's Political Caucus to discuss ways in which members of Congress could "further women's issues on the hill."[100] The president had just sent his report on the IWY to Congress, which could serve as a basis for legislative action. Weddington discussed such upcoming issues in the next Congress as abor-tion funding, veterans' preference in civil service hiring, and EEO, espe-cially on the Hill. Weddington's temperament was well suited for an old school style of "to get along, go along," as she herself noted. "In my own experience, I've certainly found a reasoned, calm approach works best *within the system* [author's emphasis]. I believe the vast majority of women agree."[101] Those same skills would also contribute to some of the conflict and hostil-ity she experienced in dealing with a few of the newly emerged women's organizations which had activist agendas.

One of the major tasks for Weddington was "communications—both communicating to the President the concerns of individual and groups of women and also communicating to them what was going on within the administration."[102] Her office published a regular series of newsletters as well as special publications on topics such as the ERA, social security, and the appointment of women to high-level posts.[103] As part of her outreach activities Weddington also arranged for White House briefings in which leaders of women's organizations could meet with policy makers in the ad-ministration, for "a dialogue between those groups."[104] For instance, mem-bers of the National Association of Commissions on the Status of Women and the President's Advisory Committee on Women attended a White House briefing in the spring of 1980, in which Madeleine Albright, a staff member for the National Security Council, gave a briefing on foreign policy and Joan Bernstein, general counsel in HHS, discussed health initiatives.[105] The NFBPWC was once again invited to participate in White House briefings. In fact, at a White House meeting organized by Weddington and attended by President Carter and the heads of women's organizations, Julie Arri, president of BPW, reported on the results of a Harris Poll on the ERA released by BPW and ERAmerica.[106]

Weddington worked to promote the record of the Carter administration through a careful cultivation of the media. For instance, she began to organize "a series of brunches, inviting 12 Administration women of Assistant Secretary rank or equivalent and 12 women from the press to each brunch, in order for them to know each other and hopefully eventually, for more word about Administration women to reach people in the various states."[107] Weddington also arranged breakfast meetings with administration women to "disseminate matters of political concern" early in 1980.[108] Weddington monitored the status of legislation and played a prominent role in directing the extension of the ERA. She organized ERA briefings for business leaders and opinion leaders of states that had yet to ratify the ERA.[109] She also assisted in congressional liaison activities through congratulatory letters to members of Congress following their election victories.[110]

The ERA was the focal point for a series of meetings Weddington organized between leaders of women's organizations, President Carter, and his top advisors, beginning late in 1979 and continuing into 1980. At a meeting between Carter and the leaders of women's organizations, Weddington suggested that the meeting not focus only on the ERA "so that it won't be a win/lose situation."[111] And the meeting broadened its agenda to include Title IX, employment, civil rights, and the impact of Carter's budget on women, with presentations by Stu Eizenstat, Eleanor Holmes Norton, Alexis Herman, and others in the administration. At the meeting, Carter identified Weddington as the White House coordinator for the ERA for groups to work with, and Secretary of Commerce Juanita Kreps as Carter's "special representative in favor of the ERA to the business community."[112] The women leaders President Carter met with December 13, 1979, represented 17 million women in the following organizations: the National Council of Negro Women, the AAUW, ERAmerica, Federally Employed Women, NWPC, President's Advisory Committee for Women (PACW), Women's Equity Action League, and the BPW. In addition, representatives from the Congressional Women's Caucus, DNC, and the Federal Women's Program attended. In the "Talking Points" prepared for the president for the event, Weddington noted the work of the League of Women Voters "in developing a strong business-for-ERA program, . . . the Business and Professional Women's Organization continues an assessment of all members to raise dollars for ERA. The AAUW has made passage of ERA their primary goal."[113] With these references and consultations, the White House was again reaching out to women through the older and more traditional women's groups. (Ellie Smeal, president of NOW was not invited. NOW threatened to picket the event, with Ellie Smeal "threatening to chain herself to the fence" similar to the action taken by the suffragettes sixty years earlier.)

The Revival of the Domestic Council

During the Nixon administration, a Domestic Council had been established in the EOP by executive order.[114] The Domestic Council was created as a means by which the president could coordinate the programs which had emerged as a part of LBJ's Great Society.[115] However, by the time of the Carter transition, the Domestic Council had been seriously weakened. Under Carter, and the direction of Eizenstat, the council was revived.

Eizenstat met "regularly with the Women's Lobby, the Women's Political Caucus, and other leading figures in the women's movement."[116] The Domestic Council provided a means by which policy concerns of women were being addressed, as they had when Armstrong was a member during the Nixon administration and John Ehrlichman headed the council. Beth Abramowitz, also active in the women's movement, did much to keep Eizenstat informed of women's issues in her work for the Domestic Council, and perhaps was more influential in getting the voices and concerns of women heard than were presidential advisors Costanza or Weddington.

With the Domestic Council having a major role in shaping the administration's domestic policy, access to Eizenstat was a key. This is similar to the situation in the Nixon administration when Ehrlichman headed the Domestic Council, and Armstrong, with cabinet rank as counselor to the president, could similarly influence Ehrlichman's policy recommendations.

Abramowitz pointed out the role of the newly formed Congressional Women's Caucus with which these same interest groups were also meeting.[117] One of the issues on the agenda of the caucus and women's organizations was ensuring participation of women in CETA job programs and expanding those eligible to include displaced homemakers.[118] Abramowitz raised the issue for consideration by the Carter administration and noted that the administration had to have a domestic agenda which included women's issues, and it could be developed in conjunction with Weddington's office.[119] The domestic agenda should be broader in focus than the ERA agenda of many women's organizations. The Domestic Council would also oversee policy recommendations arising from the IWY commission.

The President's Agenda and the IWY Commission

An outgrowth of the United Nations International Women's Year in 1975 and the United Nations General Assembly Proclamation of 1975–85 as the United Nations Decade for Women, Equality, Development, and Peace was the establishment of a National Commission on the Observance of International Women's Year.[120] A legacy from the Ford administration, this commission was planning a National Women's Conference for mid-November, 1977, in the first year of the Carter administration.

The commission and conference illustrate not only the evolution of issue networks over time, but also how the president's agenda can both be circumscribed and influenced by forces beyond the administration. Jill Ruckelshaus, who had worked in both the Nixon and Ford administrations, was the coordinator for the commission. Catherine East, who had served as an assistant to the PCSW during the Kennedy administration, worked on the agenda for IWY. The themes of the conference reflected the work that had been addressed earlier by the Kennedy Commission on the Status of Women, namely education, child care, and homemakers. In the 1977 Carter White House, the IWY fell under Costanza's jurisdiction.

The IWY and National Women's Conference were not without critics. Senator Jesse Helms (R-NC) began a series of investigations and Costanza was forced to respond to congressional inquiries as to the ideological agenda of the IWY.[121] And Costanza then had to brief cabinet heads, White House staff, women appointees, and DNC officials about these controversies.[122]

The National Women's Conference, with delegates from all fifty states and territories, was held in Houston, November 18–22, 1977. The conference was federally funded, and about forty women in appointive positions in the White House, departments, and agencies participated as speakers, while others in the administration attended the conference.[123]

The delegates to the conference adopted a National Plan of Action. Among the issues discussed were: battered women, with several bills pending in Congress and the administration yet to take a position; the creation of service centers for displaced homemakers, a topic raised by Carter in the 1976 campaign, and now in committee in Congress; the ERA, with approval needed of only three more states for ratification;[124] and rape, with several bills in committee that would "do away with the need for corroboration and redefine rape to include sexual assault upon a spouse and sexual assault on persons of the same sex [and] . . . change the rules of evidence to protect a victim of rape from being cross-examined about her prior sexual history or have her prior history weigh as a factor for the defendant."[125] In both cases, the administration had yet to take a position. Other provisions in the IWY Plan of Action included enforcing the Federal Equal Credit Opportunity Act of 1974, which prohibited sex discrimination in extending credit, and using federal funds for abortion.[126] President Carter's position was on record as opposing the use of federal funds for abortion.[127]

Both President Carter and Vice President Mondale met with the women in December to discuss the National Plan of Action and issues that would soon be facing the administration when the IWY Commission would present its Plan of Action in January, 1978, and complete its work.

The Formation of Advisory Structures

The legislation creating the IWY required that the president submit a formal report to Congress both analyzing the recommendations coming from the National Women's Conference, and then presenting his response.[128] Abramowitz on Eizenstat's Domestic Policy staff noted that "the need for follow up from IWY recommendations . . . and for a better coordinated effort in handling women's issues in general is real."[129] In addition, she also pointed out that Presidents Kennedy and Johnson had "recognized this by creating the Interdepartmental Committee on the Status of Women . . . [and] a Citizens' Advisory Council on the Status of Women [which] provide[d] external comment."[130] Rather than extend the life of the IWY Commission, or create a new commission, why not reconstitute and revitalize the existing structures, i.e the ICSW and the CACSW.

While some argued that a new commission would have different functions than the outgoing IWY Commission, it was clear that the intent of the supporters of a new commission was to extend the life of the current membership on the IWY Commission. In fact, in her argument for a new commission, Costanza noted that "failure to reappoint the Commission would result in a historic and catastrophic discontinuity in presidential commitment to the concerns of women. It would be the first time since 1961 that no commission or advisory council directly accountable to the President, was operational. To the public this could be interpreted as a retreat at the highest level of government from a commitment to equality for women."[131]

Costanza proposed an activist commission that would "take as its action agenda the National Plan of Action which consists of the recommendations adopted by the delegates to the National Women's Conference in Houston, Texas, November 18–21, 1977."[132] Costanza had also recommended the creation of an Interdepartmental Task Force, which would work with the National Commission for Women "to evaluate the impact of pertinent provisions of the National Plan of Action on [each respective department or agency's] ... programmatic and policy responsibilities."[133] The Interdepartmental Task Force, like its predecessor established by President Kennedy, was to be composed of a representative from each department.[134]

Secretary of Labor F. Ray Marshall noted that neither Presidents Johnson nor Nixon nor Carter had ever abolished Executive Order 11126, and so the authorization for an Interdepartmental Task Force, chaired by the secretary of labor, already existed.[135] Carter sought out the advice of his senior staff, and given the time constraints posed by a March 31, 1978, expiration date for the IWY Commission, the focus of Carter's advisors was on the need for a politically expedient response, which would not limit the policy options of the administration.

Jack Watson noted that "with enactment of ERA in grave danger, it is politically and substantively important that this Administration continue to give visibility to women's issues. Midge's proposal is the least expensive and likely the most effective way to do this."[136]

William M. Nichols noted that "OMB does not object to the concept of a Presidential advisory committee. . . . However, we question the use of the National Plan of Action as an action agenda in view of the fact that the recommendations in the Plan are currently under study in DPS [Domestic Policy Staff]."[137] While the management role of OMB is often overlooked, it does help keep the administration aware of existing statutes and structures, and in the case of a National Commission for Women it suggested that the role of such a commission should be examined vis-à-vis "other women's activities in the Government."[138]

Stu Eizenstat alerted the president to the fact that "if you extend the life of the current Commission, as Midge suggests, you will be required to make a decision in re-appointing the current Chairperson, Bella Abzug."[139] Eizenstat suggested that the president "not make a commitment to create a new Commission unless you want continuity with its current leadership (although you informally may want to create an advisory committee.)"[140]

Carter's Executive Order 12050, issued April 4, 1978, addressed the concerns of his senior staff, in that the new body would be an *advisory commit-*

tee, not a commission, with only thirty members, ten less than the current IWY Commission. Eizenstat's position that the administration should look at existing structures and programs already in place in the administration won out over Costanza's approach to have women continue work on a commission separate from decision-making processes in the White House or departments. The National Advisory Committee would:

> advise the President on a regular basis of initiatives needed to promote full equality for American women. . . .
>
> assist in reviewing the applicability of such initiatives, including recommendations of the 1977 National Women's Conference, to particular programs and policies . . .
>
> promote the national observance of the United Nations Decade for Women, Equality, Development and Peace (1975–1985) . . .
>
> gather and disseminate information relating to its responsibilities . . .
>
> consult regularly with the Interdepartmental Task Force. . . ."[141]

The composition of the new committee was responsive to concerns of some members of Congress that it "represent all women, all points of view, and a broad range of concerns."[142]

The Interdepartmental Task Force on Women

Carter also re-constituted an Interdepartmental Task Force, for the purpose of "reviewing the applicability of initiatives designed to promote full equality for American women, including recommendations of the 1977 National Women's Conference, to the [respective] agency's programs and policies." The task force was also to "consult regularly with the Committee." Unlike the prior task force, the secretary of labor was no longer designated as chair, an appropriate move given that the task force had languished when assigned to a cabinet secretary lacking interest in its workings.

Costanza was named chair of the Interdepartmental Task Force, which had in the past always been chaired by the secretary of labor. In spite of an expected collaboration between the task force and the National Advisory Committee, the two structures were soon in competition over resources and turf. As time went on, the problems worsened.

In the meantime, following the Houston Conference, Eizenstat's domestic policy staff had handled the administration's response to the conference for its report to Congress. It was treated the same as other domestic issues, i.e., given to the domestic policy staff to decide on the administration's position. Costanza, while having some input, did not define the final report. However, the fact that Eizenstat's office was providing the White House response to the conference meant that the conference and its recommendations were given high-level attention in the White House.

The NACW and the Interdepartmental Task Force on Women had few permanent staff, with most others detailed from other departments and agencies for periods of thirty to ninety days. As a result, there was a "a constant turnover in staff; with . . . much of the time [spent working on] shorter-term projects."[143]

That the Interdepartmental Task Force was to be rejuvenated was reflected in Weddington's coordination of the task force in her role as special assistant to the president. However, while the task force was re-established under EO 12050, at the same time the NACW (National Advisory Committee for Women) was established, the departure of Costanza and subsequent creation of the post of special assistant to the president for women's issues in September, 1978, delayed the organization and implementation of the task force. Weddington envisioned the task force having two tracks—with a policy representative from each department or agency, at least at the assistant secretary level or higher, and a staff level representative from each department and agency. The policy representatives would meet four times a year to set policy direction for the task force. The staff-level representatives would meet more regularly "to carry out the work of the Task Force and . . . work within the department and agencies on Task Force projects."[144]

However, given the small number of women at the assistant secretary level or higher, those appointed to the task force tended to be women at the level of bureau chiefs, deputy directors, or Federal Women's Program coordinators.[145] In addition, departments and agencies were slow to respond in naming a representative to the task force. Only forty-six agencies and departments had responded in identifying representatives by late November, with the first meeting of the task force scheduled for early December. Not all cabinet departments had even responded.[146]

The initial priorities of the task force were assessing "the impact of the President's inflation program on women, welfare reform proposals and their effect on child care programs and other family needs, the treatment of women under the Social Security program [and] national health insurance."[147] Thus the focus of the Interdepartmental Task Force was on federal policy and practices, which was appropriate, given Carter's delegation of policy responsibility to the department. However, with Weddington replacing the secretary of labor as the chair of the task force, the ultimate direction of the task force was moved back into the White House. And, Weddington's focus by late 1979 was more on politics than on policy, given her new responsibilities following the summer 1979 reorganization shakeup of the White House staff. Still, Weddington did work on issues of policy implementation, especially in the area of pensions and health insurance. For example, she urged Max Cleland, administrator of veterans affairs, to send out a notice to beneficiaries of a veteran's insurance program that they might want to review the benefit plan selected decades ago.[148]

The NACW Fiasco

At the time Carter's executive order was announced, the composition and chair of the National Advisory Committee had yet to be determined.[149] Shortly thereafter, it became quite clear that the fears of Eizenstat and his domestic policy staff, as well as those of OMB, regarding the role and leadership of the committee were well founded. Forty individuals, instead of thirty, were named to the new advisory committee, and Bella Abzug remained as chair, although she shared that title with Carmen Delgado Votaw, who was president of the National Conference of Puerto Rican Women.

While the NACW did represent a broad spectrum of interests, Costanza also excluded representatives of a number of interests that had long been a part of the push for women's rights, including Dorothy Height, president of the National Council of Negro Women.[150]

The NACW met for the first time in August, 1978, and focused on the participation of the United States in the U.N. Decade for Women.[151] In the fall of 1978, the NACW requested a meeting with Carter and his cabinet, in a "working session," following their receipt of a copy of the president's report to Congress on IWY recommendations.[152] Not only had the administration not circulated a draft of the report to NACW members, the name of Co-chair Carmen Delgado Votaw had been misspelled in the report.[153]

Abzug's and Votaw's request was met with a fifteen-minute session between the president and the entire NACW scheduled for the afternoon of November 22, the day before Thanksgiving, a time when many travel to see family and friends, or prepare for Thanksgiving Day. Weddington wrote to the co-chairs of the NACW a week before the scheduled meeting and indicated that the president wanted Weddington to meet with the NACW prior to his meeting with the committee. Weddington offered to rearrange her schedule to accommodate the members of the NACW in setting up such a meeting and also indicated that she and Wexler would meet with the NACW for "informal discussion and coffee in the Roosevelt Room after the session with the President."[154] This effort, like several others made by Weddington,[155] was rebuffed.

Abzug and Votaw indicated their displeasure in the brief time allotted with the President, writing to Weddington that "the Committee will not have the time to meet with you before meeting with the President because we have other business to attend to."[156] The agenda of the co-chairs was clear in that they indicated each would make a four-minute presentation, they would provide a written report to the president on their response to the President's Message to Congress on the National Plan of Action, and they wanted the press present "to take a picture."[157]

Tensions escalated when, on November 21, 1978, Abzug and Votaw canceled the meeting scheduled for the next day, by vote of the committee membership. While Abzug was absent, and at the urging of Millie Jeffrey, president of the NWPC, the NACW passed a resolution stating that "the 15 minutes allotted by the White House for the meeting was totally insufficient for a substantive discussion . . . on the major concerns of women and the issues affecting them."[158]

Weddington sent a letter on behalf of the president to Abzug and Votaw, promising a meeting at a later date. She clearly outlined the policy process to the Committee:

> As you noted, the development of domestic policy issues is currently underway although no final decisions have been made. Preliminary proposals are being discussed among the White House staff and the agencies. As a part of this effort, White House staff have been meeting with groups to discuss their concerns and ideas. These meetings are being used to help shape preliminary ideas in all areas. As issues develop, we will have additional meetings and discussions around those particular issues. I can assure you that the Advisory Committee will be involved in those discussions. In the interim, particularly in the inflation area, we can arrange sessions with key staff, if you desire. The Advisory Committee by its nature has a significant role to play in the policy development process. For this reason, although we are still in the early discussion stage, the President would like to meet with you and to have your judgment and advice on the substantive issues.[159]

The NACW, in its continuing refusal to meet with Weddington, and insistence on meeting with the president for an extended meeting, mis-read the policy formation process. In order for the president's agenda, and therefore his budget, to be inclusive of the interests of women, the president's senior advisors needed to be educated about their issues of concern. This dictated that the group meet directly with the president's advisors.

President Carter met with the NACW on January 12, 1979. The allotted time was thirty minutes, but it became an extended session. After an hour of listening to presentations by Abzug, Votaw, and five other committee members, with three more speakers still intent on speaking, President Carter interrupted the presentations indicating "he would like to share some thoughts with the Committee."[160]

His remarks were responsive to some of the issues raised by the NACW, including supporting ERA ratification, working with senators to increase the selection of women for the federal bench, reducing unemployment, and considering the effect of inflation on women. Carter also bluntly confronted the NACW with their inability to serve in an advisory capacity to the president. Noting they had prepared in advance a press release titled "President Carter Challenged on Social Priorities by National Advisory Committee for Women,"[161] he concluded, "I want to ask you to sit with Sarah Weddington and work out a two or three page paper on how to be more effective. . . . before our next meeting, we do need a sound basis for working together" (see box 6.3).[162]

Hamilton Jordan notified Abzug in person of Carter's decision to have new leadership of the committee to "enhance the relationship between the Administration and the Committee and to increase the spirit of consultation, cooperation and partnership."[164] Jordan also met with Votaw and asked her to continue on as co-chair. Following these meetings, some members of the NACW began a campaign to get the resignations of all members of the NACW, using phones in the Labor Department to pressure fellow members to resign. Several days later, Weddington recounted to the rest of Carter's senior staff what had happened:

> Their line of argument originally was that the President had "fired" Bella because the Committee failed to meet with him in November and because of the press release . . . ; that Bella had not been responsible for those actions; that the Committee members as a whole were responsible; therefore, they should share the responsibility by resigning. After a few of the representatives of major groups agreed to resign, another argument was added: this is the President versus the women's movement; are you with the movement or against it? Yesterday, Gloria Steinem added a new argument: you are a scab if you stay with the Committee; we will see that the Committee can't be effective; we will picket it if it even meets.

BOX 6.3

The President's Remarks to the National Advisory Committee for Women

I had hoped for a close consultative and supportive attitude with this Committee. This has not happened. The public thinks that you condemn my Administration and the efforts of Congress on your behalf.

You have a press release before you ever meet me that is 95% negative—or it may be 100% negative. It certainly doesn't say that we work in partnership. It would certainly help if you said we work together to achieve our goals.

I have no aversion to being criticized. We can certainly have honest differences of opinion. But for this group to stand aloof and to use precious time for condemnation or for a public relations gimmick is not appreciated.

Nothing would be more helpful than for you to meet with Sarah Weddington, my staff, and the cabinet. But the current relationship doesn't help me or Congress.

The only image that the public now has of our relationship is that you canceled our first meeting. After your press release, issued before I had a chance to respond, it will have the image that you condemn this Administration.

Every one of you was personally chosen. Half of you I know. I see the importance of your role. I know that you represent many women.

There should be no need for me or my staff to cringe when we see a meeting is scheduled with you. I'm a tough politician and I can certainly take criticism, but I thought you were to work with me.

I thought this group was to advise me, to work with me, to have a partnership in common. I never thought that you would use a trip to the White House to get in front of the cameras and criticize all that I have done.

It saps our strengths to be confrontational.

I don't feel that you are my allies. I don't feel that I can turn to you as friends.

BOX 6.3, *continued*

I am not writing off the Committee. I am anxious to work with you. But if you met every day with me, you wouldn't get as much out of it as working with Stu Eizenstat who is so familiar with every aspect of our domestic policy.

I feel discouraged. Congress after arduous debate passed the Civil Service Reform. We made a very strenuous attempt to get the veterans' preference modified. We have reorganized our equal opportunity functions to make them more effective. We extended the ERA deadline. But Congress doesn't feel that what they've done is recognized or appreciated.

This group should be bi-partisan, and to some extent it is. But there hasn't been much progress with this group.

I would like for you to consult with Sarah Weddington, with Stu Eizenstat, with Anne Wexler, with other members of my staff and my cabinet. Maybe you could establish subcommittees and they could meet with cabinet members. For example, if you had a labor committee they could meet with Ray Marshall. But now you don't have a cooperative spirit at all.

Maybe you see meeting with me more as a public relations gimmick. I know you get more TV coverage if you meet with me first. But I don't see our meetings that way, and I don't appreciate the way it's being used. . . .

I want to ask you to sit with Sarah Weddington and work out a two or three page paper on how to be more effective. Certainly subcommittees can work with cabinet members, as an example. Before our next meeting, we do need a sound basis for working together. . . .[163]

There was heavy lobbying to resign. One Committee member told me she received 8 phone calls; another told me she had never been through such pressure. Several did not want to resign, but felt they could not withstand the pressure.[165]

The splits within the women's movement were evident in the resignations. Twenty-four of forty NACW members resigned, including Votaw. However, Weddington had done her own lobbying. She met with the board of the NFBPWC, with the board of the League of Women Voters, and with Ellie Smeal and Millie Jeffrey. In the end, Marjorie Bell Chambers, president of AAUW, was named acting chair of a soon to be reconstituted NACW. Chambers, a registered Republican, had worked on Carter's 1976 election campaign on an Advisory Group on Education.[166] After the dust had settled about half of the original members of the NACW remained on the committee. Rather than fill the vacancies, the administration decided to keep the committee small in hopes that a better working relationship between the NACW and the White House could be established.[167]

The advisory potential of the NACW had been demonstrated in spite of the confrontational meeting with President Carter when the NACW had earlier met with Eizenstat in December, 1978. Eizenstat acknowledged that "the increased participation of women in the labor force has 'profound implications' for the development of public policy. He admitted that the government has not 'sensitized itself,' to that issue yet and has been negligent in failing to develop public policy on women's changing role in the economy." However, the role of the NACW, under the leadership of Abzug and Votaw, was more concerned with publicity—with press releases and statements presented to the President—than with actual policy construction.

The firing of Abzug contributed to a growing tension between different segments of the women's movement. A number of women's organizations around the country were torn between their dismay over the administration's firing of Abzug and their interests in supporting the work of Marjorie Bell Chambers and the NACW.[168] Jeanne Simon, a lawyer and former state legislator in Illinois, offered her support to Weddington, noting, "You're my kind of feminist! . . . I understand and appreciate the way you accomplish your goals."[169] Several weeks after the firing of Abzug, Carter received a threat from a California county supervisor, Susanne Wilson: "To be blunt, you were in a great deal of political trouble in California prior to the dismissal of Ms. Abzug. This kind of insensitivity [e.g., 'accepting an award for "family unity" in Salt Lake City' a stronghold of anti-ERA sentiment] to the concerns of women may lead to a 'rift' between the politically active women and your administration that time (specifically the 18 months until the June, 1980 primaries) cannot heal."[170]

In the White House press release announcing the designation of Marjorie Bell Chambers as acting chair of the NACW, the emphasis was on the *advising and consultative role for the Committee to the White House,* not the president, and that it was to *work with the President's Senior Staff,* rather than in isolation from those in the administration, and work on the agenda of the administration.[171] Weddington responded to those writing the president about the firing of Abzug, noting the White House would "continue to work with the Advisory Committee," but also "with the leadership of other groups that represent women of this country, as well as individual women."[172]

Chambers, an historian and former college president, and president of the AAUW, had had a wealth of experience in working with policy makers throughout the executive branch. The change in tone with the change in NACW leadership was evident within a month, as Chambers invited Weddington to meet with the NACW in its first meeting after the January debacle. Other senior staff from the White House also met with the committee to begin to develop a more collaborative relationship.[173]

The press release issued by NACW following the meeting reflected the new role of the committee in that the NACW had met "to reestablish their role as advisor to the President and to the Executive branch . . ." [174]

The NACW Regains its Footing

The first priorities of the new NACW were ratification of the ERA and the U.N. Mid-Decade Conference for Women. Other priorities included: "analysis and action on the reorganization of civil rights enforcement, the impact of anti-inflation guidelines on women, appointments of women to the Federal judiciary, national health insurance, welfare reform, public financing of congressional elections, and social security and pension reform."[175]

Another priority of the NACW was in the president taking action to ensure the implementation of Title IX.[176] Similar to the work of the PCSW fifteen years earlier, the long-range focus of the NACW would be "examining the role of women in today's society (the homemaker, the working mother, the head of household); and exploring a new definition of the 'extended family,' based not only on familial responsibilities, but on community relationships in caring for children and the elderly."[177]

At its March, 1979, meeting, the NACW commended the president for establishing an Interagency Task Force on Women Business Owners, holding a White House Conference on Small Business, and for creating an Interagency Committee to implement the task force recommendations. One of the recommendations was that the president issue an executive order establishing a National Women's Business Enterprise Policy. With this action, the administration would be meeting one of the resolutions of the Houston Conference's National Plan of Action "that an Executive Order establish as national policy the full integration of women entrepreneurs in government-wide business-related and procurement activities."[178]

The NACW also began to adopt the strategy of the PCSW, and various women's coalitions for appointments, identifying women for vacant posts. The judiciary was especially targeted following passage of the "Omnibus Judgeship Act" of 1978, which created 152 new lower court judgeships. Long-established traditions that Carter defer to senators in deriving the names of candidates for judicial vacancies in their respective states, however, worked against the administration's ability to include women. Carter left senators to submit names, and the NACW urged Carter to have the "Attorney General . . . supplement those lists that do not include women and minorities with qualified nominees."[179] The success of these efforts to include women in the judicial appointments will be explored to a great extent later in this chapter.

The consultative role of the NACW emerged following the change in leadership of the committee. Chambers, acting chair, forwarded copies of letters sent to the president on substantive policy issues to Weddington. Weddington, in turn, had time to follow up on these policy matters with others in the administration, in order to have a response by the time the NACW next met.[180]

The improved relationship with the White House was most evident when the remaining members of the NACW were invited to an "informal supper" with the president and Mrs. Carter in the private residence of the White House.[181]

President's Advisory Committee for Women

In May, 1979, President Carter changed the structure of the NACW through Executive Order 12135, re-establishing it as the President's Advisory Committee for Women (PACW). In addition to the individuals who had continued service on the NACW following the departure of Abzug, four new members were added. Chambers and Elizabeth Koontz, former director of the Women's Bureau, were named co-vice-chairs, and Lynda Robb, daughter of President Lyndon Johnson, was appointed chair. Robb had attended the National Women's Conference in Houston. The press release noted:

> The President's choice of Lynda Johnson Robb to chair the committee emphasizes the importance he places on women's right to choose freely among playing the role of wife and mother, combining work in the home with work outside, and pursuing a career outside the home.
>
> Robb is a homemaker with three children who is also actively involved in civic affairs and her business interests. The President feels that she can

bring to the Committee greater understanding of the concerns of women who have chosen the role of homemaker, and that she can provide these women with greater perspective on the effects of women's issues on their lives.[182]

Weddington continued in her outreach efforts to smooth the path for acceptance of this new advisory structure by lobbying Millie Jeffrey of NWPC, Ellie Smeal of NOW, and Carmen Delgado Votaw. In addition, Lynda Robb met with Bella Abzug before the Executive Order was announced and released to the press.[183]

The functions of this new advisory committee were to:

advise the President on a regular basis of initiatives needed to promote full equality for women ...

assist in reviewing the applicability of such initiatives, including recommendations of the 1977 National Women's Conference, to particular programs and policies ...

provide advice on appropriate ways to promote the national observance of the United Nations Decade for Women, Equality, Development and Peace (1975–1985) ...

gather information relating to its responsibilities and ... disseminate such information, through newsletters or other appropriate means, to the Executive Branch and to interested members of the public.

consult regularly with the Interdepartmental Task Force....[184]

Robb emphasized the PACW's advisory role. For example, in October, 1979, the president and Mrs. Carter held a reception to focus support on ERA ratification. Earlier in the day at the request of the administration, the PACW took "testimony in a confidential briefing session from selected persons from unratified states on the efforts needed for ratification. The Advisory Committee ... [was to] act as fact-finders for the President. ..."[185] Weddington's office provided logistical support, responding to questions about the administration's position on policy matters and providing lists of those who previously attended White House functions. Her office also served as an intermediary, getting input from the committee on strategies for ERA ratification, as well as sharing information with the committee.[186]

Robb also presented substantive policy recommendations on topics such as welfare, child care, education and jobs training programs, shelters, housing, and health care for the poor to Eizenstat. Robb quickly established a positive working relationship with the president's senior advisors and others in the administration. For example, when "women's groups were somewhat under-represented at the Camp David Summit" in July of 1979, she called the White House and Jack Watson responded by inviting Unita Blackwell, a member of the PACW and mayor of Mayersville, Mississippi, to the July 11 meeting along with Weddington, State Senator Polly Baca Barrigan of Colorado, Charlotte Williams, a commissioner of Flint, Michigan, and Secretary Patricia Harris.[187]

At the first meeting of the reconstituted PACW in July, 1979, the committee agreed to the following: (1) a request would be made to all cabinet and agency heads that each prepare "a full report on how their departments are implementing the planks of the Houston Plan of Action . . . relevant to their areas" by January 30, 1980; (2) the PACW would "sponsor a series of regional meetings to get . . . input on issues of concern to women"; and (3) President Carter would be strongly advised "to hold a Camp David Summit Meeting on ERA ratification."[188] Before the PACW issued a press release regarding these actions, they gave a heads-up to the White House so that the White House press office would have time to prepare a response to anticipated questions from the media. This was especially important when the president was asked to take a specific action—e.g., in holding a Camp David summit.[189] Robb did not make her recommendations directly to the president, although she did raise one particular concern directly with the president when the occasion presented itself.[190] Robb's status as a former First Daughter gave her a natural entre to the president, and she used that access to push for her strongest priority—ERA ratification. Robb and Carter both addressed the Women's Caucus of the National Association of Counties in Kansas City, and Robb was invited to fly back with the president to Washington, D.C., on Air Force One. She used that time to quietly lobby the president to hold a Camp David summit meeting on ERA ratification.[191] Robb was successful in her efforts, as Carter did hold the Camp David summit on ERA ratification.[192]

Unlike the PCSW, or the NACW, where the focus had been on the chair of the committee, the overall composition of the PACW and each constituency represented were the focus of attention. Given that the PACW began its work a year before the party primaries and caucuses, the focus in selecting members was on the states represented, as well as on the ethnic and racial representations. For instance, Weddington notified Robb of the White House's interest in adding Freddie Lang Groomes to the PACW, stating "she will be a representative from Florida; she is Black." Weddington went on to write, "I would suggest that we should add a Cuban-American after Miriam Cruz resigns. Obviously, that person should be from a state not currently represented."[193]

By 1980, the PACW had become just another one of a number of women's groups invited to the White House for briefings, along with the NWPC, BPW, and so forth. It had become an interest group, rather than an arm of the executive branch, losing its status as a special advisory body to the president.

In spite of the president's election defeat in November, 1980, Weddington pushed to have the members of the PACW recognized for their work. They presented their final report to the president on December 16, 1980, and Weddington urged that the event be a special one: "It would be nice if we could make this a more special occasion. For example, if we could have them for lunch or a dinner or if we could combine some other events that focus on women it would help build the occasion. The 30 members of the Committee have served under difficult circumstances, and I am hopeful that we can do something very special to highlight their service."[194]

The president's meeting with members of the PACW lasted less than thirty minutes, with opportunity for the press to cover the event.[195]

The Federal Courts: Appointments and Public Policy

Even though Jimmy Carter's term of office would come to an end on January 20, 1981, when Ronald Reagan took the oath of office, the influence of the Carter administration would continue on, especially through appointments made to the federal court. Given the lifetime appointments of judges to district court and appeals court positions, and the number of appointments made, the president's extended influence over the judicial branch continued to shape policy, especially with new legislation carving out rights and protections for women, long after his administration came to an end.

Carter was the first president to make a concerted effort to get women, in more than token numbers, on the bench. Carter widened the screening process through use of a newly formed Federation of Women Lawyers' Judicial Screening Panel and by persuading Democratic senators to use state nominating conventions.[196] As a means of pressuring the Senate to submit the names of women and minorities for federal court seats, Carter began "holding up the nomination of many federal judges until we see if we can get more Senators to submit the names of women and minorities."[197]

There were a number of additional actions taken by the Carter administration to help increase the number of women and minorities on the bench, including: a letter from Carter to each senator regarding the nomination; the assignment of a woman in Justice to work full time in assisting the search for women; White House briefings for women's organizations to explain the judicial selection process, and thus the need for groups to work at the state level to gain support of the key senators; and meetings between President Carter and key senators and lobbying these same senators to include women and minorities on their selection lists to help increase the number of women and minorities on the bench.[198]

The judicial appointment process, however, did not proceed smoothly, in spite of the efforts of the White House to bring this about. Tensions arose between Jordan, himself a Georgian, and others on the White House staff over the control of the selection process by fellow Georgian and friend of the President, Attorney General Griffin Bell.[199] Jordan defended Bell, in spite of the political heat others on the White House staff were feeling from women's organizations.[200] Bell, however, left halfway through Carter's term of office, and was therefore not involved in the selection process to any great extent after the Omnibus Judgeship Act created many new judgeships to fill.

Of Carter's appointments to the district courts (202), 14.4 percent went to women, and given that his immediate predecessors (Ford, Nixon, Johnson) appointed women to less than 2 percent of their district judgeships, it is not surprising that with Carter's appointments, "the proportion of women judges on the federal bench had risen from one percent to close to seven percent."[201] The administration's efforts were such that when questions were raised about the Carter record in appointing women, Weddington would note the appointment of women to executive branch posts, but would also include the efforts of the president in nominating women for federal district and appeals court positions.[202]

THE 1980 CAMPAIGN

The conflict that had emerged between the White House and certain women's organizations carried over into the 1980 campaign.

By the end of 1979, the president's re-election campaign was well under way. A challenge by Ted Kennedy was never far from the thoughts of the White House staff. Bella Abzug and company threatened to throw their support to Kennedy. Nearly one year before the election, Wexler, Weddington, and Kit Dobelle took umbrage with a story by Terry Smith in the *New York Times* in which the president's closest advisors were portrayed as all male.

They wrote to both Jordan and Powell, stating that: "In the future, when you do stories like the one in today's Times it would be better for the President's image if you included us, especially when we are trying to contrast Carter's record on women with Kennedy's. The pictures in the New York Times of the 'closest advisers' make us as vulnerable as we are trying to make Kennedy on the women's issues. Mainly through our efforts the outside world would think there are women in the inner circle. For the sake of the President, it would be good to perpetuate that myth."[203]

While Carter faced a primary challenge for his party's renomination in the spring of 1980, in part waged over the fight for the support of women voters, it would be during his administration that the rules requiring that "each state delegation [to the Democratic National Convention] be equally divided between the sexes," would finally come into practice.[204] Weddington's responsibilities were expanded to include the implementation of the equal division requirement for the Democratic Party.[205] In addition, Geraldine Ferraro was named a national deputy for the campaign.[206]

Weddington was quick to let others on the president's staff know when the percentage of women in the administration began to drop. Ever attuned to the 1980 election, Weddington thought it "crucial that we maintain the strong record the President has on appointing women. Women will play a more active role in the upcoming year than in any previous election. We cannot afford the rumblings I hear from leaders of women's organizations that we are losing ground."[207]

In the summer of 1980, Jack Watson met with the top women in the administration to brief them on their role in convention activities and in the fall campaign. He encouraged them to accept speaking invitations and fill in for the president when requested by the White House Speaker's Bureau. In addition, the women in the administration had another role when responding to requests to talk to women's groups. The White House provided a summary of the administration's record on women's issues—"The Record of President Carter on Women's Issues"—in order for the women of the administration to speak about Carter's inclusion of women in the administration, a role only assigned to the women.[208]

Carter and the ERA

The White House was under pressure to obtain ratification of the ERA, or face the opposition of members of their own party, women in particular, in the 1980 election contest. When Carter took the oath of office, the ERA had been submitted to the states and the ratification process was under way, with thirty-four states (of the needed thirty-eight) having approved of the amendment. However, in spite of thirty states having ratified the amendment by early 1973, the drive for ratification had already come to a halt. In 1978 Congress had passed legislation to extend the seven-year deadline of 1979 by three years to 1982. The push for ratification and extension became intense and intertwined with the 1980 campaign. The role of the Carter administration is well documented as part of a larger story on the fate of the ERA and the role of interest groups, the women's movement, and other governmental actors and so will not be discussed in detail here.[209]

Carter did support the amendment, and the official position of the administration was endorsement of the amendment, although Carter let personnel throughout the administration hold a different view. As a former governor, Carter would be especially attuned to the rights of states and the role of the states in the ratification process. However, as president, he had no formal role in the amendment process. Some interpreted Carter's words as backing away from a commitment to the ERA when Carter warned his staff to "explore all alternatives to the ERA ratification, just in case," in March, 1979.[210] Instead, Carter's directive reflected an active and pragmatic approach to the pursuit of women's issues, as he advised his senior staff to begin preparation for action to take in achieving the objectives of the ERA, if ratification were to fail.

Carter included the ERA in his State of the Union Address and, according to Weddington, "emphasized it in speeches he gave around the country. For example, right at the end of the campaign, he gave a speech for the ERA in Abilene, Texas, which is not your prime audience. But they responded well. We had a series of briefings for business leaders . . . here in the White House. The President himself came up with an idea of sponsoring [an] ERA fund-raiser to raise money, and he was the principal guest at the event which raised . . . about $115,000 clear, net, and was the largest single event to benefit the ERA that anyone has ever had."[211] The president's role in the ratification process is limited at best to use of the bully pulpit to persuade state legislators in fifty separate states to support the ERA. Weddington has noted that Carter "met monthly with the presidents of the national women's organizations, the largest ones, and they often had suggestions to make about ERA" i.e., how to gain support as votes came up in particular state legislatures.[212] In addition, Carter called state legislators to urge their support and made use of the family residence to host state legislators for dinner.[213] Carter also played a role in getting Congress to approve an extension when the seven years set for ratification had come to an end with only thirty-five states having ratified the amendment, three short of the thirty-eight needed. Carter, along with Vice President Mondale, "changed about seven no votes to yes votes, which did make the difference in the final passage" of the extension.[214]

CONCLUSION

In the Carter administration, attempts were made to create opportunity structures for the inclusion of women. While affirmative action began under the Nixon administration, it was given meaning through the actions of the Carter administration. This is, perhaps, one of the few times where a concerted effort was made to break down long-established barriers that restricted women's full participation in government, since the *Bakke* decision in the summer of 1978 would diminish future efforts to establish affirmative action as a federal policy. In subsequent administrations, presidents would move away from the concept of "affirmative action," and the term "quota" would be applied to actions which in reality were better termed "affirmative action," as originally conceptualized during the Nixon administration.

The policy legacy of the administration included the establishment of flex-time and part-time work in the federal sector, fulfilling one of the goals set by the PCSW in 1963. In addition, the regulations in CETA were changed to allow job training programs for displaced homemakers. A new area of law, sexual harassment, began to emerge. Consolidation of federal agencies responsible for enforcement of civil rights laws would result in stronger enforcement of Title VII and Title VI. However, the Women's Educational Equity Act's funding remained too low to authorize the use of funds to enforce Title IX provisions prohibiting sex discrimination by educational institutions and exemptions for revenue generating sports continued.[215]

An institutional structure for the inclusion of women emerged in Weddington's office, although in subsequent administrations women were appointed to the Presidential Personnel Office and the Office of Public Liaison, therefore ensuring outreach and appointments of women. In addition, the ICSW, which had suffered from neglect under Labor Secretary John Dunlop in the Ford administration, was resurrected under the guidance of Weddington.

By 1980, there was an acknowledgment that women were serving in Congress. When congressional spouses were invited to the White House, for example to briefings on the ERA, "the husbands of women members of Congress" were included on the guest list.[216]

The administration recognized that to have "women's issues . . . considered and the aspect of issues that affect women . . . considered," in the policy-making process, it helped to have women appointed to high-level positions in each department and agency. The Carter administration greatly increased the numbers of women as assistant secretaries from that of prior administrations. This was a direct response to Carter's statement made during the 1976 transition that if women were in subcabinet posts, women would be in the pipeline for future cabinet posts.

According to Weddington, the White House Office could influence actions in the departments and agencies, and elsewhere in society, through its own action. The administration applied equal employment opportunity to all offices, including the White House. The White House also worked to review guest lists at each White House briefing to see whether women were included. Yet according to Weddington, "There was, similarly, an effort in doing publications to look and see what visual images were represented there and whether or not women were included."[217] The showcasing aspect of women's inclusion continued. However, change in behavior was brought about even within the White House Office itself. Jordan, in reviewing a list of potential "kitchen cabinet" advisors for Carter, noted that "we'll get flak since no women are on the list," without the prodding by a woman assistant to the president.

By the end of the 1970s the representation of different constituencies had become an institutionalized feature of the White House Office, especially through the creation of an Office for Public Liaison. While interests institutionally began to be represented in the White House Office, it is not evident that these structural changes at a time of increasing power for presidential advisors vis-à-vis the cabinet led to increased representation of substantive policy concerns; rather these offices facilitated and enhanced symbolic representation, but also contributed to an increase in the percentage of women appointed to high-level positions within an administration.

CHAPTER 7

◉

Conclusion

Promise and Illusion

A Special Plea
In this work, when it shall be found that much is
omitted, let it not be forgotten that much likewise is
performed.
    —*Dr. Samuel Johnson*
    A Dictionary of the English Language

PRESIDENT William Jefferson Clinton
arrived at the Capitol on the night of January 19, 1999, just a month after he
had been impeached by the House of Representatives, to deliver his annual
State of the Union Address to Congress. That afternoon the Senate had lis-
tened to the president's lawyers begin their defense in the trial of the president. As an unwanted guest of the House, Clinton's quick entrance to the
enthusiastic applause of Democrats and polite applause from some Republicans replaced the traditional ritual of a president's slow movement from the
entrance of the chamber to the rostrum, being greeted by endless rounds of
applause while shaking hands down both sides of the aisle.

The impact of an impeachment decided in this very chamber seemed to
weigh heavily on the president's shoulders as he tentatively, perhaps ner-
vously, recounted the state of the union: the economy was expanding, with
low unemployment, a balanced budget, and even a surplus; peace efforts
were progressing in the Middle East and Northern Ireland; social security

was being protected, but the health care needs of senior citizens also needed to be met; and new education initiatives would be proposed.

Thirty minutes into the speech, Clinton seemed to regain his old form as he picked up the pace of delivery, with more inflection in his voice, becoming more forceful in his speech with a strong sense of conviction. The line that appeared to break the ice was a call for equal pay for equal work for both women and men by strengthening enforcement of existing laws. Receiving his loudest applause of the night thus far, Clinton turned to the Republican half of the chamber seated before him, and noted, in a more relaxed ad-lib typically seen in Clinton's speeches, that "that was encouraging, you know?—There was more balance on the see saw."

There was a certain irony in watching Democrats and Republicans applaud the president and his actions in designating equal rights for women a priority, while he stood there having been impeached for statements made under oath—designed to hide his sexual indiscretions—in a deposition that was the result of a sexual harassment lawsuit filed against him. Equally striking, perhaps, was in hearing a call for equal pay for women, when an "Equal Pay Act" had been signed into law more than thirty-five years earlier.

As recently as 1991, President George Bush's appointment of Bernadine Healy (a cardiologist and former science advisor in the Reagan White House) as director of the National Institutes of Health (NIH) came under fire. In one of her initiatives to bring about change at the NIH she worked to get Congress to fund a 625-million-dollar research project focused on women's health issues. A number of critics claimed her actions as "political showboating rather than a sensible allocation of funds."[1] However, for years women had been excluded from clinical trials and so the effects of different medical interventions on women were not known. Nor were recommended dosages of medication or possible reactions to medication known. Healy's initiative complemented efforts by women in Congress to move forward on this same agenda item.

In looking at the Clinton and Bush administrations and the status of women, it does not take long to discover that some of the same issues that were discussed in the final report of Kennedy's President's Commission on the Status of Women in 1963 remain on the national agenda—equal pay, child care, tax credits in support of child care, health care for children, volunteer service, social security protection for women, and broadened educational opportunities.[2]

Similarly, as was the case when a coalition of women's groups under the leadership of the NFBPWC in the 1960s and early 1970s joined forces to fill a talent bank with names and resumes to be used by the White House in consideration of potential presidential appointments, almost thirty years later the Coalition for Women's Appointments, "a project convened by the NWPC" for each election, continued to make recommendations for high-level appointive positions throughout the Clinton transition, and to a lesser extent, during the George W. Bush transition.[3] Included with the recommendations were detailed summaries of the educational level attained and career path taken by each woman.

The NWPC also published a guidebook during the first Bush administration and available for the Clinton transition for "women seeking appointment to a *federal board* or *commission*" [my emphasis] entitled "Don't Miss That Appointment." However, while the NWPC's list of publications in the 1990s also included pamphlets and books on women running for elective office, there were no guidebooks listed on the topic of securing the *highest* appointive posts (those positions at least at the subcabinet level).[4] More than thirty years earlier, the issue had also been one of securing appointments to *boards* and *commissions* primarily. And the NFBPWC had published similar guidebooks decades earlier.

AGENDAS AND OPPORTUNITIES FOR ACTION

When a new administration takes over the reins of government, especially if there has been a change in party control, there is an institutional learning process that must begin anew. While briefing papers are prepared on the structures of the White House or how the EOP and cabinet are to relate, or on transforming goals and pledges made in the heat of a campaign to a policy agenda, there is little preparation for dealing with the aspects of government already in place, that is, laws and statutes to be administered by the executive branch, or offices already in place to carry out policy. It is rather striking how slowly the White House Office comes to learn about the government in place. As a case in point, it was nine months before Midge Costanza learned about the Federal Women's Coordinators (FWC). Shortly before Costanza was to meet with this group, her staff prepared a briefing paper outlining the role of the FWC:

> The FWCs are responsible for the implementation of the 1972 EEO Act within the federal agencies as it relates to women. They not only deal with employment of women but with agency personnel management and policy implementation. They are the chief point of contact for the

agencies, female employees and job applicants. The FWCs are involved in discrimination complaints and the development and implementation of the Affirmative Action Plan. They counsel women on career possibilities and act as advocates of women's issues within the agencies. In their role as advocates, they get involved in improving employment benefits for women, such as access to training, interpretation of regulations, conscious-ness-raising of agency employees, both male and female.[5]

During the past forty years, each administration has inherited an agenda that includes the concerns of women. Some issues have had greater staying power, such as equal educational opportunities, while other issues, such as the ERA, have fallen by the wayside. Other issues have been redefined; consumer protection is no longer viewed as a "woman's issue." There has also been a constant push from women's organizations for the enforcement of existing statutes, such as Title IX. Presidents have reorganized and consolidated offices to facilitate the coordination of enforcement activities, but remain dependent on Congress for funds to carry out enforcement. An additional constraint comes from a regulatory process that determines the implementation of policy. In the case of Title IX, 9,700 comments were received on the proposed regulations, all of which had to be addressed before the guidelines could be put in place.

The area in which presidents have had the most interest, and thus paid more attention to and achieved success in, is the inclusion of more women in government, through both appointive positions as well as career positions in the federal government. The civil service became an early focus of attention by presidents interested in opening up employment opportunities for women. As manager of the federal government this is an area in which the president has the most direct control. For instance, John Macy's work in eliminating sex-specific jobs had a dramatic effect in opening up job opportunities for women in the Kennedy and Johnson administrations. In addition, the New Deal programs of the 1930s and Great Society programs of the 1960s expanded the size of the federal workforce, and so a president's action in opening up positions to women would have even a greater impact on society.

The president's reach over the workforce also stretched into the private sector, especially through the use of executive orders. By prohibiting sex discrimination by federal contractors, the president could influence the composition of the workforce beyond the confines of the civil service. Affirmative action, although never fully implemented in the federal sector given the Supreme Court's ruling in the *Bakke* case in 1978, did, however, become a model for state and local government and private sector employers to move forward on.

In areas where new legislation was required, change sometimes came about from legislative initiatives of the president, but more often in response to action taken by the women in Congress. With a president favorably inclined, or at least not disinclined, to expand opportunities for women, Congress added language in the 1964 Civil Rights Act and in Title IX of the 1972 Education Amendments to prohibit sex discrimination. The post-secondary and vocational school loan and grant programs begun in the 1960s and not targeted for particular programs of study or to veterans especially opened up educational opportunities for women.

Commissions and task forces, which serve the interests of the president both in responding to substantive and symbolic matters, proved useful, both directly and indirectly. The PCSW spawned the emergence of state commissions on the status of women. Members on those commissions moved in another direction in creating NOW. In the 1960s, coalitions of women's organizations came together to participate in the creation of a talent bank of women, upon which the White House could draw in making appointments to high-level positions.

APPOINTMENTS

In their speeches and press conferences, presidents and their administrations have focused on the appointment of women to high-level positions, rather than on a legislative agenda addressing issues such as equal opportunity, sex discrimination, equal rights, or women's health initiatives. From a pragmatic standpoint, while a president can control the appointment process (although not the confirmation process), the legislative agenda is shared with Congress.

Since the Truman administration there has been a political need for presidents to talk about the inclusion of women in the administration. In part this has been in response to questions from the press, but presidents have also engaged in comparing the records of their own administrations with those of their predecessors in regard to the appointment of women. This pattern slowly evolved during the Truman, Eisenhower, and Johnson administrations, but under Johnson the numbers of women appointed became the major focus in talking about women serving in the executive branch or when talking to women's groups, and this remained so until the 1990s.

This was indeed a significant development, but appointments were but one of a number of concerns. The PCSW report issued just before the assassination of President Kennedy had set out a legislative agenda that also addressed the issues of educational and training opportunities to prepare women for the workforce, as well as tax deductions for child care, and the ending of discrimination in both the private sector and in the federal workforce.

Presidents have also gone beyond the rhetoric and worked to steadily increase the numbers of women in high-level positions. Lyndon Johnson's staff soon began to realize he was serious in his intent to broaden the demographics of the administration to include women and minorities. Likewise, Jimmy Carter's staff felt similar pressure in making certain that women, in addition to First Lady Rosalynn Carter, were included in activities of the administration and on lists of potential appointees when positions became vacant.

Even while the Bush and Clinton administrations increased the percentage of women in high-level posts, each administration continued to count, compare, and contrast their records in appointing women to high-level posts with the record of preceding administrations. Yet a shift in emphasis had taken place. Initially, a few women were appointed at the highest levels in a department or agency, allowing for a "showcasing" of women (for example, Eisenhower's appointment of Oveta Culp Hobby). But with "thickening government" and thus an increase in the number of positions to fill at the level of assistant secretary and below, the numbers and percentages of women appointed would continue to increase. However, the appointments were to lower-level positions on regulatory boards and commissions, or at the level of assistant secretary in the departments.[6]

STRUCTURES WITHIN THE WHITE HOUSE OFFICE

A president can have greater control over his or her structuring of the White House Office than over the departments and agencies. Yet presidents have said and done very little about this office and the inclusion of women, and women have had a most difficult time in becoming a member of the inner circle of advisors. Anne Armstrong, in her role as counsellor to the president, gained structural access to the president and served more broadly as an advisor to the president, although such access would prove of less importance as the Watergate-induced isolation took hold in President Nixon's second term. In spite of her portfolio extending far beyond "women's organizations" and "women's issues," Armstrong did establish an office for women's programs, which in some form continued throughout the Ford and Carter administrations.

As the White House Office expanded and began to undertake and direct liaison activities to various interests and organizations, an Office of Public Liaison emerged. Not surprisingly, given the public relations aspect surrounding the appointment of women, once Armstrong left the White House in 1974 shortly after President Ford took the oath of office, the new OWP was placed under the direction of the Office of Public Liaison.

By the end of the Carter administration, a White House Office focusing on women as constituents, responding to the policy concerns of women, and increasing the number of women in high-level positions had become an institutionalized part of the White House Office. Both the Nixon-Ford and Carter White Houses had established such units to varying degrees— each administration had a high-level staff member (e.g., Counsellor to the President Anne Armstrong; Assistant to the President Sarah Weddington) responsible for women and women's issues; in subsequent administrations the office continued, although not with as high a ranking individual in charge. The institutionalization of the office lessened the need for a high-level appointee who could also fill symbolic purposes. When only one or two women were appointed to the cabinet, much attention was focused on these appointments; by the 1990s, although the appointment of women to the cabinet also fulfilled a symbolic role, the emphasis shifted to descriptive representation. Women now held a greater percentage of lower-level positions in an administration than they held top-level positions, i.e., those at the subcabinet or cabinet level.

In subsequent administrations the office would disappear, but the responsibility for outreach to women's organizations and for increasing the number of women appointed would become an institutionalized feature of the Office of Public Liaison and Presidential Personnel Office, respectively. With a proliferation of White House staff, a special assistant could be given these responsibilities. With women either heading the Office of Public Liaison or Presidential Personnel, the interests of women could be integrated within other structures in the White House Office.

However, both the Reagan and Clinton administrations went back to adding a special structure within the White House Office to focus on women. President Ronald Reagan formed a White House Coordinating Council on Women to "serve as a focal point for the coordination of politics and issues that are of particular concern to women. The Council . . . also work[ed] on the appointment of women and the development of policy and programs by regularly bringing women's concerns to the attention of the President and appropriate offices within the executive branch."[7]

President Clinton formed a "White House Office for Women's Initiatives and Outreach" a year before his re-election. The office, claiming to be the first such office, stated that it "serves as a liaison between the White House and women's organizations.... Inside and outside of the White House, the office advocates for issues that are important to women."[8]

The activities of the office were not too dissimilar to those of the Ford and Carter White House offices. According to background information provided by the White House:

> The office's primary initiative, called At the Table, is a series of roundtables across the nation with women and Administration officials to ensure that women's voices are heard at policy tables. The office has held several roundtable and media events including...the President's and First Lady's Suffrage celebration in Wyoming...; a series of roundtables hosted by the First Lady on working women's issues;... a meeting hosted by Mrs. Gore for labor women leaders; a meeting with women presidential appointees and Dr. Laura Tyson on the impact of the proposed Republican budget;... and a roundtable in the White House on the U.N. Fourth World Conference on Women, focusing on domestic economic needs.[9]

As was the case twenty years earlier, women appointees, women labor leaders, and other women leaders were targeted for special briefings and roundtable discussions. The most noticeable difference was that these sessions were often held outside of Washington, including sessions in Wyoming, California, and New Mexico.

The office remained under the direction of the Office of Public Liaison. Its profile remained low, however; so low that when this author attempted to call the White House Office for Women's Initiatives and Outreach in December, 1998,[10] a young White House staff member answered the phone and responded in an incredulous tone, "We have an 'Office for Women's Initiatives and Outreach'?" The post of director was vacant and apparently had been vacant for some time.

When the first woman, Frances Perkins, was named to the cabinet by Franklin D. Roosevelt in 1933, a great deal of media attention was given both to her nomination and confirmation. Perhaps because of this attention, and with no prior administrations by which to compare, the White

House did not necessarily make an effort to "showcase" this appointment. A photo taken in 1936 at captioned, "Roosevelt—on the White House lawn, F.D.R. and Cabinet at what news services called an 'impromptu' meeting in the spring of 1936" demonstrates this fact. In this rather formal picture, Roosevelt is surrounded by nine men, with Frances Perkins nowhere in sight.[11] In addition, while individual organizations such as the NWP urged Roosevelt to appoint women, a concerted effort to have women appointed began to be organized during the 1940s and 1950s, when a number of women's organizations were brought together in Washington, D.C. to discuss the role of women in post-war policy making. In the 1950s and 1960s, with more organizations having headquarters in Washington, D.C., similar meetings resulted in the formation of the talent bank organized by the NFBPWC. Shortly thereafter, the Coalition for Women's Appointments took over the coordination of efforts to increase the numbers of women in high-level positions.

CHANGE AND ILLUSION

With women's organizations continuing to remain active in lobbying for women, issues of symbolic representation remain important to each administration. Photo opportunities have become a means of demonstrating an administration's response. Ronald Reagan elevated Jeane Kirkpatrick's position as ambassador to the United Nations to cabinet rank, and featured her in the center of the official White House portrait of the cabinet, suggesting that an otherwise all-male administration at the highest levels was inclusive of women. Reagan had yet to appoint a woman to head a cabinet department. In 1998, Hillary Rodham Clinton, "in a departure from tradition," announced the appointment of Lt. Col. Eileen Collins as the first woman to be commander of a space shuttle mission.[12] The accompanying photo featured Hillary at the podium, with the president slightly behind her, and next to Eileen Collins. The "firsts" of women appointments continued to make headlines, and the First Lady's role contributed to the symbolism in this formal announcement.

President Clinton always included issues of concern to women on his legislative agenda, and with support from Congress, issues such as funding for women's health research, family leave, and child care are no longer viewed as unusual. But this is a relatively new phenomenon.

As demonstrated in earlier chapters, the White House has been involved in significant policy change addressing the concerns of women, especially in the areas of sex discrimination and affirmative action in the civil service, and in employment practices of government contractors, areas in which the president could more directly effect policy change. In looking at what presidents have said in public forums, little attention has been paid to other policy issues of concern to women; it is quite possible that more change could have come about if presidents had used the bully pulpit to take a leadership role in bringing about legislative as well as societal change.

One striking pattern that emerges in this study is the constant emergence and re-emergence, not only from administration to administration, but within the same administration, of various commissions, White House offices, advisory committees, task forces, and talent banks, all devoted to the question of women's inclusion and participation in government, all coming to the same conclusions, issuing a similar agenda, each administration re-inventing the wheel and claiming credit for it, while real progress proceeds in tiny increments, in fits and starts.

This book has demonstrated and discussed the social dynamics, political pressures, and institutional mechanisms within the executive branch that have brought about real change in the inclusion of women as advisors to the president, in career and appointive posts, and as constituents whose interests are being represented. The book also points out, in its examples of bureaucratic inertia, substantively overblown political showcasing of symbolic appointments and initiatives, and lackluster support of legislative goals, how an illusion of even greater change is fostered, the "myth" as Carter's advisor Sarah Weddington put it, of "women in the inner circle."

In the midst of President Clinton's second term, Ann Lewis, director of communications in the White House, was asked in an interview about the near absence of women in Clinton's inner circle of advisors in the White House, with the exception of First Lady Hillary Clinton. Lewis dismissed the assertion. However, Lewis told a reporter that the next day, while at a senior staff meeting, she looked around the room and soon realized that she was, in fact, the only woman present.[13]

APPENDIX

Party Platform Planks, 1896–2000

Election Year	Candidates	Democrats	Republicans
1896*	*McKinley*/Bryan		Equal Pay
1920*	*Harding*/Cox		Equal Pay[a]
1928*	*Hoover*/Smith	Equal Pay[b]	
1940	Roosevelt/*Wilkie*		ERA
1944	Roosevelt/*Dewey*	Equal Pay, ERA	Equal Pay,[c] ERA
1948	Truman/*Dewey*	Equal Pay, ERA	Equal Pay, ERA
1952	*Eisenhower*/Stevenson	Equal Pay, ERA	Equal Pay, ERA
1956	*Eisenhower*/Stevenson	Equal Pay, ERA	Equal Pay, ERA
1960	Kennedy/*Nixon*	Equal Pay	Equal Pay
1964	Johnson/*Goldwater*	Equal Pay	
1968	*Nixon*/Humphrey		
1972	*Nixon*/McGovern	Equal Pay,[d] ERA	Equal Pay, ERA, AA
1976	Carter/*Ford*	Equal Pay,[e] ERA, AA	ERA
1980	*Reagan*/Carter	Equal Pay,[f] ERA, AA	ERA**
1984	*Reagan*/Mondale	Equal Pay,[g] ERA, AA	Equal Pay
1988	G. *Bush*/Dukakis	ERA	Equal Pay
1992	Clinton/G. *Bush*	ERA, AA	
1996	Clinton/*Dole*	ERA, AA	
2000	G. W. *Bush*/Gore	Equal Pay,[h] ERA, AA	

Notes:

[a] "equal pay for equal service"

[b] "we favor an equal wage for equal service"

[c] "without discrimination in rate of pay because of sex"

[d] "equal pay for comparable work"

[e] "equal pay for comparable work"

[f] "equal pay for work of comparable value"

[g] "equal pay for work of comparable worth"

[h] "an equal day's pay for an equal day's work"

AA = Support for "affirmative action" for women

Equal Pay = Support for "equal pay for equal work"

ERA = Support for an "Equal Rights Amendment" to the Constitution

* = in the elections that follow, neither party includes platform planks on equal pay or the ERA, or affirmative action.

** The 1980 Republican Platform states: "We acknowledge the legitimate efforts of those who support or oppose ratification of the Equal Rights Amendment. We reaffirm our Party's historic commitment to equal rights and equality for women."

The winning candidate in each election is listed first.

Republican candidates are in italics.

HISTORICAL EVOLUTION OF STATEMENTS
IN PARTY PLATFORMS ON
THE RIGHTS OF WOMEN
Equal Rights (without explicit mention of an ERA)

1876 Republicans were the first party to specifically call for "equal rights" for women in a platform:

> "The Republican Party recognizes with approval the substantial advances recently made toward the establishment of equal rights for women, by the many important amendments effected by Republican legislatures in the laws which concern the personal and property relations of wives, mothers, and widows, and by the appointment and election of women to superintendence of education, charities, and other public trusts. The honest demands of this class of citizens for additional rights, privileges, and immunities should be treated with respectful consideration." Kirk H. Porter and Donald Bruce Johnson, comps., *National Party Platforms 1840–1964*, p. 54.

1908 Democrats.

"The Democratic party is the champion of equal rights and opportunities to all; the Republican party is the party of privilege and private monopoly." Porter and Johnson, *National Party Platforms 1840–1964*, p. 150.

1924 Democrats.

"The democratic party believes in equal rights to all and special privilege to none." Porter and Johnson, *National Party Platforms 1840–1964*, p. 243.

1928 Democrats.

"We declare for equality of women with men in all political and governmental matters." Porter and Johnson, *National Party Platforms 1840–1964*, p. 276.

Republicans.

"The Republican Party, which from the first has sought to bring this development about, accepts wholeheartedly the equality on the part of women, and in the public service it can present a record of appointments of women in the legal, diplomatic, judicial, treasury and other governmental departments." Porter and Johnson, *National Party Platforms 1840–1964*, p. 290.

1936 Democrats.

"We shall continue to guard the freedom of speech, press, radio, religion and assembly which our Constitution guarantees; with equal rights to all and special privilege to none." Porter and Johnson, *National Party Platforms 1840–1964*, p. 363.

In the following examples, "equal rights" is inferred but not explicitly stated in the platform or rights are identified in regard to a limited area:

1920 Democrats.

"We advocate full representation of women on all commissions dealing with women's work or women's interests and a reclassification of the Federal Civil Service free from discrimination on the ground of sex; a continuance of appropriations for education in sex hygiene; Federal legislation which shall insure that American women resident in the United States, but married to aliens, shall retain their American citizenship, and that the same process of naturalization shall be required for women as for men." Porter and Johnson, *National Party Platforms 1840–1964*, p. 219.

Republicans.

"Women have special problems of employment which make necessary special study. We recommend Congress for the permanent establishment of the Women's Bureau in the United States Department of Labor to serve as a source of information to the States and to Congress.

The principle of equal pay for equal service should be applied through out all branches of the Federal government in which women are employed.

Federal aid for vocational training should take into consideration the special aptitudes and needs of women workers.

We demand Federal legislation to limit the hours of employment of women engaged in intensive industry, the product of which enters into interstate commerce." Porter and Johnson, *National Party Platforms 1840–1964*, p. 238.

1940 Democrats.

We will continue our efforts to achieve equality of opportunity for men and women without impairing the social legislation that promotes true equality by safeguarding the health, safety and economic welfare of women workers." Porter and Johnson, *National Party Platforms 1840–1964*, p. 384.

1964 Democrats.

"We will support legislation to carry forward the progress already made toward full equality of opportunity for women as well as men. . . . Ending discrimination based on race, age, sex or national origin demands not only equal opportunity but the opportunity to be equal." Porter and Johnson, *National Party Platforms 1840–1964*, p. 645.

Republicans.

"continued opposition to discrimination based on race, creed, national origin or sex. We recognize that the elimination of any such discrimination is a matter of heart, conscience, and education, as well as of equal rights under the law." Porter and Johnson, *National Party Platforms 1840–1964*, p. 683.

1984 Republicans.

"The Republican Party has an historic commitment to equal rights for women. Republicans pioneered the right of women to vote, and our party was the first major party to advocate equal pay for equal work, regardless of sex." George Thomas Kurian and Jeffrey D. Schultz, eds., *The Encyclopedia of the Republican Party*, p. 725.

1988 Republicans.

"We renew our historic commitment to equal rights for women. The Republican Party pioneered the right of women to vote and initiated the rights now embodied in the Equal Pay Act, requiring equal pay for equal work." Kurian and Schultz, *The Encyclopedia of the Republican Party*, p. 755.

1992 Republicans.

"Asserting equal rights for all, we support the Bush Administration's vigorous enforcement of statutes to prevent illegal discrimination on account of sex, race, creed or national origin. Promoting opportunity, we reject efforts to replace equal rights with quotas or other preferential treatment. That is why President Bush fought so long against the Democrat Congress to win a civil rights bill worthy of that name.

We renew the historic Republican commitment to the rights of women, from the early days of the suffragist movement to the present. Because legal rights mean little without opportunity, we assert economic growth as the key to the continued progress of women in all fields of American life." Kurian and Schultz, *The Encyclopedia of the Republican Party*, p. 800.

1996 Republicans.

"The sole source of equal opportunity for all is equality before the law. Therefore, we oppose discrimination based on sex, race, age, creed, or national origin and will vigorously enforce anti-discrimination statutes. ... We renew our historic Republican commitment to equal opportunity for women. In the early days of the suffragist movement, we pioneered the women's right to vote. We take pride in this year's remarkable array of Republican women serving in and running for office and their role in leadership positions in our party, in Congress and in the states. Two women serve in our House Leadership—a record untouched by the Democrats during their 40 years in power. The full exercise of legal rights depends upon opportunity, and economic growth is the key to continuing progress for women in all fields of endeavor. Public policy must respect and accommodate women whether they are full-time homemakers or pursue a career." http://www.yologop.org/plat5.htm.

2000 Republicans.

"We also support a reasonable approach to Title IX that seeks to expand opportunities for women without adversely affecting men's teams." *CQ Almanac 2000,* p. D-28.

Equal Rights Amendment

1940 Republican.

"EQUAL RIGHTS. We favor submission by Congress to the States of an amendment to the Constitution providing for equal rights for men and women." Porter and Johnson, *National Party Platforms 1840–1964,* p. 393.

1944 Democrats.

"We recommend to Congress the submission of a Constitutional amendment on equal rights for women." Porter and Johnson, *National Party Platforms 1840–1964,* p. 403.

Republicans.

"EQUAL RIGHTS. We favor submission by Congress to the States of an amendment to the Constitution providing for equal rights for men and women." Porter and Johnson, *National Party Platforms 1840–1964,* p. 412.

1956 Democrats.

"*Equal Rights Amendment'* We of the Democratic Party recommend and indorse for submission to the Congress a Constitutional amendment providing equal rights for women." Porter and Johnson, *National Party Platforms 1840–1964,* p. 537.

Republicans.

"*Equal Rights'* We recommend to Congress the submission of a constitutional amendment providing equal rights for men and women." Porter and Johnson, *National Party Platforms 1840–1964,* p. 554.

1972 Democrats.

"*Rights of Women'* Women historically have been denied a full voice in the evolution of the political and social institutions of this country and are therefore allied with all under-represented groups in a common desire to form a more humane and compassionate society. The Democratic Party pledges the following:

A priority effort to ratify the Equal Rights Amendment;

Elimination of discrimination against women in public accommodations and public facilities, public education and in all federally-assisted programs and federally-contracted employment;

Extension of the jurisdiction of the Civil Rights Commission to include denial of civil rights on the basis of sex;

Full enforcement of all federal statutes and executive laws barring job discrimination on the basis of sex, giving the Equal Employment Opportunities Commission adequate staff and resources and power to issue cease-and-desist orders promptly;

Elimination of discriminatory features of criminal laws and administration;

Increased efforts to open educational opportunities at all levels, eliminating discrimination against women in access to education, tenure, promotion and salary;

Guarantee that all training programs are made more equitable, both in terms of the numbers of women involved and the job opportunities provided; jobs must be available on the basis of skill not sex;

Availability of maternity benefits to all working women; temporary disability benefits should cover pregnancy, childbirth, miscarriage and recovery;

Elimination of all tax inequities that affect women and children, such as higher taxes for single women; . . .

Amendment of the Internal Revenue Code to permit working families to deduct from gross income as a business expense, housekeeping and child care costs;

Equality for women on credit, mortgage, insurance, property, rental and financial contracts;

Extension of the Equal Pay Act to all workers, with amendment to read 'equal pay for comparable work';

Appointment of women to positions of top responsibility in all branches of the federal government to achieve an equitable ratio of women and men. Such positions include Cabinet members, agency and division heads and Supreme Court Justices; inclusion of women advisors in equitable ratios on all government studies, commissions and hearings; and

Laws authorizing federal grants on a matching basis for financing State Commissions of the Status of Women." Donald Bruce Johnson, comp., *National Party Platforms, vol. 2, 1960–1976*, pp. 791–92.

Republicans.

"'*Equal Rights for Women*.' The Republican Party recognizes the great con tributions women have made to our society as homemakers and moth ers, as contributors to the community through volunteer work, and as members of the labor force in careers outside the home. We fully en- dorse the principle of equal rights, equal opportunities and equal re- sponsibilities for women, and believe that progress in these areas is needed to achieve the full realization of the potentials of American women both in the home and outside the home." Johnson, *National Party Platforms*, p. 880.

1976 Republicans.

"Women, who comprise a numerical majority of the population, have been denied a just portion of our nation's rights and opportunities. We reaffirm our pledge to work to eliminate discrimination in all areas for reasons of race, color, national origin, age, creed or sex and to enforce vigorously laws guaranteeing women equal rights.

The Republican Party reaffirms its support for ratification of the Equal Rights Amendment. Our Party was the first national party to endorse the E.R.A. in 1940. We continue to believe its ratification is essential to insure equal rights for all Americans. In our 1972 Platform, the Republican Party recognized the great contributions women have made to society as home- makers and mothers, as contributors to the community through volunteer work, and as members of the labor force in careers. The Platform stated then, and repeats now, that the Republican Party 'fully endorses the prin- ciple of equal rights, equal opportunities and equal responsibilities for women.' The Equal Rights Amendment is the embodiment of this principle and therefore we support its swift ratification." Johnson, *National Party Plat- forms*, p. 976.

1980 Democrats.

"The primary route to that new horizon is ratification of the Equal Rights Amendment. A Democratic Congress, working with the women's leaders, labor, civil and religious organizations, first enacted ERA in Congress and later extended the deadline for ratification. Now, the Democratic Party must ensure that ERA at last becomes the 27th Amendment to the Consti- tution. We oppose efforts to rescind ERA in states which have already ratified the amendment, and we shall insist that past rescissions are invalid." Donald Bruce Johnson, comp., *National Party Platforms of 1980*, p. 60.

Republicans.

"We acknowledge the legitimate efforts of those who support or oppose ratification of the Equal Rights Amendment.

We reaffirm our Party's historic commitment to equal rights and equality for women." Johnson, *National Party Platforms of 1980*, p. 182.

1984 Democrats.

"*Equal Rights for Women* — A top priority of a Democratic Administration will be ratification of the unamended Equal Rights Amendment."
George Thomas Kurian and Jeffrey D. Schultz, eds., *The Encyclopedia of
the Democratic Party*, p. 802.

1988 Democrats.

"We believe that we honor our multicultural heritage by assuring equal
access to government services, employment, housing, business enterprise
and education to every citizen regardless of race, sex, national origin, religion, age, handicapping condition or sexual orientation; that these rights
are without exception too precious to be jeopardized by Federal Judges
and Justice Department officials chosen during the past seven years—by
a political party increasingly monolithic both racially and culturally—
more for their unenlightened ideological views than for their respect for
the rule of law. We further believe that we must work for the adoption of
the Equal Rights Amendment to the Constitution; that the fundamental
right of reproductive choice should be guaranteed regardless of ability to
pay; that our machinery for civil rights enforcement and legal services to
the poor should be rebuilt and vigorously utilized; and that our immigration policy should be reformed to promote fairness, non-discrimination and family reunification and to reflect our constitutional freedoms
of speech, association and travel." *CQ Almanac 1988*, p. 88A.

1992 Democrats.

"We don't have an American to waste. Democrats will continue to lead
the fight to ensure that no American suffer discrimination or depriva-
tion of rights on the basis of race, gender, language, national origin, religion, age, disability, sexual orientation, or other characteristics irrelevant
to ability. We support ratification of the Equal Rights Amendment;
affirmative action; stronger protection of voting rights for racial and ethnic minorities, including language access to voting; and continued resistance to discriminatory English-only pressure groups." Kurian and
Schultz, *The Encyclopedia of the Democratic Party*, pp. 834–35.

1996 Democrats.

"We continue to lead the fight to end discrimination on the basis of race, gender, religion, age, ethnicity, disability, and sexual orientation. The Democratic Party has always supported the Equal Rights Amendment, and we are committed to ensuring full equality for women and to vigorously enforce the Americans with Disabilities Act. We support continued efforts, like the Employment Non-Discrimination Act, to end discrimination against gay men and lesbians and further their full inclusion in the life of the nation." http://www.dncc96.org/platform.

Affirmative Action

1972 Republicans.

"Required all firms doing business with the Government to have affirmative action plans for the hiring and promotion of women." Johnson, *National Party Platforms,* p. 880.

1976 Democrats

"Accordingly, we reaffirm this Party's commitment to full and vigorous enforcement of all equal opportunities laws and affirmative action." Johnson, *National Party Platforms,* p. 918.

1984 Democrats.

"We will reverse the regressive trend of the Reagan Administration by making a commitment to increase recruitment, hiring, training, retraining, procurement, and promotional opportunity at the federal level to aid minority Americans and women. We call on the public and private sectors to live up to and enforce all civil rights laws and regulations, i.e., Equal Employment Opportunity Programs, Title VI and Title VII of the Civil Rights Act, the Fair Housing Laws, and affirmative action requirements." Kurian and Schultz, *The Encyclopedia of the Democratic Party,* p. 801.

1988 Republicans.

"We must remove remaining obstacles to women's achieving their full potential and full reward. That does not include the notion of federally mandated comparable worth, which would substitute the decisions of bureaucrats for the judgment of individuals. It does include equal rights for women who work for the Congress. We call upon the Democratic leadership of the House and Senate to join Republican members in applying to Congress the civil rights laws that apply to the rest of the nation. Women should not be second-class citizens anywhere in our country, but least of all beneath the dome of the Capitol.

Recognizing that women represent less than 5 percent of the U.S. Congress, only 12 percent of the nation's statewide offices, plus 15 percent of State legislative positions, the Republican Party strongly supports the achievements of women in seeking an equal role in the governing of our country and is committed to the vigorous recruitment, training, and campaign support of women candidates at all levels." Kurian and Schultz, *The Encyclopedia of the Republican Party,* pp. 755–56.

1992 Democrats.

"We support the ratification of the Equal Rights Amendment; affirmative action; stronger protection of voting rights for racial and ethnic minorities, including language access to voting; and continued resistance to discriminatory English-only pressure groups." Kurian and Schultz, *The Encyclopedia of the Democratic Party,* p. 835.

1996 Democrats.

"President Clinton is leading the way to reform affirmative action so that it works, it is improved, and promotes opportunity, but does not accidentally hold others back in the process. Senator Dole has promised to end affirmative action. He's wrong, and the President is right. When it comes to affirmative action, we should mend it, not end it." http://www.dncc96.org/wplatform.

NOTES

INTRODUCTION

1. Abigail Adams to John Adams, March 31, 1776, *The Book of Abigail and John: Selected Letters of the Adams Family 1762–1784*, ed. L. H. Butterfield, Marc Friedlaender and Mary-Jo Kline.
2. Ibid.
3. The different definitions of "representation" used throughout this study are drawn from the analysis done by Hanna Fenichel Pitkin in *The Concept of Representation*.
4. Social security and pensions are both issues especially of importance to women in part-time and/or low-paying jobs, or who raised children and may never have entered the workforce or have interruptions in the number of years worked.
5. Of historic note, NOW arises out of discontent on the part of several members of the State Commissions on the Status of Women meeting in a national conference of the commissions. Several members and outside observers active in national organizations were upset over the lack of movement on a policy agenda. NOW would become "an action-oriented women's organization." See Georgia Duerst-Lahti, "The Government's Role in Building the Women's Movement," *Political Science Quarterly* 104, no. 2 (1989): 264.
6. For example, see Janet M. Martin, "Women Who Govern: The President's Appointments," and Richard L. Pacelle, Jr., "A President's Legacy: Gender and Appointment to the Federal Courts," both in *The Other Elites: Women, Politics, and Power in the Executive Branch*.
7. Tanya Malich, *The Republican War Against Women: An Insider's Report from Behind the Lines*.
8. The three administrations spanning these two decades—Reagan, Bush, and Clinton—provide a range of variables to consider in examining both the president and the presidency's response to women. The two-term presidencies of Ronald Reagan and Bill Clinton in these decades can also contribute to a better understanding of the institutionalized presidency's response to women, as well as the role of the president himself in selecting advisors or cabinet members, and moving forward on an agenda.
9. For example see Nancy E. McGlen and Meredith Reid Sarkees, *Women in Foreign Policy: The Insiders;* Nancy E. McGlen and Meredith Reid Sarkees, "Style Does Matter: The Impact of Presidential Leadership on Women in Foreign Policy," in *The Other Elites;* Jean Ebbert and Marie-Beth Hall, *Crossed Currents: Navy Women from WWI to Tailhook;* Judith Hicks Stiehm, ed. *It's Our Military, Too: Women and the U.S. Military;* U.S. Presidential Commission on the Assign-

ment of Women in the Armed Forces, "Women in Combat: Report to the President." In addition to arguments in favor or against a range of Department of Defense policies and existing laws regulating the assignment of women in the military, the report includes an extensive bibliography, poll results, and summaries of studies done in the past.

10. *Judicature* routinely features articles on the status of judicial appointments within each administration and analysis of court appointments across administrations. Scholars who have written extensively on court appointments include: Sheldon Goldman, Beverly Cook, Elaine Martin, Elliot Slotnick, and Richard Pacelle. Also see Richard L. Pacelle, Jr., "The Solicitor General and Gender: Litigating the President's Agenda and Serving the Supreme Court," in *The Other Elites*.

11. For example, when Norman Y. Mineta was appointed by President Clinton in the waning days of his administration to replace William Daley as secretary of commerce, the first words used in many print and broadcast news reports in describing this appointment were "the first Asian-American cabinet secretary." Mineta's years of service as a U.S. representative from California, a committee chair, as well as his subsequent employment with Lockheed Martin Corporation, a defense contractor, were overlooked and omitted in many newscasts. However, the president and his appointee both acknowledged the significance of an appointment of an American of Asian descent to the cabinet. While the symbolic significance of the appointment is noted, the substantive implications of the inclusion of Asian Americans in governing is also presented. Mineta was a major force behind passage of the 1988 Civil Liberties Act which provided a formal apology and $20,000 to Japanese internment camp survivors, including Mineta himself. Lori Nitschke, "Mineta Likely to Win Easy Confirmation," *CQ Weekly Report*, July 1, 2000, 1594.

12. Steven A. Shull, *American Civil Rights Policy From Truman to Clinton: The Role of Presidential Leadership*.

13. See Charles E. Walcott and Karen M. Hult, *Governing the White House From Hoover Through Johnson*.

14. In particular, see chapter 6, "Looking Beyond Washington," in ibid.

15. Ibid., 119.

16. Samuel Kernell, *Going Public: New Strategies of Presidential Leadership*, 2d ed. Kernell has identified the shift from a system of institutionalized pluralism to a system of individualized pluralism resulting from increased federal programs affecting greater numbers of constituent groups outside of Washington, modern technology allowing greater communication between the White House and those around the country and ease in travel, and the decline of political parties with candidates running independent of the party.

17. Ibid.

18. While the 1961–81 time period might lend itself to interviews of those able to recollect their participation in events, I have opted not to rely on after-the-fact accounts since I have found a number of misstatements of fact or imprecision in the recollection of events. For instance, political leaders and activists have often been quoted recounting their respective party's historical record in terms of party platform support for an ERA, a platform they may have helped craft or endorsed years before. However, when looking at the actual party platforms, the historical record has frequently found these recollections in error. The re-

spective party platform positions on the issues of an ERA and equal pay listed in the Appendix were compiled out of the author's desperation in separating out historical fact from fiction caused by the inconsistencies encountered over claims to longtime support for issues of concern to women on the part of a number of party spokespersons.

19. A formal role is recognized with the establishment of The Office of the First Lady in 1978 with authorization through "The White House Personnel Authorization-Employment Act" (L. 95-570). Prior to this act Congress had allowed the use of funds for the First Lady's official activities from the "general budget line item for White House management" on an "as-needed basis." See Barbara C. Burrell, "The Office of the First Lady and Public Policymaking," in *The Other Elites,* 171.

20. Ever since Bill Clinton first ran for president, and Hillary Rodham Clinton began attracting media attention, there has been an evolving scholarship on the First lady that is beginning to examine the complexity of a position that has now become a part of the institutionalized presidency. The complexity to be found in studying the First Lady is vividly identified by Doris Kearns Goodwin in her discussion of the relationship between Eleanor Roosevelt and her daughter Anna. Anna filled in for Eleanor when the First Lady was traveling across the country, in welcoming heads of state to the White House and presiding over social events, but Anna did not want to be "officially" referred to or treated as an "assistant hostess." (Doris Kearns Goodwin, *No Ordinary Time: Franklin and Eleanor Roosevelt: The Home Front in World War II,* 489–91.) An analysis of the First Lady would require examination of the formal role and the institutionalization of the office and the symbolism attached to a position filled by women who were not the spouse of the president (e.g., daughter, sister). For example, see Betty Boyd Caroli, *First Ladies.* In one study of the political influence of First Ladies, it was found that of the thirty-eight First Ladies from Martha Washington to Hillary Rodham Clinton, thirty-one discussed politics with the president; twenty-six served as advisors; and fourteen worked to influence the selection of political appointments. These figures most likely underestimate the role of First Ladies, since information on their activities is hard to come by given social mores which dictated that wives remain in the background. See Karen O'Connor, Bernadette Nye, and Laura Van Assendelft, "Wives in the White House: The Political Influence of First Ladies," *Presidential Studies Quarterly* 26, no. 3 (Summer, 1996): 846. Robert Watson in *The Presidents' Wives: Reassessing the Office of the First Lady* reviews the status of research on the First Lady, identifying a wider range of resource material available for scholarship, especially of the twentieth-century First Ladies. Given her massive press coverage, Hillary Clinton has become the subject of public opinion polls since the 1992 campaign. Barbara Burrell fully explains the media and polling phenomena surrounding Hillary in *Public Opinion, the First Ladyship, and Hillary Rodham Clinton,* covering the 1992 campaign, transition, and first two years of the Clinton administration.

21. Stephen J. Wayne, "Approaches," in *Studying the Presidency,* ed. Stephen J. Wayne and George C. Edwards III (Knoxville: The University of Tennessee Press, 1983), 29.

22. Ian S. Lustick. "History, Historiography, and Political Science: Multiple Historical Records and the Problems of Selection Bias," *American Political Science Review* 90, no. 3 (September, 1996): 605–606.

23. Lyndon Baines Johnson, *The Vantage Point: Perspectives of the Presidency, 1963–1969*, 26.
24. Steven Greenhouse, "Companies Set to Get Tougher on Harassment," *New York Times,* Sunday, June 28, 1998, late edition, final, sec. 1, 1. I appreciate Nancy Kassop's identification of the cases: *Gebser et al. v Lago Vista Independent School District* 118 S. Ct. 1989 (1998), *Burlington Industries, Inc. v Ellerth* 118 S. Ct. 2257 (1998), and *Faragher v City of Boca Raton* 118 S. Ct. 2275 (1998).
25. Sidney M. Milkis, *The President and the Parties: The Transformation of the American Party System Since the New Deal,* viii–ix, in Charles O. Jones, *The Presidency in a Separated System,* 282.
26. Kernell, *Going Public.*
27. Milkis, *President and the Parties,* viii–ix, in Jones, *Presidency in a Separated System,* 282.

CHAPTER 1. WOMEN AND THE EXECUTIVE BRANCH

1. Ward L. Miner, "Mary Katherine Goddard," in Edward T. James, Janet Wilson James, and Paul S. Boyer, eds., *Notable American Women 1607–1950: A Biographical Dictionary,* vol. II, G–O, 55.
2. Forrest McDonald, *The American Presidency: An Intellectual History,* 226.
3. George Washington to Mary Katherine Goddard, Jan. 6, 1790, *The Writings of George Washington from the Original Manuscript Sources 1745–1799,* vol. 30, ed. John C. Fitzpatrick.
4. "Mary Katherine Goddard," 56.
5. George Washington did, however, keep a close watch over his department heads. And all presidents would follow Washington's lead in that in the areas where the president had special expertise, he would become his own secretary. For instance, "Washington was an expert in foreign affairs and war, and thus he tended to be his own foreign secretary and war secretary." McDonald, *The American Presidency,* 226.
6. One also has to bear in mind that the federal government at this time was so small that not until 1857 did Congress provide the funds necessary for a president to hire a clerk. Ibid., 280.
7. Forrest McDonald explains why these two departments were the most active. "The Treasury Department, through its port collectors, secret service, and Coast Guard, was charged with preventing counterfeiting, smuggling, piracy, and the slave trade. Through the 1820s suits for debts owed the United States were prosecuted by federal district attorneys under instructions of an auditor in Treasury, not the attorney general's office. A similar arrangement prevailed in the Post Office. In 1830 a new office, Solicitor of the Treasury, was created, and for the next three decades the solicitor directed the district attorney in all federal civil litigation except that of the Post Office. Only in appeals of suits to the Supreme Court did the attorney general participate." Ibid., 282.
8. "History of Women in the Civil Service," chapter 2, 8, in "Committee on Federal Employment Policies and Practices, Published Report, October, 1963" folder, PCSW, Box 8, John F. Kennedy Library, hereafter JFKL.
9. Terry M. Moe and William G. Howell, "The Presidential Power of Unilateral Action" (second draft), (paper presented at the annual meetings of the American Political Science Association, Boston, 1998), 2.

10. Elizabeth Brown Pryor, *Clara Barton: Professional Angel,* 56.
11. Ibid., 57.
12. Ibid. For this reason, the actual number of women working in the government would be difficult to count. At times, women succeeded their husbands and the roll continued to list their husbands or initials were used.
13. Ibid., 58–59.
14. Ibid., 73; also see chapter 5.
15. Letter, Task Force on Women's Rights to President Jimmy Carter, April 25, 1977, "OA 7801" folder, White House Central Files, (WHCF), Subject File-Executive, Jimmy Carter Library, hereafter JCL.
16. Pryor, *Clara Barton,* 91.
17. Ibid.
18. Ibid., chapter 9.
19. Ibid., 151.
20. "Women in the Public Service," August, 1957, fact sheet of the Women's Division of the Republican National Committee, "Women Appointees 1950s" folder, National Federation of Business and Professional Women's Clubs, Inc. (BPW/USA), Rawalt Center.
21. "History of Women in the Civil Service," 9.
22. For instance, recognizing the powers of Congress, Louisa Adams, wife of then Secretary of State John Quincy Adams, organized a dinner party for sixty-eight members of Congress. Adams herself labeled her lobbying efforts on behalf of her husband "'Smilin' for the Presidency." O'Connor, Nye, and Van Assendelft, "Wives in the White House," 838. In the subsequent election (1824), in which none of the four candidates gained a majority of the electoral college votes, the decision was thrown to the House of Representatives, where each state had one vote. Andrew Jackson, the popular vote winner, came in second to John Quincy Adams. Louisa Adams became First Lady. The term "First Lady" appears to have first been used in reference to Julia Grant in 1870 during the administration of Ulysses S. Grant. However, common usage of the term developed during the Rutherford B. Hayes administration, in reference to his wife, Lucy Hayes. For further discussion see Daniel C. Diller and Stephen L. Robertson, *The Presidents, First Ladies, and Vice Presidents: White House Biographies, 1789–1997.*
23. As Forrest McDonald observes, "From the point of view of administration, the history of the presidency in the twentieth century has been the history of presidents' attempts to gain control of the sprawling federal bureaucracy. As the century began, direct supervision of the administration remained where it had been for a long time, in the hands of department and bureau chiefs and the related congressional committees. McDonald, *The American Presidency,* 329. As an example, when Barton finished her work and closed the Office of Correspondence, she reported directly to Congress, which had provided the appropriations for the office.
24. "History of Women in the Civil Service," 7.
25. Ibid., 8. There was a brief period, 1932–33, in which this statute was not so interpreted.
26. Katherine Brownell Oettinger, "Address Before the Boston Council of Club Presidents," March 23, 1963, Boston, in "Committee on Federal Employment Policies and Practices: Documents #47–59 Meeting Summaries, Members Progress Reports," folder, PCSW, Box 7, JFKL.

27. "A Great Nation in Grief," *New York Times,* July 3, 1881, 1.
28. "The Federal Civil Rights Enforcement Effort—1974," vol. 5, "To Eliminate Employment Discrimination," Report of the U.S. Commission on Civil Rights, July, 1975, 9, "OA 7801" folder, WHCF, Subject File-Executive, JCL.
29. "Women at Work: A Century of Industrial Change," *U.S. Department of Labor, Women's Bureau Bulletin* 115, 18.
30. See "History of Women in the Civil Service," 13.
31. James L. Sundquist, *The Decline and Resurgence of Congress,* 47.
32. A decade later, the executive branch also gained control from Congress of the power to determine how offices and buildings in the district were to be allocated. Ibid.
33. "Women at Work."
34. See Judith Paterson, *Be Somebody: A Biography of Marguerite Rawalt,* 56.
35. "Women at Work."
36. For example, see chapter 3 in Paterson, *Be Somebody.*
37. Jo Freeman, "From Protection to Equal Opportunity: The Revolution in Women's Legal Status," in *Women, Politics, and Change,* ed. Louise A. Tilly and Patricia Gurin, 460.
38. The opinion of the attorney general of the United States on the "Appointment and Promotion of Women in the Federal Civil Service," June 14, 1962, provides a summary of the impact of the legislation passed by Congress which created a two-tier wage system for men and women. Section 165 of the revised statutes had included the following language: "'That the heads of the several departments are hereby authorized to appoint female clerks, who may be found to be competent and worthy, to any of the grades of clerkships known to the law, in the respective departments, with the compensation belonging to the class to which they may be appointed, but the number of first, second, third, and fourth class clerks shall not be increased by this section.'" Attorney General Robert Kennedy, goes on to note: "This provision was added as an amendment to a general appropriations act. The debate in both the Senate and the House of Representatives indicates that the only purpose of this provision was to clarify the existing law by specifically permitting department heads to hire women at any grade of clerkship authorized by law, and to pay equal compensation to men and women. This was considered necessary because department heads assumed that since Congress had appropriated funds for the employment of females at a lower rate of pay than the four grades of clerkships then provided for, they were without authority to employ women at these grades of clerkships," Opinion of the attorney general of the United States, "Appointment and Promotion of Women in Federal Civil Service, June 14, 1962, Robert Kennedy," in "PE 3 Fair Employment," folder, WHCF, Subject Files, Box 675, JFKL.
39. "The Federal Civil Rights Enforcement Effort—1974," 9.
40. Louise M. Young, "Women's Place in American Politics: The Historical Perspective," *Journal of Politics* (1976): 319–20.
41. Victoria Woodhull had been a candidate for the presidency on the Equal Rights Party ticket in 1872. Frederick Douglass was selected by Woodhull as her vice presidential running mate (see "The Convention at Apollo Hall," *New York Times,* May 11, 1872). For further discussion, see Barbara Goldsmith, *Other Powers: The Age of Suffrage, Spiritualism, and the Scandalous Victoria Woodhull.*

42. Paula Baker. "The Domestication of Politics: Women and American Political Society, 1780–1920," *American Historical Review* 89, no. 3 (June, 1984): 628.

43. Of course, this is not to say that this is the first political speech ever made by a woman. Women had established themselves as lobbyists for abolition and the vote, among other causes. This was the first speech at a major party convention. There is a good deal of scholarship documenting the political role of women during the 1800s. For example see Karlyn Kohrs Campbell, comp., *Man Cannot Speak For Her*, vol. 1 and *Man Cannot Speak for Her: Key Texts of the Early Feminists*, vol. 2; and Karlyn Kohrs Campbell, ed., *Women Public Speakers in the United States, 1800–1925: A Bio-critical Sourcebook* and *Women Public Speakers in the United States, 1925–1993: A Bio-critical Sourcebook*. The focus here, however, is on the intersection of women and women's groups with the presidency.

44. "Second Day of the Convention," *New York Times*, June 17, 1876. A second article on the same event, in the same newspaper and on the same page, notes, "The question of allowing Mrs. Spencer to address the house was put, and carried by a small majority." "A Plea for Woman Suffrage," *New York Times*, June 17, 1876.

45. For discussion on the controversy that ensued when suffrage for women became linked to suffrage for African American males following the Civil War, see Goldsmith, *Other Powers*.

46. "Women at the Democratic & Republican National Conventions: An Historical Overview," August 30, 1988, fact sheet, Center for the American Woman and Politics, Eagleton Institute of Politics, Rutgers University. "Women and the Republican Party," 1959, fact sheet of the Women's Division of the Republican National Committee, "Women Appointees 1950s" folder, BPW, Rawalt Center. Delegate counting by the two parties can easily be misrepresented. For example, in 1956 there were 208 women delegates at the Republican National Convention, each with a full vote, "in contrast to the many delegates in the Democrat Convention who had only a ½ vote." "Women in the Public Service." July, 1957. Women's Division, Republican National Committee in "Women Appointees—1950s" folder, BPW. Rawalt Center.

47. "Women at the Democratic & Republican National Conventions," Katie Louchheim, speech, July 11, 1960, "Louchheim, Mrs. Katie, Director of Women's Activities, DNC" folder, Records of the Democratic National Committee, Box 149, Lyndon Baines Johnson Library, hereafter LBJL.

48. M. Kent Jennings, "Women in Party Politics," in *Women, Politics, and Change*. Marguerite J. Fisher and Betty Whitehead "American Government and Politics: Women and National Party Organization" *American Political Science Review*, 38 (1944): 895–903.

49. Jennings, "Women in Party Politics."

50. "The Republican Party Structure," 1959, 11, fact sheet of the Women's Division of the Republican National Committee, "Women Appointees 1950s" folder, BPW, Rawalt Center.

51. Fisher and Whitehead, "American Government and Politics," 895–903, 900. Josephine L. Good and Clare B. Williams, "Republican Womanpower: The History of Women in Republican National Conventions and Women in the Republican National Committee," 11–15.

52. In looking at the long-term efforts by each party to include women, M. Kent Jennings found that in looking at the delegates in the time period 1948 to 1968,

women comprised 15 percent of the Republican delegates, and 13 percent of the Democratic delegates. Jennings, "Women in Party Politics," 224.

53. Kirk H. Porter and Donald Bruce Johnson, comps., *National Party Platforms 1840–1964*. Urbana: University of Illinois Press, 1966.

54. "Women and the Republican Party," 2.

55. Ibid.

56. Porter and Johnson, comps., *National Party Platforms 1840–1964*.

57. The Democratic Platform stated: "We recommend the extension of the franchise to the women of the country by the State upon the same terms as to men," 199. The last plank in the Republican Party Platform stated: "The Republican Party, reaffirming its faith in government of the people, by the people, for the people, as a measure of justice to one-half the adult population of this country, favors the extension of the suffrage to women, but recognizes the right of each state to settle this question for itself." *National Party Platforms, 1840– 1964*, 207. (All subsequent references to platforms in this chapter are taken from this volume.)

58. See Sara Hunter Graham, *Woman Suffrage and the New Democracy*, especially chapter 6.

59. Graham, *Woman Suffrage*, 114.

60. Gardener, a socially prominent member of the Congressional Committee of NAWSA, had a wide range of political contacts in Washington, including Speaker of the House of Representatives Champ Clark, who lived next door to her. See Graham, *Woman Suffrage*, 91–114.

61. Good and Williams, "Republican Womanpower," 13.

62. Eunice Fuller Barnard, "Women Who Wield Political Power," *New York Times*, Sept. 2, 1928, 6.

63. Fisher and Whitehead, "American Government and Politics," p 895–903.

64. As a side note, Luce's speech so incensed one woman listening on the radio, India Edwards, that she immediately went down to campaign for the Roosevelt-Truman ticket. According to Edwards, who lost a son during World War II, Luce "presumed to speak for the boys who had been killed [in World War II, stating] . . . if they could come back they would say to vote against Roosevelt because he was responsible for their deaths." Edwards would soon become the director of the Women's Division of the DNC. India Edwards, interview by Joe B. Frantz, Feb. 4, 1969, tape 1, 3–4, LBJL.

65. Report of the Subcommittee on Political Rights of the PCSW, March 7, 1963, "Committee on Political and Civil Rights: Documents #21–26 Meetings March 8, 1963, Property Law and Married Women" folder, PCSW, Box 10, JFKL.

66. Blanche Linden-Ward and Carol Hurd Green, *American Women in the 1960s: Changing the Future*, 412.

67. Kristi Andersen, "Working Women and Political Participation, 1952–1972," *American Journal of Political Science* 19, no. 3 (August, 1975): 450.

68. Ibid.

69. Because of the close connection between the BPW and the executive branch from the start of the organization, the history of the BPW is, in part, a history of the role of women in the executive branch—both in determining who the policy makers are, as well as in affecting policy outcomes. If members of the BPW were not at the table making decisions, they were usually nearby. Included among members of the BPW were: Eleanor Roosevelt, Bess Truman, Pat

Nixon, Margaret Chase Smith (who was president of the Maine federation), Hillary Rodham Clinton, and Janet Reno. See *A National History of the National Federation of Business and Professional Women's Clubs (BPW/USA)*, vol. III. The focus of analysis is in establishing direct links between the White House and women's organizations. For that reason, while there have been many organizations of women working on behalf of women since the 1800s, only the organizations key in establishing links, both in terms of communication as well as issue advocacy between women and the White House, are included.

70. "Women in Policy-Making Posts—A Guide," January, 1957, "Conf. On Women in Policy-Making Posts 1953—Public Affairs Project" folder, BPW, Rawalt Center.

71. Hazel Palmer, *Independent Woman*, September, 1956, reprinted in ibid.

72. Sophonisba Breckinridge, *Women in the Twentieth Century, A Study of Their Political, Social, and Economic Activities*. Fisher and Whitehead, "American Government and Politics," 900–901.

73. Press release, 1960, "BPW/ERA Historical Materials, 1960s General" folder, NFBPWC, Rawalt Center.

74. Sophonisba Breckinridge, "The Activities of Women Outside the Home," in *Recent Social Trends in the United States*, vol. 1, 739–40.

75. Paul C. Taylor, "The Entrance of Women into Party Politics: The 1920's" (unpublished Ph.D. history thesis, Harvard University, 1966).

76. "Unions and Women," Evelyn Dubrow, speech, Sept. 20, 1973, "Ruckelshaus, Lindh and Spencer File: Speech Material—Pat [Lindh]" folder, WHCF, SMOF, ALA, Box 24, Nixon Presidential Materials, hereafter NPM.

77. There are only twenty-seven amendments to the Constitution, and the most recent amendment, the Twenty-seventh, took two hundred years to be ratified by three-fourths of the states.

78. *The Autobiography of Mary Anderson as Told to Mary N. Winslow*, 91.

79. "4th Annual Message" of Theodore Roosevelt, Dec. 6, 1904, in *A Compilation of the Messages and Papers of the Presidents*, vol. XV, 6898.

80. "5th Annual Message" of Theodore Roosevelt, Dec. 5, 1905, in ibid., 6984.

81. "7th Annual Message" of Theodore Roosevelt, Dec. 3, 1907, in ibid., 7090.

82. See "Special Message to the Senate and the House," of Theodore Roosevelt, March 25, 1908, in ibid.

83. Oettinger, "Address Before the Boston Council of Club Presidents." Theodore Roosevelt, "Special Message to the Senate and the House," Feb. 15, 1909.

84. See Roosevelt, "Special Message to the Senate and House," for the recommendations of the "conference on the care of dependent children."

85. Oettinger, "Address Before the Boston Council of Club Presidents"; O'Connor, Nye, and Van Assendelft, "Wives in the White House."

86. *Autobiography of Mary Anderson*, 91–92.

87. Roger Biles, "Robert F. Wagner, Franklin D. Roosevelt, and Social Welfare Legislation in the New Deal," *Presidential Studies Quarterly* 28, no. 1 (Winter, 1998): 141.

88. The Woman in Industry Service established the first set of federal standards regarding the conditions of women in the workforce, including an eight-hour work day, a forty-eight-hour work week, and daily rest periods or breaks. The service also recommended equal pay for men and women for equal work, as well as the "appointment of women to supervisory positions." The War Labor Policies Board and the secretary of labor approved the recommendations several weeks before the armistice was signed and the standards were issued a

month later, on December 12, 1918. Over time a number of employers adopted the standards, and some were written into law. *Autobiography of Mary Anderson*, 97–101.

89. Ibid., 102.
90. Anderson already held the post, and Roosevelt continued her appointment. Ibid., 90–115.
91. *A History of the NFBPWC, Inc. (BPW/USA).*
92. U.S. House, 67th Congress, 1st session, "Hearings before the Committee on the Judiciary on the Incorporation of the National Federation of Business and Professional Women's Clubs," May 17, 1921, 4.
93. *A History of the NFBPWC, Inc. (BPW/USA)*, 1.
94. "Hearings before the Committee on the Judiciary on the Incorporation of the National Federation of Business and Professional Women's Clubs."
95. The House passed the amendment on May 21, 1919; the Senate passed the amendment on June 4, 1919. See chapter 6 for a discussion of the final efforts to get congressional approval in Graham, *Woman Suffrage.*
96. *A History of the NFBPWC, Inc. (BPW/USA)*, 2.
97. "Voluntary Organizations and Democracy: A Discussion Outline," New York, 1945, 23, BPW, Rawalt Center.
98. Ibid.
99. "Statutes at Large of the U.S. Vol. XLII from April 1921 to March, 1923," Public Law No. 97, Chapter 135, November 23, 1921 (Washington, D.C.: U.S. Government Printing Office, 1923).
100. *Fifth Annual Report of the Director of the Women's Bureau, Department of Labor, Fiscal Year Ended June 30, 1923.*
101. For example, see the *Fourteenth Annual Report of the Director of the Women's Bureau, Department of Labor, Fiscal Year Ended June 30, 1932;* or the *Twelfth Annual Report of the Director of the Women's Bureau, Department of Labor, Fiscal Year Ended June 30, 1930.*
102. *Fourteenth Annual Report.*
103. After the Civil War, presidents had already become quite active in the legislative arena in using their veto power to block private bills often centering around the issue of pensions for widows of veterans from the Civil War. See various formats and editions of public papers of the presidents for private veto messages. Also see Chapter 2 in Theda Skocpol, *Protecting Soldiers and Mothers: The Political Origins of Social Policy in the United States.*
104. "4th Annual Message" of Theodore Roosevelt, 6898.
105. The amendment passed in the House on May 21, 1919, and in the Senate on June 4, 1919.
106. Report No. 234, Jan. 8, 1918, 65th Congress, 2d session, House Committee on Woman Suffrage to accompany H.J. Res. 200, 6. [Minority views are in Report No. 234, part 2, Jan. 9, 1918.]
107. Report No. 234, Jan. 8, 1918, 65th Congress, 2d session, House Committee on Woman Suffrage to accompany H.J. Res. 200. [Minority views are in Report No. 234, part 2, Jan. 9, 1918.]
108. See Malcolm M. Willey and Stuart A. Rice, "A Sex Cleavage in the Presidential Election of 1920," *Journal of the American Statistical Association* 19 (1924): 519–20 for a study on the differences in voting patterns of women and men. The doubling of the potential electorate in 1920 was closely watched. How would

women vote since suffrage had been a non-partisan issue? Even the platforms of the two major parties were more similar than dissimilar when it came to issues of suffrage and women's rights.

109. In fact, women lawyers find positions open which are closed to them in many law firms. See Paterson, *Be Somebody.*

110. The Gallup Poll, Louis Harris and Associates, Minnesota Poll, National Opinion Research Center at the University of Chicago, Roper and Associates, and the Survey Research Center at the University of Michigan.

111. Hazel Erskine, "The Polls: Women's Role," *Public Opinion Quarterly* 35, no. 2 (Summer, 1971): 276.

112. According to Gallup, 69 percent in 1937. See Erskine, "The Polls," 279.

113. Women had become the majority of the electorate by 1944.

114. None of the national polling organizations asked a specific question on the ERA until 1970. Jane Mansbridge presents a detailed discussion of the methodological problems in interpreting the poll results on the ERA during the 1970s. See Jane J. Mansbridge, *Why We Lost the ERA,* chapter 2.

115. Eisenhower delivered the speech in Madison Square Garden on October 25, 1956, "Address at Madison Square Garden," New York City, Oct. 25, 1956, *Public Papers of the Presidents of the United States.* "Women's Party Hails Equal Rights Bid," *Christian Science Monitor,* Jan. 19, 1957, "ERA 12/5/56–1/28/58" folder, Pre-Presidential—Senate files, Box 690, JFKL.

116. Message from the President, *Congressional Record,* Jan. 16, 1957.

117. Cardinal Dougherty to Mrs. Cecil Norton Broy and Mary Sinclair Crawford, Sept. 22, 1945, "ERA 12/5/56–1/28/58" folder, Pre-Presidential—Senate files, Box 690, JFKL. Also see other correspondence in Pre-Presidential Files—Senate, Box 690, JFKL.

118. Lee C. White to Margery Leonard, Dec. 5, 1956, "ERA 12/5/56–1/28/58" folder, Pre-Presidential—Senate, Box 690, JFKL.

119. "The opposition of the ACLU is based on the fear that the amendment as phrased will freeze 'mathematical' equality into the Constitution by depriving the government of the power to enact differential legislation if and when needed to achieve true equality." See correspondence in "ERA 10/3/51–2/15/57" folder, Pre-Presidential—Senate Files, Box 762, JFKL.

120. See H.R. 4320, "Equal Pay for Equal Work," 82nd Congress, 1st session, June 4, 1951, introduced by John F. Kennedy, "Equal Pay for Equal Work (H.R. 4320) 5/10/51–6/11/51" folder, Pre-Presidential Papers, Box 3, JFKL.

121. While the AFL-CIO strongly objected to the ERA, it did support "the principle of equal pay legislation with proper safeguards to avoid interference with collective bargaining agreements," as well as "support an appropriations for the Women's Bureau of the U.S. Department of Labor, so that it may properly carry out its mandate to advance the welfare of women in industry." See Resolution "Women Workers" adopted at the December, 1957, AFL-CIO Convention, attached to letter of Andrew J. Biemiller to John F. Kennedy, Jan. 27, 1958, "ERA 12/5/56–1/28/58" folder, Pre-Presidential—Senate files, Box 690, JFKL.

122. Minnie L. Maffett, "National President's Report, 1943–44," 1944, in *Annual Reports 1940–1945 NFBPWC.* BPW, Rawalt Center.

123. The organizations were Altrusa International, American Dietetics Association, American Federation of Soroptimist Clubs, National Association of Negro Business and Professional Women's Clubs, Osteopathic Women's National

Association, the Young Women's Christian Association-Business and Professional Department of the National Board, and Zonta International.

124. "Group Action Council Report, 1942–1943," *Annual Reports 1940–1945 NFBPWC,* S-1, BPW, Rawalt Center.

125. Ibid., S-2.

126. "Legislation Committee Report, 1943–1944," ibid., 13. "Tentative Legislative Program 1944–1945, ibid., 16.

127. "Group Action Council Report, 1943–1944," ibid., 23.

128. "Group Action Council Report, 1942–1943," ibid., S-2.

129. "Education Committee Report 1943–1944," ibid., 8.

130. "Margaret Hickey, 1944–46," in Past National President's Drawer, BPW, Rawalt Center.

131. "Legislation Committee Report 1943–1944," *Annual Reports 1940–1945 NFBPWC,* 12.

132. "National President's Report 1943–1944," *Annual Reports 1940–1945 NFBPWC,* 5; "Transcripts: Proceedings, 10/2/1962," 248, PCSW, Box 5. JFKL.

133. Margaret Chase Smith, "Extension of Remarks," inserted in *Congressional Record,* June 19, 1944, Margaret Chase Smith Library, hereafter MCSL.

134. "Women in Policy-Making Set-up is Topic at White House Today," *Maine State Labor News,* MCSL.

135. "National President's Report 1943–1944," *Annual Reports 1940–1945 NFBPWC,* 5; "Transcripts: Proceedings, 10/2/1962," 248, PCSW, Box 5. JFKL.

136. "Conference at the White House," *Independent Woman,* July, 1944, MCSL.

137. Ellen S. Woodward, "My Experience at the UNRRA Conference," in transcript of "How Women May Share in Post-War Planning," General Federation of Women's Clubs, June 14, 1944, MCSL.

138. President Maffett, speech, July 14–18, 1944, "Proceedings of the Seventh Biennial Convention of the NFBPWC," NFBPWC, Rawalt Center.

139. "Public Affairs Committee Report 1943–1944," *Annual Reports 1940–1945 NFPBWC,* 22.

140. "Transcripts: Proceedings, 10/2/1962," 248, PCSW, Box 5. JFKL.

141. Ibid., 249.

142. Summary of Conference on Women in Policy-Making Posts May 15, 1953, "Conference on Women in Policy-Making Posts 1953 (Public Affairs Project)" folder, NFBPWC. Rawalt Center.

143. Ibid.; Report on Conference May 15, 1953, "Conference on Women in Policy-Making Posts 1953-Public Affairs Project" folder, NFBPWC, Rawalt Center.

144. Summary of Conference on Women in Policy-Making Posts May 15, 1953, "Conference on Women in Policy-Making Posts 1953 (Public Affairs Project)" folder, NFBPWC. Rawalt Center.

145. Ibid.

146. Ibid.

147. Ibid.

148. Paul C. Light, *Thickening Government: Federal Hierarchy and the Diffusion of Accountability,* 44–46.

149. Press release, Sept. 20, 1959, Republican National Committee, "Women Appointees 1950s" folder, NFBPWC, Rawalt Center.

150. Ibid.

151. However, there still remained obstacles to participation and representation,

especially for African Americans, which began to be addressed by voting rights legislation during the 1960s.

152. Roosevelt's cabinet was prominently featured in a Sunday *New York Times* magazine article. However, in the very formal picture of the cabinet, there is a noticeable absence of Frances Perkins, a member of Roosevelt's cabinet from 1933 to 1945.

153. Report of the Subcommittee on Political Rights of the President's Commission on the Status of Women, March 7, 1963, in "Committee on Political and Civil Rights: Documents #21–26 Meetings March 8 1963, Property Law and Married Women" folder, PCSW, Box 10, JFKL.

154. "Survey of Major Presidential Appointments of Women to Positions in Government," Dec. 8, 1960, Democratic National Committee, "Women—Role in Government" folder, Pre-Presidential Papers (Transition Files, Task Force Reports), Box 1072, JFKL.

155. Ibid. One of these issue areas was consumer policy, which Clare B. Williams had identified as well in an interview in 1958. "What Women Do In Politics," *U.S. News and World Report,* Dec. 12, 1958, 76.

CHAPTER 2. THE KENNEDY ADMINISTRATION

1. Tom Wicker, "Weather Limits Crowds at Fete," *New York Times,* Jan. 20, 1961, A1.

2. Report, "Suggested Priorities for the President-Elect," "Staff Paper I" folder, Papers of Laurin Henry, Box 2, JFKL.

3. Jones, *Presidency in a Separated System,* 135.

4. Kernell, *Going Public,* 45.

5. Austin Ranney, "The 1960 Democratic Convention: Los Angeles and Before," in *Inside Politics: The National Conventions 1960,* ed. Paul Tillett, 14.

6. Kernell, *Going Public,* 76.

7. Ibid., 46.

8. Esther Peterson, interview by Ann M. Campbell, Jan. 20, 1970, 33, JFKL. Porter and Johnson, comps., *National Party Platforms 1840–1964,* 589.

9. Cynthia Harrison, *On Account of Sex: The Politics of Women's Issues, 1945–1968,* 118.

10. Ibid., 7–8.

11. Ibid., 8.

12. Ibid.

13. Ruth Milkman, "Gender and Trade Unionism in Historical Perspective," in *Women, Politics and Change,* 95. According to Milkman, the four waves of unionization are identified as "1.) The oldest unions — the craft unions, some of which began in the 1800s; 2.) The 'new unions' emerging in the 1910s; 3.) Industrial unions emerging in the 1930s; and 4.) Service and public sector unions emerging after World War II."

14. Ibid., 95–96.

15. Freeman, "From Protection to Equal Opportunity," 457.

16. *Muller v. Oregon,* 208 U.S. 412, 422 (1908) cited in ibid., 458–59.

17. Harrison, *On Account of Sex,* 10.

18. Freeman, "From Protection to Equal Opportunity," 459.

19. Ibid. As we will see shortly, the original goals of the proponents of the ERA are revisited in the work of the PCSW during the course of the Kennedy administration.

20. Harrison, *On Account of Sex*, 19. "Women at the Democratic and Republican National Conventions: An Historical Overview," fact sheet of the Center for the American Woman and Politics (CAWP), 1988, Eagleton Institute of Politics, Rutgers University.
21. Harrison, *On Account of Sex*, 19.
22. The Democrats included support for the ERA in the 1944, 1952, and 1956 party platforms, but not in 1940, 1948, or 1960. See Porter and Johnson, comps., *National Party Platforms 1840–1964*.
23. Esther Peterson, interview by Ronald J. Grele, May 18, 1966, 1, JFKL.
24. The other two members of the "personal brain trust" were Ted Sorensen and Richard Goodwin. "Historical Materials in the John F. Kennedy Library," comp. Ronald E. Whealen (Boston: John F. Kennedy Library, 1993); Fred Burke, "Senator Kennedy's Convention Organization," in *Inside Politics*, 32. Theodore H. White, *The Making of the President*, 283–84.
25. Peterson, interview by Grele, 1; Peterson, interview by Campbell, Jan. 20, 1970, 36; Harrison, *On Account of Sex*, 86.
26. Susan Ware, *Beyond Suffrage: Women in the New Deal*, 45.
27. Ibid.
28. Peterson, interview by Grele, 7–14.
29. Peterson, interview by Campbell, Jan. 20, 1970, 31–32.
30. Ibid., 33–34.
31. Statement of Secretary of Labor Arthur Goldberg, Feb. 12, 1962, "General, Executive letters, #1–5" folder, PCSW, Box 1, JFKL.
32. Mrs. Katherine Ellickson, Executive Secretary to Mrs. Elizabeth S. Bonfils, April 24, 1962, "General Correspondence 4/1962–6/1962" folder, PCSW, Box 1, JFKL.
33. For an extended discussion of issues of representation, see Martin, "Women Who Govern," and MaryAnne Borrelli, "Campaign Promises, Transition Dilemmas: Cabinet Building and Executive Representation," both in *The Other Elites*.
34. For example, see Janet M. Martin, "The Recruitment of Women to Cabinet and Subcabinet Posts," *Western Political Quarterly* 42 (1989): 161–72.
35. For further discussion of tensions between careers, political appointees, and the White House, see Hugh Heclo, *A Government of Strangers: Executive Politics in Washington*.
36. Peterson, interview by Campbell, Jan. 20, 1970, 42–43.
37. For example, see Results from December, 1958, in *The Gallup Poll: Public Opinion 1935–71*, vol. 2, 1584.
38. Esther Peterson to Edith A. Smith, Oct. 10, 1963, "General Correspondence, 9/1963–11/1963 and Undated" folder, PCSW, Box 1, JFKL.
39. In discussion on women being considered for appointive posts, or running for elective office, Mrs. Boddy observed, "I think the Commission, . . . might urge that women exercise what is already open and available to them in the way of party work, or participation in general civic affairs, which, in turn, will acquaint them more thoroughly with the problems that face the people that make the laws . . . political work in general is not entered into by women in many areas. . . . I know that there are enthusiastic women's political clubs everywhere, but I think the average women to whom we want to address ourselves, we need to acquaint her first of all with her need to get out and find out how body politics operates and works, and then she can make herself heard." Transcripts, April 2, 1963, "Transcripts: Proceedings, 4-2-1963" folder, 421–22, PCSW, Box 5, JFKL.

40. Esther Peterson to Mrs. Wallace N. Streeter, memorandum, Jan. 18, 1962, "General Correspondence, 12/1962–3/1962" folder, PCSW, Box 1, JFKL.

41. Document 4, December, 1961, "General Meetings 2/12/1962–2/13/1962" folder, PCSW, Box 2, JFKL.

42. Ibid.

43. Document 6, Feb. 5, 1962, attached to memorandum, Executive Letter #1, from Esther Peterson, Feb. 5, 1962, "General Executive Letters #1–5" folder, PCSW, Box 1, JFKL.

44. Document 4, December, 1961.

45. Ibid.

46. Ibid. Throughout the work of the PCSW, the plight of African Americans is noted as being of primary concern; with civil rights for African Americans a top priority with which the work of the commission should not interfere. The minimum wage rose from $1.00 per hour to $1.15 per hour, effective September, 1961. *Congress and the Nation,* 639.

47. Peterson, interview by Campbell, Jan. 20, 1970, 43.

48. "Remarks to Members of the '99 Club' of Women Pilots," Public Papers of JFK, July 26, 1963, 601.

49. Report, Document 6, Feb. 5, 1962, "General Executive Letters #1–5" folder, PCSW, Box 1, JFKL.

50. Report, Document 7, Feb. 5, 1962, "General Executive Letters #1–5" folder, PCSW, Box 1, JFKL.

51. U.S. Code (1958 edition), Title 28, Chapter 121, section 1861, 5058.

52. Report, Document 8, Feb. 5, 1962, "General Executive Letters #1–5" folder, PCSW, Box 1, JFKL.

53. "The Congress, whenever two thirds of both Houses shall deem it necessary, shall propose Amendments to this Constitution, or, on the Application of the Legislatures of two thirds of several States, shall call a Convention for proposing Amendments, which, in either Case, shall be valid to all Intents and Purposes, as Part of this Constitution, when ratified by the Legislatures of three fourths of the several States, or by Conventions in three fourths thereof, as the one or the other Mode of Ratification may be proposed by the Congress."

54. The seven committees were Committee on Civil and Political Rights; Committee on Education; Committee on Federal Employment; Committee on Home and Community; Committee on Private Employment; Committee on Social Insurance and Taxes; and the Committee on Protective Labor Legislation. The commission also used ad hoc committees, and committees formed subcommittees. Sometimes there is an inconsistency in the use of the committee names in reports and memos, and for that reason readers may find references to other committees of the commission in other sources.

55. For example, President Truman's use of an executive order to desegregate the armed forces or President Bill Clinton's use of an executive order to establish policy on the treatment of gays in the military. According to Lawrence F. (Larry) O'Brien, President Kennedy did not push for a civil rights bill in the 87th Congress (1961–62), since he decided not to antagonize the Southern Democrats by pressing for passage of a civil rights bill, whose support was needed on other issues such as expanding the size of the House Rules Committee and establishing a program of federal aid to education. The administration did argue, however, that much could be accomplished in the civil rights area through the issuance of executive orders. Actions of this type were taken with

reference to non-discrimination by government contractors and government agencies, integration of transportation facilities, and non-discrimination in federally financed housing. For further discussion of Kennedy's legislative strategy see Lawrence F. O'Brien, *No More Final Victories: A Life in Politics from John F. Kennedy to Watergate.*

56. Report, "Highlights of Federal Employment," January, 1962, prepared for the PCSW by the U.S. Civil Service Commission, "General Meetings, 2/12/62–2/13/62" folder, PCSW, Box 2, JFKL.

57. Ibid.

58. Ibid.

59. Report, "Employment Policies and Practices of the Federal Government, April 9, 1962," "General Executive Letters, #1–5" folder, PCSW, Box 1, JFKL; Report, "Report of Chairman Macy of the Civil Service Commission to President's Commission on the Status of Women," June 16, 1962, "General Executive Letters #8–10" folder, PCSW, Box 1, JFKL.

60. Report, "Employment Policies and Practices of the Federal Government, April 9, 1962," "General Executive Letters, #1–5" folder, PCSW, Box 1, JFKL.

61. Ibid.

62. Ibid.

63. Ibid.

64. Ibid.

65. Ibid.

66. Ibid.

67. *Current Status,* June 29, 1962, "General, Press Releases 12/1961–7/1962" folder, PCSW, Box 3, JFKL.

68. Ibid.

69. John F. Kennedy to Eleanor Roosevelt, June 15, 1962, "General Executive Letters #8–10" folder, PCSW, Box 1, JFKL.

70. For example, see Janet M. Martin, *Lessons from the Hill: The Legislative Journey of an Education Program,* especially chapter 2.

71. "Transcript: Proceedings February 13, 1962" folder, 106, PCSW, Box 4, JFKL.

72. One commission member, a Texan serving at the request of Vice President Lyndon Johnson and not a part of the Washington community represented on the commission, asked, "What will equal pay for equal work be exactly?" (Ibid., 108–109.) She thought that working women took too much time off from work and therefore they should not get the same pay as men. "I have heard a great many complaints from people who employ women that their absenteeism is very high. I think if that is true, they may be penalized. . . . We aren't telling somebody we expect them to pay women whether they are there or not." (Ibid., 106, 109–10.)

73. Ibid., 118.

74. Ibid., 118–19.

75. Katherine Ellickson to PCSW Members, Feb. 21, 1962, Executive letter No. 3, "General Executive Letters #1–5" folder, PCSW, Box 1, JFKL.

76. Esther Peterson recounts a delightful tale from her experiences on the commission. According to Peterson, Vice President Johnson and his wife, Lady Bird, hosted the commission members for a reception. "There was a car and driver for Mrs. Roosevelt and me. We had just had our first day's meetings, and Mrs. Boddy pulled us all up so many times because she'd ask, 'Well, what is a minimum wage?' . . . I'll never forget Mrs. Roosevelt's question to me on the way in the car. She said, . . . 'Where did you get Mrs. Boddy?' . . . I said this was someone the vice

president asked us to put on. . . . The only political appointee on that whole commission—a very small price to pay, I thought. . . . When we got out to the House there was a receiving line and I was introducing people to Mrs. Roosevelt and the vice president. . . . Here came Mrs. Boddy. After she got through, Mrs. Roosevelt turned to the vice president and said, 'I wonder where they found her. She doesn't know from anything.' I just gasped. . . . Later on . . . when we were taking Mrs. Roosevelt back, she said, 'You know, I didn't turn to look at you for fear we would have smiled.'" Peterson, interview by Campbell, Jan. 20, 1970, 78.

Mrs. Boddy herself admitted to commission members why she had to ask these basic questions: "I read the things that you have sent me very faithfully when I get them. And yet when I come up here, I have to ask a good many questions, because I don't have a background in any of this sort of thing. I have to look at it like the average ordinary clubswoman who reads the headlines and gets the wrong impression. And that is why I am very much opposed to making any endorsements in the first place which I can't explain for sure when I get home, and in the second place involving ourselves in anything." "Transcripts Proceedings, 2/13/1962" folder, 113, PCSW, Box 4, JFKL.

77. Jones, *Presidency in a Separated System,* 133.
78. O'Brien, *No More Final Victories,* 143.
79. Harrison, *On Account of Sex,* 93.
80. "Bill W." to "Arthur," May 4, 1961, attached to Secretary of Labor to David Bell, July 14, 1961, folder LL-2-1, Box 75, RG174 (Goldberg), National Archives, quoted in ibid.
81. *CQ Almanac 1962,* 412.
82. Peterson, interview by Campbell, Jan. 20, 1970, 48.
83. Ibid., 47.
84. Ibid., 51.
85. Ibid., 55.
86. Minutes, April 1–2, 1963, "General Meetings, 4/1/1963–4/2/1963 (folder 1)" folder, PCSW, Box 3, JFKL.
87. *Current Status,* November, 1962, "General Background Information and Newsletters" folder, PCSW, Box 1, JFKL.
88. For an extended discussion of the legislative history of equal pay bills, see Harrison, *On Account of Sex,* especially chapter 6.
89. Peterson, interview by Campbell, Jan. 20, 1970, 54.
90. See Harrison, *On Account of Sex,* chapter 6.
91. Document 1, "Committee on Federal Employment Policies and Practices," June 8, 1962, "General Executive Letters, #8–10" folder, PCSW, Box 1, JFKL.
92. Document 8, "Committee on Federal Employment Policies and Practices," Jan. 30, 1963, "General Executive Letters, #16–18" folder, PCSW, Box 2, JFKL.
93. Ibid.
94. For an extended discussion on women in the military, see Ebbert and Hall, *Crossed Currents.*
95. Report, October 1–2, 1962, "Committee on Social Insurance and Taxes: Documents #22–25 Deductions for Child Care and Disabled Dependents" folder, PCSW, Box 13, JFKL; Transcripts, October 2, 1962, "Transcripts: Proceedings 10/2/1962" folder, PCSW, Box 5, JFKL; Minutes, February 11–12, 1963, "General, Executive letters, #20" folder, PCSW, Box 2, JFKL.
96. Minutes, April 1–2, 1963, "General, Meetings, 4/1/1963–4/2/1963 (folder 1)" folder, PCSW, Box 3, JFKL.

97. Minutes, October 1–2, 1962, "General, Executive Letters, #15" folder, PCSW, Box 2, JFKL.

98. Peterson to Smith, Oct. 10, 1963.

99. "The Gender Gap," fact sheet of the CAWP, 1987, Eagleton Institute of Politics, Rutgers University.

100. What might be most surprising to those noting the close association between the National Education Association and Democratic administrations in subsequent years, especially that of Presidents Carter and Clinton, is that one of the two most important qualities looked for in candidates was "1. Independence from NEA domination." Dan H. Fenn, Jr., to Ralph A. Dungan, memorandum, July 31, 1962, obtained from an exhibit at the JFK Museum; original document in LBJL.

101. Ibid.

102. See Martin, "Women Who Govern."

103. Peterson, interview by Campbell, Jan. 20, 1970, 35–36.

104. Ibid., 36.

105. Ibid., 32.

106. Ibid., 33.

107. Ibid., 31.

108. Eona Gatchell to President Kennedy, copied to Mrs. Roosevelt, May 1, 1962, "General, Correspondence 4/1962–6/1962" folder, PCSW, Box 1, JFKL.

109. Transcripts, Oct. 2, 1962, "Transcripts: Proceedings, 10/2/62" folder, 253, PCSW, Box 5, JFKL.

110. Ibid., 255.

111. Peterson, interview by Campbell, Jan. 20, 1970, 36.

112. Ibid.

113. Peterson, interview by Grele, 18.

114. Ibid., 21.

115. Ibid., 19.

116. Transcripts, Oct. 2, 1962, 257.

117. See Ware, *Beyond Suffrage.*

118. Transcripts, Oct. 2, 1962, 257.

119. Ibid., 258.

120. Ibid., 263.

121. Ibid., 264.

122. Ibid., 267.

123. Ibid., 243.

124. Minutes, 4th Meeting, Oct. 1–2, 1962, "General, Exec Letters #15" folder, PCSW, Box 2, JFKL.

125. Graham T. Allison, *Essence of Decision: Explaining the Cuban Missile Crisis,* chapter 2.

126. Allison, *Essence of Decision,* 1.

127. Katherine Ellickson to Commission Members, Executive Letter #15, Oct. 25, 1962, "General, Executive Letters #15" folder, PCSW, Box 2, JFKL; Katherine Ellickson to Esther Peterson, memorandum, Oct. 31, 1962, "General, Correspondence 9/1962–1/1963" folder, PCSW, Box 1, JFKL.

128. Document 8, "Committee on Federal Employment Policies and Practices Document #8," Jan. 30, 1963.

129. "Chapter 10 Political Executives," October, 1963, "Committee on Federal Employment Policies and Practices, Published Report, 10/1963" folder, PCSW, Box 8, JFKL.

130. Transcripts, Oct. 12, 1963, "Transcripts: Proceedings, October 12, 1963" folder, 388, PCSW, Box 5, JFKL.

131. Document 29, Feb. 4, 1963, Committee on Government Contracts, "General, Executive Letters #19" folder, PCSW, Box 2, JFKL.

132. Report, "Draft Proposal for National Roster of Women Executives," Spring, 1963, "Committee on Federal Employment Policies and Practices: Documents #36–46 Military, Women Executives" folder, PCSW, Box 7, JFKL.

133. Report, August, 1963, "Committee on Federal Employment Policies and Practices: Document #60 Final Draft of Report" folder, PCSW, Box 7, JFKL.

134. Esther Peterson to Cabinet Secretaries, memorandum, draft, Sept. 16, 1963, "General Correspondence 9/1963–11/1963 and undated" folder, PCSW, Box 1, JFKL.

135. Transcripts, April 24, 1963, "Transcripts: Proceedings, 4-24-63" folder, 306–307, PCSW, Box 6, JFKL.

136. Memo to Members of the President's Commission on the Status of Women, Jan. 28, 1963, "General Executive Letters #16–18" folder, PCSW, Box 2, JFKL.

137. "Special Message to the Congress: The Manpower Report of the President," Public Papers of JFK, March 11, 1963, 255.

138. Stephen J. Wayne, *The Road to the White House 1996*, (post-election edition), 102.

CHAPTER 3. THE JOHNSON ADMINISTRATION

1. *CQ Almanac 1963*, 68–70.

2. Jane Grant to President Johnson, Dec. 5, 1963, "GEN LE/HU 3" folder, LE/HU 3, Box 72, LBJL.

3. Esther Peterson to Myer Feldman, memorandum, Dec. 31, 1963, "GEN LE/HU 3" folder, LE/HU 3, Box 72, LBJL.

4. Ibid.

5. James F. Frey to Don Furtado, memorandum, Oct. 5, 1967, "GEN HU3 1023/65" folder, WHCF, HU3, Box 58, LBJL.

6. Myer Feldman to Jane Grant, Dec. 31, 1963, "GEN LE/HU 3" folder, LE/HU 3, Box 72, LBJL.

7. Early in January, 1964, at a meeting of the cabinet, the issue of civil rights was thoroughly discussed. In notes prepared for the president before the meeting, Lee C. White, who had been chairing the Subcabinet Committee on Civil Rights, suggested that there be "a firm statement of Presidential policy regarding strong efforts to employ and promote on the basis of ability and without regard to race, color or creed." Lee C. White to President Johnson, memorandum, Jan. 6, 1964, "Cabinet Meeting, 1-6-64" folder, Cabinet Papers, Box 1, LBJL. There was no mention of the inclusion of equal rights for women in discussion of the administration's civil rights policy rights until after passage of the 1964 Civil Rights Act, which had been quietly amended to include "sex" in Title VII provisions.

8. For example, see George Christian to Margery Leonard, Oct. 12, 1967, "GEN HU3 10/23/65" folder, WHCF, HU3, Box 58, LBJL.

9. National Woman's Party, memorandum, n.d., "EX FG 737 Pres. Commission on the Status of Women" folder, WHCF, FG 737, Box 404, LBJL.

10. Mrs. Hermine Tobolowsky and Mrs. Modell Scruggs, to President Johnson, Jan.

23, 1965, "GEN HU3 Equality for Women 9/1/64–10/22/65" folder, WHCF, HU 3, Box 58, LBJL.

11. National Woman's Party to President Johnson, telegram, Oct. 28, 1964, "GEN HU3 9/1/64–10/22/65" folder, WHCF, GEN HU3, Box 58, LBJL. The 1964 Democratic Platform instead stated, "We will support *legislation* [emphasis added] to carry forward the progress already made towards full equality of opportunity for women as well as men." In fact, the platform goes on to state: "We are firmly pledged to continue the Nation's work towards the goals of equal opportunity and equal treatment for all Americans regardless of race, creed, color or national origin." "Democratic Party Platform 1964" in Porter and Johnson, comps., *National Party Platforms 1840–1964*, 649.

12. Ralph A. Dungan to Dorothy M. Ford, Oct. 17, 1964, "GEN 737" folder, WHCF, FG 737, Box 404, LBJL.

13. Bob Fleming to Will Sparks, memorandum, ca. October, 1967, "EX HU3 11/1/67–9/30/68" folder, WHCF, HU3, Box 58, LBJL.

14. Elizabeth Wickenden (Mrs. Arthur Goldschmidt), interview by Paige Mulhollan, June 3, 1969, 87, LBJL.

15. Peterson, interview by Greele, 77.

16. See Executive Order 11126, Nov. 1, 1963.

17. I greatly appreciate the work of the archivists at the Lyndon Johnson Library in tracking down this speech for me. "5/21/62, Remarks by Vice President at Democratic Women's National Conference, Washington, D.C.," Box 65, LBJL. Johnson has contributed some of the more memorable remarks concerning the role of women in government. As vice president, Johnson spoke before the Democratic Women's National Conference in Washington, D.C. in 1962 and recounted the history of women in the party: "The woman pioneers who set the proud pattern for the Democratic Party were burden-bearers, not orchid-wearers. [Paragraph break] Eleanor Roosevelt, Carolina O'Day, Frances Perkins, Mary Norton, Emily Newell Blair . . . they cared, they got things done."

18. "What the Administration has Done for Women," memorandum, April 20, 1964, "Panzer: Women" folder, Office Files of Fred Panzer, Box 522, LBJL.

19. John Macy, interview by David McComb, April 25, 1969, tape 2, 16, LBJL.

20. Ibid., 14–15.

21. Ibid., 18.

22. Wickenden, interview by Mulhollan, 88–89.

23. See Executive Order 11126.

24. Mary D. Keyserling, interview by David G. McComb, Oct. 31, 1968, tape 2, 4–5, LBJL.

25. Press Release, 1-16-64, "Panzer Women" folder, Office Files of Fred Panzer, Box 500, LBJL.

26. Press announcement from the Office of Information, Publications, and Reports, Department of Labor, Jan. 20, 1964, "EX FG 686" folder, WHCF, FG 686, Box 385, LBJL.

27. Ibid.

28. Ibid.

29. Keyserling, interview by McComb, Oct. 31, 1968, tape 2, 4–5.

30. Among the issues confronting the president were tensions between Greece and Turkey over Cyprus, the escalating situation in the Gulf of Tonkin, and "coups and counter coups in Saigon." See Robert Dallek, *Flawed Giant: Lyndon Johnson and His Times, 1961–1973*, 238. Johnson, *Vantage Point*, chapters 3 and 6.

31. President Johnson to W. Willard Wirtz, Aug. 20, 1964, "EX PE 2 8/16/64–9/25/64" folder, WHCF, PE 2, Box 8, LBJL.

32. Isabelle Shelton, "Women Gaining in Opportunities," ca. October, 1964, "Panzer: Women" folder, Office Files of Fred Panzer, Box 522, LBJL.

33. Esther Peterson, interview by Ann M. Campbell, Feb. 11, 1970, 78–79, JFKL.

34. Light, *Thickening Government.*

35. For example, see *Fifth Annual Report of the Director of the Women's Bureau for the Fiscal Year Ended June 30, 1923.*

36. This figure excludes employees in the CIA, NSA, and temporary Christmas postal workers.

37. Mary D. Keyserling, interview by David G. McComb, Oct. 22, 1968, tape 1, 13, LBJL.

38. See Duerst-Lahti, "Government's Role in Building the Women's Movement."

39. For historical context, it was not until 1966 that "a Federal court held for the first time that the Equal Protection Clause of the Fourteenth Amendment applies to discrimination against women. The three-judge Federal Court in Alabama held that the State jury statute excluding women was in violation of that Amendment. This decision was a major step in realizing a most important and far-reaching recommendation of the President's Commission on the Status of Women." Report, "What the Administration is Doing for Women," July 18, 1966, "Women's Bureau" folder, Office Files of Fred Panzer, Box 548, LBJL.

40. See Keyserling, interview by McComb, Oct. 22, 1968, tapes 1 and 2; "Computer Fails the Women," *The Evening Star,* July 29, 1965; Remarks by the President, June 21, 1968, "Committee on the Status of Women" folder, Office Files of Harry McPherson, Box 55, LBJL; *Public Papers of the Presidents of the United States: Lyndon B. Johnson,* July 29, 1965, 807–809.

41. Keyserling, interview by McComb, Oct. 31, 1968, tape 2, 7.

42. Duerst-Lahti, "Government's Role in Building the Women's Movement."

43. For example, see Jo Freeman, *Politics of Women's Liberation.* As Georgia Duerst-Lahti notes, "Jo Freeman can be credited with the best overall account of the politics of the current women's movement."

44. Kathryn F. Clarenbach to President Johnson, Nov. 11, 1966, "GEN HU 3 10/23/65—" folder, WHCF, HU 3, Box 58, LBJL.

45. Stephen N. Shulman to W. Marvin Watson, memorandum, Nov. 23, 1966, "GEN HU 3 10/23/65—" folder, WHCF, HU 3, Box 58, LBJL.

46. Harry McPherson to Marvin Watson, handwritten note, Sept. 25, 1967, "GEN HU 3 10/23/65—" folder, WHCF, HU 3, Box 58, LBJL; Betty Friedan to President Johnson, Sept. 18, 1967, "GEN HU 3 10/23/65—" folder, WHCF, HU 3, Box 58. LBJL.

47. Judith Hole, "National Organization for Women (NOW)," in *The Reader's Companion to U.S. Women's History,* ed. Wilma Mankiller, Gwendolyn Mink, Marysa Navarro, Barbara Smith, and Gloria Steinem. *A History of the National Federation of Business and Professional Women's Clubs, Inc., (BPW/USA),* vol. III, compiled by Mariwyn D. Heath (Washington, D.C.: National Federation of Business and Professional Women's Clubs, Inc., BPW/USA, 1994), 24.

48. Jones, *Presidency in a Separated System.* 19.

49. Johnson, *Vantage Point,* 37–38.

50. For example, see John C. Donovan, *The Politics of Poverty,* for a full discussion of the origins and programs of the Economic Opportunity Act of 1964 targeting poverty.

51. For example, see Christopher Weeks, *Job Corps, Dollars and Dropouts* and Edith Green, interview by Janet Kerr-Tener, Aug. 23, 1985, tapes 1 and 2, LBJL.

52. Green, interview by Kerr-Tener, tape 1 of 2, 41.

53. Report, "What the Administration is Doing for Women," July 18, 1966, "Women's Bureau" folder, Office Files of Fred Panzer, Box 548, LBJL. For a more detailed discussion of this provision, see Green, interview by Kerr-Tener, tapes 1 and 2. See also Weeks, *Jobs Corps.*

54. Chapter 3, "Labor Standards," sec. G, "Equal Pay" in "Administrative History of the Department of Labor," vol. I, vol. II, pt. 1; "Vol. II (2), Pt. 1 [2 of 2] Programs of the Dept. Of Labor" folder, LBJL.

55. Ibid.

56. See Eric L. Davis, "The Johnson White House and the 1964 Civil Rights Act" (paper presented at the American Political Science Association meetings, Atlanta, Ga., Aug. 31–Sept. 3, 1989).

57. Keyserling, interview by McComb, Oct. 22, 1968, tape 1, 18–19.

58. Ibid., 17–18.

59. Esther Peterson to Mrs. Cecil Norton Broy, March 27, 1964, "GEN HU 3 Equality for Women 11/22/63–4/30/64" folder, WHCF HU3, Box 58, LBJL.

60. Chapter 3, "Labor Standards," sec. G, "Equal Pay."

61. Chapter 3, "Labor Standards," sec. 3, "Women Workers," in "Administrative History of the Department of Labor," vol. I, vol. II, pt. 1, 446; "Vol. II (2), Pt. 1 [2 of 2] Programs of the Dept. Of Labor" folder, LBJL.

62. Ibid.

63. See Peterson, interview by Greele, 84–86.

64. Ibid., 93.

65. In looking at the entries in the *U.S. Government Manual* drawn from information provided by the White House, scholars are correct in noting no women appear to reach the level of special assistant to the president until Johnson's appointment of Betty Furness in 1967. However, Esther Peterson was appointed special assistant to President Johnson in 1964, while retaining her position as assistant secretary for labor standards, although her salary came out of the Department of Labor's budget and not the White House budget. See Joe Califano to President Johnson, memorandum, April 21, 1967, "EX FG 11-8-1/Furness, Betty 11/23/63–5/1/67" folder, WHCF, FG 11-8-1/Furness, Betty, Box 83, LBJL.

66. Esther Peterson, interview by Michael L. Gillette, Oct. 29, 1974, 37–39, LBJL.

67. Robert E. Kintner to Gardner Ackley, memorandum, Aug. 8, 1966, "Cabinet Meeting 8-11-66 [2 of 4]" folder, Cabinet Papers, Box 7, LBJL.

68. Press release, Jan. 3, 1964, "Women's Appointments" folder, Office Files of Fred Panzer, O.A. Box 27, LBJL.

69. Jack Valenti to President Johnson, memorandum, Dec. 5, 1964, "Valenti, Jack 1963–64" folder, Office of the President Files, Box 12, LBJL.

70. In a memo to the president, Jack Valenti presented an organization chart of the White House and noted that "each staff member has a special province that is uniquely his. If he feels that he has a substantive role, if he feels he is making a contribution, he is a happier man. If he seems isolated or drifting, he is a millstone around your neck and will cause annoyance to you and within himself." Valenti observes that there is need for "some kind of inner staff hierarchy . . . that will check things out with the others and cut down the physical access to you. This would be supplied by Moyers, Bundy, Valenti, and Reedy, and possibly one more staff member. (More than five men reporting to the President will

erode the President's time and will be unwieldy.)" Jack Valenti to President Johnson, memorandum, Dec. 6, 1964, "Valenti, Jack 1963–64" folder, Office of the President Files, Box 12, LBJL. A year and a half later, when Robert E. Kintner was asked by the president "to prepare a description of what each of the Special Assistants and the Counsel do," Esther Peterson was again omitted from the list of special assistants. The only woman included on the list was Juanita Roberts, personal secretary to the president. Robert E. Kintner to President Johnson, memorandum, May 19, 1966, "Kintner, Robert" folder, Office of the President Files, Box 6, LBJL.

71. Consider the Offices of Congressional Liaison, Personnel, and the Bureau of the Budget and its successor, Office of Management and Budget, all in the Executive Office of the President.

72. Memo, March 25, 1965, "Cabinet Meetings [2 of 2] 3/25/65" folder, Cabinet Papers, Box 2, LBJL; see Boxes 1–15 in the Cabinet Papers Collection, LBJL, for attendance lists of all of the cabinet meetings.

73. Bill Moyers to President Johnson, memorandum, March 30, 1966, "EX FG 11-8-1/P" folder, WHCF, EX FG 11-8-1/P, Box 103, LBJL.

74. Statement, March 3, 1967, "EX FG 11-8-1/P" folder, WHCF, EX FG 11-8-1/P, Box 103, LBJL.

75. John W. Macy, Jr., to President Johnson, memorandum, Feb. 8, 1967, "EX FG 717 9/27/66–5/1/67" folder, WHCF, Box 396, LBJL.

76. Ibid.

77. Ibid.

78. Joe Califano to President Johnson, memorandum, Feb. 9, 1967, "EX FG 717 9/27/66–5/1/67" folder, WHCF, Box 396, LBJL.

79. Liz Carpenter to President Johnson, memorandum, Nov. 4, 1966, "Carpenter, Elizabeth" folder, Office of the President Files, Box 1, LBJL.

80. Report, by Esther Peterson, March 3, 1967, "EX FG 11-8-1/P" folder, WHCF, EX FG 11-8-1/P, Box 103, LBJL.

81. Vera Glaser, "Women Abandon Top-Level Posts," March 2, 1967, [St. Louis *Globe-Democrat*], "Betty Furness" folder, Office Files of Fred Panzer, Box 553, LBJL.

82. Fred Panzer to Joe Califano, memorandum, March 13, 1967, "EX FG 717 9/27/66–5/1/67" folder, WHCF, FG 717, Box 396, LBJL; Memo for the Record, Larry Levinson, March 18, 1967, "EX FG 11-8-1/Furness, Betty 11/23/63–5/1/67" folder, WHCF, FG 11-8-1/Furness, Betty, Box 83, LBJL.

83. Fred Panzer to President Johnson, memorandum, March 8, 1967, "EX FG 11-8-1/Furness, Betty 11/23/63–5/1/67" folder, WHCF, FG 11-8-1/Furness, Betty, Box 83, LBJL.

84. Fred Panzer to Robert Kintner, memorandum, April 27, 1967, "EX FG 11-8-1/Furness, Betty 11/23/63–5/1/67" folder, WHCF FG 11-8-1/Furness, Betty, Box 83, LBJL.

85. *Public Papers of the President of the United States: Lyndon B. Johnson,* May 1, 1967, 489.

86. Ibid.

87. Letter, Joseph Califano to a number of those writing about the Furness appointment, May, 1967, "Betty Furness Swearing In" folder, Office Files of Fred Panzer, Box 551, LBJL.

88. Given that Esther Peterson had been serving as the chair of this committee, from an organizational structure perspective it had made sense to have the

committee function at the assistant secretary level, since Peterson herself was an assistant secretary. However, Peterson was also a special assistant for consumer affairs.

89. Califano wrote to Johnson that Esther Peterson had a "long-standing commitment to address the Association of Industrial Hygienists in Chicago on occupational health and safety problems . . . [which] are among the responsibilities she has as Assistant Secretary of Labor." Joe Califano to President Johnson, May 1, 1967, "Peterson, Esther (2 of 2)" folder, WHCF Name File, Box 163, LBJL.

90. Liz Carpenter to President Johnson, memorandum, March 10, 1967, "Carpenter, Elizabeth" folder, Office of the President Files, Box 1, LBJL.

91. Keyserling, interview by McComb, Oct. 22, 1968, tape 2, 9.

92. Johnson, *The Vantage Point.*

93. A longtime family friend, Elizabeth Wickenden, observed that Lady Bird "influences him a great deal by indirection. I don't think she tells him straight-out what she thinks he should be doing at any given moment, but I think she kind of edges him in." Wickenden, interview by Mulhollan, 84–85.

   Katie Louchheim, who also had known the Johnsons for many years, especially through her work at the DNC, stated that "I believe the President when he says he never really made a decision without her. He really had great respect and affection for his mother; he thought she was an extraordinary women and I think he turned around and the reason he picked Lady Bird was because she too had extraordinary sensitivity as well as a great deal of intelligence and a fine character." Kathleen C. Louchheim, interview by Paige E. Mulhollan, April 1, 1969, tape 1, 18, LBJL.

94. Keyserling, interview by McComb, Oct. 22, 1968, tape 2, 7.

95. Lewis L. Gould, foreword to *Ruffles and Flourishes*, by Liz Carpenter.

96. Horace Busby to President Johnson, memorandum, n.d. (shortly after 1964 election), "Busby, Horace" folder, Office of the President Files, Box 1, LBJL.

97. Not until 1971 would women be allowed at the National Press Club. National Press Club, telephone interview with author, March 31, 1997.

98. See memos from Liz Carpenter to the President (or President and Mrs. Johnson) in "Carpenter, Elizabeth" folder, Office of the President Files, Box 1, LBJL, or "EX PE 2 11/16/66–12/5/66" folder, WHCF, PE 2, Box 11, LBJL.

99. Listing, from Liz Carpenter, "Pending Vacancies to Which Women Might Be Appointed," Jan. 16, 1964, "EX PE 2 11/22/63–2/14/64" folder, WHCF, PE 2, Box 7, LBJL.

100. Valenti to Johnson, memorandum, Dec. 5, 1964.

101. "Notes of Meeting on the Cabinet," memorandum, Sept. 11, 1967, "Cabinet Meetings, 9/20/67 [4 of 4]" folder, Cabinet Papers, Box 10, LBJL.

102. Carpenter, *Ruffles & Flourishes,* 13.

103. Liz Carpenter to President Johnson, memorandum, Jan. 29, 1964, "EX PE 2 11/22/63–2/14/64" folder, WHCF, PE 2, Box 7, LBJL.

104. Liz Carpenter, interview by Joe B. Frantz, Dec. 3, 1968, interview I, tape 1, 11, LBJL.

105. Ralph Dungan, interview by Paige Mulhollan, April 18, 1969, 18–19, LBJL.

106. Ibid., 19. In the oral history interview of Ralph Dungan, following a discussion of the recruitment of women, the interviewer asks: "Did it get harder to recruit good *men* [my emphasis] for President Johnson as compared to what had been in your role with Kennedy?" The interview was done in 1969, and so at the time the question may not have been as surprising, but that it followed a discussion of women it is most curious. (Dungan, interview by Mulhollan, 19.)

107. Liz Carpenter to Jack Valenti, memorandum, Nov. 19, 1964, "EX PR 18 11/6/64–11/30/64" folder, WHCF, EX PR 18, Box 356, LBJL.

108. Liz Carpenter to President Johnson, memorandum, Jan. 15, 1966, "EX ND 19/CO 312 1/15/66–1/21/66" folder, WHCF, EX ND 19/CO312, Box 218, LBJL.

109. Keyserling, interview by David G. McComb, Oct. 31, 1968, tape 2, 3.

110. For example, see David E. Bell to Ralph A. Dungan, memorandum, March 5, 1964, "Misc Women" folder, Office Files of John Macy, Box 850, LBJL.

111. Charles L. Schultze to President Johnson, memorandum, Nov. 21, 1966, EX PE 2 11/16/66–12/5/66" folder, WHCF, PE 2, Box 11, LBJL.

112. Ralph A. Dungan to Heads of Departments and Independent Establishments, memorandum, Jan. 27, 1964, "EX FG 686" folder, WHCF, FG 686, Box 385, LBJL.

113. Edward Sherman to Ralph A. Dungan, memorandum, Feb. 14, 1964, "EX PE 2 2/15/64–3/9/64" folder, WHCF, PE 2, Box 7, LBJL.

114. Liz Carpenter to "Anyone Interested in Women," memorandum, Feb. 24, 1964, "EX PE 2 2/15/64–3/9/64" folder, PE 2, Box 7, LBJL.

115. See a series of memos in "EX PE 2 2/15/64–3-9/64" folder, WHCF, PE 2, Box 7, LBJL.

116. Anthony Celebrezze to President Johnson, memorandum, Feb. 24, 1964, "EX PE 2 2/15/64–3/9/64" folder, WHCF, PE 2, Box 7, WHCF PE 2, LBJL.

117. John C. Donovan to Bill Moyers, memorandum, Feb. 24, 1964, "EX PE 2 2/15/64–3/9/64" folder, WHCF, PE 2, Box 7, LBJL.

118. Luther H. Hodges to President Johnson, memorandum, Feb. 24, 1964, "EX PE 2 2/15/64–3/9/64" folder, WHCF, PE 2, Box 7, WHCF, PE 2, Box 7, LBJL.

119. Memorandum of Meeting, Feb. 24, 1964, "Misc. Women—Agency Contacts—Women" folder, Office Files of John Macy, Box 850, LBJL.

120. "Remarks to the Winners of the Federal Woman's Award," Public Papers of LBJ, March 3, 1964, 330.

121. Ralph A. Dungan to Salinger, Carpenter, Jenkins, and Valenti, memorandum, March 11, 1964, "EX PE 2 3/10/64–4/27/64" folder, PE 2, Box 7, LBJL.

122. Keyserling, interview by McComb, Oct. 22, 1968, tape 1, 1.

123. "Johnson Picks Woman for 5 Key U.S. Posts," The Evening Star, March 29, 1964, in "Panzer: Women" folder, Office Files of Fred Panzer, Box 522, LBJL; for an excellent account of some of the appointments and the problems Johnson's approach created for those in his administration, see "'Something for the Girls,'" Newsweek, March 16, 1964, 29–30.

124. Edward Sherman to Ralph Dungan, memorandum, Feb. 29, 1964, "EX PE 2 2/15/64–3/9/64" folder, PE 2, Box 7, LBJL.

125. Jack Valenti to George Reedy, memorandum, June 8, 1964, "EX PE 2 5/26/64–6/17/64" folder, PE 2, Box 8, LBJL.

126. Recent presidents have tended to turn more to the Washington community for their appointments if they inherited an administration of the same party, or even as their own term of office progressed and familiarity with the Washington community grew. For further discussion, see Martin, "Women Who Govern."

127. "Administrative History of the U.S. Civil Service Commission, Volume I, Pt. II, Chapter XV—Presidential Appointments from the Career Service," LBJL.

128. "Talent Search for Womanpower," n.d., "Misc. Women" folder, Office Files of John Macy, Box 850, LBJL.

129. For instance, Justice had a solid record in hiring women as attorneys in the department. The percentage of women lawyers in Justice was higher than the

percentage of women lawyers across the country. This figure was probably the result of two factors: (1) Women were finding barriers to being hired in the top law firms in the country; and (2) With the directives from President Kennedy and John Macy in 1961 and 1962 ending the classification of most federal jobs by sex, positions opened up to women. William A. Geoghegan to William Moyers, memorandum, Feb. 20, 1964, "EX PE 2 2/15/64–3/9/64" folder, WHCF, PE 2, Box 7, LBJL.

130. Ibid.

131. For example, see memos in "EX PE 2 2/15/64–3/9/64" and "EX PE 2 3/10/64–4/27/64" folders, WHCF, PE 2, Box 7, LBJL and "EX FI 1-2 4/1/64–5/6/64" folder, WHCF, FI 1-2, Box 4, LBJL.

132. Liz Carpenter to President Johnson, memorandum, Feb. 25, 1964, "EX PE 2 2/15/64–3/9/64" folder, WHCF, PE 2, Box 7, LBJL.

133. Marjorie Hunter, "Margaret Chase Smith Seeks Presidency," *New York Times,* Jan. 28, 1964, 1.

134. President Johnson to Margaret Chase Smith, Dec. 17, 1964, "Smith, Margaret Chase (Senator)" folder, WHCF, Name File, Box 402, LBJL.

135. Harold W. Stanley and Richard G. Niemi, *Vital Statistics on American Politics,* 77.

136. Data are from the U.S. Bureau of the Census, Current Population Reports, Series P-20, "Voting and Registration in the Election of November 1964" and subsequent report years. Reported in "Sex Differences in Voter Turnout," fact sheet of the CAWP, Eagleton Institute of Politics, Rutgers University.

137. And, in fact, Johnson would receive a greater percentage of support among women than among men in 1964. This pattern would continue through the 1996 elections except in 1976, when the Democratic candidate, challenger Jimmy Carter, won a greater percentage of votes among men than among women. Stanley and Niemi, *Vital Statistics,* 4th ed., 105, reproduced in Nelson W. Polsby and Aaron Wildavsky, *Presidential Elections: Strategies and Structures in American Politics,* 9th ed. 45.

138. James G. Morton to Bill D. Moyers, memorandum, July 14, 1964, and press release, "Women in a Man's World by Eugene D. Fleming," "EX PE 6/11/64–12/10/64" folder, WHCF, EX PE, Box 1, LBJL.

139. Frank Mankiewicz to Bill Moyers, memorandum, June 15, 1966, "Personnel" folder, Office Files of Bill Moyers, Box 74, LBJL.

140. "Remarks at the Sixth Annual Federal Woman's Award Ceremony," Public Papers of LBJ, Feb. 28, 1966, 226–27.

141. Report, "Federal Woman's Award Study Group on Careers for Women: Progress Report to the President," March 3, 1967, "EX MA 1/D-F" folder, MA 1/F*, Box 2, LBJL.

142. See Executive Order 11375, Oct. 13, 1967.

143. "Federal Women's Award Study Group on Careers for Women."

144. See Executive Order 11375, Oct. 13, 1967.

145. Robert E. Kintner to President Johnson, memorandum, Jan. 20, 1967, "CF WH 10 Staff meetings (1967–)" folder, CF WH 10, Box 99. LBJL.

146. Ibid.

147. "Suggestions for Filling Top Government Jobs from Cabinet Members," memorandum, June 1, 1966, "Cabinet Meeting, 6-1-66 [2 of 2]" folder, Cabinet Papers, Box 5, LBJL.

148. Memorandum for President Johnson, Oct. 6, 1966, "EX PE 2 10/5/66–11/15/66"

folder, PE 2, Box 11, LBJL; however, John Macy did send ongoing reports of major appointments by just about any imaginable category, including: experience, state and regional breakdowns, department and agency, full and part time from Texas, women, Phi Beta Kappas, Rhodes Scholars, college presidents, ABA ratings of judges, parties of judges, and university records of cabinet and White House staff. See "EX PE 2 9/17/66–10/4/66" folder, PE 2, Box 11, LBJL, as well as other folders in the PE 2 series, especially Boxes 7, 12, and 14, and reports in the Cabinet Papers, LBJL.

149. Marvin to President Johnson, Jan. 22, 1968, and Tom Johnson to President Johnson, memorandum, Jan, 22, 1968, "EX PE 12 11/8/67–5/15/68" folder, WHCF, EX PE 12, Box 38, LBJL.

150. Joe Califano to President Johnson, memorandum, May 1, 1968, "Cabinet Meeting, 5/1/68 [2 of 4]" folder, Cabinet Papers, Box 13, LBJL.

151. Patricia Roberts Harris, interview by Steve Goodell, May 19, 1969, 22, LBJL.

152. Ibid., 24.

CHAPTER 4. THE NIXON ADMINISTRATION

1. Rep. Dwyer to President Nixon, memorandum, July 6, 1969, "[GEN] HU 2-5 Women 1/1/70–12/31/70" folder, WHCF, Subject Files HU, Box 22, NPM.

2. President Abraham Lincoln issued a proclamation on September 22, 1862, announcing the forthcoming Emancipation Proclamation, thus giving one hundred days' notice to the states of the Confederacy. *A Compilation of the Messages and Papers of the Presidents, 1789–1897,* comp. James D. Richardson, vol. VI.

3. See Executive Order 9981, July 26, 1948.

4. Robert D. Loevy, "Introduction: The Background and Setting of the Civil Rights Act of 1964," in *The Civil Rights Act of 1964: The Passage of the Law that Ended Racial Segregation,* ed. Robert D. Loevy, 14.

5. See Joel D. Aberbach and Bert A. Rockman, "Clashing Beliefs Within the Executive Branch: The Nixon Administration Bureaucracy," *American Political Science Review* 70, no. 2 (June, 1976): 456–68.

6. For example, see Walcott and Hult, *Governing the White House,* and for an in-depth analysis of the Executive Office of the President see John Hart, *The Presidential Branch: From Washington to Clinton,* 2d ed.

7. For instance, leaders of the NFBPWC wondered with whom to have contact in this new administration—the Justice Department? the White House? If so, with whom? Nearly simultaneously, different advisors within the White House initiated contact with the NFBPWC, to solicit recommendations of names for commission vacancies.

8. Statement by Richard M. Nixon, press release of the RNC, Oct. 17, 1968, "ERA [1 of 3]" folder, WHCF, SMOF, ALA, Box 7, NPM.

9. Ruth M. Easterling to President Nixon, June 25, 1971, "Outside Women's Organizations File, [NFBPWC 1 of 4]" folder, WHCF, SMOF, Anne Armstrong, Box 63, NPM.

10. "Address to the Nation Announcing Intention to Nominate Lewis F. Powell, Jr., and William H. Rehnquist to be Associate Justices of the Supreme Court of the United States," Public Papers of Nixon, Oct. 21, 1971, 1056.

11. Several months later, Rehnquist was appointed associate justice of the Supreme Court.

12. Helen Delich Bentley to the President, July 20, 1971, "Fred Malek, July 1971" folder, WHCF, SMOF, HR Haldeman, Box 82, NPM. Len Garment, while alerting H. R. Haldeman to the letter, noted how "mild" in tone it was, just asking "that the President reaffirm his 1968 position on the Equal Rights Amendment." Garment then went on to note that "although the letter does not demonstrate good judgment, . . . it is well intended and should not be interpreted as a mutiny within the ranks." Fred Malek to H. R. Haldeman, July 22, 1971, "Fred Malek July 1971" folder, WHCF, SMOF, H.R. Haldeman, Box 82, NPM.

13. Statement of Richard M. Nixon, May 10, 1972, "Outside Women's Organizations File, [NFBPWC 2 of 4]" folder, WHCF, SMOF, ALA, Box 63, NPM.

14. The ERA has received attention from a number of scholars, with several comprehensive analyses of its support and defeat. For example, see Mansbridge, *Why We Lost the ERA.* Given these studies, the ERA is only discussed here in the broader context of the Nixon White House, and its relations with a number of women's organizations, as well as major policy priorities of the administration: the limited constitutional role of a president in regards to the passage and ratification of amendments; the limited involvement, specifically, of President Nixon in the battle for the ERA; the passing of the amendment in Congress with little administration input; and the fact that the ratification process will extend through two more administrations, once Nixon resigns.

15. Florence Dwyer to Richard M. Nixon, Feb. 26, 1969, "[GEN] HU 2-5 Women Beginning 6/30/69" folder, WHCF, Subject File, HU, Box 22, NPM.

16. Elizabeth Boyer to Richard M. Nixon, March 21, 1969, "Women—Beginning—6-30-69" folder, WHCF, Subject Files, HU, Box 22, NPM.

17. Press release, Sept. 22, 1969, "September 22" folder, White House Press Releases 9/16/69–10/31/69, Box 5, NPM.

18. Press Conference of Arthur Burns, Sept. 22, 1969, "September 22" folder, White House Press Releases 9/16/69–10/31/69, Box 5, NPM.

19. See the Arthur F. Burns Papers, White House Series, 1969–70, Gerald R. Ford Library, hereafter GRFL.

20. Daniel Patrick Moynihan to President Nixon, memorandum, Aug. 20, 1969, "[EX] HU 2-5 Women Beginning 12/31/69" folder, WHCF, Subject Files, HU, Box 21, NPM.

21. John D. Ehrlichman to President Nixon, memorandum, Sept. 29, 1969, [EX] HU 2-5 Women Beginning 12/31/69" folder, WHCF, Subject Files, HU, Box 21, NPM.

22. Ibid.

23. Peter M. Flanigan to Staff Secretary, memorandum, Aug. 25, 1969. "[EX] HU 2-5 Women Beginning—12/31/69" folder, WHCF, Subject Files, HU, Box 21, NPM.

24. For example, see Peter Babcox, "Meet the Women of the Revolution, 1969," *New York Times Magazine,* Feb. 9, 1969.

25. For example, President Nixon sent a letter to Dr. Lois M. Jones stating, "I was very pleased to read a news report that you will head the first team of women to study at American bases in the Antarctic. You are joining another very proud group of pioneers in science and I have every hope that each of you will find challenge and fulfillment in this new and exciting assignment." President Nixon to Lois M. Jones, Oct. 6, 1969, "[EX] HU 2-5 Women Beginning-12/31/69" folder, WHCF, Subject Files, HU, NPM.

26. For example, Title II, public accommodations, which would allow women to have access to all business establishments.

27. The amendment of Title IV and IX to authorize the attorney general to assist women and girls in the bringing of suits in cases of sex discrimination in access to or in the area of public education.

28. Executive Order 11246 had been signed by President Johnson in October, 1967; it went into effect in October, 1968; it had yet to be implemented by the secretary of labor.

29. "A Matter of Simple Justice, The Report of the President's Task Force on Women's Rights and Responsibilities," April, 1970, "Publications File: A Matter of Simple Justice, The Report of the President's Task Force on Women's Rights and Responsibilities" folder, WHCF, SMOF, ALA, Box 68, NPM. Given the long time from when the final report was submitted to the president until it was publicly released, there are a number of versions of the report, including one entitled "Report of the Presidential Task Force on Women's Rights and Responsibilities," December, 1969, in the archive of the NFBPWC. There are minor variations in the wording of the different versions.

30. Memo, Charlie Clapp to John Ehrlichman and Ken Cole, memorandum, May 26, 1970, "EX FG 221 10/1/69–[1/70–6/70] [2 of 3]" folder, WHCF, Subject Files, FG 221 Task Forces, Box 1, NPM.

31. Philip Shandler, "HEW's Mrs. Hitt Due for New Post," *Evening Star,* Feb. 14, 1973, in Press Clippings, Vertical File, "Hitt, Patricia (Reilly) Hamilton (1918–) Health, Education and Welfare," folder, NPM; "Pat Nixon," *Biography A&E,* 1999, Cat. No. AAE-17492.

32. Bryce Harlow to Staff Secretary, memorandum, Aug. 21, 1969, "[EX] HU 2-5 Women Beginning–12/31/69" folder, WHCF, Subject Files, HU, NPM.

33. Shandler, "HEW's Mrs. Hitt Due for New Post."

34. Patricia Reilly Hitt, speech, July, 1969, National Business and Professional Women's Clubs convention, Marguerite Rawalt Center, St. Louis, Mo.

35. For example, when President Nixon met with the Republican women members of the House of Representatives (Florence Dwyer, Charlotte Reid, Catherine May, and Margaret Heckler), to discuss the role of women in the federal government, Hitt was not present, nor briefed after the meeting.

   Shortly thereafter, in giving a speech to members of the NFBPWC, Hitt could only relate that "it is my understanding that he found their observations highly valuable and they, in turn, were generally pleased with the results of that meeting." Hitt, speech, July, 1969.

   In this dual role, Pat Hitt had an "off the record" meeting with Betty Friedan and other officers of NOW. She wrote Friedan, after the meeting, indicating how she had responded to their concerns:
   "I want you to know that I have lived up to my half of the bargain and did so sometime ago. I forwarded to the White House the copy of the materials which you left with us and have stated that I believe the Equal Rights Amendment for Women should be passed.

   Regarding the creating and expansion of child care centers, I am diligently pursuing this in several directions. I have made it known to the Secretary of Health, Education, and Welfare, and to the Voluntary Action Program, that it is my unequivocal opinion that the matter of proper care for the children of working mothers underlies most of the basic problems facing us in the inner-city for which we must find solutions.

As to the creation of an executive level post concerned with the problems of women, as I told you that day I had already made this suggestion sometime prior to our meeting. Obviously, I can neither promise nor guarantee either, but I can assure you that I am giving these points active and continuing support."

Patricia Reilly Hitt to Betty Friedan, July 1, 1969, "[GEN] HU 2-5 Women Beginning 7/1/69–12/31/69" folder, WHCF, Subject Files, HU, Box 22, NPM.

36. Patricia Reilly Hitt to John Ehrlichman, memorandum, April 15, 1970, "[EX] HU 2-5 Women 1/1/70–12/31/70" folder, WHCF, Subject Files, HU, Box 21, NPM.

37. Lucille H. Shriver to John D. Ehrlichman, memorandum, Feb. 5, 1970, "Subject File: NFBPWC" folder, WHSF, SMOF, Charles Colson, Box 90, NPM.

38. Appointment schedule, Feb. 12, 1970, "Subject File: NFBPWC" folder, WHSF, SMOF, Charles Colson, Box 90, NPM.

39. Chuck Colson to H. R. Haldeman, memorandum, Feb. 26, 1970, "Subject File: NFBPWC" folder, WHSF, SMOF, Charles Colson, Box 90, NPM.

40. Ibid.

41. Ibid.

42. Clark Mollenhoff to President Nixon, memorandum, Feb. 3, 1970, "Len Garment-Chron-Feb. 1970" folder, WHSF, SMOF, H. R. Haldeman, Box 209, NPM.

43. John Keats, "She's the American Traveler's Best Friend," *Readers' Digest* (February, 1970).

44. Peter Flanigan to Bob Haldeman, memorandum and note on memorandum, Feb. 16, 1970, "Len Garment—Chron-Feb. 1970" folder, WHSF, SMOF, H. R. Haldeman Files, Box 209, NPM.

45. See H. R. Haldeman to Charles Colson, memorandum, March 4, 1970, "Subject File: NFBPWC" folder, WHSF, SMOF, Charles Colson, Box 90, NPM.

46. Elizabeth Duncan Koontz to John Ehrlichman, memorandum, June 1, 1970, "EX FG 221-40 Women's Rights and Responsibilities [1969–70]" folder, WHCF, Subject Files, FG 221 Task Forces, Box 7, NPM.

47. Elizabeth Duncan Koontz, press conference, June 9, 1970, "June 9" folder, White House Press Releases, 5/1/70–6/15/70, Box 10, NPM.

48. Ibid.

49. George T. Bell to H. R. Haldeman, memorandum, Sept. 25, 1970, "1970 Memos for T. Brown File" folder, WHSF, SMOF, H. R. Haldeman, Box 272, NPM.

50. The Committee on Administrative Management (the Brownlow Committee) was appointed in 1936 and completed a draft report later that year, and in 1937 the report was printed and distributed. "Brownlow Committee," in *A Historical Guide to the U.S. Government,* ed. George Thomas Kurian.

51. See Susan Borches to Lyn Nofziger, memorandum, Feb. 23, 1971, "ERA [1 of 3]" folder, WHCF, SMOF, ALA, Box 7, NPM.

52. See "Digest of other White House Announcements," June 9, 1970, and "Task Force on Women's Rights and Responsibilities," October 1, 1969, in *Weekly Compilation of Presidential Documents,* "ERA [1 of 3]" folder, WHCF, SMOF, ALA, Box 7, NPM.

53. George T. Bell to Lucille Shriver, June 9, 1970, "Subject File: NFBPWC" folder, WHSF, SMOF, Charles Colson, Box 90, NPM.

54. Helen Bentley chaired the Federal Maritime Commission, 1969–75.

55. H. R. Haldeman to Mr. Finch, memorandum, Sept. 8, 1970, "[EX] HU 2-5 Women 1/1/70–12/31/70" folder, WHCF, Subject Files, HU, Box 21, NPM.

56. Statement by Richard M. Nixon, press release of the RNC, Oct. 16, 1968, "ERA [1 of 3]" folder, WHCF, SMOF, ALA, Box 7, NPM.

57. Bryce N. Harlow to President Nixon, memorandum, July 8, 1969, "[CF]HU 2-5 women [1969–70]" folder, WHSF-WHCF, Subject Files, Confidential Files 1969–74, Box 35, NPM. The only woman in the Senate, Republican Margaret Chase Smith of Maine, did not participate.

58. Ibid.

59. Memo for the President's File, by Peter M. Flanigan, July 12, 1969, "Beginning July 6, 1969" folder, WHSF, POF, Memoranda for the President, Box 78, NPM.

60. Ibid.

61. List, November 11, 1969, "November 11" folder, White House Press Release 11/1/69–12/5/69, Box 6, NPM; Memo for the President's File, by Peter M. Flanigan, November 11, 1969, "Beginning November 9, 1969" folder, WHSF, POF, Memoranda for the President, Box 78, NPM.

62. For example, see list, "Women Appointed or Reappointed by the Nixon Administration," ca. July 8, 1969, "[CF] HU 2-5 Women [1969–70]" folder, WHSF-WHCF, Subject Files, Confidential Files 1969–1974, Box 35, NPM.

63. Executive Order 11478 included the following: "Section 1. It is the policy of the Government of the United States . . . to promote the full realization of equal employment opportunity through a continuing affirmative program in each executive department and agency. . . . Sec. 2. The head of each executive department and agency shall establish and maintain an affirmative program of equal employment. . . . It is the responsibility of each department and agency head to . . . provide sufficient resources to administer such a program in a positive and effective manner; assure that recruitment activities reach all sources of job candidates; utilize to the fullest extent the present skills of each employee; provide the maximum feasible opportunity to employees to enhance their skills so they may perform at their highest potential and advance in accordance with their abilities; provide training and advice to managers and supervisors to assure their understanding and implementation of the policy expressed in this Order. . . . "

64. "The President's News Conference of February 6, 1969," Public Papers of Nixon, 75–76.

65. For instance, in 1969 as positions were being filled throughout the administration, John Ehrlichman asked Peter Flanigan about the "possibility of including a woman in the field of environment who could participate in formulating our program and possibly be a member of a future council of environmental advisors." Clay T. Whitehead to John Ehrlichman, memorandum, Nov. 18, 1969, "[EX] HU 2-5 Women Beginning-12/31/67" folder, WHCF, Subject Files, Box 21, NPM.

66. Ibid.

67. See "[CF] PE 2 Employment-Appointments 1-1-69 to 8-31-69 [1969–70]" folder, WHSF-WHCF, Subject Files, Confidential Files, NPM.

68. In response to an inquiry regarding whether the president was "reneging on his commitment to place women in high government positions," Stephen Bull, staff assistant to the president, wrote: "Mr. H.R. Haldeman has asked me to reply to your note. . . . Based on the recent appointments of two ladies—Mrs. Elizabeth Koontz, who will head up the Women's Bureau of the Department of Labor, and Mrs. Patricia Hitt, who has recently been appointed as Assistant Secretary of Health, Education and Welfare Department—the implicit suggestion

is unfounded. The primary criteria for appointment to Federal office is the individual's qualifications to perform the functions of the office. Other considerations, such as race, sex, and religion are superficial and unimportant. I am confident that many women will ultimately be appointed to positions of responsibility, but their appointments will reflect their qualifications rather than their sex." Stephen Bull to Mrs. Louis A. Bassion, Feb. 4, 1969, "[GEN] HU 2-5 Women Beginning 6-30-69" folder, WHCF, Subject Files, HU, Box 22, NPM.

69. In a letter from Charles B. Wilkinson, special consultant to the president to Nola Smith, who appeared to be working for Senator John Tower: "Senator Tower asked this office in a letter dated April 21 if we or the personnel people in the White House had been able to identify specific jobs that might be available for outstanding women. In pursuing the matter further, I checked with Harry Flemming in the personnel office. He tells me that at the moment he has no jobs that could appropriately be reserved for women. He plans to report to the National Committee within the next few weeks about what this Administration has done so far for women, and what its future plans are. I'm sure that this material would be made available to you if you so desire. The boards and commissions 'of interest to the President' have been assigned for liaison among the members of the White House staff. We are in the process of analyzing each one that has been assigned to us and should there appear to be openings for women on any that come under our review; I will be in touch with you." Charles B. Wilkinson to Nola F. Smith, April 29, 1969, "[GEN] HU 2-5 Women Beginning-6/30/69" folder, WHCF, Subject Files, HU, Box 22, NPM.

70. The National Federation of Business and Professional Women even forwarded Archibald Cox, special assistant to the attorney general, the names of several prominent attorneys in the talent bank database who could join his investigation. Lucille H. Shriver to Archibald Cox, May 30, 1973, "Ruckelshaus, Lindh, and Spencer File: B.W." folder, WHCF, SMOF, ALA, Box 18, NPM.

71. Participating organizations in the talent bank, as of the fall of 1970, were the AAUW, the American Home Economics Association, the American Medical Women's Association, the Association of American Women Dentists, B'nai B'rith Women, Church Women United, the National Association of Women Deans and Counselors, the National Council of Administrative Women in Education, the National Council of Catholic Women, the NFBPWC, the National Home Fashions League, the National League for Nursing, Ninety-Nines, Inc., Quota International, and Soroptimist.

72. Charles W. Colson to Irene Schlueter, April 24, 1970, "Subject File: NFBPWC" folder, WHSF, SMOF, Charles Colson, Box 90, NPM.

73. Osta Underwood to President Nixon, telegram, Oct. 22, 1971, "[NFBPWC 1 of 4]" folder, WHCF, SMOF, ALA, Box 63, NPM.

74. See Pacelle, "A President's Legacy" and "The Solicitor General and Gender" and Freeman, "From Protection to Equal Opportunity."

75. Herbert B. Asher, *Presidential Elections and American Politics: Voters, Candidates and Campaigns since 1952*, 182.

76. See Jules Witcover, "Making of a Landslide—How Nixon Did It," *Los Angeles Times*, Dec. 29, 1972.

77. For example, see Dwight Chapin to Larry Higby, memorandum, March 11, 1971, "[EX] HU 2-5 Women 1/1/71–12/31/71" folder, WHCF, Subject Files, HU, Box 21, NPM.

78. Polsby and Wildavsky, *Presidential Elections* 45. In 1968, while 66 percent of women reported voting, a percentage smaller than that for men (70 percent), since 1964 the actual number of women voters exceeded the number of men voting. "Sex Differences in Voter Turnout," July, 1987, fact sheet of CAWP, Eagleton Institute, Rutgers University. Turnout data from "Table 1—Age and Sex—Reported Voter Participation and Registration For Persons of Voting Age, By Race, For the United States: November 1968," *Current Population Reports,* "Voting and Registration in the Election of November 1968," Series P-20, No. 192, December 2, 1969.

79. For example, see Lisa Sergio, speech, July 24, 1972, "NFBPWC Convention News Release," in "Outside Women's Organizations Files: [NFBPWC 2 of 4]" folder, WHCF, SMOF, ALA, Box 63, NPM.

80. For example, see memorandums in "ERA [2 of 3]" folder, WHCF, SMOF, ALA, Box 7, NPM.

81. Roy Morey to Ken Cole, memorandum, July 28, 1972, "[EX] HU 2-5 Women 4/1/72–12/31/72" folder, WHCF, Subject Files, HU, Box 21, NPM.

82. Rita E. Hauser to President Nixon, memorandum, April 12, 1971, "[EX] HU 2-5 Women 1/1/71–12/31/71" folder, WHCF, Subject Files, HU, Box 21, NPM.

83. Harry Dent to Dave Parker, memorandum, May 10, 1971, "[EX] HU 2-5 Women 1/1/71–12/31/71" folder, WHCF, Subject Files, HU, Box 21, NPM.

84. Fred Malek to Dave Parker, memorandum, May 12, 1971, "[EX] HU 2-5 Women 1/1/71–12/31/71" folder, WHCF, Subject Files, HU, Box 21, NPM.

85. Witcover, "Making of a Landslide."

86. Malek to Parker, memorandum, May 12, 1971.

87. Charles Colson to David Parker, memorandum, May 4, 1971, "[EX] HU 2-5 Women 1/1/71–12/31/71" folder, WHCF, Subject Files, HU, Box 21, NPM.

88. Herbert G. Klein to President Nixon, memorandum, July 8, 1971, "Herbert Klein July 1971" folder, WHSF, SMOF, H. R. Haldeman, Box 82, NPM.

89. Ibid.

90. Memo, Robert H. Finch to President Nixon, memorandum, April 15, 1971, "President's Handwriting April 1–15, 1971" folder, WHSF, President's Office Files, Box 10, NPM.

91. "Memorandum About Women in Government," April 21, 1971, 581, and White House announcement, Public Papers of Nixon, April 22, 1971, 582. While Franklin's position was staff assistant, in letters sent out to the press, Margita White, assistant deputy director of communications identified her as a "Special Assistant to the President," indicating a rank much higher than that she was given. For example, see Margita E. White to Mrs. Denny Griswold, May 10, 1971, "[GEN] HU 2-5 Women 1/1/71–9/30/71" folder, WHCF, Subject Files, Box 22, NPM.

92. According to Finch, "At present, there are over 78,000 people employed by the Government in part-time positions at GS-12 level and above with about 60% in the regions around the country. Only 1100 of these are women. Therefore, we have an opportunity to employ large numbers of additional women in attractive positions. This can be a valuable public relations tool since it is so aptly geared to the plight of millions of professional women who must also be homemakers. I am confident that enactment of the program outlined above can provide a real talking point for you during the campaign next year." Finch to Nixon, memorandum, April 15, 1971.

93. Ibid.

94. Fred Malek for the President's File, memorandum, "Beginning 4-25-71" folder, WHSF, POF, Memoranda for the President files, Box 84, NPM. I am most appreciative of the archivists at the NPM project who directed me to the "Memoranda for the President" files. They are a wonderfully rich and detailed accounting of the president's meetings in the Oval Office with various individuals. At times there is more than one account available, and the particular interests and biases of the White House staff can begin to be detected.

95. Stephen Bull to President Nixon, memorandum, April 21, 1971, "[EX] HU 2-5 Women 1/1/71–12/31/71" folder, WHCF, Subject Files, HU, Box 21, NPM.

96. Fred Malek for Staff Secretary, memorandum, April 21, 1971, "Beginning 4-18-71" folder, WHSF, POF, Memoranda for the President files, Box 84, NPM.

97. Richard A. Moore for the File, memorandum, April 21, 1971, "Beginning April 18, 1971" folder, WHSF, POF, Memoranda for the President files, Box 84, NPM.

98. "Women Appointees 1970" folder, NFBPWC, Rawalt Center, and see the series of memos in "[EX] HU 2-5 Women 1/1/71–12/31/71" folder, WHCF, Subject Files, HU, Box 21, NPM.

99. Fred Malek to Bruce Kehrli, memorandum, July 2, 1971, "Fred Malek July 1971" folder, WHSF, SMOF, H.R. Haldeman, Box 82, NPM.

100. Witcover, "Making of a Landslide."

101. Penciled in were the following additions: Dr. Helen Edmonds, the first black woman deputy to the United Nations; Elizabeth Duncan Koontz, the first black woman to head the Women's Bureau; Dr. Zelma George, the first black woman member of the Corporation for Public broadcasting; Ersa Poston, the first black woman to chair the Advisory Committee on Intergovernmental Personnel Policy; Sallyanne Payton, a black woman to serve on the Domestic Council staff; Dr. E. Corinne Brown Galvin, a black woman as member of the Citizens Advisory Committee on Environmental Quality Control; and Jewel Lafontant, a black woman to U.S. Advisory Committee on International Education and Culture. Barbara Hackman Franklin, speech before NFBPWC Convention, July 28, 1971, "Outside Women's Organization File-[NFBPWC 1 of 4]" folder, WHCF, SMOF, Armstrong, Box 63, NPM.

102. Ibid.

103. Ibid.

104. For example, see Barbara Hackman Franklin to Theresa Humphreyville, Nov. 22, 1971, "[GEN] HU 2-5 Women 10/1/71–12/31/71" folder, WHCF, Subject Files, HU, Box 22, NPM. In a letter to the vice president of the National Association of Manufacturers, Franklin wrote, "[T]he President is deeply committed to the appointment of more women to policy-making posts in government. To that end, I am searching the country and building a talent bank of top women. I would be pleased to have any suggestions you might have." Barbara H. Franklin to Phyllis H. Moehrle, Oct. 20, 1971, "[GEN] HU 2-5 Women 10/1/71–12/31/71" folder, WHCF, Subject Files, HU, Box 22, NPM.

105. Anne Armstrong, in a speech before the NFBPWC in 1973, acknowledged the role of the organizations in establishing the talent bank. Anne Armstrong, "Meet Your Challenge for Commitment," reprinted in *National Business Woman* 54, no. 8 (Sept., 1973), in "Outside Women's Organization File—[NFBPWC 4 of 4]" folder, WHCF, SMOF, ALA, Box 63, NPM.

106. Barbara Franklin to Fred Malek, memorandum, Dec. 9, 1971, "[EX] HU 2-5 Women 1/1/71–12/31/71" folder, WHCF, Subject Files, HU, Box 21, NPM.

107. Press release, April 28, 1972, "Ruckelshaus, Lindh, and Spence: Speeches by Others on ERA, etc. Women" folder, WHCF, SMOF, ALA, Box 21, NPM.

108. Handwritten note, April 19, 1972, memo from Barbara Franklin, "[EX] HU 2-5 Women 4/1/72—" folder, WHCF, Subject Files, HU, Box 21, NPM.

109. Fact sheet, April 28, 1972, "Ruckelshaus, Lindh, and Spencer: Speeches by Others on ERA, etc. Women" folder, WHCF, SMOF, ALA, Box 24, NPM.

110. Press release, April 28, 1972, "April 28" folder, White House Press Releases, 3/26/72–4/30/72, Box 27, NPM.

111. For example, in a memo sent to Pendleton James, Barbara Franklin noted "there have been more than 700 women placed in mid-level positions (GS 13-15) between April and December [1971] as a result of the President's program. We can specifically take credit for about 30 of those." Barbara Franklin to Pen James, memorandum, Jan. 27, 1972, "[EX] HU 2-5 Women 1/1/72–3/31/72" folder, WHCF, Subject Files, HU, Box 21, NPM.

112. Peter A. Michel to Barbara Franklin, memorandum, Aug. 15, 1972, "[EX] HU 2-5 Women 4/1/72–12/31/72" folder, WHCF, Subject Files, HU; "Fact Sheet: Women in the Federal Executive Government," ca. April, 1974, "Jill Ruckelshaus, Patricia Lindh, Jean Spencer File—Briefing Papers—Women and My Office" folder, WHCF, SMOF, ALA, Box 18, NPM.

113. For an extended discussion of civil rights policy and priorities in the Nixon administration, see Chapter 3 in Joan Hoff, *Nixon Reconsidered.*

114. For a discussion on public opinion and polling at this point in time, see Mansbridge, *Why We Lost the ERA?*

115. Myra Marx Ferree, "A Woman for President? Changing Responses: 1958–1972," *Public Opinion Quarterly* 38 (Fall, 1974): 390–99.

116. Fact sheet, "Women in the Federal Government," ca. April, 1974, "Jill Ruckelshaus, Patricia Lindh, Jean Spencer File—Briefing Papers—Women and My Office" folder, WHCF, SMOF, ALA, Box 18, NPM.

117. "[EX] HU 2-5 Women 1/1/72–3/31/72" folder, WHCF, Subject Files, HU, Box 21, NPM.

118. For example, see correspondence between Jeanne C. Squire of the NFBPWC and Barbara Hackman Franklin, Sept. 15, 1972, "Outside Women's Organization Files: [NFBPWC 2 of 4]" folder, WHCF, SMOF, ALA, Box 63, NPM.

119. Barbara Franklin to Dan Kingsley, memorandum, Feb. 14, 1972, "[EX] HU 2-5 Women 1/1/72–3/31/72" folder, WHCF, Subject Files, HU, Box 21, NPM.

120. This was part of a broader campaign strategy to send out "surrogates" to different constituencies to tout the accomplishments of the Nixon administration. Witcover, "Making of a Landslide."

121. List of Women Surrogates, Sept. 18, 1972, "Beginning September 17, 1972" folder, WHSF, SMOF, Memoranda for the President files, Box 89, NPM. Given the uncertainty in how to view women, or include women, it is not surprising, although ironic, that President Nixon, in meeting with the "surrogates," would not distinguish between women married to appointees and women who were themselves appointees. Memo for the President's File, by Barbara Franklin, Sept. 18, 1972, "Beginning September 17, 1972" folder, WHSF, POF, Memoranda for the President files, Box 89, NPM.

122. Judy Cole to Barbara Franklin, memorandum, Nov. 7, 1972, "[Appearances by Women Appointees, # 1]" folder, WHSF, SMOF, Staff Secretary, Box 87, NPM.

123. Evaluations, 11/7/72, "[Appearances by Women Appointees, # 1]" folder, WHSF, SMOF, Staff Secretary, Box 87, NPM.

124. For example, see National Federation of Business and Professional Women to President Nixon, telegram, Dec. 5, 1972, "Outside Women's Organizations File: [NFBPWC 2 of 4]" folder, WHCF, SMOF, ALA, Box 63, NPM.

125. The written historical record presents ambiguity as to Armstrong's title. President Nixon seemed to think Armstrong was co-chair, but Bob Dole and the RNC did not seem to agree. She is omitted from the list of RNC officials in their own publications. However, in the White House announcement of her appointment as Counsellor-Designate to the President she is referred to as "Co-Chairman of the Republican National Committee." Nixon Public Papers, 1972, A28, E20. In briefing the president before his first meeting with Armstrong in 1971 when she was co-chairman of the RNC, Harry S. Dent noted that Armstrong "gives the impression of having a keen understanding of politics for a lady." Harry S. Dent to President Nixon, memorandum, April 22, 1971, "[EX] HU 2-5 Women 1/1/71–12/31/71" folder, WHCF, Subject Files, HU, Box 21, NPM.

126. Anne Armstrong to President Nixon, April 28, 1971, "[EX] HU 2-5 Women 1/1/71–12/31/71" folder, WHCF, Subject Files, HU, Box 21, NPM.

127. Loose folder—press releases vertical file, Anne Armstrong [Legendre] (1927–), NPM.

128. Mrs. Tobin Armstrong to Madera Spencer, WHCF, SMOF, ALA, Box 4, Alphabetical File, ALA(S) [1 of 2], NPM.

129. Mrs. Tobin Armstrong to Pearl Watts, WHCF, SMOF, ALA, Box 4, Alphabetical File, ALA(W), NPM.

130. Isabelle Shelton, "Workload in White House: President Piles It On," *The Evening Star*, March 11, 1973, in Loose Folder—press releases vertical file Anne Armstrong [Legendre] (1927–), NPM.

131. Anne Armstrong, counsellor to the president, draft, "Op-Ed," in "Ruckelshaus, Lindh and Spencer File: Speech Material—Pat [Lindh]" folder, WHCF, SMOF, ALA, Box 24, NPM.

132. Shelton, "Workload in White House."

133. "Speech Suggestions," attached to Anne Armstrong to Bruce Kehrli, memorandum, Sept. 21, 1973, "Adm. File: (ALA) Kehrli Rdg. File" folder, WHCF, SMOF, ALA, Box 4, NPM.

134. Anne Armstrong to Secretary Weinberger, memorandum, Dec. 12, 1973, "Ruckelshaus, Lindh, & Spencer File: Dr. Jean Spencer" folder, WHCF, SMOF, ALA, Box 24, NPM.

135. Barbara Franklin to Ron Ziegler, memorandum, Jan. 31, 1973; Anne Armstrong to Ron Ziegler, memorandum, Feb. 1, 1973; and Anne Armstrong to Ronald L. Ziegler, memorandum, March 14, 1973, "Administration File: (ALA) Ziegler Reading File" folder, WHCF, SMOF, ALA, Box 4, NPM.

136. Annual Message to the Congress on the State of the Union, Jan. 30, 1974, *Public Papers of the Presidents of the United States: Richard M. Nixon*, 77.

137. Ibid.

138. Annual Message to the Congress: The Economic Report of the President, Feb. 1, 1974, *Public Papers of the Presidents of the United States: Richard M. Nixon*, 110.

139. Memo for the President's File, Feb. 13, 1974, from Anne Armstrong, "Beginning 1-20-74" folder, WHCF, POF, Memoranda for the President files, Box 93, NPM.

140. Anne Armstrong to Bruce Kehrli, memorandum, Sept. 10, 1973, "Adm. File: (ALA) Kehrli Rdg. File" folder, WHCF, SMOF, ALA, Box 4, NPM.

141. Ibid.

142. Anne Armstrong to Doris L. Sassover, June 19, 1973, "[EX] HU 2-5 Women [Folder 1 of 2] 6-19-73" folder, WHCF, Subject Files, HU, Box 21, NPM.

143. Regarding Franklin's new responsibilities on the CPSC, the issue of "consumers" would begin to be viewed as an issue with a broader constituent base. This issue had evolved as a "women's issue" during World War II when war rations and tight budgets affected the quality of daily life, and it was the women who managed households and held jobs.

144. "Statement for the Record by the White House Office of Women's Programs, Joint Economic Committee Hearing on Economic Problems of Women, July 1973," "Staff Miscellany File, July 73" folder, WHCF, SMOF, ALA, Box 16, NPM.

145. Vera Hirschberg to Anne Armstrong, memorandum and attachment, June 13, 1973, "Staff Miscellany file — June 1973" folder, WHCF, SMOF, ALA, Box 16, NPM. Thirty of the required thirty-eight states had ratified the ERA by early 1973. Mansbridge, *Why We Lost the ERA,* 12–13.

146. "Statement for the Record by the White House Office of Women's Programs, Joint Economic Committee Hearing on Economic Problems of Women, July 1973."

147. Fred Slight to Anne Armstrong, memorandum, Aug. 1, 1974, "Miscellaneous Correspondence and Staff memos, 4 of 4 [August 1974]" folder, WHCF, SMOF, ALA, Box 7, NPM.

148. *Public Papers of the Presidents of the United States: Richard M. Nixon,* March 13, 1973, 187–91.

149. Ibid., 190.

150. For a discussion of the status of women in the foreign service at this point in time, see McGlen and Sarkees, "Style Does Matter."

151. See Martin, "Women Who Govern."

152. Of Nixon's total appointments to full-time, Senate-confirmed positions in the executive departments and agencies, 3 percent went to women. See Martin, "Women Who Govern."

153. Press Conference, April 28, 1972, "April 28" folder, White House Press Releases 3/26/72–4/30/72, Box 27, NPM.

154. Ibid.

155. Anne Armstrong to Tim Austin, memorandum, May 14, 1973, "Subject File [Personnel] D-E-F [D] [1 of 3] [CFOA 1293]" folder, WHCF, SMOF, ALA, Box 8, NPM.

156. See Martin, "Women Who Govern."

157. Betsy Ancker-Johnson to Anne Armstrong, memorandum, May 10, 1973, "Subject File [Personnel] G-H-I-J-K [I-J-K] [3 of 3] [CFOA 1293]" folder, WHCF, SMOF, ALA, Box 8, NPM.

158. William F. Rhatican to Ehrlichman, Shultz, and Weber, memorandum, Sept. 16, 1971, "[EX]HU 2-5 Women 1/1/71–12/31/71" folder, WHCF, Subject Files, HU, Box 21, NPM.

159. Secretary to John D. Ehrlichman, memorandum, Jan. 12, 1972, "[EX] HU 2-5 Women 1/1/72–3/31/72" folder, WHCF, Subject Files, HU, Box 21, NPM.

160. Ann Dore McLaughlin was director of communications in Nixon's reelection campaign, and also on the 1973 inaugural staff; Elizabeth Dole was deputy director of the Office of Consumer Affairs from 1969 to 1973.

CHAPTER 5. THE FORD ADMINISTRATION

1. This amendment was prompted by President Eisenhower's heart attack in 1955; the assassination of President Kennedy in 1963 expedited passage of the amendment in both the House and Senate in 1965 and ratification by thirty-eight states two years later.

2. Andrew Johnson was impeached by the House of Representatives in 1868, saved from removal of office by a single vote in the Senate trial; Bill Clinton was impeached by the House of Representatives along nearly partisan lines on December 19, 1998, and acquitted in the Senate by a bipartisan vote in February, 1999.

3. "Congress Approved Ford Nomination for Vice President," *CQ Almanac 1973*, 1060.

4. The vote in the House was 387-35 (December 6, 1973), and in the Senate 92-3 (November 27, 1973). "Congress Approved Ford Nomination for Vice President," 1065.

5. Richard L. Spears to Anne Armstrong, Aug. 30, 1974, "HU 2-5 8/9/74–9/30/74 General" folder, WHCF, Subject File, HU 2-5, Box 10, GRFL.

6. James Cannon, *Time and Chance: Gerald Ford's Appointment with History*, 356–58.

7. Helen Thomas, "Transition Officially Over," Press advance, UPI, "Women (1) 12-21-74 Helen Thomas teletype" folder, Warren and White Files, Box 29, GRFL.

8. Minutes, Women appointees and Anne Armstrong and Betty Ford, Sept. 4, 1974, "Women Appointees-Sept. 4, 1974" folder, Lindh and Holm Files, Office of Public Liaison, Box 1, GRFL.

9. Anne Armstrong to President Ford, memorandum, Sept. 13, 1974, "HU 2-5 9/1/74–9/30/74 Executive" folder, WHCF, Subject File, HU 2-5, Box 9, GRFL.

10. Pat Lindh to Nola Haerle, Sept. 16, 1974, "PE 2 Employment-Appointments 7/31/74–9/30/74 General" folder, WHCF, Subject File, Box 5, GRFL.

11. For example, shortly after taking on the job as press secretary, Ron Nessen let Anne Armstrong know that "hiring a woman is one of my top priorities." Ron Nessen to Anne Armstrong, memorandum, Sept. 25, 1974, "HU 2-5 9/1/74–9/30/74" folder, WHCF, Subject Files, Executive HU 2-5, Box 9, GRFL.

12. For example, see Anne Armstrong to Rogers C. B. Morton, secretary of the interior, Sept. 27, 1974, "Chronological Files, Armstrong, Anne-Correspondence and Memos" folder, White House Staff Files, Anne Armstrong, GRFL.

13. Patricia S. Lindh, interview by David Horrocks, June 24, 1996, GRFL.

14. "Finding Aid," White House Staff Files—Lindh and Holm Files, GRFL.

15. For instance, Lindh began efforts to have Ford meet with women appointees in August, 1975, and was only successful eight months later, when the women appointees met with the president in April, 1976.

16. For a discussion of the evolution and changes in the Executive Office of the President and the White House Office in particular, see Hart, *Presidential Branch*; and Walcott and Hult, *Governing the White House*.

17. Anne Armstrong to Rebecca Benites, Oct. 3, 1974, "HU 2-5 10/1/74–10/15/74 General" folder, WHCF, Subject Files, Box 11, GRFL.

18. Charles Jones has clearly made this point in *Presidency in a Separated System*.

19. David Gergen to Anne Armstrong, memorandum, Aug. 15, 1974, "Anne Armstrong" folder, Office of White House Operations—Al Haig Files, Box 1, GRFL; and Anne Armstrong to Robert Hartmann, memorandum, Aug. 13, 1974, "Anne Armstrong" folder, Office of White House Operations—Al Haig Files, Box 1, GRFL.

20. For example, see a series of memos regarding appointments in Hartman, Box 84, GRFL.

21. "Women," "President Ford '76 Fact Book," http://www.ford.utexas.edu/library/document/factbook/women.html.

22. The new status of some of these organizations is revealed in the White House press briefing on this meeting, which listed the Women's Equity Action League as "We'll" rather than WEAL. "Women's Organization Leaders—Sept. 6, 1974, M/W President" folder, Lindh and Holm Files, Box 1, GRFL.

23. The organizations represented included: AAUW; Church Women United; NFBPWC; NOW; Women's Zionist Organization; Interstate Commissions on the Status of Women; and the Women's Equity Action League. See Name File, [including: Arvonne Fraser, Dorothy Height, Marie Bowden, Mary Lou Burg, Betty Butler, Ruth Clusen, Karen DeCrow, Clair Fulcher, Elizabeth Genne, Rhea Hammer, Clair Collin Harvey, Mrs. Henry Stewart Jones, Ione Kubby, Rose Matzkin, Mary Katherine Miller, Ethel Phillips, Joy Simonson, Mary Louise Smith, and Bernice Lilly], GRFL.

24. "Meeting with the Leaders of the Major Women's Organizations," Sept. 5, 1974, Memo from Anne Armstrong, "HU 2-5 9/1/74–9/30/74 Executive" folder, WHCF, Subject File, HU 2-5, Box 9, GRFL; also see "Drop-by Meeting of Top Women Presidential Appointees," Sept. 3, 1974, "PE 2 9/1/74–9/11/74 Executive" folder, WHCF, Subject Files, Box 2, GRFL.

25. For example, Ford signed the Housing and Community Development Act of 1974 which "include[d] a section prohibiting discrimination in housing and mortgage credit lending on the basis of sex." Meeting with the Leaders of the Major Women's Organizations, Sept. 5, 1974, Memo from Anne Armstrong, "HU 2-5 9/1/74–9/30/74 Executive" folder, WHCF, Subject File, HU 2-5, Box 9, GRFL.

26. Minutes, Women's Advisory Committee, Oct. 10, 1974, "Women's Advisory Committee—October 10, 1974" folder, Lindh and Holm, Box 1, GRFL.

27. Attendees at the October 10, 1974, meeting included: Virginia Allen, deputy assistant secretary for public affairs, state; Gwen Anderson, assistant to counselor Dean Burch; Catherine Bedell, chairman, U.S. Tariff Commission; Helen Bentley, chairman, Federal Maritime Commission; Barbara Franklin, commissioner, Consumer Product Safety Commission; Margaret Heckler, representative from Massachusetts; Carla Hills, assistant attorney general, Civil Division, Justice; Jeanne Holm, major general, air force; Jewell LaFontant, deputy solicitor general, Justice; Ruckelshaus. See ibid.

28. For example, see Karen Keesling to Anne Armstrong, memorandum, Oct. 7, 1974, "HU 2-5 10/1/74–10/31/74 Executive" folder, WHCF, Subject Files, HU 2-5, Box 9, GRFL.

29. "Summary of Suggestions from Prior Meetings," Oct. 7, 1974, "HU 2-5 10/1/74–10/31/74 Executive" folder, WHCF, Subject Files, HU 2-5, Box 9, GRFL.

30. See Martin, "Women Who Govern."

31. Anne Armstrong to David Abshire, Nov. 15, 1974, "HU 2-5 11/1/74–12/31/74" folder, WHCF, Subject File, Box 9, GRFL.

32. Annette L. Buckland to Anne Armstrong, Nov. 18, 1974, "Annette Buckland" Folder, Name File, GRFL.

33. For example, see Stan Scott to Greg Lebedev, memorandum, Nov. 19, 1974, "FG 11 11/1/74–11/31/74 Executive" folder, WHCF, Subject Files, Box 73, GRFL.

34. Annette L. Buckland to L. Dean Brown, Nov. 18, 1974, "Annette Buckland" folder, Name File, GRFL.

35. Anne Armstrong to Women Appointees, memorandum, Nov. 26, 1974, "HU 2-5 11/1/74–12/31/74 Executive" folder, WHCF, Subject Files, Box 9, GRFL.

36. Annette L. Buckland to L. Dean Brown, Nov. 18, 1974, "Annette Buckland" folder, Name File, GRFL.

37. Ibid.

38. Ibid.

39. Ibid.

40. Mike Causey, "The Status of Women is Left in Doubt," Washington Post, Dec. 16, 1974, D13.

41. See a series of memos in "PE 2 11/1/74–11/30/74 Executive" WHCF, Subject Files, PE 2, Box 3, GRFL and in "HU 2-5 11/1/74–12/31/74 Executive" folder, WHCF, Subject Files, Box 9, GRFL.

42. Causey, "The Status of Women," D13.

43. Press release, Jan. 14, 1976, "Women Presidential Appointees" folder, White House Staff files—Patricia Lindh and Jeanne Holm Files, Box 16, GRFL.

44. Sam Schulhof to Pat Lindh, memorandum, Aug. 15, 1974, "PE 2 Employment—Appointments 8/6/74–8/31/74 Executive" folder, WHCF, Subject File, Box 2, GRFL.

45. Among the names listed for senior-level positions were those of Jane Cahill, vice president for communications of IBM; Martha Wallace, executive director of the Luce Foundation; Constance Cook, a member of the New York Assembly; Patricia Jane Carry, president of the investment banking firm of Knight, Carry, Bliss and Company; Patricia R. Hitt, former assistant secretary for communities and field services in the Department of HEW; Rita Hauser, former U.S. Representative to the U.N. Commission on Human Rights; and Margaret Heckler, a representative from Massachusetts. List, "Women's Talent Search," "Transition (1974)—Possible Candidates for Appointments to Positions. ca. 8/74 (1 and 2)" folder, White House Operations—Richard Cheney Files, Box 12, GRFL.

46. For example, see Lindh to Shirley Temple Black, Sept. 18, 1974, "HU 2-5 9/1/74–9/30/74 Executive" folder, WHCF, Subject Files, GRFL.

47. See "Oversized Attachment 3307-A," September, 1974, WHCF, HU 2-5, GRFL.

48. The talent search was proposed by Ford's special assistant to the president for minority affairs. Stanley S. Scott to William N. Walker, memorandum, Feb. 7, 1975, "PE 2 1/1/75–3/31/75" folder, WHCF, Subject Files, Box 3, GRFL.

49. For a discussion of Hartmann's role as an advisor, see Cannon, Time and Chance.

50. Samuel Schulhof for the President, memorandum, Oct. 30, 1974, "PPO 10/29–31/74" folder, Counsellors to the President—Robert T. Hartmann Files, Box 79, GRFL.

51. Robert T. Hartmann to Samuel A. Schulhof, note on memo, 10-30-74, Samuel A. Schulhof to Robert Hartmann, Robert Hartmann Files, Box 79, GRFL. Rep. William H. Hudnut was defeated in 1974.

52. For a detailed discussion of the confirmation process, see G. Calvin Mackenzie's The Politics of Presidential Appointments.

53. Jack Marsh to Bill Walker, memorandum, Dec. 27, 1974, "PE 2 12/1/74–12/31/74 Exec" folder, WHCF, Subject Files, Box 3, GRFL.

54. Douglas Bennett to Christopher J. Dodd, April 2, 1975, "PE 2 4/1/75–4/8/75 Exec" folder, WHCF, Subject File, Box 3, GRFL.

55. See "Transition (1974)—Possible Candidates for Appointments to Positions, ca. 8/74 (1)" folder, White House Operations—Richard Cheney Files, Box 12, GRFL.

56. Office of the Historian, U.S. House of Representatives *Women in Congress: 1917–1990*.

57. David J. Wimer through Alexander Haig to President Ford, memorandum, Sept. 25, 1974, "PPO 9/25–26/74" folder, Counsellors to the President-Robert T. Hartmann Files, Box 78, GRFL.

58. Ibid.

59. Ibid.

60. "President Names 10 to Advisory Panels," *New York Times*, Nov. 3, 1974; Helmi Raaska, archivist at GRFL, personal communication with author, Feb. 21, 2002, GRFL.

61. Most student interns were Republican.

62. See Walcott and Hult, *Governing the White House*. An historical perspective on outreach activities by earlier administrations is presented in chapter 6. Walcott and Hult note that "the Office of Public Liaison formalized the stepped-up group outreach activities of Charles Colson and his staff under Richard Nixon," 310.

63. Patricia S. Lindh to Francis Acost, Oct. 16, 1975, "HU 2-5 10/1/75–11/15/75 Executive" Folder, WHCF, Subject Files, HU 2-5, Box 10, GRFL.

64. Ibid.

65. Karen Keesling to Amelia Ann Koch, June 17, 1975, "FG 147 Interdepartmental Commission on the Status of Women-General" folder, WHCF, Subject Files, Box 159, GRFL.

66. Karen Keesling to Don Dotts, Oct. 29, 1974, "HU 2-5 10/1/74–10/31/74 Executive" folder, WHCF, Subject File, HU 2-5, Box 9, GRFL.

67. Pat Lindh to Wayne Valis, memorandum, June 2, 1975, "HU 2-5 5/1/75–6/30/75" folder, WHCF, Subject Files, HU 2-5, Box 9, GRFL.

68. Pat Lindh to Bill Baroody, memorandum, Aug. 1, 1975, "American Federation of Government Employees—July 30, 1975" folder, Lindh and Holm Files of Public Liaison Office, Box 2, GRFL.

69. Pat Lindh to Martha Roundtree, Nov. 4, 1975, "HU 2-5 11/1/75–1/7/76 General" folder, WHCF, Subject File, HU 2-5, Box 11, GRFL.

70. Pat Lindh to Maxine Hays, Feb. 4, 1976, "MC 1/1/76–4/30/76 Executive" folder, WHCF, Subject File, Box 1, GRFL.

71. Pat Lindh to Doug Bennett, memorandum, Sept. 5, 1975, "HU 2-5 8/1/75–9/30/75 Executive" folder, WHCF, Subject File, HU 2-5, Box 9, GRFL.

72. Karen Keesling to Margaret Heckler, Dec, 6, 1974, "PE 2 12/1/74–12/31/74 Executive" folder, WHCF, Subject File, Box 3, GRFL.

73. Beth Gordon to Pat Lindh, memorandum, Jan. 3, 1975, "Chronological Files, Gordon, Beth—Correspondence and Memos," Anne Armstrong, Box 1, GRFL. Still, computerized lists of appointees by fields were lacking through the Bush administration; it is not until the Clinton administration that we see the organized listing of appointments with readily identifiable fields such as "sex."

74. Ted Marrs for Warren Rustand, memorandum, Feb. 28, 1975, "MC 4 3/20/75–3/31/75 Executive" folder, WHCF, Subject Files, Box 14, GRFL.

75. Lindh, interview by Horrocks.

76. The following advisors all spoke to the group: William J. Baroody, assistant to

the president for public liaison; John Marsh, Jr., counsellor to the president; Donald Rumsfeld, assistant to the president; Philip Buchen, counsel to the president; Robert Hartmann, counsellor to the president; Warren Rustand, director of scheduling; and James Cannon, executive director of the domestic council.

77. Pat Lindh, schedule proposal, March 17, 1975, "MC 4 3/20/75–3/31/75 Executive" folder, WHCF, Subject Files, Box 14, GRFL.

78. For example, see Pat Lindh to James Cannon, memorandum, Feb. 19, 1975, "HU 2-5 1/1/75–2/28/75 Executive" folder, WHCF, Subject File, Box 9, GRFL.

79. For an analysis of the diversity of groups comprising the women's movement, see Anne Costain, *Inviting Women's Rebellion: A Political Process Interpretation of the Women's Movement.*

80. See "Clearinghouse on Women's Issues" folder, Lindh and Holm Files, Box 33, GRFL.

81. For example, see Frances Tarlton Farenthold to President Ford, May 21, 1975, "National Women's Political Caucus # 2-2" folder, Lindh and Holm Files, Box 37, GRFL.

82. Maxine R. Hacke to Douglas Bennett, Oct. 15, 1975, "Name File—Marjorie Lynch," GRFL.

83. However, with no more vacancies during the Ford administration and President Carter having no vacancies to fill during his four-year term, it would not be until President Reagan made his first appointment to the Court when a woman would finally be named to the Court.

84. John Mackenzie, "2 Women on List for Court," *Washington Post,* Nov. 20, 1975, A13.

85. Pat Lindh through William Baroody, memorandum, Nov. 17, 1975, "Supreme Court—Appointment of Women" folder, Lindh and Holm, Box 13, GRFL.

86. Mackenzie, "2 Women on List for Court," A13.

87. Douglas Bennett to President Ford, memorandum, n.d., "Supreme Ct. Nominations—Background on Recommended Candidates" folder, White House Operations—Richard Cheney Files, Box 11, GRFL.

88. Ibid.

89. Ibid.

90. Ibid.

91. See Ware, *Beyond Suffrage.*

92. See Paterson, *Be Somebody,* 51. Paterson's biography of Rawalt provides insight in to the social and political networks of women in Washington, in particular from the 1930s to the 1980s.

93. Patricia S. Lindh to Judith Connor, March 8, 1976, "Judith Connor" folder, Name File, GRFL.

94. Finding Aid, White House Staff Files—Jeanne Marjorie Holm, GRFL.

95. Jim Connor to Dick Cheney, memorandum, Jan. 22, 1976, "White House Staff—Female Appointees" folder, James E. Connor Files, Box 21, GRFL.

96. See a series of memos in: "White House Staff—Female Appointees" folder, James E. Connor Files, Box 21, GRFL.

97. Press release, March 8, 1976, UPI, "Women Presidential Appointees" folder, Lindh and Holm Files, White House Staff Files, Box 16, GRFL.

98. William T. Coleman, Jr., to President Ford, April 12, 1976, "MC 3 5/1/76–5/10/76 Executive" folder, WHCF, Subject Files, Box 3, GRFL.

99. Jeanne M. Holm to William F. Gorog, May 3, 1976, "MC 3 5/1/76–5/10/76 Executive" folder, WHCF, Subject Files, Box 3, GRFL.

100. Jeanne M. Holm to Bill Baroody, memorandum, May 6, 1976, "FG 1 4/1/76–5/18/76 Executive" Folder, WHCF, Subject Files, Box 5, GRFL.

101. Ibid.

102. Jeanne Holm to Dave Gergen, memorandum, Sept. 1, 1976, "HU 2-5 8/1/76–10/31/76 Executive" Folder, WHCF, Subject File, Box 10 HU 2-5, GRFL.

103. Jimmy Carter, *Keeping Faith: Memoirs of a President.*

104. Carter would usher in a new style election campaign—a response to the reforms of the Democratic National Party which emerged from the painful 1968 convention and loss.

105. For instance, see Cannon, *Time and Chance,* chapter 21.

106. "Congress Approved Ford Nomination for Vice President," 1069.

107. Ibid., 1062.

108. Jeanne Holm to Mike Duval, memorandum, Aug. 3, 1976, "Campaign of 1976—Republican Platform Regarding Women's Concerns" folder, WH Staff Files—Patricia Lindh and Jeanne Holm Files, Box 7, GRFL.

109. For example, see "The Gender Gap: Voting Choices, Party Identification, and Presidential Performance Ratings," 1996, fact sheet of CAWP, Eagleton Institute of Politics, Rutgers University.

110. "The Gender Gap," Fact Sheet, August, 1994, CAWP, Eagleton Institute of Politics, Rutgers University.

111. Public Papers of Ford, June 7, 1976, 1855.

112. R. W. Apple, "President Favors a Running Mate in Middle of Road," *New York Times,* Aug. 9, 1976, 12.

113. "'Best Chance' Strategy to Win," Aug. 1, 1976, "National Surveys—Strategy Book Memorandum, August 1976 (2)" folder, Robert Teeter Papers, National Surveys, July, 1976, Box 54, GRFL.

114. Ibid.

115. Robert Teeter for President Ford, memorandum, Aug. 16, 1976, "U.S. National Survey Data Analysis. August 1976 (1)" folder, Robert Teeter Papers, National Surveys, July, 1976, Box 54, GRFL.

116. "Ford Defeats Reagan for GOP Presidential Nod, Selects Sen. Dole of Kansas as Running Mate," *Facts on File* 36, no. 1867 (Aug. 21, 1976): 598.

117. Jeanne Holm to Doug Bennett, memorandum, Sept. 24, 1976, "PE 2 9/1/76–9/30/76 Executive" folder, WHCF, Subject File, Box 5, GRFL.

118. "Appointments," "Campaign of 1976—Campaign Issues Book on Women's Issues (1)" folder, White House Staff Files—Patricia Lindh and Jeanne Holm Files, Box 7, GRFL.

119. President Ford to Attorney General Edward H. Levi, signed June 30, 1976, "HU 2-5 7/1/76–7/30/76 Executive" folder, WHCF, Subject File, HU 2-5, Box 10, GRFL.

120. Jim Connor to President Ford, note, June 29, 1976, "HU 2-5 7/1/76–7/30/76 Executive" folder, WHCF, Subject File, HU 2-5, Box 10, GRFL.

121. Public Papers of Ford, July 1, 1976, 1946.

122. Mansbridge, *Why We Lost the ERA,* 13.

123. For an in-depth discussion see Walcott and Hult, *Governing the White House* and Hart, *Presidential Branch.*

124. See Lindh, interview by Horrocks, 6.

125. Wayne, *Road to the White House 1996,* 117.

CHAPTER 6. THE CARTER ADMINISTRATION

1. George Bush is the exception, although it is interesting to note that his two sons are governors, Jeb of Florida and George W. of Texas, and George W. became the forty-third president in 2001.

2. "Sex Differences in Voter Turnout," August, 1994, fact sheet of the CAWP, Eagleton Institute, Rutgers University; Polsby and Wildavsky, *Presidential Elections.*

3. Hamilton Jordan, quoted in Hedrick Smith, "Carter Urges Aides to Find a Broad `Mix' for Posts in Cabinet," *New York Times,* Nov. 19, 1976, 1.

4. For instance, the NWPC sent almost daily mailgrams and letters as soon as the election had been decided. See NWPC to President-elect Carter, memorandum, Nov. 19, 1976, "Recommendations—[General] Unanswered [O/A 10,621]" folder, Hamilton Jordan Papers, Box 10, Jimmy Carter Library, hereafter JCL.

5. See Hamilton Jordan Papers, transition boxes, JCL. Millie Jeffrey to President-elect Carter, mailgram, Dec. 14, 1976, "[Health, Education and Welfare—Recommendations] [O/A 10,625]" folder, Hamilton Jordan Papers, Box 5, JCL. Millie Jeffrey to President-elect Carter, mailgram, Dec. 14, 1976, "[Cabinet Level Positions—Recommendations General] [O/A 10,628]" folder, Hamilton Jordan Papers, Box 1, JCL.

6. Joanne Massey Howes to Randy Kinder, Dec. 21, 1976, "D.O.T. Recs [O/A 10,623]" folder, Hamilton Jordan Papers, Box 31, JCL. While recent presidents entering the White House through a party transition tend to look beyond Washington for initial appointments, and then turn to the Washington community to fill vacancies as their term progresses, in the case of women, presidents have tended to draw on the Washington community early on in their administration. This is a pattern that begins with Carter's appointments and continues through the Clinton administration. But men tend to have had more federal administrative experience than have women. Thus women were selected from a broader pool reflecting a network of women living in the Washington area yet working both in government and in the private sector, and the need for the NWPC and other women's organizations to continue their activity in promoting women already in government service to move up. See Martin, "Women Who Govern."

7. The Talent Advisory Group consisted of Lucy Wilson Benson, Owen Cooper, Marian Wright Edelman, Carol Tucker Foreman, Patricia Roberts Harris, Theodore Hesburgh, Vernon Jordan, Lane Kirkland, Hank Lacayo, Irving Shapiro, and Robert Strauss. In looking at the recommendations of Patricia Roberts Harris, of those whom she knew personally and could "recommend for serious consideration on the basis of my personal knowledge of their ability, personality and character," eight of the twenty-one names were women. These were Julia Walsh, Matina Horner, Lois Rice, Mary Lou Munts, Sara Alyce Wright, Jill Wine Volner, Jewel Cobb, and Alice Rivlin.

   In addition, "talent search assignments" were identified for key transition members, leaving the Departments of State and Defense, the National Security Council, and the CIA for President-elect Carter and Vice President-elect Mondale. Of the ten individuals assisting the president-elect and vice president-elect was one woman, Anne Wexler, with the responsibility for the Commerce Department, which Juanita Kreps was appointed to lead.

8. Mary King to Hamilton Jordan, memorandum, Dec. 15, 1976, "[Women Appts. —Mary King Memo 1-15-77] [O/A 10,620], Hamilton Jordan Papers, Box 32, JCL.

9. "Meeting with Mary King," memorandum, Dec. 16, 1976, "[Women Appt.s— Mary King Memo, 12/76–1/77] [O/A 10,622]" folder, Hamilton Jordan Papers, Box 32, JCL.

10. Ibid.

11. Ibid.

12. Ibid.

13. Ibid.

14. Minutes, Meeting of Subcommittee of Women in Government, Dec. 20, 1976, "[Women Appts.—Mary King Memos, 12/76–1/77] [O/A 10,622]" folder, Hamilton Jordan Papers, Box 32, JCL.

15. For example, see a series of memos in "Pres. Appts., 1976–77 [CF, O/A 414]" folder, early in 1977, Hamilton Jordan Papers, Box 51, JCL. Patricia Roberts Harris to President Carter, memorandum, Feb. 14, 1977, "FG 23 1/20/77–3/31/77" folder, WHCF Subject Files-Executive, Box FG-136, JCL.

16. For example, see Hubert Humphrey to Hamilton Jordan, Jan. 14, 1977, Hamilton Jordan Papers, Box 9 or letters from Arvonne Fraser and others writing on her behalf in December, 1976, Hamilton Jordan Papers, Letters to Carter and the transition team, JCL.

17. Ronnie Feit to Midge Costanza, memorandum, Feb. 11, 1977, "FG 6-1-1/ Costanza, Margaret 1/20/77–2/28/77" folder, WHCF, Subject Files-Executive, Box FG-37, JCL. Hamilton Jordan to President Carter, memorandum, and notations by Carter, Jan. 21, 1977, "Pres. Appts. 1976–77 [CF, O/A 414]" folder, Hamilton Jordan Papers, Box 51, JCL.

18. "Firsts in Women Appointments," n.d., "Women/Appts. [1]" folder, Sarah Weddington Papers, Box 18, JCL. For example, see "Women Presidential Appointees by Administration, 1912–1978" n.d., "Women/Appts. [1]" folder, Sarah Weddington Papers, Box 18, JCL.

19. Smith, "Carter Urges Aides," 1.

20. Political Action Task Force to President Carter, Feb. 5, 1978, "HU 1-6 1/1/78– 9/30/78" folder, WHCF Subject File-General, Box HU-17, JCL.

21. James F. Gamill, Jr., to Political Action Task Force, Feb. 23, 1978, "HU 1-6 1/1/78– 9/30/78" folder, WHCF Subject File-General, Box HU-17, JCL. According to the Carter White House records, Ford made "2096 appointments, 273, or 12.9% . . . women. Of the 2096, 592 are full-time positions and 1504 are part-time positions. Of the 592 full-time positions, 28, or 4.7 percent, are women. Of the 1504 part-time positions, 245, or 16.2 percent are women; 43 of the 245 were appointed to the Commission for the Observance of International Women's Year." "President Ford's Appointments of Women," n.d., "Women/Appts. [1]" folder, Sarah Weddington Papers, Box 18, JCL.

22. Martin, "Women Who Govern."

23. Patricia Bario to Judy Karst, Nov. 30, 1977, "PE 2 10/1/77–12/31/77" folder, WHCF, Subject File-Executive, Box PE-6, JCL.

24. "Women Appointed to Top Positions by President Carter," March, 1979, "Women/Appointments [1]" folder, Sarah Weddington Papers, Box 18, JCL.

25. "Women Appointed to Top Government Posts by President Jimmy Carter," December, 1979, "Women and Minorities—Women Appointed to Top Government Posts" folder, Sarah Weddington Papers, Box 92, JCL.

26. Margaret Costanza to President Carter, memorandum, Dec. 5, 1977, "HU 1-6 11/1/77–12/31/77" folder, WHCF, Subject File-Executive, Box HU-14, JCL.

27. Anne Wexler to Hamilton Jordan, memorandum, May 4, 1978, "Cabinet Representatives—Meetings with the White House Staff [CF O/A 103]" folder, Hamilton Jordan Papers, Box 41, JCL.

28. Ibid.

29. President Carter to Cabinet Officers and Heads of Agencies, memorandum, June 13, 1979, "PE 2 5/1/79–6/28/79" folder, WHCF, Subject File-Executive, Box PE-7, JCL. Tim Kraft and Arnie Miller to Hamilton Jordan, memorandum, July 23, 1979, "Candidates for Sub-Cabinet Positions [CF, O/A 646]" folder, Hamilton Jordan Papers, Box 41, JCL.

30. See Harry Schwartz to Stu Eizenstat and Bert Carp, memorandum, July 24, 1979, "FG 6/1/79–7/31/79" folder WHCF, Subject File-Executive, Box FG-3, JCL.

31. Stuart E. Eizenstat to Patricia Roberts Harris, Feb. 29, 1980, "[Folder-Patricia Roberts Harris] Patricia Roberts Harris" folder, Name File, JCL.

32. Carter to Cabinet Officers and Heads of Agencies, memorandum, June 13, 1979.

33. Kraft and Miller to Jordan, memorandum, July 23, 1979.

34. Ibid.

35. Sarah Weddington to President Carter, memorandum, Dec. 3, 1979, "Chron. Files-Dec. 1979 [3]" folder, Sarah Weddington Papers, Box 7, JCL.

36. Ibid.

37. Ibid.

38. Sarah Weddington to Shirley Hufstedler, Dec. 12, 1979, "Chron. Files-Dec. 1979 [2]" folder, Sarah Weddington Papers, Box 7, JCL.

39. Patricia Roberts Harris, remarks at the NWPC Convention, July 14, 1979, "FG 23 4/1/79–8/31/79" folder, WHCF, Subject File—Executive, Box FG-138, JCL.

40. Ibid.

41. See James T. Wooten, "Carter Considering Splitting CIA Post Between 2 Persons," New York Times, Dec. 19, 1976; James T. Wooten, "Carter Names Friend as Attorney General and Selects Woman," New York Times, Dec. 21, 1976.

42. Juanita Kreps to President Carter, ca. Feb. 1, 1977, "HU 1-6 1/20/77–2/28/77" folder, WHCF, Subject File-Executive, Box HU-14, JCL.

43. Ibid.

44. Isabel E. Hyde to Sarah Weddington, memorandum, Sept. 22, 1978, "FG 6-1-1/ Weddington, Sarah 1/20/77–10/31/78" folder, WHCF, Subject File-Executive, Box FG-70, JCL. Light, in *Thickening Government,* provides an excellent discussion of political appointees and career executives and the layers of management resulting from a proliferation of positions in each department. The addition of layers adds to the isolation of a secretary making policy from those in the civil service implementing a policy. The growth in high-level staff positions, in close proximity to the secretary, with political and policy agreement, and therefore increased power, has paralleled the thickening of government.

45. President Carter to Heads of Executive Departments and Agencies, memorandum, Aug. 26, 1977, "HU 1-2 6/1/77–8/31/77" folder, WHCF, Subject File-Executive, Box HU-9, JCL.

46. Sarah Weddington, exit interview by Emily Soapes, Jan. 2, 1981, 13, JCL.

47. Ibid.

48. See "HU 1-2 9/1/77–9/30/77" folder and "HU 1-2 10/1/77–12/3/77" folder, WHCF, Subject File-Executive, Box HU-10, JCL.

49. Weddington, exit interview by Soapes, 16.

50. President Ford to Heads of Departments and Agencies, memorandum, March 6, 1975, "HU 1-2 10/1/77–12/31/77" folder, WHCF, Subject File-Executive, Box HU-10, JCL.

51. Hamilton Jordan and Frank Moore to President Carter, memorandum, April 14, 1978, "Cabinet, 1978 [CF, O/A 413]" folder, Hamilton Jordan Papers, Box 41, JCL.

52. President Carter to Heads of Departments and Agencies, memorandum, Nov. 17, 1977, "HU 1-2 10/1/77–12/31/77" folder, WHCF, Subject File-Executive, Box HU-10, JCL.

53. W. W. to Rick Hutcheson, note, Nov. 15, 1977, "HU 1-2 10/1/77–12/31/77" folder, WHCF, Subject File-Executive, Box HU-10.

54. Richard Pettigrew to Rick Hutcheson, note, ca. November, 1977, HU 1-2 10/1/77–12/31/77" folder, WHCF, Subject File-Executive, Box HU-10, JCL.

55. Data revealed that "Government-wide, of 397 SES appointments made from July 13, 1979, to January 1, 1980, sixty-five (16.4 percent) were women—more than three times their original SES representation of 4.9 percent. Minority representation in these new appointments was thirty-nine members (9.8 percent). In contrast, minorities made up only 5.6 percent of the SES in July." "The Senior Executive Service," in "Civil Service Report: A Report on the First Year," January, 1980, "Background Information [Women Federal Workers]" folder, Weddington-Publications Files, Box 50, JCL.

56. For example, see Jane Wales to Anne Wexler and Mike Chanin, memorandum, Jan. 5, 1979, "HU 1-2 8/1/78–4/30/79" folder, WHCF, Subject File-Executive, Box HU-11, JCL.

57. For further discussion, see Janet M. Martin, "George Bush and the Executive Branch," in *Leadership and the Bush Presidency,* ed. Ryan J. Barilleaux and Mary E. Stuckey.

58. For example, see Thomas G. Kobus to Zbigniew Brzezinski, Feb. 28, 1977, "PE 2 1/20/77–3/31/77" folder, WHCF, Subject File-General, Box PE-8, JCL.

59. Margaret Heckler and Donna Shalala headed the newly created Department of Health and Human Services, which emerged after the creation of a separate Department of Education.

60. Alan K. Campbell to President Carter, memorandum, Aug. 6, 1979, "HU 1-2 7/1/79–3/31/80" folder, WHCF, Subject File-Executive, Box HU-11, JCL.

61. Jimmy Carter, note on Alan K. Campbell to President Carter, memorandum, Aug. 6, 1979, "HU 1-2 7/1/79–3/31/80" folder, WHCF, Subject File-Executive, Box HU-11, JCL.

62. See memos in "HU 1-2 1/20/77–4/30/77" folder, WHCF, Subject File-Executive, Box HU-9, JCL.

63. In January, 1995, Congress ended its exemption from eleven statutes, including the Fair Labor Standards Act of 1938 and the Civil Rights Act of 1964. See *CQ Almanac 1995,* 1–33.

64. President Jimmy Carter and Vice President Walter Mondale to Alan Campbell, memorandum, May 24, 1977, "HU 1-2 5/1/77–5/31/77" folder, WHCF, Subject File-Executive, Box HU-9, JCL.

65. For example, see memos in "Senior Staff Mtg.-Agenda [CF, O/A 647]" folder, Hamilton Jordan Papers, Box 55, JCL.

66. *CQ Almanac 1978,* 796.

67. Figures on the size of the White House staff are from Stanley and Niemi, *Vital Statistics on American Politics.*
68. *CQ Almanac 1978,* 797.
69. Ibid.
70. The visible role of Hillary Clinton as presidential advisor has spurred new and in-depth research on the role of the First Lady. For example, see O'Connor, Nye, and Van Assendelft, "Wives in the White House;" Burrell, "The Office of the First Lady and Public Policymaking," and Robert Watson, *The Presidents' Wives: Reassessing the Office of First Lady.*
71. For example, see Sarah Weddington to Jack Watson and Arnie Miller, Nov. 27, 1979, "FG 6-1-1 1/20/77–1/20/81" folder, WHCF, Subject File-Executive, Box FG-23, JCL.
72. President Carter to Stu Eizenstat, note on Eizenstat to Carter, memorandum, Sept. 1, 1978, "FG 194 1/20/77–1/20/81" folder, Box FG-95, JCL.
73. Hamilton Jordan to President Carter, memorandum, n.d. (ca. 1978), "Senior Advisers with President 1978" folder, Hamilton Jordan Papers, Box 37, JCL.
74. Vivian Cadden, "Midge Costanza: One Door from the Oval Office," *MS,* January, 1978.
75. Hamilton Jordan to Millicent Eisenberg, May 28, 1977, "FG 6-1 1/20/77–1/20/81" folder, WHCF, Subject File-Executive, Box FG-21, JCL.
76. Janice K. Mendenhall to Midge Costanza, Jan. 24, 1977, "FG 6-1-1/Costanza 3/1/77–5/31/77" folder, WHCF, Subject File-Executive, Box FG-37, JCL.
77. Jordan to Eisenberg, May 28, 1977.
78. See series of memos from Hamilton Jordan to senior staff, "Staff and Other Meetings—Memos [CF, O/A 413]" folder, Hamilton Jordan Papers, Box 55, JCL. At the time of Costanza's resignation, the organizational structure of the White House placed her in the second tier of presidential advisors. The first tier included Vice President Mondale, Eizenstat, Jordan, Kraft, Lipshutz, Moore, Powell, Watson, Wexler, Brzezinski, McIntyre, and Schultze. The second tier included Bourne, Hugh Carter, Esther Peterson, Rafshoon, Hutcheson, as well as First Lady Rosalynn Carter. For the record, Tom Jones, memo distribution list, July 24, 1978, "HU 1-6 7/1/78–8/31/78" folder, WHCF, Subject File-Executive, Box HU-15, JCL.
79. Margaret Costanza to Jere Hathaway Wright, Dec. 8, 1977, "HU 1-6 11/1/77–12/31/77" folder, WHCF, Subject File, Box HU-14, JCL.
80. The amendment, named for its sponsor, Representative Henry Hyde, a Republican from Illinois, banned federal funding of abortion unless the life of the mother was in danger.
81. Cadden, "Midge Costanza."
82. For example, see memos, "HU 1-6 9/1/77–10/31/77" folder, WHCF, Subject File-Executive, Box HU-14, JCL.
83. President Carter to Heads of Departments and Agencies, memorandum, July 20, 1978, "HU 1-6 7/1/78–8/31/78" folder, WHCF, Subject File-Executive, Box HU-15, JCL.
84. Margaret Costanza to President Carter, July 31, 1978, "FG 6-1-1/Costanza 11/1/77–1/20/81" folder, WHCF, Subject File-Executive, Box FG-37, JCL.
85. See "FG 6-1-1/Peterson, Esther" folder, WHCF, Subject File-Executive, Box FG-57, JCL; and Esther Peterson, exit interview by Emily Soapes, Jan. 5, 1981, JCL.
86. Hamilton Jordan to President Carter, memorandum, April 19, 1978, "White House Staff Reorganization [CF, O/A 414]" folder, Hamilton Jordan Papers, Box 57, JCL.

87. Ibid.

88. Wexler to Jordan, memorandum, May 4, 1978.

89. Hamilton Jordan to Stu, Jody, Tim, Frank, Anne, memorandum, May 2, 1978, "Cabinet Representatives—Meetings with the White House Staff [CF, O/A 103]" folder, Hamilton Jordan Papers, Box 41, JCL.

90. Anne Wexler to Richard L. Lesher, Oct. 31, 1978, "FG 20-13 1/20/77–1/20/81" folder, WHCF, Subject File-Executive, Box FG-129, JCL.

91. Anne Wexler to Frank Horton, July 24, 1978, "FG 6-1-1/Wexler 1/20/77–8/31/78" folder, WHCF, Subject File-Executive, Box FG-73, JCL.

92. Anne L. Wexler to Mrs. John L. McCain, Dec. 18, 1978, "FG 6-1-1/Wexler, Anne, 11/1/78–12/31/78" folder, WHCF, Subject File-General, Box FG-74, JCL.

93. Weddington, exit interview by Soapes, 1.

94. Ibid., 2.

95. David Broder, "Kraft to be Carter's Campaign Chief," *Washington Post*, Aug. 11, 1979.

96. Finding Aid, Sarah Weddington Papers, JCL.

97. Sarah Weddington to White House Staff, memorandum, Oct. 4, 1979, "FG 6-1-1 7/1/79–12/31/79" folder, WHCF, Subject File-Executive, Box FG-22, JCL.

98. Sarah Weddington to her staff and the Interdepartmental Task Force, memorandum, "[Admin. Personnel] [1]" folder, Sarah Weddington Papers, Box 56, JCL. Finding Aid, Sarah Weddington Papers, JCL.

99. Weddington, exit interview by Soapes, 17.

100. Memorandum of Meeting, Oct. 27, 1978, "FG 6-1-1/Weddington, Sarah 1/20/77–10/31/78" folder, WHCF, Subject File-Executive, Box FG-70, JCL.

101. Sarah Weddington to Nathalie Vaughan, Jan. 31, 1979, "FG 300 1/20/77–1/20/81" folder, WHCF, Subject File-Executive, Box FG-221, JCL.

102. Weddington, exit interview by Soapes, 17.

103. See materials in "Publications of the Office of Sarah Weddington," Box 44, Sarah Weddington Papers, JCL.

104. Weddington, interview by Soapes, 18. The groups covered a wide spectrum of interests, including the Association of Junior Leagues, the Coalition of Labor Union Women, the General Federation of Women's Clubs, Girl Scouts, League of Women Voters, NWPC, NFBPWC, YWCA, the National Association of Commissions on the Status of Women, the PACW, the Women's Equity Action League, and a number of organizations representing various religious denominations and ethnic and racial groups. Absent was NOW. See list, "President of National Women's Organizations," April 22, 1980, "Meetings w/Carter 4/22/80" folder, Sarah Weddington Papers, Box 34, JCL.

105. See "National Commission on the Status of Women 4-8-80" folder, Sarah Weddington Papers, Box 2, JCL.

106. "Meeting with Presidents of Women's Organizations," Jan. 30, 1980, "Meetings-Presidents of Women's Organizations w/President Carter 1/30/80 [1]" folder, Sarah Weddington Papers, Box 35, JCL.

107. Sarah Weddington to Lee Z. Steele, March 29, 1979, "HU 1-6 3/1/79–12/31/79" folder, WHCF, Subject File-Executive, Box HU-17, JCL.

108. See correspondence in "Mtgs-Adm. Women 2-2-80" folder, Sarah Weddington Papers, Box 34, JCL, or "Meeting w/ Administration Women 7/8/80" folder, Sarah Weddington Papers, Box 4, JCL.

109. For example, see correspondence in "MC 3 2/1/80–2/29/80" folder, WHCF, Subject File-Executive, Box MC-8, JCL.

110. See correspondence in a series of folders, "FG 6-1-1 Weddington, Sarah," Boxes FG-70 and FG-71, JCL.

111. Sarah Weddington to President Carter, memorandum, Dec. 3, 1979, "Chron. File-December 1979 [3]" folder, Sarah Weddington Papers, Box 7, JCL.

112. Sarah Weddington to President Carter, memorandum, "Talking Points," Dec. 13, 1979, "Meetings-with Carter 12/13/79" folder, Sarah Weddington Papers, Box 34, JCL.

113. Sarah Weddington to President Carter, memorandum, Dec. 13, 1979; and "Meeting with Presidents of Women's Organizations," talking points, Dec. 13, 1979, "Meetings—Presidents of Women's Organizations, 12/13/79–2/28/80" folder, Sarah Weddington Papers, Box 35, JCL.

114. Executive Order 11541, July 1, 1970.

115. All from Ray Calamero to Senator Mondale/Governor Carter, memorandum, ca. Dec. 13, 1976, "[Reorganization Domestic Policy Council] [O/A 10,622]" folder, Hamilton Jordan Papers, Box 10, JCL.

116. Beth Abramowitz to Stu Eizenstat, memorandum, March 1, 1978, "FG 6-1-1/ Eizenstat, 3-1-78 to 5-31-78" folder, WHCF, Subject File-Executive, Box FG-41, JCL.

117. Abramowitz noted the caucus was "an almost invisible federation of Congressional women. Their major legislative agenda items are displaced homemakers and flexi-time/part-time work for federal employees. The caucus plans to call a meeting of administration officials to discuss flexi-time/part-time legislation now pending in Congress. The bills are not likely to pass in both houses in this session; therefore, there is no urgent need to meet with the Congressional Women's Caucus. However, before the session ends, such a meeting would be desirable to show administration concern for women's issues generally," ibid. For a discussion of the evolution of the Congresswomen's Caucus into the Congressional Caucus for Women's Issues, see Joan Hulse Thompson, "The Congressional Caucus for Women's Issues: A Study in Organizational Change" (paper delivered at the annual meeting of the American Political Science Association, Washington, D.C., Sept., 1993).

118. "Displaced homemakers" was the term used to designate women over the age of forty who were unmarried, divorced, or widowed. Beth Abramowitz to Stu Eizenstat, memorandum, Feb. 13, 1978, "LA 2 1/1/78–2/28/78" folder, WHCF, Subject File-Executive, Box LA-3, JCL.

119. Beth Abramowitz to Stu Eizenstat, memorandum, April 5, 1979, "HU 1-6 4/1/79–5/31/79" folder, WHCF, Subject File-Executive, Box HU-15, JCL.

120. "Executive Order Establishing a National Commission for Women," draft by Margaret Costanza, ca. March, 1978, "FG-300 1/20/77–1/20/81" folder, WHCF, Subject File-Executive, Box FG-221, JCL.

121. For example, see Margaret Costanza to Rep. Bob Michel, Sept. 28, 1977, "HO/ International W 1/20/77–1/20/81" folder, WHCF, Subject File-Executive, Box HO-3, JCL; Margaret (Midge) Costanza to Rep. Allen E. Ertel, Nov. 14, 1977, "HU 1-6 11/1/77–12/31/77" folder, WHCF Subject File, Box HU-14, JCL.

122. Jan Peterson to Margaret Costanza, memorandum, Sept. 6, 1977, "MC 3 9/1/77–9/30/77" folder, WHCF, Subject Files-Executive, Box MC 3, JCL.

123. President Carter chose not to attend the conference in Houston scheduled just four days before his planned departure for a nine-country trip. However, Carter had postponed the trip early in November when it looked like his energy program would not be passed in Congress before his scheduled departure. President Carter to Bella Abzug, Oct. 27, 1977, "(NACW) Items Pre 1/12/79" folder, Sarah Weddington Papers, Box 13, JCL.

124. Thirty-eight states were needed for ratification of a constitutional amendment.
125. Margaret Costanza, "Meeting with Administration Women on IWY Conference," Dec. 13, 1977, "HU 1-6 11/1/77–12/31/77" folder, WHCF, Subject Files, Box HU-14, JCL.
126. Ibid.
127. Ibid.
128. Stu Eizenstat to Domestic Policy Staff, memorandum, Jan. 30, 1978, "HU 1-6 1/1/78–3/31/78" folder, WHCF, Subject File, Box HU-14, JCL.
129. Beth Abramowitz to Stu Eizenstat, memorandum, March 14, 1978, WHCF, Subject File-Executive, JCL.
130. Ibid.
131. Margaret Costanza to President Carter, memorandum, March 16, 1978, "FG 300 1/20/77–1/20/81" folder, WHCF, Subject File-Executive, Box FG-221, JCL.
132. Draft Executive Order establishing a National Commission for Women, "FG 300 1/20/77–1/20/81" folder, WHCF, Subject File-Executive, Box FG-221, JCL.
133. Ibid.
134. Ibid.
135. Ray Marshall to President Carter, March 20, 1978, "FG 300 1/20/77–1/20/81" folder, WHCF Subject File-Executive, Box FG-221, JCL.
136. Jack Watson to Rick Hutcheson, memorandum, March 17, 1978, "FG 300 1/20/77–1/20/81" folder, WHCF, Subject File-Executive, Box FG-221, JCL.
137. William M. Nichols for James T. McIntyre to Rick Hutcheson, memorandum, March 17, 1978, "FG 300 1/20/77–1/20/81" folder, WHCF, Subject File-Executive, Box FG-221, JCL.
138. Ibid.
139. Stu Eizenstat to President Carter, memorandum, March 21, 1978, "FG 300 1/20/77–1/20/81" folder, WHCF, Subject File-Executive, Box FG-221, JCL.
140. Ibid.
141. Executive Order 12050, *Federal Register* 43, no. 67, April 6, 1978, "Women's Advisory Committee [CF, O/A 647]" folder, Hamilton Jordan Papers, Box 57, JCL.
142. For example, see Margaret Costanza to Dan Marriott, July 3, 1978, "FG-300 1/20/77–1/20/81" folder, WHCF, Subject File-Executive, Box FG-221, JCL.
143. Weddington, exit interview by Soapes, 9.
144. Sarah Weddington to Donna Shalala, Oct. 27, 1978, "FG 23 6/1/78–10/31/78" folder, WHCF, Subject File-Executive, Box FG-137, JCL.
145. See Martin, "Women Who Govern."
146. The cabinet departments which had responded by mid-November included: Housing and Urban Development; Transportation; Justice; Health, Education and Welfare; Energy; Treasury; Agriculture; and Labor. See correspondence in "FG 258-5 11/1/78–12/31/78" folder, WHCF, Subject File-Executive, Box FG-207, JCL.
147. Sarah Weddington to Christine M. Shannon, memorandum, Jan. 11, 1979, "FG 258-5 1/20/77–1/20/81" folder, WHCF, Subject File-General, Box FG 207, JCL.
148. Sarah Weddington to Max Cleland, Oct. 5, 1979, "FG 258-5 1/1/79–1/20/81" folder, WHCF, Subject File-Executive, Box FG-207, JCL.
149. For example, see Margaret Costanza to John J. Rhodes, April 14, 1978, "FG 300 1/20/77–1/20/81" folder, WHCF, Subject File-Executive, Box FG-221, JCL.
150. Beth Abramowitz sought to remedy this slight on the part of Midge Costanza, who had made the recommendations for the appointments, and urged Eizenstat that Height be considered for the Medal of Freedom. As Abramowitz argued,

"Mrs. Height is the only living female member of the early civil rights struggle. Her organization, which was founded by the late Mary McCloud Bethune—a member of Roosevelt's Kitchen Cabinet, is the largest and oldest organization of black women in this country.

Miss Height is a vigorous woman of advanced years who should be honored in her lifetime. Honoring her will spread more goodwill in the black community, than meeting with Jesse Jackson. Midge Costanza unfortunately failed to appoint Miss Height or any other member of the only national organization of black women, to the National Advisory Council on Women. This oversight, which was brought to Midge's attention several times, has cost needless support and has been interpreted by many black women as a snub of Miss Height and the National Council of Negro Women."

Beth Abramowitz to Stu Eizenstat, memorandum, Aug. 10, 1978, "FG 300 1/20/77–1/20/81" folder, WHCF, Subject File—Executive, Box FG-221, JCL.

151. Carmen Delgado Votaw and Bella S. Abzug to President Carter, memorandum, Aug. 22, 1978, HU 1-6 7/7/78–8/31/78" folder, WHCF, Subject File-Executive, Box HU-15, JCL.

152. NACW to President Carter, Oct. 6, 1978, "FG 194 1/20/77–1/20/81" folder, WHCF, Subject File-Executive, Box FG-195. JCL.

153. Carmen Delgado Votaw to President Carter, Oct. 9, 1978, "(NACW) Items Pre 1/12/79" folder, Sarah Weddington Papers, Box 13, JCL.

154. Sarah Weddington to Bella Abzug and Carmen Delgado Votaw, memorandum, Nov. 16, 1978, "(NACW) Items Pre 1/12/79" folder, Sarah Weddington Papers, Box 13, JCL.

155. Sarah Weddington to Bella Abzug and Carmen Delgado Votaw, memorandum, Nov. 14, 1978, "(NACW) Items Pre 1/12/79" folder, Sarah Weddington Papers, Box 13, JCL.

156. Bella Abzug and Carmen Delgado Votaw to Sarah Weddington, memorandum, Nov. 17, 1978, "(NACW) Items Pre 1/12/79" folder, Sarah Weddington Papers, Box 13, JCL.

157. Ibid.

158. Abzug and Votaw to President Carter, Nov. 21, 1978, "(NACW) Items Pre 1/12/79" folder, Sarah Weddington Papers, Box 13, JCL; and Sarah Weddington to President Carter, memorandum, Nov. 22, 1978, "(NACW) Items Pre 1/12/79" folder, Sarah Weddington Papers, Box 13, JCL.

159. Sarah Weddington to Bella Abzug and Carmen Delgado Votaw, Nov. 22, 1978, "(NACW) Items Pre 1/12/79" folder, Sarah Weddington Papers, Box 13, JCL.

160. See Sarah Weddington to Senior Staff, memorandum, Jan. 14, 1979, "(NACW) Items on 1/12/79" folder, Sarah Weddington Papers, Box 19, JCL.

161. See press release, Jan. 12, 1979, "Women's Advisory Committee [CF, O/A 647]" folder, Hamilton Jordan Papers, Box 57, JCL.

162. "The President's Remarks to the National Advisory Committee for Women," "(NACW) Items on 1/12/79" folder, Sarah Weddington Papers, Box 14, JCL.

163. Ibid.

164. Hamilton Jordan to Bella Abzug, Jan. 12, 1979, "Women's Advisory Committee [CF, O/A 647]" folder, Hamilton Jordan Papers, Box 57, JCL.

165. See Sarah Weddington to Senior Staff, memorandum, Jan. 14, 1979.

166. Ibid.

167. See letters from Sarah Weddington to various individuals, "FG 300 1/20/77–1/20/81" folder, WHCF, Subject File-General, Box FG-221, JCL.

168. See correspondence in "FG 300 1/20/77–1/20/81" folder, WHCF, Subject File-Executive, Box FG-221, JCL.

169. Jeanne Simon to Sarah Weddington, Feb. 12, 1979, "FG 6-1-1/Weddington, Sarah 1/1/79–2/28/79" folder, WHCF, Subject Files-Executive, JCL.

170. Susanne Wilson to President Carter, Jan. 25, 1979, "FG 300 1/20/77–1/20/81" folder, WHCF, Subject File, Box FG 221, JCL.

171. White House press release, Jan. 19, 1979, "FG 300/A 1/1/79–1/20/81" folder, WHCF, Subject File-Executive, Box FG-221, JCL.

172. Sarah Weddington, to Concerned Citizen(s), form letter, Jan. 31, 1979, "FG 300 1/20/77–1/20/81" folder, WHCF, Subject File-General, Box FG-221, JCL.

173. Marjorie Bell Chambers to President Carter, Feb. 16, 1979, "(NACW) Correspondence" folder, Sarah Weddington files, Box 13, JCL.

174. Press release, NACW, Feb. 22, 1979, "(NACW) Items after 1/12/79" folder, Sarah Weddington Papers, Box 14, JCL.

175. Ibid.

176. Press release, NACW, March 27, 1979, "(NACW) Items after 1/12/79" folder, Sarah Weddington Papers, Box 14, JCL.

177. Press release, NACW, Feb. 22, 1979.

178. Marjorie Bell Chambers to President Carter, March 27, 1979, "(NACW) Correspondence" folder, Sarah Weddington Papers, Box 13, JCL.

179. Marjorie Bell Chambers to President Carter, March 23, 1979, "(NACW) Items after 1/12/79" folder, Sarah Weddington Papers, Box 14, JCL.

180. See Marjorie Bell Chambers to President Carter, March 27, 1979, and Sarah Weddington to Marjorie Bell Chambers, March 29, 1979, "HU 1-6 3/1/79–3/31/79" folder, WHCF, Subject File-Executive, Box HU-15, JCL.

181. Sarah Weddington to Judith Fannin, March 29, 1979, "FG 300 1/20/77–1/20/81" folder, WHCF, Subject File-Executive, Box FG221, JCL.

182. White House press release, May 9, 1979, "FG 300 1/20/77–1/20/81" folder, WHCF Subject File-Executive, Box FG-221, JCL.

183. Sarah Weddington to President Carter, memorandum, May 9, 1979, "FG 300 1/20/77–1/20/81" folder, WHCF, Subject File-Executive, Box FG-221, JCL.

184. Executive Order 12135, May 9, 1979, "FG 300 1/20/77–1/20/81" folder, WHCF, Subject File-Executive, Box FG-221, JCL.

185. Sarah Weddington to Mrs. Obera Bergdall, Oct. 12, 1979, "HU 1-6 10/1/79–10/31/79" folder, WHCF, Subject File-Executive, Box HU-16, JCL.

186. See correspondence in "FG 300 1/20/77–1/20/81" folder, WHCF, Subject File-Executive, Box FG-221, JCL.

187. See Lynda Johnson Robb, speech, July 14, 1979, at the NWPC, "[Correspondence]-to S[arah] W[eddington] (from Lynda [Johnson] Robb)" folder, Sarah Weddington Papers, Box 7, JCL; Sarah Weddington to Lynda Robb, memorandum, July 12, 1979, "FG 300 1/20/77–1/20/81" folder, WHCF, Subject File-Executive, Box FG-221, JCL; and see letters, "FG 6-1-1/Wexler, Anne 6/1/79–4/30/80" folder, WHCF, Subject File-Executive, Box FG-73, JCL.

188. Robb, speech, July 14, 1979.

189. Sarah Weddington to Rex Granum, memorandum, July 13, 1979, "FG 300 1/20/77–1/20/81" folder, WHCF, Subject File-Executive, Box FG-221, JCL.

190. See, letters in "[Correspondence]-to S[arah] W[eddington] (from Lynda [Johnson] Robb)" folder, Sarah Weddington Papers, Box 7, JCL.

191. See Lynda Johnson Robb, speech, Jan. 14, 1979, at the NWPC, "[Correspondence]-to S[arah] W[eddington] (from Lynda [Johnson] Robb)" folder, Sarah Weddington Papers, Box 7, JCL.

192. Sarah Weddington to Fran Voorde and Phil Wise, memorandum, July 19, 1979, "FG 300 1/20/77–1/20/81" folder, WHCF, Subject File-Executive, Box FG-221, JCL.

193. Sarah Weddington to Lynda J. Robb, memorandum, Oct. 12, 1979, "FG 300 1/20/77–1/20/81" folder, WHCF, Subject File-Executive, Box FG-221, JCL.

194. Sarah Weddington to Phil Wise and Fran Voorde, memorandum, Nov. 13, 1980, "FG 300 1/20/77–1/20/81" folder, WHCF, Subject File-Executive, Box FG-221, JCL.

195. "The Daily Diary of President Jimmy Carter," Dec. 16, 1980, JCL.

196. See Sheldon Goldman, "Carter's Judicial Appointments: A Lasting Legacy," Ju9dicature 64, no. 8 (March, 1981): 344–55.

197. Sarah Weddington to Beverly Clark, Feb. 26, 1979, "FG 6-1-1/Weddington 1/1/79–2/28/79" folder, WHCF, Subject File-Executive, Box FG-71, JCL.

198. Sarah Weddington to Lois Kram Turner, Feb. 26, 1979, "HU 1-6 1/1/79–2/28/79" folder, WHCF, Subject File—General, Box HU-17, JCL.

199. Doug Huron to Hamilton Jordan, memorandum, Jan. 12, 1979, "Women's Advisory Committee [CF, O/A 647]" folder, Hamilton Jordan Papers, Box 57, JCL.

200. Hamilton Jordan, note on Doug Huron to Hamilton Jordan, memorandum, Jan. 12, 1979, "Women's Advisory Committee [CF, O/A 647]" folder, Hamilton Jordan Papers, Box 57, JCL.

201. Goldman, "Carter's Judicial Appointments," 349.

202. For example, see Sarah Weddington to Lee Z. Steele, March 29, 1979, "HU 1-6 3/1/79–12/31/79" folder, WHCF, Subject File—General, Box HU-17. JCL.

203. Anne Wexler, Sarah Weddington and Kit Dobelle to Hamilton Jordan and Jody Powell, memorandum, Nov. 6, 1979, "White House Staff Reorg. 1979 [CF, O/A 647]" folder, Hamilton Jordan Papers, Box 57, JCL.

204. Wayne, *Road to the White House 1996.*

205. Sarah Weddington to Susanne Wilson, Feb. 26, 1979, "FG 300 1/20/77–1/20/81" folder, WHCF, Subject File-Executive, Box FG-221, JCL.

206. Weddington, exit interview by Soapes, 4–5.

207. Sarah Weddington to Jack Watson and Arnie Miller, memorandum, Nov. 27, 1979, "HU 1-6 3/1/79–12/31/79" folder, WHCF, Subject File-General, Box HU-17, JCL.

208. Sarah Weddington to Jack Watson, memorandum, July 8, 1980, "Meeting w/ Administration Women 7/8/80" folder, Sarah Weddington Papers, Box 4, JCL.

209. For example, see Mansbridge, *Why We Lost the ERA.*

210. President Carter, note on Sarah Weddington to President Carter and First Lady Rosalynn Carter, memorandum, March 27, 1979, "SO3 1/1/79–10/17/79" folder, WHCF, Subject File-Executive, Box SO-2, JCL.

211. Weddington, exit interview by Soapes, 14.

212. Ibid., 15.

213. Ibid., 20.

214. Ibid., 13.

215. See Sarah Weddington Papers, Box 13, for further discussion of these issues.

216. Weddington, exit interview by Soapes, 13.
217. Ibid., 12.

CHAPTER 7. CONCLUSION

1. James Fallows, "The Political Scientist," *The New Yorker*, June 7, 1999, 69.
2. For a list of the recommendations of the PCSW, see their final report, or a report of one of its committees, for example, "Recommendations of the President's Commission on the Status of Women," *Report of the Committee on Civil and Political Rights* (Washington, D.C.: President's Commission on the Status of Women, 1963).
3. For further discussion of the George W. Bush transition see Janet M. Martin and MaryAnne Borrelli, "Campaign Promises and Presidential Appointments: Women in the George W. Bush Administration" (paper delivered at the annual meetings of the American Political Science Association, San Francisco, September, 2001).
4. "NWPC Publications," *Women's Political Times* (Washington, D.C.: NWPC, 1995).
5. Jan Peterson and Ruth Sanchez-Dirks to Margaret Costanza, memorandum Oct. 21, 1977, "HO/International W 1/20/77–1/20/81" folder, WHCF, Subject File-EX" folder, Box HO-3, JCL.
6. For further discussion see Martin, "Women Who Govern."
7. "Announcement of the Formation and Membership of the White House Coordinating Council on Women," August 27, 1982, *Public Papers of the Presidents of the United States: Ronald Reagan*, 1084.
8. http://www.whitehouse.gov/WH/EOP/women/OWIO, Nov. 7, 1995.
9. Ibid.
10. The call took place during the time when the House of Representatives was debating the articles of impeachment which had been brought against President Clinton.
11. Thomas E. Cronin, "Conflict Over the Cabinet," *New York Times*, Aug. 12, 1979, sec. VI, 24.
12. Associated Press, "First Woman to Be Space Commander Named," *New York Times*, March 6, 1998, A12.
13. Alexis Simendinger of *National Journal*, conversation with author, 1997.

BIBLIOGRAPHY

"1980 Republican Platform Text," *CQ Weekly,* July 19, 1980, 2033.

Adams, Abigail. Letter to John Adams. March 31, 1776. In *The Book of Abigail and John: Selected Letters of the Adams Family 1762-1784,* edited by L. H. Butterfield, Marc Friedlaender and Mary-Jo Kline. Cambridge: Harvard University Press, 1975.

Aberbach, Joel D., and Bert A. Rockman. "Clashing Beliefs Within the Executive Branch: The Nixon Administration Bureaucracy." *American Political Science Review* 70, no. 2 (June 1976): 456–68.

Allison, Graham T. *Essence of Decision: Explaining the Cuban Missile Crisis.* Boston: Little, Brown, and Company, 1971.

Andersen, Kristi. "Working Women and Political Participation, 1952–1972." *American Journal of Political Science* (August, 1975).

Asher, Herbert B. *Presidential Elections and American Politics: Voters, Candidates and Campaigns since 1952.* Homewood, Ill.: The Dorsey Press, 1976.

The Autobiography of Mary Anderson as Told to Mary N. Winslow. Minneapolis: University of Minnesota Press, 1951.

Baker, Paula. "The Domestication of Politics: Women and American Political Society, 1780–1920." *American Historical Review* (1984).

Bennetts, Leslie. "Women's Group Gets Appeal by Reagan." *New York Times,* Oct. 21 1980, electronic, 7B.

———. "Feminists Dismayed by the Election and Unsure of What Future Holds." *New York Times,* Nov. 7 1980, late edition, electronic, 16A.

Biles, Roger. "Robert F. Wagner, Franklin D. Roosevelt, and Social Welfare Legislation in the New Deal." *Presidential Studies Quarterly* 28, no. 1 (Winter, 1998): 139–52.

Borrelli, MaryAnne. "Gender, Credibility, and Politics: The Senate Nomination Hearings of Cabinet Secretaries-Designate, 1975 to 1993." *Political Research Quarterly* 50 (March, 1997): 171–97.

———. *The President's Cabinet: Gender, Power, and Representation.* Boulder, Colo.: Lynne Rienner Publishers, Inc., 2002.

Borrelli, MaryAnne, and Janet M. Martin, eds. *The Other Elites: Women, Politics, and Power in the Executive Branch.* Boulder, Colo.: Lynne Rienner Publishers, Inc., 1997.

Bornet, Vaughn Davis. *The Presidency of Lyndon B. Johnson.* Lawrence: University Press of Kansas, 1983.

Breckinridge, Sophonisba P. "The Activities of Women Outside the Home." In *Recent Social Trends in the United States.* Vol. 1. Report of the President's Research Committee on Social Trends, 739–40. New York: McGraw-Hill Book Co., Inc., 1933.

———. *Women in the Twentieth Century, A Study of Their Political, Social, and Economic Activities.* New York and London: McGraw-Hill Book Company, Inc., 1933.

Broder, David. "Kraft to be Carter's Campaign Chief." *Washington Post,* Aug. 11, 1979.

Buchanan, Sara Louise. *The Legal Status of Women in the United States as of January 1, 1948, Summary for all States Combined.* Bulletin of the Women's Bureau. No. 157— United States Summary (Revised). Washington, D.C.: Government Printing Office, 1951.

Burrell, Barbara C. *Public Opinion, the First Ladyship and Hillary Rodham Clinton.* New York: Garland Press, 1997.

Cadden, Vivian. "Midge Constanza: One Door from the Oval Office." *MS* (January, 1978).

Campbell, Colin, and Bert A. Rockman, eds. *The Clinton Presidency: First Appraisals.* Chatham, N.J.: Chatham House Publishers, 1996.

Campbell, Karlyn Kohrs, comp. *Man Cannot Speak for Her.* Vol. 1. New York: Greenwood, 1989.

———, comp. *Man Cannot Speak for Her: Key Texts of the Early Feminists.* Vol. 2. New York: Greenwood, 1989.

———, ed. *Women Public Speakers in the United States, 1800–1925: A Bio-critical Sourcebook.* Westport, Conn.: Greenwood Press, 1993.

———, ed. *Women Public Speakers in the United States, 1925–1993: A Bio-critical Sourcebook,* Westport, Conn.: Greenwood Press, 1994.

Cannon, James. *Time and Chance: Gerald Ford's Appointment with History.* New York: Harper Collins, 1994.

Carpenter, Liz. *Ruffles & Flourishes.* College Station: Texas A&M University Press, 1969.

Caroli, Betty Boyd. *First Ladies.* New York: Oxford University Press, 1995.

Carter, Jimmy. *Keeping Faith: Memoirs of a President.* New York: Bantam Books, 1982.

Carroll, Susan. *Women as Candidates in American Politics.* 2d ed. Bloomington: Indiana University Press, 1994.

Carroll, Susan, and Barbara Geiger-Parker. *Women Appointed to the Carter Administration: A Comparison with Men.* New Brunswick, N.J.: Center for the American Women and Politics, Eagleton Institute of Politics, Rutgers University, 1983.

Catt, Carrie Chapman, and Nettie Rogers Shuler. *Woman Suffrage and Politics: The Inner Story of the Suffrage Movement.* New York: C. Scribner's Sons, 1923.

Center for the American Woman and Politics (CAWP). Eagleton Institute of Politics, Rutgers University. Fact Sheets.

Cohen, Jeffrey E. *The Politics of the U.S. Cabinet: Representation in the Executive Branch, 1789–1984.* Pittsburgh: University of Pittsburgh Press, 1988.

A Compilation of the Messages and Papers of the Presidents, 1789–1897. Compiled by James D. Richardson. Vol. VI. Washington, D.C.: Government Printing Office, 1897.

A Compilation of the Messages and Papers of the Presidents. Vol. XV. New York: Bureau of National Literature, Inc.

Congress and the Nation. Washington, D.C.: Congressional Quarterly, Inc., 1969.

Cook, Elizabeth Adell, and Clyde Wilcox. "Feminism and the Gender Gap: A Second Look." *Journal of Politics* 53 (1991): 1111–22.

Cook, Elizabeth Adell, Sue Thomas, and Clyde Wilcox, eds. *The Year of the Woman: Myths and Realities.* Boulder: Westview Press, 1994.

Cook, Rhodes. "Carter Locks up Nomination Early," *Congressional Quarterly Weekly Report* (August 16, 1980): 2351.

Costain, Anne. *Inviting Women's Rebellion: A Political Process Interpretation of the Women's Movement.* Baltimore: Johns Hopkins University Press, 1992.

CQ Almanac 1962. Washington, D.C.: Congressional Quarterly, Inc., 1963.

CQ Almanac 1963. Washington, D.C.: Congressional Quarterly, Inc., 1964.

CQ Almanac 1973. Washington, D.C.: Congressional Quarterly, Inc., 1974.

CQ Almanac 1978. Washington, D.C.: Congressional Quarterly, Inc., 1979.

CQ Almanac 1988. Washington, D.C.: Congressional Quarterly, Inc., 1989.

CQ Almanac 1995. Washington, D.C.: Congressional Quarterly, Inc., 1996.

CQ Almanac 2000. Washington, D.C.: Congressional Quarterly, Inc., 2001.

Dallek, Robert. *Flawed Giant: Lyndon Johnson and His Times, 1961–1973.* New York: Oxford University Press, 1998.

Darcy, R., Susan Welch, and Janet Clark. *Women, Elections, and Representation.* 2d ed., revised. Lincoln: University of Nebraska Press, 1994.

Davis, Eric L. "The Johnson White House and the 1964 Civil Rights Act." Paper presented at the annual meetings of the American Political Science Association, Atlanta, Ga., Aug. 31–Sept. 3, 1989.

Diller, Daniel C. and Stephen L. Robertson. *The Presidents, First Ladies, and Vice Presidents: White House Biographies, 1789–1997.* Washington, D.C.: Congressional Quarterly, Inc., 1997.

Donovan, John C. *The Politics of Poverty.* Indianapolis: Pegasus, 1967.

Duerst-Lahti, Georgia. "The Government's Role in Building the Women's Movement." *Political Science Quarterly* 104, no. 2 (1989): 67–120.

Duerst-Lahti, Georgia, and Rita Mae Kelly, eds. *Gender Power, Leadership, and Governance.* Ann Arbor: University of Michigan Press, 1995.

Ebbert, Jean, and Marie-Beth Hall. *Crossed Currents: Navy Women from WWI to Tailhook.* Washington, D.C.: Brassey's, 1993.

Erskine, Hazel. "The Polls: Women's Role." *Public Opinion Quarterly* 35, no. 2 (1971).

Fenno, Richard F. *The President's Cabinet, An Analysis in the Period from Wilson to Eisenhower.* Cambridge, Mass.: Harvard University Press, 1959.

Ferree, Myra Marx. "A Woman for President? Changing Responses: 1958–1972." *Public Opinion Quarterly* 38 (Fall, 1974): 390–99.

Fifth Annual Report of the Director of the Women's Bureau, Department of Labor. Washington, D.C.: U.S. Government Printing Office, 1923.

Fisher, Marguerite J. and Betty Whitehead. "American Government and Politics: Women and National Party Organization." *American Political Science Review* 38 (1944).

Fourteenth Annual Report of the Director of the Women's Bureau, Department of Labor, Fiscal Year Ended June 30, 1932. Washington, D.C.: U.S. Government Printing Office, 1932.

Freeman, Jo. *Politics of Women's Liberation.* New York: David McKay Co., 1976.

The Gallup Poll: Public Opinion 1935-71. Vol. 2. New York: Random House, 1972.

Gelb, Joyce, and Marian Lief Palley. *Women and Public Policies: Reassessing Gender Politics.* Rev. ed. Charlottesville: University of Virginia Press, 1996.

Genovese, Michael A., ed. *Women as National Leaders.* Newbury Park, Calif.: Sage Publications, 1993.

Goldman, Sheldon. "Carter's Judicial Appointments: A Lasting Legacy." *Judicature* 64, no. 8 (March, 1981): 344–55.

Goldsmith, Barbara. *Other Powers: The Age of Suffrage, Spiritualism, and the Scandalous Victoria Woodhull.* New York: Alfred A. Knopf, 1998.

Good, Josephine L., and Clare B. Williams. "Republican Womanpower: The History of Women in Republican National Conventions and Women in the Republican National Committee." Washington, D.C.: Women's Division, Republican National Committee, 1963.

Goodwin, Doris Kearns. *No Ordinary Time: Franklin and Eleanor Roosevelt: The Home Front in World War II.* New York: Simon and Schuster, 1994.

Graham, Sara Hunter. *Woman Suffrage and the New Democracy.* New Haven: Yale University Press, 1996.

Harrison, Cynthia. *On Account of Sex: The Politics of Women's Issues, 1945–1968.* Berkeley: University of California Press, 1988.

Hart, John. *The Presidential Branch: From Washington to Clinton.* 2d ed. Chatham, N.J.: Chatham House, 1995.

Heclo, Hugh. *A Government of Strangers: Executive Politics in Washington.* Washington, D.C.: Brookings, 1977.

Hess, Stephen. *Organizing the Presidency.* Washington, D.C.: Brookings Institution, 1988.

Hinckley, Barbara. *Less Than Meets the Eye: Foreign Policy Making and the Myth of the Assertive Congress.* Chicago: University of Chicago Press, 1994.

A History of the NFBPWC, Inc. (BPW/USA). Vol. III. Washington, D.C.: BPW, 1994.

Hoff, Joan. *Nixon Reconsidered.* New York: Basic Books, 1994.

Holm, Jeanne M. "Ford's Record on Women's Rights," *Washington Post,* October 19, 1976, A19.

James, Edward T., Janet Wilson James, and Paul S. Boyer, eds. *Notable American Women 1607–1950: A Biographical Dictionary.* Vol. II, G–O. Cambridge: Belknap Press of Harvard University Press, 1971.

Jamieson, Kathleen Hall. *Beyond the Double Bind: Women and Leadership.* New York: Oxford University Press, 1995.

Johnson, Donald Bruce, comp. *National Party Platforms, vol. 2, 1960–1976.* Rev. ed. Urbana and London: University of Illinois Press, 1978.

———, comp. *National Party Platforms of 1980.* Urbana and London: University of Illinois Press, 1982.

Johnson, Lyndon Baines. *The Vantage Point, Perspectives of the Presidency, 1963–1969.* New York: Popular Library, 1971.

Jones, Charles O. *The Presidency in a Separated System.* Washington, D.C.: The Brookings Institution, 1994.

Keats, John. "She's the American Traveler's Best Friend." *Reader's Digest* (February, 1970).

Kernell, Samuel. *Going Public: New Strategies of Presidential Leadership.* 2d ed. Washington, D.C.: Congressional Quarterly, Inc, 1993.

Kurian, George Thomas, ed. *A Historical Guide to the U.S. Government.* New York: Oxford University Press, 1998.

Kurian, George Thomas, and Jeffrey D. Schultz, eds. *The Encyclopedia of the Democratic Party.* Armonk, N.Y.: Sharpe Reference, 1997.

———, eds. *The Encyclopedia of the Republican Party.* Armonk, N.Y.: Sharpe Reference, 1997.

Linden-Ward, Blanche, and Carol Hurd Green. *American Women in the 1960s: Changing the Future.* New York: Twayne Publishers, 1992.

Light, Paul C. *Thickening Government: Federal Hierarchy and the Diffusion of Accountability.* Washington, D.C.: Brookings Institution, 1995.

Loevy, Robert D., ed. *The Civil Rights Act of 1964: The Passage of the Law that Ended Racial Segregation.* Albany: SUNY Press, 1997.

Mackenzie, G. Calvin. *The Politics of Presidential Appointments.* New York: Free Press, 1981.

Mackenzie, G. Calvin, ed. *The In-and-Outers: Presidential Appointees and Transient Government in Washington.* Baltimore: Johns Hopkins University Press, 1987.

Malich, Tanya. *The Republican War Against Women: An Insider's Report from Behind the Lines.* New York: Bantam Books, 1996.

Mankiller, Wilma, Gwendolyn Mink, Marysa Navarro, Barbara Smith, and Gloria Steinem, eds. *The Reader's Companion to U.S. Women's History.* Boston: Houghton Mifflin Company, 1998.

Mansbridge, Jane J. *Why We Lost the ERA.* Chicago: University of Chicago Press, 1986.

Martin, Janet M. "An Examination of Executive Branch Appointments in the Reagan Administration by Background and Gender." *Western Political Quarterly* 44 (1991): 173–84.

———. "George Bush and the Executive Branch." In *Leadership and the Bush Presidency,* ed. Ryan J. Barilleaux and Mary E. Stuckey. Westport, Conn.: Praeger, 1992.

———. *Lessons from the Hill: The Legislative Journey of an Education Program.* New York: St. Martin's Press, 1994.

———. "The Recruitment of Women to Cabinet and Subcabinet Posts." *Western Political Quarterly* 42 (1989): 161–72.

Martin, Janet. M., and MaryAnne Borrelli. "Campaign Promises and Presidential Appointments: Women in the George W. Bush Administration." Paper delivered at the annual meetings of the American Political Science Association, San Francisco, Sept., 2001.

McDonald, Forrest. *The American Presidency: An Intellectual History.* Lawrence: University of Kansas Press, 1994.

McGlen, Nancy E., and Meredith Reid Sarkees. *Women in Foreign Policy: The Insiders.* New York: Routledge, 1993.

McGlen, Nancy E., and Karen O'Connor. *Women, Politics, and American Society.* Englewood Cliffs, N.J.: Prentice Hall, 1995.

Means, Marianne. *The Women in the White House.* New York: Signet Press, 1963.

Milkis, Sidney M. *The President and the Parties: The Transformation of the American Party System Since the New Deal.* New York: Oxford University Press, 1993.

Nathan, Richard P. *The Administrative Presidency.* New York: Macmillan, 1986.

A National History of the National Federation of Business and Professional Women's Clubs (BPW/USA). Vol. III. Washington, D.C.: National Federation of Business and Professional Women's Clubs, Inc. BPW/USA, 1994.

Neustadt, Richard E. *Presidential Power and the Modern Presidents: The Politics of Leadership from Roosevelt to Reagan.* New York: Free Press, 1990.

O'Brien, Lawrence F. *No More Final Victories: A Life in Politics from John F. Kennedy to Watergate.* Garden City, N.Y.: Doubleday & Company, Inc., 1974.

O'Connor, Karen, Bernadette Nye, and Laura Van Assendelft. "Wives in the White House: The Political Influence of First Ladies." *Presidential Studies Quarterly* 26, no. 3 (Summer, 1996): 835–53.

Office of the Historian. U.S. House of Representatives. *Women in Congress: 1917–1990.* Washington, D.C.: U.S. Government Printing Office, 1991.

Ornstein, Norman J., Thomas E. Mann, Michael J. Malbin, and John F. Bibby. *Vital Statistics on Congress, 1982.* Washington, D.C.: AEI for Public Policy Research, 1982.

Paterson, Judith. *Be Somebody: A Biography of Marguerite Rawalt.* Austin: Eakin Press, 1986.

Pfiffner, James, ed. *The Managerial Presidency.* Pacific Grove, Calif.: Brooks/Cole Publishing Company, 1991.

Pitkin, Hanna Fenichel. *The Concept of Representation*. Berkeley: University of California Press, 1967.

Polsby, Nelson W. "Presidential Cabinet Making: Lessons for the Political System." *Political Science Quarterly* 93 (1978): 15–25.

Polsby, Nelson W., and Aaron Wildavsky. *Presidential Elections: Strategies and Structures in American Politics*. 9th ed. Chatham, N.J.: Chatham House Publishers, 1996.

Porter, Kirk H., and Donald Bruce Johnson, comps. *National Party Platforms 1840–1964*. Urbana and London: University of Illinois Press, 1966.

President's Committee on Administrative Management ["Brownlow Committee"]. "Administrative Management in the Government of the United States." Washington, D.C.: United States Government Printing Office, 1937.

Pryor, Elizabeth Brown. *Clara Barton: Professional Angel*. Philadelphia: University of Pennsylvania Press, 1987.

Public Papers of the Presidents of the United States: Dwight D. Eisenhower, Washington, D.C.: Government Printing Office, 1953–61.

Public Papers of the Presidents of the United States: George Bush, Washington, D.C.: Government Printing Office, 1989–93.

Public Papers of the Presidents of the United States: Gerald R. Ford, Washington, D.C.: Government Printing Office, 1974–77.

Public Papers of the Presidents of the United States: Harry S. Truman, Washington, D.C.: Government Printing Office, 1945–53.

Public Papers of the Presidents of the United States: Herbert Hoover, Washington, D.C.: Government Printing Office, 1932–33.

Public Papers of the Presidents of the United States: John F. Kennedy, Washington, D.C.: Government Printing Office, 1961–63.

Public Papers of the Presidents of the United States: Jimmy Carter, Washington, D.C.: Government Printing Office, 1977–81.

Public Papers of the Presidents of the United States: Lyndon B. Johnson, Washington, D.C.: Government Printing Office, 1963–69.

Public Papers of the Presidents of the United States: Richard M. Nixon, Washington, D.C.: Government Printing Office, 1969–74.

Public Papers of the Presidents of the United States: Ronald Reagan, Washington, D.C.: Government Printing Office, 1981–89.

Public Papers of the Presidents of the United States: William J. Clinton, Washington, D.C.: Government Printing Office, 1993–2001.

Rather, Dan, and Gary Paul Gates. *The Palace Guard*. New York: Harper and Row, 1974.

Recent Social Trends in the United States. New York: McGraw-Hill Book Co., Inc. 1933.

Rinehart, Sue Tolleson. "Madam Secretary: The Careers of Women in the U.S. Cabinet, 1932–1988." Paper presented at the Annual Meeting of the Southern Political Association, Atlanta, Ga., Nov., 1988.

Rourke, Francis E. "The 1993 John Gaus Lecture: Whose Bureaucracy is This, Anyway? Congress, the President, and Public Administration." *PS* 26, no. 4 (Dec., 1993): 687–92.

Salokar, Rebecca. *The Solicitor General: The Politics of Law*. Philadelphia: Temple University Press, 1992.

Shull, Steven A. *American Civil Rights Policy From Truman to Clinton: The Role of Presidential Leadership*. Armonk, N.Y.: M.E. Sharpe, 1999.

Skocpol, Theda. *Protecting Soldiers and Mothers: The Political Origins of Social Policy in the United States*. 1992; reprint, Cambridge: Belknap Press of Harvard University Press, 1995.

Stanley, David T., Dean E. Mann, and Jameson W. Doig. *Men Who Govern: A Biographical Profile of Federal Political Executives*. Washington, D.C.: Brookings Institution, 1967.

Stanley, Harold W., and Richard G. Niemi. *Vital Statistics on American Politics*. Washington, D.C.: CQ Press, 1988.

Stiehm, Judith Hicks, ed. *It's Our Military, Too: Women and the U.S. Military*. Philadelphia: Temple University Press, 1996.

Sundquist, James L. *The Decline and Resurgence of Congress*. Washington, D.C.: The Brookings Institution, 1981.

Taylor, Paul C. 1966. "The Entrance of Women into Party Politics: The 1920's." Unpublished Ph.D. history thesis. Harvard University.

Thomas, Helen. *Front Row at the White House: My Life and Times*. New York: Simon and Schuster, 1999.

Thompson, Joan Hulse. "The Congressional Caucus for Women's Issues: A Study in Organization Change." Paper delivered at the annual meetings of the American Political Science Association, Washington, Sept., 1993.

Tillett, Paul, ed. *Inside Politics: The National Conventions 1960*. Dobbs Ferry, N.Y.: Oceana Publications, Inc., 1962.

Tilly, Louise A., and Patricia Gurin, eds. *Women, Politics, and Change*. New York: Russell Sage Foundation, 1992.

Tinker, Irene, ed. *Women in Washington: Advocates for Public Policy*. Beverly Hills: Sage Publications, 1983.

Twelfth Annual Report of the Director of the Women's Bureau, Department of Labor, Fiscal Year Ended June 30, 1930. Washington, D.C.: Government Printing Office, 1930.

U.S. Bureau of the Census, Current Population Reports, Series P-20.

U.S. Presidential Commission on the Assignment of Women in the Armed Forces. "Women in Combat: Report to the President." Washington, D.C.: Brassey's, 1993.

Walcott, Charles E., and Karen M. Hult. *Governing the White House From Hoover Through Johnson*. Lawrence: University of Kansas Press, 1995.

Ware, Susan. *Beyond Suffrage: Women in the New Deal*. Cambridge, Mass.: Harvard University Press, 1981.

Washington, George. Letter to Mary Katherine Goddard, Jan. 6, 1790. In *The Writings of George Washington from the Original Manuscript Sources 1745–1799*, edited by John C. Fitzpatrick. Vol. 30. Washington, D.C.: U.S. Government Printing Office.

Watson, Robert P. "The First Lady Reconsidered: Presidential Partner and Political Institution." *Presidential Studies Quarterly* 27, no. 4 (Fall, 1997): 805–18.

————. *The Presidents' Wives: Reassessing the Office of First Lady*. Boulder: Lynne Rienner Publishers, Inc., 1999.

Wayne, Stephen J. *The Road to the White House 1996*. Post-election ed. New York: St. Martin's Press, 1997.

Wayne, Stephen J., and George C. Edwards III, eds. *Studying the Presidency*. Knoxville: The University of Tennessee Press, 1983.

Weeks, Christopher. *Job Corps, Dollars and Dropouts*. Boston: Little, Brown and Company, 1967.

Weisberg, Herbert F., ed. *Democracy's Feast: Elections in America*. Chatham, N.J.: Chatham House Publishers, 1995.

West, Darrell M. "Constituencies and Travel Allocations in the 1980 Presidential Campaign," *American Journal of Political Science* 27, no. 3 (Aug. 3, 1983).

Wheeler, Marjorie Spruill, ed. *Votes for Women: The Woman Suffrage Movement in Tennessee, the South, and the Nation.* Knoxville: University of Tennessee Press, 1995.

White, Theodore H. *The Making of the President.* New York: Atheneum Publishers, 1962.

Willey, Malcolm M., and Stuart Rice. "A Sex Cleavage in the Presidential Election of 1920." *Journal of The American Statistical Association* 19 (1924).

"Women at Work: A Century of Industrial Change," *U.S. Department of Labor, Women's Bureau Bulletin* 115. Washington, D.C.: U.S. Government Printing Office, 1934.

Woodward, Bob. *The Agenda: Inside the Clinton White House.* New York: Simon and Schuster, 1994.

Young, Louise M. "Women's Place in American Politics: The Historical Perspective." *Journal of Politics* 38, no. 3 (1976).

ARCHIVES, COLLECTIONS, AND ORAL HISTORIES
John F. Kennedy Library

Collections	Boxes
CF WH 10	99
Democratic National Committee	
Women-Role in Government	1072
Papers of Laurin Henry	2
PCSW	1, 2, 3, 4, 5, 7, 8, 10
Committee on Federal Employment Policies	7, 8
Committee on Social Insurance and Taxes	13
General Background Info. and Newsletters	1
General Correspondence 4/1962–6/1962	1
General Correspondence 9/1963–11/1963	1
General, Executive Letters #1–5	1
General, Executive Letters #8–10	2
General, Executive Letters #15	2
General, Executive Letters #16–18	2
General, Executive Letters #19	2
General, Executive Letters #20	2
General Meetings 2/12/1962–2/13/1962	2
General Meetings 4/1/1963–4/2/1963	3
General Press Releases 12/1961–7/1962	3
Transcripts: Proceedings, 4/13/1962	4
Transcripts: Proceedings, 10/2/1962	5
Transcripts: Proceedings, 4/2/1963	5
Transcripts: Proceedings, 4/24/1963	5
Transcripts: Proceedings, 10/12/1963	5

Pre-Presidential Papers 3
Pre-Presidential-Senate Files 544, 690, 762
WHCF 675

Oral Histories
Peterson, Esther, oral history interview by Ronald J. Grele, May 18, 1966.
Peterson, Esther, oral history interview by Ann M. Campbell,
Jan. 20, 1970.

Lyndon Baines Johnson Library

Collections	Boxes
CF WH 10	99
LE/HU 3	
GEN LE/Hu 3	72
WHCF	
EX FG 11-8-1/P	103
EX FG 11-8-1/Furness, Betty	83
EX FG 717	396
EX MA	2
EX ND 19/ CO312	218
EX PE	1
EX PE 2	7, 11
EX PE 12	38
EX PR 18	356
FG 500	351
FG 686	385
FG 737	404
FI 1-2	4
GEN HU3 1023/65	58
HU3	58
PE 2	7, 8, 11, 12, 14
Name file	163, 306, 402
5/21/62, Remarks by Vice President at Democratic Women's National Conference	65
Cabinet Papers	1, 2, 5, 7, 10, 13
Office Files of Fred Panzer	27, 500, 522, 548, 551, 553
Office Files of Harry McPherson	55
Office Files of Bill Moyers	74
Office Files of John Macy	850
Office of the President Files	6, 12
Programs of the Dept. of Labor	
Records of the Democratic National Committee	149

Administrative History of the Department of Labor
Administrative History of the U.S. Civil Service Commission

Oral Histories

Carpenter, Liz, oral history interview by Joe B. Frantz, Dec. 3, 1968.
Dungan, Ralph, oral history interview by Paige Mulhollan, April 18, 1969.
Edwards, India, oral history interview by Joe B. Frantz, Feb. 4, 1969.
Green, Edith, oral history interview by Janet Kerr-Tener, Aug. 23, 1985.
Harris, Patricia Roberts, oral history interview by Steve Goodell, May 19, 1969.
Keyserling, Mary, oral history interview by David McComb, Oct. 22, 1968.
Keyserling, Mary, oral history (2nd) interview by David McComb, Oct. 31, 1968.
Louchheim, Katie, oral history interview by Paige Mulhollan, April 1, 1969.
Macy, John, oral history interview by David McComb, April 25, 1969.
Peterson, Esther, oral history interview by Michael L. Gilette, Oct. 29, 1974.
Wickenden, Elizabeth (Mrs. Goldschmidt), oral history interview by Paige Mulhollan, June 3, 1969.

Nixon Presidential Materials (National Archives)

Files	*Boxes*
WHCF	
Subject Files HU	21, 22
Subject Files FG 221 Task Forces	1, 2, 7
SMOF: ALA	4, 7, 8, 16, 18, 24, 63, 68
Subject files: Missing Title	21
WHSF-WHCF Subject files Confidential Files 1969–74	35
WHSF	
SMOF: Charles Colson	90
SMOF: H.R. Haldeman	82
SMOF: Anne Armstrong	63
SMOF: Staff Secretary	87
SMOF: Frederic Malek Files	82
POF: Memoranda for the President	78, 84, 89
President's Office Files	10
White House Press Releases 9/16/69–10/31/69	5
White House Press Releases 5/1/70–6/15/70	10
White House Press Releases 4/21/71–5/31/71	19
White House Press Releases 1/1/72–2/10/72	25
White House Press Releases 3/26/72–4/30/72	27

Gerald R. Ford Library

Files	*Boxes*
Arthur F. Burns Papers, White House Series 1969–70	
James E. Conner Files	21, 48
Alexander Haig Files	1, 3
Robert T. Hartmann, Counsellors to the President	78, 79, 84, 86

Lindh and Holm Files
    Campaign of 1976   7
    Office of Public Liaison   1, 2, 4, 13, 16, 33, 37
    Republican Women's Task Force   37
    Supreme Court—Appointment of Women   13
    Women and Business   4
    Women Presidential Appointees   16
Robert Teeter Papers   54
Warren and White Files   29
WHCF
    FG 1 4/1/76–5/18/76 Executive   10
    FG 147 Interdepartmental Commission   159
    MC 1/1/76–4/30/76 Executive   1
    MC 3 5/1/76–5/10/76 Executive   5
    MC 4 3/20/75–3/31/75 Executive   14
    Name File—Annette Buckland
    Name File—Judith Connor
    Name File—Majorie Lynch
    Subject File Executive HU 2-5   9, 10
    Subject File General HU 2-5   10, 11
    Subject File PE 2 General   5
    Subject File PE 2 Executive   3, 5
        Subject files   1, 2, 3, 5, 9, 10, 11, 12, 14, 29
White House Staff Files
    Anne Amstrong   1
    Patricia Lindh and Jeanne Holm Files   1, 7, 16
White House Operations—Richard Cheney Files 1, 11, 12, 18

Oral History
Lindh, Patricia, oral history interview by David Horrocks, June 24, 1996.

Jimmy Carter Presidential Library

Files   *Boxes*
Hamilton Jordan Papers   1, 5, 9, 10, 31, 32, 37, 41, 51, 55, 57
Sarah Weddington Papers   2, 4, 7, 12, 13, 14, 18, 19, 34, 35, 50, 56, 92

FG 194 1/20/77–1/20/81   FG-95
WHCF
    Subject Files-Executive   ED-2, FG-21, FG-22,
                               FG-37, FG-41, FG-57,
                               FG-70, FG-71, FG-73,
                               FG-129, FG-136,
                               FG-137, FG-138,
                               FG-221, HO-3, HU-9,
                               HU-10, HU-11, HU-14,
                               HU-15, HU-17, LA-3,

Subject Files-General

MC-8, PE-5, PE-6,
PE-7, PE-8
FG-74, FG-207,
HU-17, PE-8

The Daily Diary of President Carter
Name File
"[Folder-Patricia Roberts Harris]
Patricia Roberts Harris" folder

Oral History
Weddington, Sarah. Oral history interview by Emily Soapes, Jan. 2, 1981.

Rawalt Center

Folder
BPW/ERA Historical Materials, 1960's General
Conference on Women in Policy-Making Posts 1953-Public Affairs Project
National Business and Professional Women's Clubs
Past National Presidents
Proceedings of the Seventh Biennial Convention of the NFBPWC
Voluntary Organizations and Democracy: A Discussion Outline
Women Appointees 1950's
Women Appointees 1970's

Annual Reports 1940–1945 NFBPWC
"Margaret Hickey, 1944–46," in Past National Presidents' Drawer
Speech by Patricia Reilly Hitt, July, 1969, Convention of the NFBPWC, St. Louis, Mo.

Margaret Chase Smith Library
Newspaper files: *Maine State Labor News*

INDEX

abortion, 221–22

Abramowitz, Beth, 227–28, 229, 323n. 150

Abzug, Bella, 220, 230; dismissal and California politics, 238; Kennedy primary challenge and, 244; as NACW chair, 233–35

Adams, Abigail, 3–4, 18

Adams, John, 3, 4

Addams, Jane, 32

Adkins, Bertha, 45–46

administrative state, 38

affirmative action, 143–44, 252–53, 303n. 63; Carter and, 209–10, 214–15, 247–48; Nixon and, 143–44, 149 Box 4.5, 155–56 Box 4.6

African American(s): Civil Rights Act of 1964 and, 86; civil rights and the executive branch, 86, 123–24; as focus of Johnson civil rights agenda, 97, 98; suffrage, 284n. 151; talent search for, 178; women's wages, 62

Agnew, Spiro T., 167

Aiken, Senator George D., 59

Albers, Bill, 224–25

Albert, Representative Carl, 194–95

Albright, Madeleine K., 226

Allan, Virginia, 96, 128, 157 Box 4.7, 160

Allison, Graham T., 81

Amalgamated Clothing Workers (ACW), 53

American Association of University Women (AAUW), 29

American Bar Association (ABA), 178; Standing Committee on the Judiciary, 186

American Civil Liberties Union (ACLU), 41, 283n. 119

American Federation of Government Employees, 183

"American Women at the Crossroads: Directions for the Future" (conference), 134

Anderson, Kristi, 29

Anderson, Mary, 32, 33, 95

Anthony, Susan B., 32

appointment(s), 253–54; Carter administration, 195, 204–13, 208–209, 254, 317n. 21; Congress as pool for, 179–81; counted and compared, 253, 254; Eisenhower administration, 45–47; firsts, 257; Ford administraton, 174–75, 177–82, 208–209, 317n. 21; geographic balance in, 181; George Washington's delegation of sub-cabinet, 17–18, 276n.5; Johnson administration, 107, 120–21; judicial, 140, 144, 186–89, 240, 243–44; Kennedy administraton, 75–83; NFBPWC and, 144; Nixon administraton, 47, 139–42, 148, 150 Table 4.1; OWP tracking of, 184; party factions and, 181–82; and presidential leadership, 35; symbolic v. substantive representation of, 79–80; White House Fellows counted as, 143; women's organizations and, 77, 132, 140, 144, 151–53, 185–86, 208–209, 250–51, 253, 257, 304n. 71

armed forces: desegregation of, 19; women and, 42, 73–74, 154

Armstrong, Anne L., 143, 148, 158, 165; career summary, 158–59, 177; counselor to the president with cabinet rank, 158–62, 254–55; during 1976 Ford campaign and transition,

ISBN 1-58544-245-3